Vanguard College Library
12140 103 Street
Edmonton, Alberta
T5G 2J9

D0977596

THINGS ARE POSSIBLE

The Healing & Charismatic
Revivals in Modern
America

VANGUARD COLLEGE LIBRARY
12140 - 103 STREET
EDMONTON, AB T5G 2J9

Discard

ALL
THINGS ARE
POSSIBLE

*The Healing & Charismatic
Revivals in Modern
America*

David Edwin Harrell, Jr.

Indiana University Press

BLOOMINGTON AND INDIANAPOLIS

This book is a publication of

Indiana University Press
601 North Morton Street
Bloomington, Indiana 47404-3797 USA

http://iupress.indiana.edu

Telephone orders 800-842-6796
Fax orders 812-855-7931
Orders by e-mail iuporder@indiana.edu

First Indiana University Press paperback edition 1978
© 1975 by Indiana University Press
All rights reserved

No part of this book may be reproduced or utilized in any form or by any
means, electronic or mechanical, including photocopying and recording,
or by any information storage and retrieval system, without permission in
writing from the publisher. The Association of American University Presses'
Resolution on Permissions constitutes the only exception to this prohibition.

The paper used in this publication meets the minimum requirements of
American National Standard for Information Sciences—Permanence of Paper
for Printed Library Materials, ANSI Z39.48-1984.

Manufactured in the United States of America

Library of Congress Cataloging-in-Publication Data

Harrell, David Edwin.
All things are possible.

Bibliography
1. Revivals—United States. 2. Faith-cure—History.
3. Pentecostalism—History. I. Title.
BV3773.H37   1975   269'2'0973   75-1937
ISBN 0-253-20221-3 (pbk.)

17 18 19 20 21 09 08 07 06 05 04

To Millie, Eddie, Elizabeth,

Lee, and Robert

CONTENTS

CONTENTS

PREFACE

IT HAS NOT BEEN EASY TO BE OBJECTIVE about the healing and charismatic religious movements. Healing revivalism invites caricature, but this book is based on the belief that the movement is too important to be handled carelessly or flippantly. My quest for objectivity has led me into the frequent, and perhaps tedious, use of quotations. But there is some advantage in letting the men who know the revival best tell the story. Their language is frequently unschooled, but I have avoided pointing the finger of [sic] at quoted material unless something in it seemed to require clarification. In another effort to avoid needlessly cluttering the manuscript, I have not often used labels such as *allegedly* and *reportedly* when relating the stories of healings and other miracles as viewed through the eyes of the believers. No one should understand this as an endorsement of the testimonies. Belief in miracles is a theological issue and this book is not intended to argue that point. Those who read this book will discover some, though by no means all, of the pros and cons on that question. As it happens, I do not share the religious presuppositions of the charismatic revivalists, but in my many conversations with them, I have insisted that my own religious views are, if I do my job properly, irrelevant to the telling of the story.

Pentecostals use certain terms—such as *pentecostalism, charismatic movement,* and *neopentecostalism*—in a confusing variety of ways. I use *pentecostalism* and the *charismatic movement* to include all those who believe in the gifts of the Holy Spirit. I have chosen to distinguish the two phases of the revival by calling the first the *healing revival* and the second the *charismatic revival.* The reader will discover that the first phase of the revival was a relatively homogeneous cultural unit that particularly emphasized the gift of healing. The second phase was culturally mixed and displayed a broader interest in all of the gifts of the Spirit. I have used the term *neopentecostal* to describe all those members of traditional churches who accept the charismatic experience. The word is widely used in this sense by pentecostals, although many of the more sophisticated neopentecostals use the term to mean only those who have abandoned old-time pentecostal theology and culture and place the charismatic experience within their own church tradition.

The bibliographical essay at the end of the book describes the variety of sources available to the student of this subject. There I have listed people with whom I taped formal interviews. In my footnote citations of these interviews I have not identified the specific person quoted. This may be inconvenient for some readers, but I felt obliged to give some public protection to the many people within the movement who spoke candidly to me about controversial issues. Students who are interested in pursuing this general subject will find copies of most of the interviews in the Pentecostal Collection at Oral Roberts University. Any scholar wishing information about a specific citation may feel free to address an inquiry to me. I want to express my deepest appreciation to the twenty-six individuals whom I formally interviewed and to the hundreds of other participants of the revival who shared their impressions with me. There exists a vast amount of written material on the charismatic experience and the pentecostal tradition, but both are best understood orally.

The major research center for this subject is the Pentecostal Collection at Oral Roberts University. I am deeply indebted to Mrs. Juanita Raudszus for the many kindnesses she extended to me in Tulsa. Mrs. Raudszus spent hours discussing this work with me and made many valuable suggestions during the last five years. The entire staff of the Oral Roberts University library was most helpful. I also gratefully acknowledge the assistance of the University of Alabama in Birmingham. Dr. George E. Passey, Dean of the School of Social and Behavioral Sciences, has done much to encourage my research. I received two research grants from the Faculty Research Committee of the university, which made possible the extensive travel required in gathering materials. I am deeply grateful for the confidence of the committee and its chairman, Dean Samuel B. Barker. The final revision of this manuscript was made while I was in residence as a Fellow of the Institute for Ecumenical and Cultural Research in Collegeville, Minnesota. The facilities and atmosphere of the Institute surpass the dreams of a research scholar.

A number of colleagues and friends read the manuscript and made helpful suggestions. Professor Martin Marty of the University of Chicago and Professor Kilian McDonnell, osb, of St. John's University and Abbey in Collegeville, Minnesota, read the entire manuscript and made valuable suggestions. Professor McDonnell was especially helpful in deepening my knowledge of the neopentecostal and Roman Catholic charismatic movements. My two good friends, Harold Dowdy and

Harold Comer, read the manuscript and offered helpful criticism and needed encouragement.

I am also grateful to those who helped to prepare the manuscript. The secretaries of the history department of the University of Alabama in Birmingham, Mrs. Deborah McCain and Mrs. Pat Davis, spent many hours typing the manuscript. Deborah McCain was frequently an able editor and critic as well. Sister Romaine Theisen, OSB, typed the entire manuscript in revised form. Mr. Alan Pitts, a graduate assistant at the university of Alabama in Birmingham, helped to solve problems in the final preparation. I also express appreciation to my wife, Deedie, and to my children, for, as always, arranging their lives around my exasperating work schedule.

My friend John Gallman, editorial director of Indiana University Press, has been both a prod toward excellence and a source of encouragement. His unflagging interest and his gentle urging helped to keep this work moving. J. M. Matthew, a sensitive editor, improved the manuscript in countless ways.

DAVID EDWIN HARRELL, JR.
Birmingham, Alabama

---

*Prayer for
the Sick*

1

Introduction

ONCE AN OBJECT OF DERISION, in the 1970s pentecostal religion became almost fashionable. Many judged the charismatic movement the most vital single force in American religion. The gifts of the Holy Spirit (charisms), speaking in tongues (glossolalia), and divine healing were subjects studied in nearly every American church, and cells of charismatic believers appeared in most American denominations. By 1975, perhaps 5,000,000 or more Americans were taking part in the charismatic revival.

Pentecostal, or charismatic, religion in the 1970s was a many-faceted phenomenon. Most prominent were the many small churches which had grown out of the pentecostal message in the early twentieth century; they were popularly lumped into a category called classical pentecostalism or old-line pentecostalism, although they varied vastly in size, sophistication, and doctrine. There were also many members of traditional Protestant churches who, during the 1960s, had accepted a type of pentecostal theology while remaining in their own churches. This growing movement, generally made up of the sophisticated and the well-to-do, came to be labeled neopentecostalism. A similar outbreak that erupted in the American Roman Catholic Church in 1967 was called Catholic pentecostalism to distinguish it from the earlier neopentecostal movement. Considerable differences in beliefs and behavior existed both between and within the groups, but they were united by the conviction that they had received the outpouring of God's Holy Spirit.

Finally, there was a group of revival ministries which were in a large part responsible for the unexpected growth of pentecostalism in modern America. Since World War II, hundreds of ministers, most of them in the 1950s coming from the ranks of classical pentecostalism but later from a variety of backgrounds, established independent evangelistic associations. These associations lived or died with the charisma of the evangelist, and some became multimillion dollar organizations. Taken together, they were a powerful independent force in modern American religion and won the religious loyalty and financial support of millions of Americans. Little understood by the public, the faith healing revivalists were the main actors in the postwar pentecostal drama. By the 1970s, the independent ministries had become as diverse as pentecostalism itself. Their organizations were the only bridge that spanned the entire expanse of pentecostalism and they are the chief subject of this book.

Americans have long been fascinated by the bizarre world of faith healers. The Elmer Gantry stereotype was given new life in 1972 with the release of the popular motion picture *Marjoe*. The movie and subsequent book about its producer, Marjoe Gortner, once again explored the themes of greed, fraud, exploitation, and hardened showmanship long associated with healing revivlaism.[1] Marjoe's exposé was the work of an acknowledged insider, and it reopened deep wounds that charismatic leaders had worked hard to heal. Marjoe demonstrated that spiritual hustlers were still around (no one knew it better than the leaders of the charismatic revival). His attack once again challenged objective observers to distinguish charlatans from true believers. In the process, Marjoe brought once again into full view the whole curious world of hullabaloo and hope found in the tents and tabernacles of American pentecostal subculture. Once again, the religious rituals of the poor and lowly had piqued the interest of better-off Americans.

More important in bringing the charismatic message into public view than the new notoriety of Marjoe Gortner was the emergence of a sophisticated and respected charismatic leadership. Once scorned by most of the nation's religious leaders and the press, by the 1970s Oral Roberts had become a man of prestige and stature. In 1974, pentecostal leader David J. duPlessis was included in a list of the eleven most influential Christians in the world, based on an informal poll conducted by seven major church magazines.[2] Kathryn Kuhlman's ministry was both successful and respectable. The Full Gospel Business Men's Fellowship International took the charismatic message into the banquet halls of the best hotels of the world and boasted among its members some of the world's wealthiest, most glamorous, and most powerful. The snow white dove was still seen scribbled on ghetto walls, but it was also molded into lapel pins worn by the mighty.

There were other forces at work in American society which allowed the revival to expand from the shabby tabernacles of the poor to the temples of the comfortable—all of them, to the faithful, evidence of the powerful work of God. The affluence of the time allowed many independent revivalists to build far stronger financial organizations than ever had been possible before. Ecstatic religion, with its emphasis on divine healing and the physical presence of the Holy Spirit, had long filled an important place in the barren emotional lives of the poor. Increasingly in the 1950s and 1960s sophisticated Americans awoke to the emotional insecurity of their own cultural anonymity. The youth revolt of the 1960s quickly established contact with the fundamentalist religious tradition—including the charismatic movement. At the same time, many middle-class Americans, beset by their own frustrations, were romantically attracted to the occult, psychic phenomena, and divine healing. The charismatic movement became a vital but amorphous phenomenon, ranging from tent healers and old-time pentecostals to sophisticated Episcopalians and Roman Catholics who discovered anew the gifts of the Holy Spirit.

The charismatic revival was born in the small pentecostal churches in the aftermath of World War II and nurtured by the generation of charismatic evangelists who established independent ministries in the late 1940s and early 1950s. The most successful of the revivalists quickly freed themselves from the domination of the small pentecostal churches and became autonomous powers in the pentecostal world. By the mid-1950s most of the pentecostal denominations, for a variety of reasons, had withdrawn their endorsements of the traveling evangelists. Some of the smaller revivalists were crushed by this development and forced to stop campaigning; the most successful had to reassess their plans and change their methods to build new bases of support.

The great revival that launched the careers of the independent ministers lasted roughly from 1947 to 1958 and was preeminently a healing revival. In some ways the charismatic evangelists looked much like other revivalists in American history. They studied the techniques of figures such as Billy Sunday and Dwight L. Moody. They admired the success of Billy Graham. But they were not a part of the same revivalistic stream—theirs was a signs-gifts-healing, a salvation-deliverance, a Holy Ghost–miracle revival. Salvation from sin was preached, but, whatever the intention of the evangelists, it was never the central theme of their meetings. All the gifts of the Holy Spirit, including speaking in tongues and prophesying, and all the expressions of joy so common in pentecostal worship were present in the early revivals, but they were not the central theme. The common heartbeat of every service was the miracle—the hypnotic moment when the Spirit moved to heal the sick and raise the dead.

As will become apparent to the reader of this book, the variety of the thousands of services held under the big tents and in auditoriums throughout the country was as broad as the genius of the magnetic men who led the revival. All the evangelists preached in their own styles, all relying heavily on rehearsals of the miracles of Jesus, on stories of miracles in their own lives, and on tales of fantastic healings which they had witnessed. Some depended upon professional musicians to set the mood. They used a wide variety of high and low pressure tactics to raise the funds so quickly guzzled by their growing organizations. Most used lively associate ministers to prepare the audiences for the dramatic appearance of the anointed evangelist. Frequently, the services lasted four or five hours. But, whatever else happened, finally came the climactic moment, the moment for which the thousands had assembled, when silent expectation filled the air, when all the audience bowed their heads, raised their arms, and in the hushed silence whispered, "God, do it now"—the moment of the man and the miracle.

The healing techniques of the evangelists were disparate. Unanimously, however, those who succeeded had a powerful control over their audiences and an unwavering confidence in their own charisma. Most were dedicated to back-breaking work and spent long grueling hours in the centers of the platforms of the big tents praying, clapping, shouting, pleading with the crippled to walk, commanding the blind to see, and bowing dramatically amidst shouts of "Praise the Lord" and "Hallelujah." It was an exhausting, grinding, draining way of life. William Branham was a broken man after little more than a year; Jack Coe was physically exhausted at the time of his death; A. A. Allen, an incredibly tough campaigner, tottered constantly on the brink of psychological collapse; the resilience of Oral Roberts became a legend among his peers.

Part 2 of this book tells the story of these men and their healing revival. It is an account first of men—imposing, flamboyant, compelling preachers. Each independent minister has his own story; each deserves to be told. Chapters 3 and 4 trace the careers of the major leaders of the revival to 1958 and glance at some of the minor figures. But there is also a common scenario shared by all the actors. The revival had a life of its own, composed of the common doctrines, claims, successes, and failures of the revivalists. Chapter 5 analyzes the principal themes of the revival. The revivalists' teachings on healing, prophecy, ecumenism, evangelism, and a number of other subjects had a lasting impact on American religion. Chapter 5 also considers the apparent weaknesses of the revival. Internal tensions existed from the beginning, and, as the revival boomed in the early 1950s, pressures built. Misunderstood and caricatured by the press, disparaged by the medical profession, repudiated by most other Christian groups, and finally ostracized by the major pentecostal churches, the independent evangelists came to face seemingly insurmountable obstacles. By 1958, nearly all recognized that what had begun in 1947 was over. To survive, the independent revivalists looked for new paths to follow.

Part 3 of this book traces the development of independent charismatic ministries in America after 1958. Since that time, the old healing revival has been replaced by a much broader charismatic revival, whose ministries, some old and some new, have been varied. Some of the evangelists were learned; others were earthy prophets of the poor. They all owed a historical debt to the healing revival of the previous decade, but the variegated charismatic revival they have helped forge has had a distinctive life of its own.

The immediate reason that the old ministries changed after 1958 was the loss of financial support. Chiefly responsible for the decline was the opposition of the pentecostal churches. But there were many other reasons. Miracles became too commonplace, claims too unbelievable, prophets too available. Honest participants in the revival were disturbed by the popularity of frauds and extremists. The old revival died a slow and introspective death.

Fortunately for them, new opportunities were clearly visible to the evangelists by the late 1950s. Thousands of people in the traditional churches had become interested in the charismatic message; hundreds of thousands of religious Americans were dissatisfied with their own lethargic denominations and were searching for a more dynamic experience. Chapter 6 discusses the death pangs of the old healing revival and the sources of new spiritual strength upon which the charismatic revival was built.

As the charismatic movement took shape in the 1960s, most of the evangelistic ministries began to change in response. Frequently they turned into missionary or benevolent societies, while continuing the healing campaigns when feasible. Many still depended on loyal old-line pentecostals for support, but others, consciously or unconsciously, adapted to meet the blossoming interest in the charismatic message in the traditional churches. Most evangelists became teachers more than healers and recast their revival teams into teaching organizations.

Not all of the old-time Holy Ghost revivalists made the demanding transition successfully, and their places in the revival were taken by new and accomplished teachers. Some of these, most notably Kathryn Kuhlman, had long been active in a healing ministry, but the charismatic revival carried them to new heights. Scores of bright and forceful young men, most of them abandoning ministerial careers in the traditional denominations, established independent ministries in the late 1960s and early 1970s, bursting into the movement with a great surge of energy. Chapter 7 gives a sampling of how the old ministries changed and how the new ministries emerged.

Chapter 8 is a discussion of the persistence of healing campaigning since 1958. Some of the revivalists refused to fold their tents when hard times came. Some well understood the limitations of their gifts, some already had concluded bitterly that they would have to live or die without the support of pentecostal denominational leaders, and some were trapped by their own radical characters. A few survived and grew. They generally appealed to the abjectly poor—to blacks, Indians, Puerto Ricans, and poor whites. A. A. Allen was their leader, but scores of small evangelists travelled the sawdust trail to them. By the 1970s, the nation's fairgrounds and civic auditoriums once again were filled not only with disciples of Allen, but also with new young campaigners who had powerful revival ministries of their own.

Thus, the healing revival of the postwar period mushroomed into a complex charismatic movement. The later revival was vastly different from the original outbreak and some of its differences are discussed in Chapter 9. Healing was no longer the dominant theme, although it remained an important doctrinal—and promotional—plank. The new movement was much more genuinely charismatic—interested in all of the gifts of the Holy Spirit. In many ministries, financial prosperity replaced divine healing as the most advertised miracle. In general, the doctrinal interests of the independent ministers came to span a much wider range.

The revival also became much more diverse in style. Even the recent tent campaigners could not recapture the uniform and spontaneous milieu of the early meetings. In general, the campaigns became more stereotyped, more staged, and more professional. Among the sophisticated, the revival moved into Hilton Hotels and ornate churches; and revival services were replaced by charismatic conferences and seminars. If the same Spirit provoked the testimonies of corporate executives and four-star generals and the ecstatic shouts and dances of spirit-filled Navaho, it chose to do so in quite different locales under the ministries of quite different servants.

This book does not set out to study all independent charismatic revivalists. That would be an impossible task for one volume. Rather, I intend to explore the overall dimensions of the revival and to omit no one who had an important impact on the course of the movement. Generally, only the most prominent leaders of such people's religious movements reach the view of the wider public, and then too often only in polemical tracts or sensational exposés. They deserve better. These men are persistent types of prophets in the Christian tradition—enigmatic and illusive characters in their own day and little more than fuzzy myths when subsequent generations return to study them. Few learned observers recognized the significance of the huge healing campaigns of the 1950s; not many of those enthralled by the charismatic movement today understand its origins. This book does not answer all of the questions raised by the postwar miracle revivals, but it does place the charismatic movement in a historical perspective that allows some useful generalizations and gives coherence to a confusing patchwork of independent religious associations.

2

Origins

FEW CHRISTIAN RITUALS have a more legitimate ancestry than prayer for the sick. Most Christians in all ages have believed in the miraculous intervention of God in the affairs of men. A recent report on the charismatic movement among Roman Catholics emphasized the precedent for the gifts of the spirit in the historical church:

> It should not be forgotten that in the course of the Church's history the Holy Spirit and his charisms were not absent. The Holy Spirit manifested himself in a multiplicity of ways in various epochs of the Church's history. One could mention the lay monastic movements, the founding of religious orders, the prayer gifts in the Church's mystical tradition.[1]

The tradition of divine healing in the church, both eastern and western, is long and revered. The exorcism of demons, recently a matter of popular attention, has long been an established part of Christian thought and practice. It is one of the powers conferred on persons preparing to be Roman Catholic priests.

In spite of the charismatic tradition in Roman Catholicism, in the twentieth century miraculous religion came more and more to be associated with evangelical Protestantism. By the end of the nineteenth century, the literature of evangelical Christians showed a strong interest

in the supernatural and in healing the sick by prayer. In 1885, a Divine
Healing Conference in London drew supporters from all over the world.
Out of this yearning for a new outpouring of the Holy Spirit rose the
impoverished but energetic pentecostal movement at the beginning of
the twentieth century.

The roots of American pentecostalism reach deep into the history of
ecstatic Christianity. Pentecostal leaders trace their origins through
George Fox and the Quakers, John Wesley and early Methodism, the
Plymouth Brethren, William Booth and the Salvation Army, and other
similar men and movements. More recently, American pentecostalism
grew out of a deepening of spiritual life associated with the holiness
movement at the end of the nineteenth century. Participants in this
nebulous movement, both in America and abroad, looked beyond the
conversion experience to continual personal encounters with God for the
Christian.[2] Around the turn of the century some of these reformers
began to teach that the baptism of the Holy Ghost, accompanied by
speaking in tongues, was the final, and pentecostal, work of grace to be
sought by every Christian.

Organized pentecostalism in America emerged in many different
places. One center in western North Carolina and eastern Tennessee
came to be associated with the name of A. J. Tomlinson and the Church
of God. In the Midwest the pioneer pentecostal was Charles G. Parham,
a Methodist minister and teacher. Many date the beginnings of
American pentecostalism from a meeting held in the Azusa Street
mission in Los Angeles in 1906. At any rate, the amorphous movement
slowly took shape in the 1920s as a confusing patchwork of small sects
frequently divided by seemingly trivial points of doctrine. By the end of
World War II, the three largest churches were the Assemblies of God,
the Church of God, and the Pentecostal Holiness church. Pentecostal
religion was especially successful in the South, but all over the nation
small churches began to spring up, drawing members from the poor and
those discontented in the traditional churches.[3]

The central doctrine of pentecostalism, according to one of the
movement's best known leaders, is "the abiding possibility and importance of the supernatural element . . . particularly as contained in the
manifestation of the Spirit."[4] The holiness movement of the late
nineteenth century stressed personal holiness, or "entire sanctification,"
as an evidence of the indwelling of the Holy Spirit. Pentecostals took
this emphasis a step further in what some called a "third work of grace,"
while others omitted sanctification and considered "baptism in the
spirit" the only subsequent experience to conversion. The consecrated

Christian who received the baptism of the Holy Ghost was set apart by speaking in tongues. In addition to the baptism of the Holy Ghost, pentecostals believed that nine Biblical gifts of the Spirit—the word of wisdom, the word of knowledge, the gift of faith, the gift of healing, the gift of miracles, the gift of prophecy, the gift of discerning spirits, the gift of tongues, and the gift of interpretation of tongues—were available to Christians today.[5] Those anointed by God with these charismatic gifts had miraculous powers which would build the faith of others. A recent pentecostal author summed up the message: "Jesus Christ is the Savior, the Healer, and the Baptizer in the Spirit." [6] This "full gospel" message gave a degree of unity to the movement, although a bewildering variety of interpretations of these works of the Spirit led to seemingly endless schisms in the small churches.

A number of other issues also proved particularly divisive to the pentecostal movement. Some pentecostals, such as the Assemblies of God, emphasized the independence of local congregations in the Baptist tradition; others, including most of the forms of the Church of God, formed centralized organizations in the Methodist tradition. The movement was further deeply divided by an unusual unitarian–trinitarian split. A number of the early leaders in the movement believed that Jesus, God, and the Holy Spirit were all one person, whose name was Jesus. In 1916, a group of these ministers were forced out of the Assemblies of God. A number of splinter sects were formed, generally referred to as "Jesus only" or "oneness" churches. In 1945, a large number of oneness pentecostals merged as the United Pentecostal Church.[7]

Rigidly conservative on moral teaching, pentecostals repeatedly divided over interpretations of Biblical commands on marriage and divorce and other moral issues. In the 1930s, the Pentecostal Fire–Baptized Holiness church separated from the Pentecostal Holiness church because of the "neck-tie issue," believing that the acceptance of relaxed standards of dress was a sinful compromise with the world. By that time, the small pentecostal churches were probably expending more energy fighting one another than they were preaching their full gospel message to others.

The pentecostal message was born before the warring sects, however, and it continued to nourish independent charismatic figures who somehow lifted themselves above the doctrinal bickering in the churches. A number of celebrated healers ministered to the entire movement in the early twentieth century. They were the legitimate ancestors of the charismatic revivalists of the post–World War II period. Some, such as A. J. Gordon, a respected Boston Baptist, and A. B. Simpson, a Presbyterian who established the Christian and Missionary Alliance, were simply honored as pioneer teachers on divine healing. Others were the trailblazers of healing revivalism in America.

Alexander Dowie

The father of healing revivalism in America was the enigmatic Alexander Dowie.[8] Dowie was born in Scotland in 1847 but was reared in Australia where he very early felt called to the ministry. He was trained for the Congregational ministry and held a number of pastorates in Australia before deciding in 1878 to establish an independent congregation. In 1882, Dowie began preaching divine healing, and in the stormy years that followed, this teaching was his theme in attracting followers. In 1888, after several years of uneven success in Australia, Dowie came to America. He settled in Chicago in 1893.

In Chicago, Dowie began a spectacular ministry which brought him worldwide fame. Beginning with a small congregation, his divine healing successes soon attracted public attention. He was frequently arrrested and fought a running battle with local authorities who, he believed, resented his scathing denunciations of public sin. But he attracted thousands of supporters. In 1896, he formed the Christian Catholic Church, and, in a dramatic move in 1900, he announced the purchase of 6,000 acres of land north of Chicago where he intended to build the city of Zion, a paradise for the righteous. Within two years over 10,000 people had moved to his new city of God.

Dowie was able and lusty, but he was also tyrannical and unpredictable. A prolific writer, he circulated his magazine, *Leaves of Healing*, all over the world. He ruled Zion with an iron hand, and his financial irresponsibility and taste for personal luxury soon caused some disciples to have second thoughts. Doubts were also raised by Dowie's claims to repeated divine revelations exalting his personal status: in 1901 he announced that he was "Elijah the Prophet" and somewhat later he proclaimed himself the "first apostle" of the church. The ridicule which followed these pronouncements, along with growing financial problems in the city of Zion, led to a revolt which ousted him from control of his church in 1906, just a year before he died.

Dowie was the first man to bring national attention to divine healing in twentieth-century America. No charismatic leader of the post–World

[1 3

War II revival was directly influenced by Dowie, but the indirect ties were many and important. Gordon Lindsay, one of the most knowledgeable leaders of the postwar revival, wrote of Dowie's influence:

> Out of Zion came F. F. Bosworth, and his brother B. B. Bosworth, whose healing campaigns in the Twenties filled great auditoriums, seating many thousands of people. From Zion went forth John G. Lake with a message that stirred all of South Africa, and resulted in the establishing of hundreds of churches that remain to this day. . . . Raymond T. Richey who was only a lad at the time, unconsciously absorbed the atmosphere of faith that pervaded the city, and later his healing ministry became the phenomenon of that time. . . . From the ministry of these men and others we might mention, there has arisen a host of men of faith who have had powerful ministries. The Full Gospel movement which sprang into existence, coincidentally, as Dowie passed from the scene, owes Zion a debt that it perhaps little realizes.[9]

Among those who carried the mark of Zion was Lindsay himself.

Smith Wigglesworth

By the end of World War I, a number of healing evangelists began building independent revival ministries. Several British evangelists made tours of the United States in the 1920s and 1930s. Perhaps the most lasting foreign influence came through the work of Smith Wigglesworth. For many years Wigglesworth was a plumber and volunteer worker in Salvation Army missions in Bradford, England, but by the 1920s he had become a well-known healing revivalist. He never officially identified with any denomination, although he received the strong backing of the Assemblies of God in Great Britain. Wigglesworth visited America in 1923 and included on his itinerary a meeting in Springfield, Missouri, the location of the headquarters of the Assemblies of God. "When in America," recalled pentecostal editor Stanley Frodsham, "he filled the biggest halls, ministered to record crowds, prayed for thousands of people." [10] Wigglesworth died in 1944, but his work was remembered by a generation of pentecostals and his writings served as a guide for the next generation of revivalists.

F. F. Bosworth

More important were a small coterie of American healing revivalists who established independent ministries in the 1920s. One of the most successful was Fred F. Bosworth of Zion. His family had moved there while he was a youth and he served as band director at Dowie's church.[11] About 1910, Bosworth moved to Dallas where he built a strong independent charismatic church and pastored it for ten years. Then, after World War I, he began conducting revivals. His reputation grew rapidly. "By the late twenties," wrote an admirer, "the Bosworth Revival had electrified dozens of cities in the United States and Canada and the work of this man had already had a profound impact on an entire generation of Americans." [12] Reportedly, in one Bosworth rally in 1924, "some 12,000 sought the Lord for salvation." [13] Bosworth became a pioneer of radio evangelism when he established National Radio Revival Missionary Crusaders as a nonprofit Illinois corporation and began broadcasting regularly over WJJD in Chicago. In a few years his radio ministry processed more than a quarter of a million letters.[14]

Bosworth's ministry declined during the depression, and when the post–World War II revival broke out he had retired to Florida. He was an important advisor to postwar revivalists, and his knowledge of revival techniques and healing theology was widely sought. T. L. Osborn, one of the most successful of the postwar preachers, reminisced in 1972, "Old F. F. Bosworth used to share a lot of secrets with us. You remember, years and years ago (he was about 80 then) and we were young ones. . . . I always loved to talk with him." [15] When Bosworth died in January 1958, at the age of 81, he was one of the few charismatic evangelists in the nation who had participated in the hopeful beginnings of the 1920s and the explosive revival of the 1950s.

Wyatt, Lake, Woodworth-Etter

A number of other healing evangelists earned national reputations during the 1920s. Thomas Wyatt was a well-known revivalist in the Midwest before settling down to pastor an independent church in Portland, Oregon, in 1937. Wyatt and the organization he built made important contributions to the postwar revival, but he never again became a touring evangelist. John G. Lake, the protege of Alexander Dowie, spent five years in Africa as a missionary before returning to Spokane, Washington, about 1910, where he built a large charismatic church. Lake had an inspirational ministry in Spokane; according to Gordon Lindsay, "100,000 healings were recorded in five years." He later began a church in Portland, Oregon, in which Gordon Lindsay was converted. Lindsay believed that Lake "had the ability to build faith in his audiences as no other man of his time." [16] Lake always pastored a local church, but he also was an active travelling evangelist during the

1920s and 1930s. Mrs. M. B. Woodworth-Etter had an influential healing ministry which began in 1876 while she was a member of the United Brethren church. She later associated herself with the Methodist Holiness church and spent several decades as an itinerant evangelist preaching divine healing in the nebulous pentecostal movement. In the early twentieth century she built a famous tabernacle in Indianapolis and remained active as a revivalist into the 1920s.[17]

Raymond T. Richey

Some of the revivalists of the early twentieth century were associated closely with a particular pentecostal sect. Raymond T. Richey was generally identified with the Assemblies of God.[18] Richey nevertheless pioneered in the techniques of healing revivalism in the 1920s and was one of the few major revivalists of that early period who also had a major ministry in the postwar revival.[19] During the depression, Richey was forced to leave the evangelistic field and settle into a pastorate at his independent Evangelistic Temple in Houston, Texas. He also headed a bible college and continued to conduct sporadic campaigns during the 1930s and 1940s. In 1951, in the midst of the great revival, he once again became a full-time revivalist.[20]

Aimee Semple McPherson

The most famous of the healing evangelists of the 1920s was Aimee Semple McPherson. She was a Canadian farm girl whose beauty and magnetic personality made her name a household word. After an unhappy early personal life, she became a touring healing revivalist in 1918 at the age of 28. A startling success from the beginning, in 1923 she built her famous church, Angelus Temple, in Los Angeles and began publishing a monthly magazine, *The Bridal Call*. She seemed to thrive on controversy and scandal. Despite open feuding with her domineering mother over control of the church, persistent rumors of indiscreet conduct, and a sensational court case in 1926 after she was allegedly kidnapped, the evangelist's work survived and grew. "During the decade 1926–1937," wrote her biographer, "Aimee Semple McPherson's name appeared on the front pages of the Los Angeles newspapers an average of three times a week." [21] At the peak of her success McPherson decided to build her own sect, the Foursquare Gospel church. When she died in 1944, American pentecostalism lost its most widely known public figure.[22]

Charles S. Price

The man who probably influenced the healing revivalists of the postwar period most directly was Dr. Charles S. Price. Born in England, Price received a law degree from Oxford and immigrated to Canada while still a young man.[23] Price went through a series of spiritual crises. He became a Methodist minister, and then, after moving to the United States, received the baptism of the Holy Ghost under the influence of Aimee Semple McPherson's preaching. For a time he ministered to an independent church in Lodi, California, but in 1922 he decided to become a full-time evangelist. Price was a man of rare talent and education in the early pentecostal movement, and he was immediately successful. He held city-wide auditorium meetings throughout the 1920s and strongly resisted the breakup of the movement into warring sects. He refused to identify with any of the pentecostal organizations, and in 1928 announced in his monthly magazine, *Golden Grain*:

> We are to remain as we always have been . . . independent . . . Full Gospel . . . Holy Ghost teachers and preachers . . . coveting the cooperation of all God's blood-washed children and laboring in His vineyard for the salvation of souls.[24]

Price began publishing *Golden Grain* in 1925, and it is perhaps the best record of the successes and hardships of charismatic revivalism before World War II. His own ministry flourished in the 1920s and then met hard times. In a prophetic move, Price maintained his ministry in the 1930s largely by appealing to nonpentecostal Christians. "I am a Holy Ghost preacher," wrote Price in 1937, "and have not and will not compromise on my message. I am proclaiming the gospel of Jesus Christ and all of its fullness, including the Baptism of the Holy Ghost and Divine healing for the days in which we live." [25]

Charles S. Price died in 1947, shortly before the outbreak of the postwar revival. More than any other early independent evangelist, he sensed the nearness of the revival. He felt a cooperative spirit growing. In February 1947, just before his death, he wrote:

> We are in receipt of a letter from a minister who is, evidently, the pastor of a prominent church telling of his dissatisfaction with the fellowship to which he belongs. This man is hungry for God. His letter is one of many we have received, from various parts of the country. Everywhere the spirit is working in the hearts of men drawing them away from their own traditional path into the walk of communion and fellowship with Him. . . . God is moving wonderfully in the hearts of His people in this Divinely appointed hour.[26]

For a time, Price's ministry was carried on by Canadian Lorne Fox, who had been healed in a Price campaign in 1923. Fox edited *Golden Grain* for several years and began holding meetings on the West Coast in 1947. He was on the scene in 1947 when the revival erupted and has been an active evangelist ever since.[27]

Price was not the only revivalist to run up against the harsh financial realities of the depression. During the 1930s, it proved almost impossible to finance large campaigns in the field. The touring ministries of figures such as Raymond T. Richey, F. F. Bosworth, and Aimee Semple McPherson gradually tapered off.[28]

Equally debilitating to the independent revivalists was the friction among the pentecostal sects. Evangelist David Nunn described the situation in the 1930s: "They began to have divisions, splits and controversies. Soon they began to split their splits. Nearly every church was either a split or a splinter!" [29] In 1936, Charles Price had warned that the pentecostal message was being lost amidst the "new cults and doctrines which seem to be springing up everywhere, like mushrooms growing up over night." [30] Doctrinal haggling and suspicions made union meetings impossible.

The pentecostal psyche had already been dealt a crushing blow in 1928, when a national fundamentalist organization refused to admit pentecostal churches. The ravages of the depression further forced the attention of the pentecostal sects inward and put them on the psychological defensive. R. O. Corvin, an influential postwar pentecostal educator, recalled those times:

> Persecution against Pentecostals was both real and imaginary. Preachers who identified themselves with the churches entered the arena of life fighting. . . . They preached in school houses, under brush arbors, in store buildings, on street corners, under tents, in homes, on radios. They built inferior frame structures and large tabernacles.[31]

Immediately after World War II, the psychology of the pentecostal movement began to change. One minister remembered 1946 as the "year of preparation"; others, as had Charles Price, sensed a new mood of anticipation.[32] There was a longing for a renewal of the divine healing and the manifestation of the gifts of the Spirit that seemed to be disappearing from the church. People who professed to believe in healing were anxious to actually witness a miracle.[33] A new generation was hungry for a revival in its own time. Soon, international pentecostal leader Donald Gee was observing "a very noticeable renewed emphasis upon divine healing in connection with evangelism in the U. S. A. and Canada." [34]

Particularly important was the cooperative mood of the pentecostal churches by 1946. The churches were filled with a new generation less belligerent about divisive doctrinal issues as well as hungry for a demonstration of miraculous power. There had been a marked mellowing of sectarian traits among the larger pentecostal denominations. No longer was the membership of these churches largely poor or lower class: their social status had risen sharply during the war years.[35] The pentecostal denominations finally won recognition by organized evangelical religion in America. In 1943, a number of churches joined the National Association of Evangelicals, which, in a sense, was the successor of the fundamentalist movement that had repudiated pentecostalism in 1928.[36] Cautiously entering the NAE, some pentecostal leaders met each other for the first time. In 1947, American pentecostals participated in a world convention of pentecostals at Zurich, and, in 1948, eight major pentecostal churches formed the Pentecostal Fellowship of North America. All this meant changes, as R. O. Corvin has written:

> With this new acceptance in relationship, the Pentecostal preachers became less antagonistic toward the historical churches. . . . They had to adjust their sermons with more charity and their conduct with more peace. . . . Great church structures were lifting the prestige from the lower classes to the middle and upper classes.[37]

The great healing revival which erupted in 1947 was made possible by these changes in organized pentecostalism. David J. duPlessis, probably the most prominent world pentecostal leader of today, believed that the revival was totally the product of this new ecumenical mood:

> The general effects of these international and national conferences have been noticed particularly in city-wide and in county-wide Union Meetings held by Pentecostal evangelists. The pastors and people from almost every Full Gospel Church in the neighborhood attend such campaigns, where it is not uncommon to find from 5,000 to 10,000 and more. Such meetings were unheard of before the first World Conference of 1947.[38]

It was fitting that Oral Roberts, the most famous of the postwar revivalists, was the featured speaker at the constitutional convention of the Pentecostal Fellowship of North America in 1948. One participant expressed well the sense of unity and revival that permeated that meeting: "As the many hundreds of ministers left this great convention there was in all of our hearts an assurance of closer fellowship and unity as we press on in this great age of revivals until Jesus comes." [39]

And so, the times were ripe. Pentecostalism had become affluent enough to support mass evangelism. It had become tolerant enough to overlook doctrinal differences. Convictions were still deep enough that there was a longing for revival. As the older generation thrilled to memories of the miracle ministries of the 1920s, the young yearned for a new rain of miracles.[40]

The need of the hour was for leaders. "The deaths of Charles Price and Smith Wigglesworth within a few days of each other early in 1947," wrote Donald Gee in 1956, "certainly fired many pure young hearts with a holy desire to pick up the torch of their ministry and carry it forward to new achievements." [41] The deaths of these pioneer evangelists, along with that of Aimee Semple McPherson, left a void. Some troubled older pentecostals wondered if the days of revival were over. In fact, the greatest pentecostal revival, identified by some as a part of the prophetic "latter rain," was about to begin. The pioneers of divine healing revivalism were gone, "but almost simultaneously with their passing, God raised up . . . many others to carry on a new wave of revival that has reached nearly every nation of the free world." [42]

The revival erupted in 1947 with astonishing force. The practice of praying for the sick, wrote historian John T. Nichol, "was revived on a scale hitherto unknown." [43] David J. duPlessis wrote:

> The sudden move towards mass evangelism lately, has been just as unexpected and has been equally as little prepared for, as the phenomenal growth . . . 50 years ago. It cannot be attributed to anything else than the spontaneous move of the Holy Spirit upon all flesh.[44]

Almost unanimously pentecostals received the first wave of the revival as a mighty work from God. Stanley Frodsham, for twenty-eight years editor of the *Pentecostal Evangel*, the official magazine of the Assemblies of God, heartily approved of what came in 1948 and 1949, including not only the healing revival but the more controversial "latter rain" emphasis on prophecy which divided many pentecostal churches. The aging editor resigned his position under pressure in 1949 because his support of the revival and the latter rain doctrine was unacceptable to most of his church's leaders. But he, and others like him, had provided an initial friendly atmosphere which allowed the revivalists to win the support of many old-line pentecostals.[45]

The revival that began in 1947 was, to say the least, numerically an astonishing success. "Vast crowds have gathered in many places in the world," wrote Donald Gee in 1956, "that far exceeded those of the former generation of evangelists." [46] The postwar healing revival dwarfed the successes of earlier charismatic revivalists; it had a dramatic impact on the image of American pentecostalism and set off a period of world-wide pentecostal growth. A generation grew up that would never forget the ecstatic years from 1947 to 1952, years filled with long nights of tense anticipation, a hypnotic yearning for the Holy Spirit, and stunning miracles for the believers performed by God's anointed revivalists. In the hallowed atmosphere under the big tents, it seemed most surely that all things were possible.

The Healing

Revival

1947–1958

PROLOGUE

THE HEALING REVIVAL THAT ERUPTED in 1947 thrust into positions of world-wide prominence a group of unsuspecting men. Chapter 3 discusses the two men who first came to the forefront—the two giants of the healing revival, William Branham and Oral Roberts. They were remarkably different personalities, but they quickly recognized one another as the premier leaders of the revival.

Most of the participants of the revival looked upon Branham as its initiator. Out of his massive union meetings in 1947 spread reports of hundreds of miracles and marvels. Branham seemed an unlikely leader. He had long been a pastor in a small independent Baptist church; he was introduced to the pentecostal world by the despised oneness pentecostals; his preaching was halting and simple beyond belief. But William Branham became a prophet to a generation. A small, meek, middle-aged man with piercing eyes, he held audiences spellbound with tales of constant communication with God and angels. Night after night, before thousands of awed believers, he discerned the diseases of the sick and pronounced them healed.

The second giant of the healing revival was Oral Roberts. The success of Roberts was as predictable as Branham's was unpredictable. Only twenty-nine years old when he launched his ministry, he was a tall, handsome Oklahoman thoroughly versed in the nuánces of pentecostal theology and worship. Roberts quickly became the aristocrat of the revival. The son of a pentecostal minister, he had a smattering of college education and was a man of immense common sense. The services under his big tent, which seemed disorderly and crude to millions of Americans who watched them in the early days of television, were models of propriety and decency within the pentecostal context. Oral Roberts' combination of talent and organizational skill quickly pushed him to the first rank of the revival.

The unexpected force of the revival demanded unprecedented amounts of talent. The call for miracle revival came at once from every community. Hundreds of charismatic evangelists, veterans of years of poverty-stricken service in pentecostal churches, rushed to answer the call. The revival gave opportunity to the fascinating variety of gifted ministers who will be studied in chapter 4. They brought to the revival both creativity and a perplexing variety of problems.

Each of the ministers who became prominent within the movement had his own special approach, whether they were able to establish permanent organizations or only flamed brilliantly for a time. Gordon Lindsay, a bright young Assembly of God minister with an impeccable pentecostal background and a wide circle of acquaintances, became the organizer and publicist of the revival. Until his death, Jack Coe, a hulking, friendly man with a raucous wit and a reckless boldness, challenged Oral Roberts as the foremost hero of the people. T. L. Osborn was a young missionary who built a desire to take the revival abroad into a powerful empire. A. A. Allen, whose turbulent personality was both his greatest asset and his deadliest enemy, repeatedly turned adversity into victory. Scores of other evangelists established national reputations and ministered to thousands of believers. Each was different, each made his own contribution to the revival, each fought his own battle to survive. Their stories are the stuff of the revival.

While each independent ministry was unique, they all shared the common hopes and problems outlined in chapter 5. They tried to develop a common doctrine of healing, but they tolerated great diversity. From the beginning they sought support where they could find it and were never afraid to experiment. In the process, they forged a theology which was unique to the independent ministries and their revival.

The revival was nevertheless united more by its problems than by a common theology. The revivalists pondered long the perplexing persistence of healing failures. More serious were the practical enemies that threatened the life of all of the independent ministries. In the early morning hours after a night's campaign, the evangelists frequently could be found huddled around tables in all-night cafes anxiously discussing among themselves their troubles with the press, or denominational leaders, or the government. As crowds dwindled in the late 1950s, these anxieties increasingly bred frustration, anger, and innovation in the movement.

3

Two Giants

WILLIAM MARRION BRANHAM

"THE STORY OF THE LIFE of William Branham," wrote his friend Gordon Lindsay, "is so out of this world and beyond the ordinary that were there not available a host of infallible proofs which document and attest its authenticity, one might well be excused from considering it farfetched and incredible." [1] The climactic chapter in Branham's life began on May 7, 1946, when he received an angelic visitation which was to thrust him to the front of the revival. In the two decades that followed, Branham repeated the story of his vision before hundreds of thousands of listeners:

> Then along in the night, at about the eleventh hour I had quit praying and was sitting up when I noticed a light flickering in the room. . . . As the light was spreading, of course I became excited and started from the chair, but as I looked up, there hung the great star. However, it did not have five points like a star, but looked more like a ball of fire or light shining down upon the floor. Just then I heard someone walking across the floor, which startled me again. . . . He appeared to be a man who, in human weight, would weigh about two hundred pounds, clothed in a white robe. He had a smooth face, no beard, dark hair down to his shoulders, rather dark-complexioned, with a very pleasant countenance, and coming closer, his eyes caught with mine. Seeing

how fearful I was, he began to speak. "Fear not. I am sent from the presence of Almighty God to tell you that your peculiar life and your misunderstood ways have been to indicate that God has sent you to take a gift of divine healing to the people of the world. IF YOU WILL BE SINCERE, AND CAN GET THE PEOPLE TO BELIEVE YOU, NOTHING SHALL STAND BEFORE YOUR PRAYER, NOT EVEN CANCER." [2]

Among "many other things," the angel told Branham that he would be able to detect diseases by vibrations on his left hand.[3]

William Branham was born on April 6, 1909, in a dirt-floored log cabin in the remote mountains of eastern Kentucky. At the time his mother was fifteen and his father eighteen. When he was very young his family moved to a farm near Jeffersonville, Indiana, where he was reared in deep poverty. At the age of nineteen he wandered to Phoenix where he worked for several years on a ranch and began a career as a professional boxer, but he returned home when his brother died. To his neighbors the early life of Branham seemed unsingular. His family was abjectly poor and his father was a heavy drinker, but they seemed typical of the times. William Branham was a dependable youth; he "always lived a clean, moral, quiet life." Later his early acquaintances would remember that he "always seemed to be a little different." [4]

Upon his return to Jeffersonville young Branham began a search "to seek and find God." Religion had long had an important and mystical influence in his life, although his family had not been active church members. Gordon Lindsay reported that God first spoke to Branham at age seven and told him to never drink or smoke—an edict which he claimed never to have violated. Branham later recalled that God had visited him at age three and told him that he would live near a city called New Albany.[5] It is not strange that this young man who returned to his home in the depths of the depression physically weak and spiritually hungry found little to sustain him in the established churches. After visiting many of them, he finally went to a small church and was anointed with oil and received a personal healing. Then, about six months after his religious quest began, he felt the call to preach.

Ordained an independent Baptist minister, Branham attracted a small group of followers who furnished him with a tent. At the age of twenty-four he launched his career with an impressive success. He filled his tent in a revival in Jeffersonville in June 1933; he later estimated that as many as 3,000 people attended the services in a single evening. Branham reported that "at the baptismal service which followed the revival, some 130 people were baptized in water." [6] Even this early ministry, Branham disciples believed, was accompanied by unusual signs.

"It was at this time," reported his friend Pearry Green, "that a heavenly light appeared above him as he was about to baptize the seventeenth person." [7] After the revival, his supporters built a small meeting house in Jeffersonville which came to be called Branham Tabernacle.

Branham's church seemed to flourish for a few years, but the financial condition of the small group was at best precarious. Branham's lower-class supporters were hard-hit by the depression; he preached for them without compensation. [8] The young minister's mysticism estranged him from the more sedate independent Baptists of his community. A Baptist friend later recalled, "He always drifted out into some sort of conversation which I did not grasp, and later came to disregard as entirely visionary, and finally to dismiss his strange cogitations as useless and irrational. I had been a Baptist preacher for many years and had been taught to disregard such ideas and concepts of spiritual things as visions, talking with the Lord, and kindred things." [9]

During these harsh years, Branham, by coincidence, attended a "Jesus only" pentecostal assembly and was invited to preach. Subsequently, he was invited to conduct revivals in several pentecostal churches. He seriously considered working with such groups but was finally persuaded to refuse the offers because of the dubious social reputation of the pentecostals. He later believed that his anointing left him for five years because of this decision, and when the opportunity came a second time he was ready.

William Branham's personal life at that time was a study in the suffering and tragedy of the depression. At the height of his ministry, his halting tales of personal hardship generated a magical empathy with his audiences. He unashamedly told of having his easy chair repossessed by a finance company. With pathos he told of losing his wife and child when the Ohio River flooded in 1937. He was the poorest of the poor. He worked at different jobs before becoming an Indiana game warden, the position he held when he received his famous angelic visit in 1946. [10]

By the end of World War II, William Branham's life had begun to brighten, and he was full of anticipation. His small band of followers believed deeply that he was a man of destiny. "We realized," recalled one church member, "that God gave him some special phenomenon, but we did not know just what it would be." In late 1945 and early 1946 Branham repeatedly told his congregation of new visions. Then, on May 7, 1946, Branham described the angel's visit, the promise of the gift of healing, and a revelation that he would be standing before thousands in packed auditoriums. One of his members later recalled:

Now for a carnally-minded person this seemed absolutely impossible, as this boy was a humble worker, a very poor peasant type, and uneducated. But we had seen other visions come to pass, and he spoke this with such certainty, and openly declared it to everyone, that we were sure this would come to pass also.[11]

In the midst of that Sunday evening service, Branham received a telegram from a minister friend, Robert Daugherty, urging him to come to St. Louis to pray for Daugherty's sick daughter. Branham's congregation "got enough money together to pay his way over and back by train coach," he borrowed some clothes from his brothers, and departed for St. Louis.[12] He had embarked on a journey that would take him around the world five times: the most incredible miracle of all was beginning to take shape in "Brother Bill's" life.

After Branham prayed for her, Daughterty's daughter improved; Branham returned to St. Louis in June to conduct a revival in Daugherty's church. From June 14 to June 25, 1946, Branham preached and prayed for the sick, and his reputation began to spread through the small churches associated with the oneness movement, which had recently merged to form the United Pentecostal church. Shortly after closing his meeting in St. Louis, Branham was invited to hold a revival in the Bible Hour Tabernacle in Jonesboro, Arkansas. Events in Jonesboro set off a flurry of excitement among pentecostals in the surrounding region. Gordon Lindsay later reported that "people gathered to the little city from twenty-eight states and Mexico, and some 25,000 people, it was estimated, attended the meeting."[13] Branham had struck into the heartland of fervent pentecostalism—a heartland starved for a message of old-time miracle power. Branham had also won the approval of W.E. Kidson, one of the pioneer oneness pentecostal ministers and editors.[14] From Jonesboro, Branham was conducted by Kidson from town to town, followed by an entourage of campers. In Jonesboro, he was reported to have raised a dead man; in Camden, a supernatural light appeared behind his head when his picture was taken. An admirer celebrated the beginning of the "sensational gospel ministry of Rev. William Branham . . . bringing salvation and healing to throngs of anxious seekers who dared believe his story of angelic visitation and endowment of the healing power of Jesus Christ."[15]

Among those who attended the Branham revival in Arkansas were some of the members of the oneness pentecostal church in Shreveport, Louisiana, pastored by building contractor Jack Moore. The Shreveport visitors brought back "incredible reports of what they saw" and Branham was invited to the church for a revival.[16] Moore's daughter later recalled his arrival at their home:

All things we heard about him seemed quite incredible; but as he was traveling southward, he stopped with us . . . and since that time we have never really doubted that William Branham is truly a prophet sent from God. Could I ever forget the first time I saw him—that Sunday afternoon in 1947 when a little '38 Ford turned in our driveway, and a slight, tired man with the deep eyes of a mystic got out and looked around. As I watched from the window, I began to weep for no apparent reason, except that my heart seemed to break.[17]

Branham's meeting in Shreveport was a spectacular success, but, more important, he asked Jack Moore and Young Brown of Shreveport to accompany him and help to manage his meetings so that Kidson could return to his church in Houston. Branham had begun to build his first team. Jack Moore remained a valued friend through the remainder of Branham's life and periodically travelled with him, and the revivalist's last major meeting before his death was held in Shreveport.

Leaving Shreveport, accompanied by Moore, Branham held revivals in San Antonio, Phoenix, and in several cities in California in the early spring. While in Oakland, Jack Moore wrote a fateful letter to an old friend in Ashland, Oregon, Gordon Lindsay. Lindsay had spent several years as an Assemblies of God evangelist before settling down in Oregon as a pastor. In an act of tolerance unusual in the 1930s, Lindsay had been allowed to conduct a revival in the Jesus Only church in Shreveport. The personal friendship between Lindsay and Moore proved to be a crucial bridge between the oneness and trinitarian pentecostals in the beginning of the revival. Moore wrote to his friend:

I know you will be surprised to hear from me here in Oakland, California, but this is what happened. We had a Brother Branham from Jeffersonville, Indiana, a Baptist minister who has received the Holy Ghost, and has great success in praying for the sick on such a scale as I have never seen before. So Brother Brown and myself came along with him out here to fill some engagements he had made. We haven't found buildings large enough to take care of the crowds. . . . So we will be in this part of the country for several days and I would like to see you and would like for you to see what this brother is doing.[18]

A few days later Moore visited Lindsay to persuade him to attend the Branham revival in Sacramento.

As Lindsay listened to Branham preach, he was convinced—"this man had indeed received a special visitation from God." He wondered why God had chosen a man out of the Baptist movement—he probably wondered even more why a prophet would rise among the oneness pentecostals—but he was impressed by Branham's emphasis on unity and his humility. After the service Lindsay met with Branham and Moore, who asked him to join them. He wrote, "Because our associations had been in the larger Full Gospel circles, it suggested itself to Brother Branham and Brother Moore, that perhaps I might be the one to introduce him to the ministers of these groups." [19] Until then, the Branham revivals, for all their success, had been mostly in churches, and totally with the United Pentecostals. Lindsay could open doors in the Assemblies of God and the other major pentecostal groups. The two men talked excitedly about the possibility of a united effort to bring the message of deliverance to all the people, avoiding controversial subjects. Lindsay believed it could be done. "Brother Branham," he reported, "was enthusiastic about the idea, for indeed the uniting of believers had been the burden of his heart from the time that the angel had visited him." [20] In addition, Branham recognized that he was no organizer;[21] in Lindsay he had found the most talented promoter of the early years of the revival. The two immediately agreed that Lindsay would arrange a series of meetings in the Northwest for the fall of 1947.

That campaign was a stunning success. During the first meeting in Vancouver, British Columbia, Branham added to his team W. J. Ern Baxter, a colorful Canadian minister who remained an important charismatic speaker into the 1970s. "In fourteen days of services, in four cities, with only a modest amount of advertising," wrote Lindsay, "some 70,000 people attended." [22] The meetings were conducted on an "inter-evangelical basis" and were marked by long hours of prayer for the sick and supernatural occurrences. The crowds were pentecostal, but it was a new generation. Lindsay was astonished that "there had been such an evident falling away in actual practice that we discovered that ninety per cent of these people who attended the meetings had never previously witnessed a single miracle." [23] In January the team toured Florida and held large revivals in Miami and Pensacola. In the spring they conducted a huge campaign in Kansas City and were visited by a young minister who had just launched a ministry of his own, Oral Roberts. In the late spring the team scheduled a series of revivals on the West Coast. Suddenly, in Eugene, Oregon, in May 1948, just as he was beginning to attract world-wide attention, Branham announced that he was ill and would be forced to leave the field.[24] His announcement brought to an end, in evangelist Del Grant's words, "a healing itinerary such as perhaps was never paralleled outside of Christ's and the Apostles' sojourns with the sick of their day." [25]

Lindsay was dismayed by Branham's announcement. He had a "suitcase full" of invitations and had plans to hold campaigns in all the large cities of America. Furthermore, just a few weeks before Branham's announcement, Lindsay, Jack Moore, and Moore's daughter Anna Jeanne, at the instigation of the revivalist, had begun publication of a magazine, *The Voice of Healing,* to promote the Branham meetings. Branham bluntly told his colleagues that his retirement "might be a year or it might be forever." [26] *The Voice of Healing,* he told Lindsay and Moore, was their responsibility. Lindsay felt deserted, and, although the team did work together again, Lindsay never again promoted Branham's work exclusively.[27]

Branham's illness sent a shock through the nascent world of healing revivalism. Oral Roberts, the emerging popular hero, praised the "humble, devout man of God" who was now ill and called upon "God's believing people everywhere to immediately go on their knees, calling Brother Branham's name in prayer, that he may be restored to strength for the mighty work that still awaits his labors." [28] Some privately questioned whether Branham was really ill, speculating that he already sensed an unholy atmosphere entering the meetings. But unquestionably the long gruelling nights of ministering to the sick had taken their toll. In his last meetings he was said to have been tottering and staggering from intense fatigue. Branham later told audiences that he was suffering from nervous exhaustion from the pressure of his work. He also reported that "Mayo Clinic's verdict" was that "you will never be entirely over 'nerves' because of your father's 'drinking.' ".[29]

As suddenly as he had retired from the field, Branham announced in October that he was returning to the revival circuit. He sent word to *The Voice of Healing* that he was gaining rapidly and expressed "sincere appreciation to his many friends who have been so loyal and faithful in their moral and prayerful support." [30] Beginning in late 1948 Branham made a successful tour which included meetings in California and at Alexander Dowie's old church in Zion, Illinois. In November 1949, he returned to Shreveport to visit Jack Moore and Gordon Lindsay. Lindsay reported:

> When we met him, he told us at once that the angel of the Lord had again appeared to him, and that he was to minister in a series of campaigns in America. After that he was to go overseas. He wanted to know if we would go with him in these meetings. After some days of prayerful consideration, we felt it was the will of God and so informed him.[31]

During the five-month interlude of Branham's illness, the world of healing revivalism had erupted. The ministry of Oral Roberts was booming and *The Voice of Healing* had become the publicity magazine for a number of new ministries. But Branham's reentry on the field, perhaps hastened by the success of his competitors, placed him once again at the head of the movement. Branham told Lindsay and Moore that he did not resent the proliferation of ministries:

> Though God did use my ministry in a special way in the earliest days of this special visitation, the Lord is now raising up others. God has made it plain that each has his part in this great move. Let none of us think of himself greater than he ought to think.[32]

At the same time, he declared that "the greatest part of his ministry" was just ahead, and he apparently realized with some surprise that the adoring masses had followed others readily during his absence. Lindsay reported that special arrangements had been made to feature the Branham meetings in *The Voice of Healing*, and that he and Jack Moore would again be accompanying Branham.[33]

In January 1950, Branham, accompanied by Moore, Lindsay, Ern Baxter, and F. F. Bosworth, conducted a dramatic and important campaign in Houston. The meeting began in the City Auditorium but was later moved to the Coliseum because of the size of the crowds. Reportedly, as many as 8,000 people attended a single service. The presence of Bosworth was particularly significant. Bosworth's career, as noted earlier, stretched from Dowie to Branham; without question Branham received inspiration and instruction in pentecostal doctrine and campaigning techniques from Bosworth. Since Branham's crusade in Miami in January 1948, Bosworth had been a loyal supporter and his presence lent enormous prestige to the team. Until his death in 1958, he remained a staunch supporter of the Branham work.[34] During the Houston campaign, Bosworth debated W. E. Best, pastor of the Houston Tabernacle Baptist Church, who had challenged Branham to defend his teachings on divine healing. The affair received considerable attention in the press, a kind of publicity which came to be prized by the revivalists.

An incident occurred during the Houston campaign which later became a legend among Branham followers. Best hired two professional photographers to take his picture during the services. Gordon Lindsay reported the startling results in *The Voice of Healing*:

> Every one of the shots taken were absolutely blank. But a shot taken of Rev. Branham, upon development showed a supernatural halo of light above his head. This completely convinced the photographers, one of whom had been skeptical.[35]

When Branham was informed of the "amazing photograph," he was "not greatly surprised over the circumstances, as a number of times before similar things had happened in his ministry." [36] The photograph became perhaps the most famous relic in the history of the revival.

In April 1950, Branham, Moore, Lindsay, and Baxter made the first journey to Europe by a major American healing revivalist. The group set a precedent of touring which became one of the marks of salvation-healing revivalism in the postwar period. Branham was invited to Finland by a Finnish pastor who had attended one of his campaigns in Arkansas.[37] Scandinavia had long been a center of pentecostalism, but the success of the Branham campaign there was startling. Over 7,000 people filled Finland's largest auditorium night after night and numerous miracles were reported. The campaign brought international publicity to the emerging phenomenon of healing revivalism. *Pentecost*, a magazine published in London and the voice of international pentecostalism, took note of the Branham campaign in 1950. Its respected editor Donald Gee wrote, "Every service held in this hall witnessed a capacity crowd, while hundreds, and in some cases thousands, stood outside." [38] After preaching in a number of places in Finland, Branham toured Norway and Sweden before returning home. By that time, Branham had become a celebrity in his hometown and an internationally acclaimed healer and revivalist.

For the next several years the Branham campaigns were singularly successful. One pentecostal historian wrote, "Branham filled the largest stadiums and meeting halls in the world. He was reported in the newspapers, sometimes favourably, often critically, and in fact in most cases unfavourably." [39] Whatever the slant, he was news. In 1952, accompanied by Bosworth, Baxter, and his son Billy Paul, he held a series of "great revivals" in Africa.[40] In 1955, he made another triumphant tour through Europe.

The Branham team changed from time to time—the growth of Gordon Lindsay's own work caused him to leave Branham after four years—but nothing slowed the pace of Branham's success. The Branham party had no problems financially; Gordon Lindsay noted that many evangelists had to "beat the people" to get funds but that "with the Branham meetings all we did was to pass the pans, practically." [41] Branham's miracles were unsurpassed. In 1951, in Los Angeles, Branham effected one of the more famous healings in the revival's history on William D. Upshaw, a former United States congressman and a widely-known temperance advocate. At Branham's urging Upshaw was able "to walk normally, unaided, after 59 of his 66 years were spent on crutches, and seven years in bed." [42] Branham's healing power became a world-wide legend; there were continued reports that he raised the dead. As early as 1949, thousands of "anointed ribbons, prayed over and anointed by Brother Branham," were being distributed throughout the world.[43]

By the 1950s, the field had become crowded with charismatic healers, but Branham's name awed even the boldest newcomers. Branham's stature was most clearly reflected by the honor he drew from Oral Roberts, the energetic and talented evangelist who increasingly dominated the revival. Roberts deeply respected Branham; he prized a "rare photograph" taken during his 1948 visit to Branham's Kansas City campaign.[44] Roberts was no follower; his mushrooming ministry was his own. But he was obviously flattered when Branham attended his Tampa crusade in 1949. In a dramatic meeting the two "embraced and bowed before the Lord in appreciation of what the Master was doing through their humble lives, and each asked God's richest blessings upon the other's ministry during these last days." *The Voice of Healing* saw the meeting as a demonstration of the "great and big" character of Branham.[45] Roberts' own magazine, *Healing Waters*, also viewed the meeting as a momentous event:

> It was wonderful beyond words to watch these two faithful men, both called of God, both having heard the voice of the same wonderful Savior, both commissioned of the Lord to deliver humanity, as they talked of the marvelous things of God. . . . Both had heard the voice of God, both felt the healing power in their hands. Brother Branham in his left through vibrations, Brother Roberts in his right with power to detect the presence, names and numbers of demons.[46]

Roberts continued to publicize the Branham meetings for several years after his own work had begun its unparalleled growth.

The younger deliverance evangelists viewed Branham as a man "set apart, just like Moses was set apart." [47] "He was number one," said evangelist H. Richard Hall; "Of the common run of evangelists that we have now, put twenty of them on one end and William Branham on the other end and he would outweigh them." [48] He was, said old friend Jack Moore, "the most gifted of all." [49]

William Branham's initial ascendency in the signs-gifts revival was based partly on his reputation—spread by the skillful publicity of Gordon Lindsay and Anna Jeanne Moore—as the "man sent from God." His long nights of ministering inspired many emulators, but also left a generation of awed witnesses who were ever ready to recount hundreds of tales of Branham's unique powers. "When the gift is operating," wrote the aged F. F. Bosworth in 1950, "Brother Branham is the most sensitive person to the presence and working of the Holy Spirit and to spiritual realities of any person I have ever known." [50]

Increasingly Branham became dependent upon the presence of an angel while ministering to the sick. "He does not begin to pray for the healing of the afflicted in body in the healing line each night," wrote F. F. Bosworth, "until God anoints him for the operation of the gift, and until he is conscious of the presence of the Angel with him on the platform. Without this consciousness, he seems to be perfectly help-less." [51] But when "conscious of the Angel's presence, he seems to break through the veil of the flesh into the world of spirit, to be struck through and through with a sense of the unseen." [52]

The first sign received by Branham as a confirmation that he was a healing agent was "vibrations" that he felt in his left hand. In Bosworth's description:

> When the Angel appeared to Brother Branham, he told him how he would be able to detect and diagnose all diseases and afflictions; that when the gift was operating, by taking the right hand [Branham said left] of the patient he would feel various physical vibrations or pulsations which would indicate to him the various diseases from which each patient was suffering. Germ diseases, which indicated the presence and working of an "oppressing" (Acts 10:38) spirit of affliction can be distinctly felt. When the afflicting spirit comes into contact with the gift it sets up such a physical commotion that it becomes visible on Brother Branham's hand, and so real that it will stop his wrist watch instantly. This feels to Brother Branham like taking hold of a live wire with too much electric current in it. When the oppressing spirit is cast out in Jesus' Name, you can see Brother Branham's red and swollen hand return to its normal condition. [53]

Branham later reported that this sign had been greatly misunderstood by many people. It did not imply, he insisted, that "I would have power in my left hand to heal people." His ability to "take hold of the person's left hand" (Bosworth was apparently mistaken in reporting the right hand) and discern his illness did not give him a magical healing power; it was simply a sign that God was with him. [54]

The second sign granted to Branham, and the one which most amazed the tens of thousands who witnessed it, was a gift of the "word of knowledge." Again, Bosworth described the gift:

> The Angel told him that the anointing would cause him to see and enable him to tell the suffering many of the events of their lives from their childhood down to the present time. . . . The great audience hears all this over the

[37

public address system. Brother Branham actually sees it enacted and pushing the microphone away so the audience won't hear it, he tells the patient any unconfessed and unforsaken sins in their lives which must be given up before the gift will operate for their deliverance. As soon as such persons acknowledge and promise to forsake the sin, . . . their healing often comes in a moment before Brother Branham has time to pray for them.

This gift, which many insisted was "exactly 100 per cent" successful, made Branham "a channel for more than the mere gift of healing"—it made him a "Seer as were the Old Testament prophets." [55]

The second sign began to work in Branham's ministry about 1949, after his brief retirement, and it greatly impressed his peers. A modern pentecostal historian, who worked as translator for Branham in one of his campaigns in Switzerland, wrote, "I am not aware of any case in which he was mistaken in the often detailed statements he made." [56] Donald Gee, a usually critical observer, believed that Branham was "remarkably accurate"; to him it seemed "impossible to deny something of the Spirit of God in his revelations." [57] A contemporary evangelist recalled: "I've been with him when he would meet a person that he had never seen and immediately call him by name." [58] This gift did much to further the growing Branham legend. "Branham came to town and called a few people's names," remembered a friend, "and the people would be there out of curiosity." [59]

In his early campaigns Branham often labored for hours praying for the sick. During a 1949 meeting in Zion, Illinois, night after night he "preached and prayed with the sick from three to four hours until taken bodily from the platform." [60] His power was often so great, reported his supporters, that there was no such thing as a hard case for him. In one 1950 meeting, Bosworth reported, "nine deaf mutes came in the prayer line and all nine were healed." [61] Finally, in the early 1950s, Branham felt compelled because of "the limits of physical strength" no longer to "pray for all that throng his meeting." More and more he came to depend on the "word of knowledge." [62]

Perhaps the most impressive facet of the early Branham meetings was his quiet mastery of his audiences. He was notably "gentle and quiet spoken in all his dealings with the people." In marked contrast to the flamboyant tactics of many of the revivalists, Branham seldom "raised his voice or got excited or disturbed." His sermons were largely stories of his personal experiences. With little showmanship, his gifts of knowledge and healing could stir an audience. One observer recorded an occasion when Branham called a woman from the audience, discerned her name and hometown and revealed that she had two growths in her stomach:

When he said this, pandemonium broke out among the great crowd. It seemed that everyone was weeping and sobbing and shouting all at once. Something happened to me inside, and I know that I shall never be the same again. Please don't suggest that there was any fake about all this—the very atmosphere of the place, and the spirit of the man would make such a thought almost sacrilegious.[63]

The trait which most impressed Branham's audiences and won the respect of his colleagues was his "outstandingly humble spirit." [64] "There is nothing boisterous or arrogant about him," wrote an observer, "he is a meek and humble man. . . . He is a man loved by all. No one begrudges him any of his success or is envious of his great popularity." [65] This humility, combined with his refusal to discuss controversial doctrinal matters, won him the support of a wide range of pentecostals through the early fifties. Branham also steadfastly declined to start a new sect, although he obviously could have done so. He insisted that his "great task" was "calling His people to unity of spirit." [66]

In 1955 Branham's career suddenly began to falter. The weaknesses in the ministry that had seemed unimportant during the peak of the revival began to surface. The fact that Branham lived in a different world from other men was not an unmixed blessing. His lack of sophistication left him unprepared to match wits with people who would take selfish and subtle advantage of him.[67] Many felt that his managers had unfairly used him for their own financial gain.[68]

Thus, after nine successful years on the field, Branham faced financial difficulties. He had always been careless about his finances and vowed never to stress money in his campaigns. During the flush years of the revival it had never been necessary. It was easy then for him to be nonchalant toward all business matters; Gordon Lindsay recalled that he was "almost childish in some ways." [69] He sometimes missed scheduled meetings and was totally unconcerned about business details. Some of his business associates came to feel that he was culpably irresponsible. At any rate, Branham came to write:

For nine years, the Lord met every need without my having to pull for money. Then, in 1955, in each of three of my greatest meetings, the income fell far short of expenses and others stepped in to make up large deficits.[70]

The distraught evangelist soberly informed his family that he might leave the ministry and return to one of his old jobs.[71]

Branham's difficulties became more complicated in 1956 when the Internal Revenue Service filed a tax evasion suit against him. While his manager had paid personal income taxes on nearly $80,000 in one year,

Branham had claimed a personal income of only about $7,000. The unsophisticated Branham, apparently little interested in personal wealth, had made no systematic effort to account for the thousands of dollars that flowed through his ministry. After several years of legal negotiation, the Branham ministry settled the case out of court, agreeing to a penalty of about $40,000. For the remainder of his life Branham worked under the burden of that debt, and the larger part of it remained when he died.[72]

Further, the climate that Branham had helped create was beginning to suffocate him. In the Branham meetings "scores of evangelists and pastors received a new anointing upon their lives and launched out into an enlarged ministry." Quite a number developed ministries of national prominence.[73] Gordon Lindsay repeatedly pointed out that the purpose of the Branham meetings was not to encourage a great number to attempt to conduct vast campaigns, but rather to enable pastors to take "new inspiration . . . back to their own churches and begin a real ministry of deliverance."[74] Nevertheless, the deluge came; by the early 1950s Branham could only cordially welcome the charismatic newcomers. "For a while," wrote Lindsay, "he carried, as it were, the weight of a suffering world upon his frail shoulders, until at last God made it known unto him that the responsibility must be shared by others."[75]

Branham accepted the new deliverance evangelists (he really had little choice), but as the aspirants multiplied he more and more felt led to establish a unique ministry. Always hopeful, he believed that some more spectacular miracle was just ahead. When asked by an interviewer in 1951 if he was contemplating retiring from the ministry, Branham replied, "Very much to the contrary, I believe that God will grant me a greater ministry than I have ever had—something else that will go beyond this present revival."[76] He was always concerned not to be considered envious of the other healing ministers, but he remained sure that "something greater than what has been given me is yet at the door."[77] In December 1955, in the midst of his financial difficulties and personal despair, Branham received a famous vision of "a great huge tent" which was "packed and lined everywhere with people."[78] As the years passed, some of Branham's followers found the tent vision their major source of "hope in his own life and ministry."[79]

As Branham became more and more hedged in by the proliferation of healing "imitators," he talked of a "third pull" which would be dramatically different. "Nobody will be able to imitate this one," he told his followers.[80] His prophetic revelations seemed to confirm his growing sense of uniqueness. A personality cult gathered around the charismatic evangelist, even though many of his earlier friends felt that he was not personally responsible for its development.[81] Always outside the mainstream of pentecostalism, Branham's teachings became increasingly unique and divisive as the first flush of enthusiasm wore thin.

Branham's sense of differentness was fed by new prophetic revelations. In 1955, Branham reported that the angel which had given him his original gift had reappeared and together they "descended into a little room." The message he received would have to be kept "secret the rest of my life," but the clear implication was that Branham was now privy to special divine knowledge.[82] In 1957, Leo Mercier, one of Branham's workers, revealed a dream which had stirred his heart and which "our dear Brother Branham has told me . . . has spiritual significance." The dream revealed Branham ministering in a "white disk" above a pyramid. A voice from heaven proclaimed that no other man could stand in the disk "unless he die or be killed," that Branham was "the only one who can and will stand there." While Mercier did not attempt to interpret the dream, he suggested to his readers that "perhaps the Holy Spirit may lead you to know the meaning of it." He did reveal, however, that Branham had confirmed that God had told him that he would receive a new ministry and that "no one could impersonate this last ministry that will be given to him." [83]

By 1958, William Branham, in concert with most of the other deliverance evangelists, was deeply reassessing his ministry. Joseph Mattsson-Boze, a long-time friend, wrote an optimistic notice of the Branham ministry at the beginning of 1958: "In Rev. Branham's office there are at present invitations to 400 of the leading cities of the United States and the largest churches on file. They are writing and they are calling and they are begging Rev. Branham to come. Besides all these calls in the United States and Canada there are invitations to many countries in the world." And yet, reported Mattsson-Boze, Branham was not "at liberty to move too freely as yet" and "instead he has for the time being taken a few smaller meetings." He revealed that Branham had, in the past year, "spent much time alone with God" and assured the prophet's followers that "his greatest ministry is not in the past but in the future." [84] William Branham was searching deep in his psyche for new "leadings" from God.

GRANVILLE ORAL ROBERTS

Granville Oral Roberts, the young man who in 1947 came quickly to rival and then surpassed William Branham as the leader of the salvation-healing revival, had a much more stable early life. In fact, the childhood of Roberts, though it might seem fanatically religious to some, was much more tranquil and secure than those of most of the healing evangelists. Roberts was born in 1918, the fifth son of honest and poor parents. His father was a minister in the Pentecostal Holiness church. Roberts later recalled, "From a child I knew the Lord was with my parents." [1] The great turning point in Roberts' early life came when he was seventeen years old. While playing in a high school basketball game, he collapsed. A short time after his illness was diagnosed as tuberculosis, he felt he was healed of the disease during a tent revival conducted in Ada, Oklahoma, by a traveling evangelist. At the same time he was cured of stuttering and soon began to preach.

From 1935 Roberts spent eleven years preaching in small Pentecostal Holiness churches and learning the hard lessons of poverty and ridicule shared by most American pentecostals before the war years. Never satisfied with this life, Roberts tried to improve himself. While ministering in Enid, Oklahoma, in 1946 he attended the Disciples of Christ's Phillips University and taught occasional classes at a small denominational school, Southwestern Bible College. Defeated and discouraged, yet feeling a compelling call to the ministry and a yearning for more important work, Roberts fasted and prayed intensively in 1947. He then decided to launch an independent ministry.

Oral Roberts' early methods in his independent deliverance ministry may have been influenced by his observation of William Branham. Gordon Lindsay recalled that Roberts discussed the matter with the Branham team in Tulsa in the summer of 1947 and again when he attended a Branham meeting in Kansas City in 1948.[2] But Roberts was no imitator: he was a thoughtful and bold man who clearly made his own decisions. He later reported that he spent "seven months prior to May 1947 . . . fasting and praying in a wholehearted search for God's plan for my life." [3] Roberts conducted his first auditorium revival in May 1947, in Enid, Oklahoma. In quick steps he added healing to his meetings and began emphasizing that his campaigns were interdenominational.[4]

With characteristic vigor and decisiveness, Roberts made a series of crucial administrative decisions. In June 1947, having resigned his pastorate, he moved to Tulsa. In the fall, in a meeting sponsored by three churches in Muskogee, Oklahoma, Roberts reported his first major healing—he removed the braces from the legs of a young polio victim and reported that she was healed.[5] Perhaps his most important early decision was to publish his own magazine, *Healing Waters*. It began in November 1947 with an issue of 10,000 and gave Roberts preeminent visibility in the world of healing revivalism; he has continued to consider it his primary system of communication with his followers.[6]

In the first issue of *Healing Waters*, the basic outlines of the Roberts ministry were already apparent. The magazine not only told of his healing campaign in Muskogee but also offered for sale his first book, *If You Need Healing—Do These Things!* Roberts also issued an appeal for "Partners for Deliverance": "Many have volunteered their work, but yet we need help. We need prayer. We need warriors who will fast. We need financial help. Will you make an investment in human deliverance?" [7] Finally, the "Healing Waters Radio Log" revealed that Roberts was being heard regularly over five radio stations.

Rapidly, Roberts built an organization and a revival team. In 1948, he established Healing Waters, Incorporated, a nontaxable religious corporation with all its "assets bound up in an irrevocable trust made to the retired ministers of the larger Pentecostal groups of America who sponsor his programme." [8] The early staff of *Healing Waters* consisted of five stenographers; Oral Roberts, Founder and Director; Mrs. Oral Roberts, office manager; and L. V. Roberts, Oral's brother, who was in charge of public relations.[9] Roberts and his wife Evelyn worked tirelessly during those early months. The line between financial success and failure was very thin during the early months of expansion. Roberts wrote that when Lee Braxton, a successful North Carolina banker and businessman, visited Tulsa in 1948, he found the staff "struggling to answer our mail. He saw me laying out the proof pages of our monthly magazine on the floor. There was literally no room elsewhere in the house." Braxton immediately advised the young evangelist, "You've got to build an office and do this work in a businesslike way instead of piecemeal like you're having to do here." Roberts instinctively "understood that what he said was right" and resolved to develop an efficient organization. He later wrote: "This incident in my life was large at the time. It has helped me in much larger ones since, for through the growth of this ministry I've been forced to become not only an evangelist, but a businessman." [10] In the first decade of his ministry, Roberts revealed a sure gift for selecting able men to help him. Among his important early staff additions were Braxton and G. H. Montgomery, influential editor of the *Pentecostal Holiness Advocate*, whose facile pen served Roberts well until 1961.

The need for efficient organization was obvious. During the spring and summer of 1948, Roberts' office staff answered 25,000 letters, mailed 30,000 anointed handkerchiefs, distributed 15,000 books, and dispensed 90,000 copies of his magazine. By October, the office staff had grown to seven. Each year the ministry reported impressive growth. In 1952,

Healing Waters, Incorporated received 280,355 letters and mailed out 140,177 prayer cloths.[11] The circulation of the monthly magazine grew from 115,000 in 1951 to 175,000 in 1952 and 265,000 in 1953.[12]

To keep pace, Roberts supervised a series of major building programs. By 1951, a "beautiful Healing Waters Office" had been located in modest quarters in Tulsa. In August 1954, the organization moved into a new three-story, $400,000 office building, but even that soon proved inadequate. By 1958, Roberts had begun construction of a much larger headquarters building.[13]

Meanwhile, Roberts' ministry in the field went through a similar growth. He announced in January 1948, that he had ordered a "tent cathedral" to seat 2,000. In a great step of faith he borrowed $15,000 to make the purchase, convinced that he could raise enough money during his summer revivals to pay the debt. The tent was an immediate success. It let him hold revivals where city auditoriums were not available. Gordon Lindsay wrote in *The Voice of Healing*, "Brother Roberts has provided himself with perhaps the greatest and most complete equipment ever used by an American evangelist in gospel work." [14]

Roberts quickly assembled a team of competent assistants for his revivals. In the spring of 1951 he was joined by Robert DeWeese, a minister who had supervised his Tacoma, Washington, campaign in 1949. DeWeese, who retired from the organization in 1974, remained Roberts' platform assistant until Roberts stopped conducting revivals. By 1952, Roberts' field staff had grown to ten members.

In the late summer of 1950, a crisis struck. In the midst of a tent campaign in Amarillo, Texas, Roberts' tent and equipment were demolished by a storm. The evangelist faced—as many deliverance evangelists later faced—a crushing financial crisis. His friend Lee Braxton flew from North Carolina to his side and gave him "new strength and courage." [15] Oral Roberts had come too far to turn back. In what he always considered a major turning point in his career, he announced that he would conduct several meetings in auditoriums, but that he was immediately ordering a new $65,000 tent. His credit was good and his spirit was undampened.[16]

Early in 1951, Roberts began using his new tent, which seated 7,500. His belief that God would reward his faith seemed confirmed when just two years later the evangelist was forced to purchase a new tent seating 12,500.[17] His audiences grew as rapidly as his tents. In 1948, Roberts calculated that in ten revivals he "prayed for 50,000 sick" and had 7,000 "saved." [18] In one 1950 campaign in Columbia, South Carolina, there were 13,500 "altar calls." [19] In eleven tent campaigns in 1952, reportedly attended by 1,500,000 people, the organization recorded 66,000 people prayed for in the healing lines and 38,457 conversions.[20]

All the while, Roberts blazed the trail for deliverance revivalists in mass communications. His radio network grew steadily: by summer 1950 he was preaching on eighty-five stations. Lee Braxton led a concerted drive to secure "radio partners" to support this work; it grew rapidly in the next several years. His network included 114 stations at the end of 1951, 175 at the end of 1952, and over 300 by the end of 1953. In January 1952, his radio budget was $240,000 a year, but the publicity rewards of such saturation programing were unquestionably large.[21]

Perhaps the boldest venture of faith Roberts ever made was to launch a television ministry. As early as fall 1951 Roberts toyed with the idea and asked the readers of *Healing Waters* if they believed he should undertake such an expensive move. He pointed out that Billy Graham, whom he always admired, had begun a successful television ministry. In early 1952, he revealed that he had made a survey showing that a network of fifty stations would cost approximately a million dollars a year—a staggering sum for a young man who four years earlier had prayerfully borrowed $15,000 to purchase a tent. Not quite ready just then for television, Roberts made a film about his ministry, *Venture of Faith*, which was shown in hundreds of churches throughout the country.[22]

Meanwhile, Roberts worked feverishly to prepare for television. In January 1954, he began broadcasting over nine stations. The initial filming cost was $104,000; station costs seemed overwhelming, even for the maturing ministry of Roberts. The evangelist candidly explained the economics of television to the readers of *Healing Waters*, listing the available stations and their rates and frankly admitting that he could not penetrate any of the major markets without immediate sponsors. Once again, Roberts' supporters answered his appeal; by mid-1955, his program was being aired weekly on 91 domestic and two foreign television stations. He still had managed to support telecasts in only three large cities (Los Angeles, Washington, D.C., and New York City), but he hoped to be on 200 stations by the end of the year. Three years later his network had grown to 136 stations.[23]

In his first ten years of healing revivalism, Oral Roberts repeatedly explored new techniques and won the admiration and respect of his fellow revivalists, who well appreciated his judgment and skill. A modern revivalist, remembering those early days, recalled: "Roberts was as the, you know how the Presbyterians are to the Methodists and the Baptists. I think they are the elite of that group. And that's the way Roberts was among the Pentecostals." [24] Roberts early attracted the attention of the international pentecostal press and soon was a world-wide celebrity. Already by 1949, he was recognized as a giant in the pentecostal world. When the meeting of pentecostal leaders from North America was held in 1948 to form the North American Pentecostal Fellowship, Roberts was chosen to deliver the closing address.

During the first few years of his ministry, Roberts frequently identified his work with the larger healing revival. Reg Hanson, Roberts' early manager, was an old-time friend of Lorne Fox and publicized this link with the past in *Healing Waters*. F. F. Bosworth visited and commended Roberts' early work, though he never worked with Roberts. Roberts was obviously gratified that his ministry had received the approval of William Branham.[25] Until 1952, Roberts continued to publicize occasionally the work of other deliverance ministers in *Healing Waters*, although only a few ever received the seal of Roberts' approval—Branham, T. L. Osborn ("a Tulsa boy"), and the flamboyant Jack Coe. Roberts called Coe a man of "great faith," [26] although the two clashed occasionally and had vastly different personalities.

More and more, as Roberts surged far into the leadership of the independent revivalists and as the ministries began to vary widely in quality and integrity, Roberts isolated himself. Roberts never had an official relationship with the Voice of Healing, the association central to the beginning of most of the other important ministries. He did have a cordial relationship with Gordon Lindsay and on occasion spoke at Voice of Healing conventions, but Roberts had little to gain by linking his ministry to those of less gifted and frequently less responsible men. By the early 1950s, the extreme tactics of some of the revivalists clearly concerned the serious and moderate Roberts, but he never openly criticized another evangelist.

Roberts' aloofness also helped him maintain cordial relations with the pentecostal churches. He carefully courted the churches and, of all the deliverance evangelists, was the most successful in winning sponsoring pastors. He was fortunate to belong to the Pentecostal Holiness church; the larger and more powerful Assemblies of God in the early 1950s began a concerted effort to control its evangelists, but Roberts' much smaller church, while not always enthusiastic about his independence, was not strong enough to challenge him openly.

Roberts' support from the Pentecostal denominations was no accident. From the beginning, he was determined to be free of denominational control and yet to work within the bounds of organized religion. He made a revealing choice when a group of local pastors demanded certain changes in a 1948 meeting:

If I were to have the cooperation of the organized church I'd have to do what they said. Or I'd have to turn away from the church and do it the way I had started. I've always been a churchman so I agreed with them and made that change in the latter part of the crusade.[27]

Few deliverance evangelists were so cooperative. "Having been a pastor for ten years before becoming an evangelist," wrote one of Roberts' supporters, "Reverend Roberts knew and understood the needs of these ministers. And he let them know how much he appreciated them." [28] Precampaign banquets for sponsoring pastors became a common technique to rally supporters; the presence of a high official of a pentecostal denomination at a campaign was likely to receive attention in *Healing Waters*.[29]

Through all his cooperation, Roberts steadfastly maintained his independence of any denominational hierarchy. Although his early meetings were heavily pentecostal and sponsored totally by full gospel churches, he very early emphasized that his ministry was intended for all churches. Lee Braxton wrote in 1951:

Oral Roberts recognizes good in all denominations, and is a strong believer in Church Organizations, but feels that he is called to bring Bible Deliverance to all people of all Faiths. People from almost all denominations attend the Roberts Campaigns, subscribe to *Healing Waters* Magazine, and support the Radio Broadcast. Oral Roberts has received and preaches the Full Gospel experience. But he works with many denominations. He is called to bring deliverance to *The People* and he has no quarrel with some who might not see eye to eye with him on some fine point of theology or doctrine.[30]

Roberts' work became more ecumenical with time. During a 1957 campaign in Raleigh, North Carolina, he listed among the churches represented in his audiences: Assemblies of God, Roman Catholic, Baptist, African Methodist Episcopal, Christian Science, Church of God, Episcopal, Free Will Holiness, Lutheran, Greek Orthodox, Missionary Alliance, Methodist, Glad Tiding Tabernacle, Presbyterian, Missionary Baptist, Pentecostal Holiness, and United Brethren.[31]

The most serious hindrance to Roberts' good relations with the churches was his financial success. The financial expansion of the Roberts' ministry seemed to some a direct threat to the local churches and denominations that supported his work. As early as 1949, a rival minister charged that Roberts was "a racketeer and a fraud." [32] Few things could prod Roberts into open confrontation, but the charges of financial chicanery that followed him through the years occasionally brought a reply. He repeatedly insisted that he had vowed "to touch neither the gold nor the glory"; in truth, his honesty and ethics seemed to be among the more exemplary in the revival.[33]

By the mid-1950s, Roberts had established a financial policy which seemed to him both fair and practical. He reported that he used no funds sent to Healing Waters for his personal benefit and received from the organization only a modest salary. For years, he contributed that salary to evangelistic work. Rather than the organization supporting him, he argued, he supported it:

> I would like to strengthen that statement by declaring that none of my support is received in any way, shape, or form from the Foundation. Conversely, I help to support the Foundation from the love offerings that I receive in the campaigns and from the royalties that I receive from the sale of my books.[34]

Roberts was determined that his campaigns not put an "improper emphasis on money." He recalled that "just prior to my launching out I had attended a healing revival where, from all outward evidence, the evangelist's chief concern was on raising money." That spectacle, reported the evangelist, "made me sick at heart." Consequently, Roberts developed an open and orderly financial scheme:

> During a 10-day meeting under the tent we receive eight expense offerings for the budget, one love offering for me, and pastors who sponsor the campaign. (We began doing the latter in late 1955 and expect to continue.) The local committee is informed of these offerings throughout the campaign. Several times during each meeting the audience is told how much money has been raised and for what purpose. We allow ourselves and the sponsoring pastors, or whoever takes up the offering in the meeting, only three minutes to state the need, offer prayer, and send the ushers to receive the offering.[35]

Roberts' formula, much more open and responsible than was common, astutely provided a financial incentive for local pastors. The fact that the "proceeds from the assets [of the foundation] shall be given to the full gospel churches supporting my meetings and are to be used exclusively for foreign missions and the support of their aged ministers" also did something to salve the feelings of denominational leaders.[36]

Roberts never hesitated to admit that he was personally prosperous. He retained the copyright on six of the thirty books he had written by 1957, and his "love offerings" were admittedly large. The evangelist believed that God did not want his followers to suffer from poverty, and he did not intend to do so himself. He was not ashamed that he had been able to accumulate a modest personal estate.[37] About 1960, his love offerings became so large that Roberts said he felt uncomfortable and placed himself on a salary of $15,000 a year. In the 1970s, the evangelist revealed, with a degree of pride, that despite his success and fame he was not "personally wealthy." [38]

As early as 1954 Roberts predicted that his followers' gifts would be returned to them by God seven times, as he believed that his own works would be rewarded.[39] Under the initial pressure to raise funds for television in 1954, Roberts initiated his "blessing-pact" plan. He offered to earnestly pray that any gift given to his ministry would be returned "in its entirety from a totally unexpected source." If, after one year, this had not happened, the "Evangelistic Association will refund you the same amount immediately and no questions asked." By 1961, Roberts reported that over half the funds for his ministry came from the systematic gifts of his partners.[40]

In the long run, Roberts' financial success depended mainly on his ability to attract and mobilize a growing group of successful charismatic businessmen. The presence of a prominent person or major supporter in one of his campaigns seldom escaped his attention. As early as 1949, Roberts held a businessmen's luncheon during his campaign in Tacoma, Washington. At his instigation, eventually there was formed the Full Gospel Business Men's Fellowship International, which was to have an enormous impact on the charismatic revival in the late 1950s and 1960s.[41] Roberts had a direct and close connection with the organization from the beginning (Lee Braxton was an original vice-president) and greatly influenced its development. Demos Shakarian, the founder of the FGBMFI, remained one of Roberts' strongest supporters and a trustee of the Oral Roberts Evangelistic Association. In 1953, Roberts invited nine prominent supporters to a special conference at his home in Tulsa; conferences with key supporters became annual affairs, and by 1957 the gatherings had grown to include 14,000 people.[42]

Of course, Oral Roberts' initial success and his continuing appeal rested on the healing ministry that began in 1947. His early preaching strongly emphasized the miraculous. By 1954, among the five things that Roberts believed God had shown him, were "a visitation of men by angels as in Bible times," "a new world-wide emphasis on healing and supernatural deliverance," and "mass healings among large audiences." [43] William Branham testified in 1949 that Roberts' "commanding power over demons, over disease and over sin was the most amazing thing he had ever seen in the work of God." [44] In the years that followed, thousands passed through the Roberts healing lines and reported healings of diseases ranging from headaches to terminal cancer. Roberts felt a "manifestation of God's presence in his right hand" which supplied a "point of contact" between the believer and the healing power of God. This gave him "an assurance that resulted in the healing of thousands of people." [45]

Roberts' healing message was essentially positive and practical and was aimed at activating the faith of the supplicant. In his early book, *If You Need Healing—Do These Things!* he listed "six steps to your deliverance:" "1. Know that God's will is to heal you." "2. Remember that healing begins within." "3. Use a point of contact for the release of your faith." "4. Turn your faith loose—now!" "5. Close the case for victory." "6. Join yourself to companions of faith." [46]

Roberts' thought was more than positive thinking. Demons loomed large in his early healing ministry. The sensitivity in his right hand gave him the "power to detect the presence, names and numbers of demons" in afflicted people.[47] Concerning demons, he wrote: "A demon is a strange, abnormal personality of evil. He lost his celestial body, spiritual illumination, godly knowledge and balance. He is now a miserable, disfranchised, homeless, psychopathic creature." [48] Roberts believed that demons were responsible for insanity, one of man's most formidable enemies. In 1948, the unsophisticated young minister reported to his readers: "While I was studying Psychiatry in Phillips University, my professor pointed out that about one-tenth of the population was either insane now or would be before their death." [49]

Roberts' ministry was never one simply of healing, and as time passed, his approach became more and more varied. He was a versatile man, and he believed his ministry was meant to answer a number of needs. He was always interested in evangelism and was a talented preacher. In 1958, Roberts revealed that God had given him seven messages since healing him of tuberculosis as a child. The first four had to do with divine healing. The sixth and seventh had to do with the need for evangelism.[50]

The fifth message, given to him in Miami in 1950, instructed him to "emphasize the power and presence of the Holy Ghost and tell the people to have an expectation for Jesus to come during 1950!"—all through the early 1950s Roberts' evangelism was colored by a fervent end-time emphasis. In 1950, he indeed seemed to be preaching that Jesus would return that year; he later explained that his message had simply been that people should live in the "expectation" that Jesus would return.[51] Subsequently, he continued to proclaim the second coming, writing in 1953, "I feel the soon-coming of the Lord so powerfully and consistently that my soul burns within me." [52] The next year he predicted "a coming together of God's anointed for the final revival." [53]

It was this fervent eschatology that led Roberts in the summer of 1953 to invite nine businessmen to his home in Tulsa to solicit their support for a plan to win a million souls in his campaigns during the next three years.[54] After this goal was accomplished, God, he said, spoke to him for the seventh time in 1956, while he was in Hong Kong, and gave him a master plan for the conversion of ten million people in the next decade.[55] By spring 1958, the team was on schedule with over two million reported conversions.[56]

The 1956 master plan provided for "seven world outreaches of Oral Roberts' Ministry." They included crusades in America, a missionary ministry abroad, the radio and television ministries, a ministry to "the Jews through the placing of Bibles in the hands of the people of Israel," special work among the American Indians, an "outreach for the world's children," and a literature crusade.[57] This multifaceted program was in many ways a summary of the types of ministries developed during the first decade of deliverance revivalism. It was difficult to read the future, but the astute Roberts spread his wings to cover a variety of potentially important works.

Roberts' reevaluation of his work in the mid-1950s was also a part of the general pattern in deliverance evangelism. Finding it increasingly difficult to get the support of the organized pentecostal churches and beset by criticism from the press and other religious leaders, Roberts had serious misgivings about the future. In 1954, he began to wonder if he was reaching a "leveling off place." Would his anointing diminish, he asked himself, would "the Crusades dwindle away?"[58] In 1967, Roberts recalled, "a few years ago, it seemed that the gathering forces of the ministry were coming to a climax and that from that point on the ministry would begin to subside."[59] In fact, "at one period, during late 1957 and early 1958, a shortage of funds threatened to stop our ministry entirely."[60] But Roberts was not intimidated. He refused to stop construction on his new headquarters building, arranged the necessary credit, and increased his labor to raise the needed contributions.

Nevertheless, the Roberts' ministry began to change directions in subtle ways. The tent revivals continued, but other aspects of the ministry became more prominent. Healing was still important in his meetings but evangelism came to be the dominant theme. Furthermore, Roberts began reaching for a new clientele as the pentecostal churches became colder to the deliverance revivalists. He had always ministered to members of traditional churches, but his ministry through the early fifties was heavily pentecostal. By 1956, he was clearly highlighting the appeal of his work to traditional Christians. Quietly, with no public explanation, Roberts' magazine began publication in April 1957, as the organ of the "Oral Roberts Evangelistic Association, Inc." A major reorganization had wiped out the old Healing Waters foundation with its financial ties to the pentecostal churches.[61] Some old patterns persisted, but the first phase of Oral Roberts' healing ministry had come to a troubled close.

4

The Flowering of the

Healing Revival

GORDON LINDSAY *and the Voice of Healing*

MORE THAN ANY SINGLE MAN, Gordon Lindsay brought system and unity to the healing revival. Lindsay contributed to the revival an orderly mind, a keen business sense, boundless energy, badly needed literary skills, and an ecumenical spirit. He very correctly surmised that the revival needed a coordinator and publicist much more than another evangelist. Lindsay's calm temperament, his career as an itinerant evangelist in the 1930s, and a well-deserved reputation for integrity pushed him quickly to the foreground.[1]

The life of Gordon Lindsay singularly equipped him for leadership in the healing and charismatic movements. His father was a teacher and his mother, who came from a moderately well-to-do family, was a woman of profound faith. The Lindsays were deeply religious; Gordon Lindsay was born in 1906 in Zion City where his parents had come as disciples of Alexander Dowie. While still a baby Lindsay saw the pioneer healer, though he did not later remember the event. When Zion plunged into financial difficulties in 1904, the Lindsays migrated west. A few years later they joined another religious communal experiment in southern California, Pisgah Grande, under the leadership of Phinias Yoakum.

[53

After about six months, the Lindsays, again disillusioned, abandoned Pisgah Grande and settled permanently near Portland, Oregon. In his youth Lindsay fell under the influence of Dr. John G. Lake, who had established a church in Portland in 1920. Adding one other hallowed pentecostal name to his experience, the young Lindsay was converted under the preaching of the pioneer of American pentecostalism, Charles G. Parham.

When only eighteen Lindsay decided he wanted to preach, and, with the help of Lake, he began a career as a traveling evangelist. For the next eighteen years, first alone and then with his family, Lindsay traveled across the country holding revivals in full gospel churches. He later estimated that during those years he conducted over 150 campaigns. This period of travel prepared him as perhaps no other man in the nation to establish communication among a variety of pentecostals. Most of his work was with the Assemblies of God, but for a short period after his marriage he was a minister in the Foursquare Gospel church, and he had many friends in other pentecostal groups. When World War II began, Lindsay felt compelled to give up his evangelistic wanderings because of the hardships created for his young family and accepted a call to pastor a church in Ashland, Oregon.

The decision to resign his pastorate in 1947 and become William Branham's manager was hard for a prudent man like Lindsay. His managerial talents were soon obvious in the Branham campaigns, and in April 1948, he opened wide the door of the revival when he edited the first issue of *The Voice of Healing*. It was at this crucial point that Branham informed the bewildered Lindsay that he "would not continue on the field more than a few weeks more." [2] Lindsay, in another difficult personal decision, decided to invest his own savings to continue the publication of the new magazine in cooperation with his long-time friends, Jack Moore and his talented daughter Anna Jeanne Moore.

Lindsay's only alternative was to find new revivalists to publicize. "Already a large number of evangelists had received a new vision of apostolic ministry and were beginning to hold campaigns that were drawing large audiences," recalled Lindsay—the field seemed open. Lindsay learned of a young minister named William Freeman who had been "holding meetings in small churches" and visited one of his campaigns. Freeman at once asked Lindsay to work with him in a series of campaigns if he "felt it was the will of God." [3] A successful series was immediately launched and, through 1948, *The Voice of Healing* featured the miracles of the Freeman campaigns.

In March 1949, Gordon Lindsay reported to his readers the

phenomenal success of the first year of *The Voice of Healing*. The circulation had grown to nearly 30,000 per month and was expanding at an ever accelerating rate. "During this period," wrote Lindsay, "we have seen this publication grow from a small paper to a magazine of national and international circulation, reaching into all states of the union and many foreign countries."[4] *The Voice of Healing* became the firebrand in the night spreading the word of revival throughout the whole world.

In December 1949, Lindsay arranged the first convention of healing revivalists in Dallas, Texas. The assembly was addressed by Branham, Lindsay, Moore, old-timers such as F. F. Bosworth and Raymond T. Richey, and a number of rising revivalists including O. L. Jaggers, Gayle Jackson, Velmer Gardner, and Clifton Erickson. This "historic conference" symbolized the vitality and cohesion of the revival.[5]

The following year, the evangelists, about 1,000 strong, met in Kansas City. Conspicuously absent were William Branham and Oral Roberts, but virtually every other important revivalist in the nation attended this Voice of Healing convention. Lindsay intended to coordinate and direct the mushrooming revival through the convention. The movement was old enough to have revealed several points of danger and tension. He tried to define them and to propose guidelines for the future.

Most important, Lindsay tried desperately to avert a clash between the evangelists and the pentecostal churches; in fact, many felt he deferred too much to the Assemblies of God hierarchy. He gave firm assurance that the Voice of Healing conventions would not lead to a new denomination or fellowship to compete with the older pentecostal churches. In an article announcing "the purpose, plan and policy of the Voice of Healing Convention," he scored extremists in the churches and among the independents. He denounced "free-lancers who violently and indiscriminately attack organization in general." These evangelists, asserted Lindsay, "break fellowship, and then pity themselves because they fail to have fellowship." On the other hand, he believed "it is wrong for organizations to persecute independent churches." He urged avoidance of "novel prophetic interpretations, dogmatic doctrinal assertions, sectarian predilections, theological hair-splitting."[6]

In effect, this 1950 meeting made the Voice of Healing convention into a loose association of healing revivalists. The evangelists officially associated with *The Voice of Healing* magazine held "family meetings" at the conventions, at the same time maintaining their desire to "prove to the world that those associated with *The Voice of Healing* have no intention to organize another movement."[7] Through the decade the Voice of Healing conventions were showcases for healing revivalism. The conference programs were workshops on the problems of healing evangelists. Typical topics were "prayer and fasting," "preparation for a campaign," "the follow-up work after a campaign," "the system of cards for the prayer tent and the healing line." In one meeting, which included many local pastors as well as the revivalists, Jack Coe discussed the delicate subject of finances and outlined a plan which reportedly was received with "great satisfaction" by the pastors. As the association grew in importance in the 1950s, the program frequently was headed by Roberts or Branham; every new revivalist aspired to be a speaker on the program.[8]

And so, after 1950 the Voice of Healing was more than a magazine—it had become a loose fellowship of ministers working under loose rules. In return for their support of the magazine, the ministers received publicity and advice from Lindsay. By 1952 he had built a new headquarters building in Dallas and had drawn up general rules governing the admission of new ministers:

> Briefly we may say that they should: (1) Have a mature healing ministry. (2) Be willing to accept and abide by the articles of the constitution. (3) Have a character that is without reproach. (4) Be willing to practice the ideal of THE VOICE OF HEALING fellowship. (5) Labor for the unity of God's people. (6) Be willing to help to the best of their ability in increasing the circulation of the magazine. (7) Be an evangelist and not a pastor.[9]

Lindsay repeatedly emphasized that his fellowship did not compete with churches and did not "include all men whom God is using in the deliverance ministry by any means." It was, in effect, a central advertising bureau for evangelists with proven ministries. Lindsay rejected many applications for membership because "full information is not available at the time that the evangelist's ministry has reached . . . maturity." He also demanded that the Voice of Healing ministers show "consideration for the pastors" and maintain the respect of local pentecostal churches. As late as 1953, he boasted that his group had "the confidence of the Full Gospel organization"; he worked hard, but ineffectually, to maintain that relationship. Ministers who stopped supporting the Voice of Healing, either by beginning their own publication or by retiring to a local church, were dropped from Lindsay's listing.[10]

The Voice of Healing roster of evangelists flowered in the early 1950s. Lindsay continued to publicize Branham's work, although he was not formally associated with the organization; the nucleus of the fellowship was an influential clique which included O. L. Jaggers, William Freeman, Jack Coe, T. L. Osborn, A. A. Allen, and Velmer

Gardner. Attrition soon set in when O. L. Jaggers and Jack Coe began their own publications in 1953, and in the years that followed the most successful of the revivalists tended to abandon Lindsay's fellowship.[11] Nevertheless, by 1954 the "associate editors and evangelists" listed in *The Voice of Healing* numbered nearly fifty; it was a directory of the successes and failures of the next decade.

Lindsay for a time contemplated becoming an active revivalist himself. In 1949, he wrote, "Up till now we have not assumed any great responsibility in praying for the sick. We ask our readers to pray for us that the Lord will guide us. If time and strength is available it may be we shall hold some healing campaigns ourselves." [12] Lindsay did take to the field on several occasions in company with other revivalists such as T. L. Osborn, but more and more he confined his work to organization and management.[13] His success there led him to decide against a permanent tie to any ministry and he determined to build the Voice of Healing into a major work in its own right.[14]

By the end of a decade of independent work, Lindsay's ministry had become an important one by any standard. His wife reported in 1956 that the expenses of the Voice of Healing were running $1000 a day.[15] In addition to the national and regional conventions sponsored by his organization, Lindsay also began to sponsor missions and a radio program.

Lindsay's overview of the deliverance-healing revival was without equal. He visited the revivalists' meetings constantly and received frequent reports from most of them. In an article published in 1954 he announced that during the "past couple of months" he had attended a Branham auditorium meeting in Denver and an A. A. Allen campaign in Bellflower; he had been with Gayle Jackson in Evansville, David Nunn in Zanesville, Morris Cerullo in South Bend, R. W. Culpepper in Baltimore, and Richard Vinyard in Moosic, Pennsylvania. In addition, he reported on the "mighty momentum" of the foreign campaigns of Tommy Hicks in Argentina, of T. L. Osborn in Indonesia, and of James Daoud in India. "It is evident," he concluded, "that the salvation-healing revivals, in most places, instead of diminishing, are increasing in power." [16]

Lindsay was more than an advisor during the first decade of the healing revival; he was much like the director of an unruly orchestra. He tried desperately to control the proliferation of ministries in an effort to keep the revival respectable. He repeatedly advised, "It is better for one to go slow. Get your ministry on a solid foundation. . . . By all means avoid Hollywood press agent stuff." [17] While he wanted to "as fully and

[57

fairly represent the field as is possible," Lindsay took seriously the character clause of the general rules an evangelist was asked to observe if he hoped to receive the highly-prized publicity in the pages of *The Voice of Healing*. Lindsay was particularly wary of those evangelists who seemed to "have an inordinate ambition to magnify themselves" and those who seemed to hope to "amass money for personal comfort." [18] Lindsay clearly saw and certainly expressed more openly than any other man the destructive and divisive excesses in the movement. He tried his best to direct and control its expansion, but in the end it outgrew his ability to direct. Many of the evangelists came to resent the coercive power he exercised. Many of the new leaders of the early 1950s owed their early success to the literary support of Gordon Lindsay, but success brought independence and independence led to a chaotic clash of competing ministries. By 1958, many of the revivalists believed that Lindsay's work was over. Some told him directly that he should retire.[19]

JACK COE

Jack Coe, an ordained Assemblies of God evangelist, swept to the front of the revival in the early 1950s. Born in Oklahoma City in 1918, he was abandoned by his father and mother and was reared in an orphanage. He left the orphanage at age 17 and soon "was deep in sin." He became a heavy drinker but all the while struggled with a stern pentecostal conscience. Finally, while in the army during World War II, he "received a miraculous healing" and decided to become a minister. Coe began conducting healing revivals while still in service, and in early 1944 he was ordained an Assemblies of God minister.[1]

A large, self-assured man with a brash sense of humor, Coe had a dynamic personality and stage presence. He played to the crowd brilliantly. He was sometimes saucy, sometimes angry, sometimes flippant, sometimes humble, always nervy. He rented his first tent in 1947 and launched a short-lived magazine to publicize his ministry. Although his ministry was small, Coe was an established evangelist when the revival exploded in 1947.[2]

Of all the charismatic evangelists, only Jack Coe seriously challenged Oral Roberts as the popular leader of the revival. Gordon Lindsay spoke of his "tremendous hold on the common man," and judged that his appeal to the masses was greater than Roberts'.[3] But where Roberts was able to use his small Pentecostal Holiness church as a base without its seriously threatening his independence, Coe was up against the much larger Assemblies of God, which was more able to control its evangelists.

Coe's dash and flair thrilled his audiences and at the same time irritated his church's leaders.

Lindsay recalled vividly the first time he attended a Coe revival in 1948:

He knew of me, because I was then engaged in large campaigns with Brother Branham. In those days Brother Coe was generally regarded as an extremist. . . . By the time the service was over I realized that although the evangelist was new in the art of preaching, he possessed a dynamic personality and had the ability to present the Gospel message with unusual power. I saw that he had possibilities of going far.[4]

Coe quickly won the respect of his peers and the allegiance of thousands. He was a preacher with a sting. He thrived on controversy and drew lots of it with his rough and ready tactics. He appeared to enjoy a fight. A fearless healer, he looked for hard cases. "Coe was a bold man, recklessly bold," recalled a contemporary evangelist.[5] Gordon Lindsay found him good at heart but noted, "In growing up it was root hog or die. For that reason he tangled." When Coe died in 1957, Lindsay wrote his obituary: "Jack Coe, lovable, impulsive, bold in spirit yet tenderhearted, beloved of thousands, though not without bitter enemies." [6]

Coe did everything frenetically. He preached in blunt words, calling the apostles "uneducated smelly fishermen." Juanita Coe, his wife and colleague, wrote, "Some say that he isn't as dignified as a minister should be." [7] He attracted large numbers of blacks to his campaigns—the first evangelist to do so. His claims of miracles were among the more extreme. He on occasion said that those who opposed his work were likely to be struck dead by God.[8] Above all, he was the ultimate healer:

In . . . Alabama he had 103 people in wheelchairs and crutches all in a line. So he goes down through the line—there's none, not any, that's ever followed after him—but he would go down the line and pick people up out of the wheelchairs. If they fell, he'd say you didn't have faith. If they walked, and there was 63 of them in this one meeting in Birmingham, one night, walked out of their wheelchairs, got up off their beds, and they were afflicted. . . . There was no make-believe; it was true.[9]

Coe was in constant conflict with his colleagues—or competitors. Some ministers, wrote Mrs. Coe in 1956, "to this day hate him" because of his "plain speaking." [10] Oral Roberts called Coe a man of great faith,[11] but even he was not immune to Coe's needling. Coe visited a Roberts meeting, measured the Tulsa evangelist's tent, and then ordered one slightly larger. In July 1951, he ran a notice in *The Voice of Healing*:

A letter from the Smith Manufacturing Co., Dalton, Ga., declares that according to his measurements the Coe tent is by a slight margin the largest

[59

Gospel tent in the world. Since Oral Roberts has a prayer tent 90′ × 130′, Brother Roberts has the largest amount of tent equipment. Both the Coe and Roberts tents are larger than the Ringling Brothers big top.[12]

According to Gordon Lindsay, Roberts was irritated by the article and complained to him. "Jack had no business doing that," Lindsay agreed, but he urged Roberts to overlook the matter since his own ministry was so great.[13] Coe never let the issue rest. Declaring that he was not in competition with others, he repeatedly mentioned over the years that he had the biggest tent in the world. Writing about that tent, Coe could boast, lecture his fellow evangelists, and appear humble and victimized all at the same time:

> I bought my present tent to accommodate the crowds attending my meetings. . . . When evangelists make statements about the size of their tent, they could dispel much of the controversy by giving the actual length and width. Then people would not feel that someone was telling a lie or exaggerating. I'm not saying this to belittle or condemn some other evangelist, but many have claimed that we are exaggerating when others beside myself state that they have the world's largest tent. If they do have . . . I praise God for it! If they will write me, telling me the size of their tent . . . I will print this information in my magazine, admitting that mine is only the second or third largest.[14]

Coe began to publish his own magazine, originally entitled the *Herald of Healing,* in 1950. That same year he also opened a children's home near Dallas, a project recalling his own days as an orphan. He was aided, Juanita Coe wrote later, by his ability as a manager and by the support of wealthy business men.[15]

The magazine originally listed a number of field editors—W. V. Grant, Wilbur Ogilvie, Gayle Jackson, Mildred Wicks, Velmer Gardner, Clifton Erickson, and Gordon Lindsay, among others. But soon it became simply the voice of his own ministry.

> This magazine is a voice to cause people to see Christ first, and to help them to realize that the fullness of the Gospel-Salvation, Divine Healing Baptism of the Holy Spirit, and the Soon Coming of the Lord is all in the blood of Jesus Christ.[16]

The magazine flourished. Within a year circulation had reached 35,000; by 1956 it had reached 250,000. The masthead boasted that the *Herald of Healing* was one of the fastest growing magazines, with almost a hundred percent renewal each year.[17]

Coe was not so successful in conciliating the leaders of his denomination, the Assemblies of God. To the degree that his volcanic personality would allow, he tried. When he held a meeting in 1952 in Springfield, Missouri, the headquarters of the church, a report noted that Coe urged the people to read *The Pentecostal Evangel* and obtained 120 subscriptions to the paper.[18] The evangelist was also said to have refrained from begging or pleading for money and to have been "led to take offerings to be given to missions and other causes." [19] The Assistant Superintendent of the Assemblies of God, R. M. Riggs, wrote to Coe, "You are doing an excellent work, and I want you to know that I am standing with you in love and prayer." [20]

Nevertheless, it was in the same year that Coe, chaffing under all restraints, decided to build an independent congregation in Dallas. The first meetings were in a theater. Church leaders were frustrated by his extreme independence and embarrassed by some of his methods. In a dramatic feud, he was expelled from the Assemblies of God ministry in 1953 and a period of bitter recrimination followed. For a while, Coe apparently considered establishing a competing group to be called the Fundamental Assemblies of God.[21] But in the end, he simply went on his extremely individual way. He raised $350,000 in six months to complete his church building and, in 1954, the Dallas Revival Center was opened with a gala celebration featuring sermons by leading revival figures such as O. L. Jaggers, A. A. Allen, Gayle Jackson, W. V. Grant, Mildred Wicks, and the new leader of the Full Gospel Business Men's Fellowship International, Demos Shakarian. Within two years, it was one of the largest churches in Dallas.[22]

Coe's reach sometimes exceeded his grasp. In 1954, he announced the beginning of a television series that would soon grow into "a vast weekly network of Gospel television programs," but only a few shows were aired on small stations. Coe complained that it was virtually impossible to "locate Christian cameramen who will be able to faithfully photograph healings as they occur and give us complete television films on schedule," but also television placed obvious financial strains on his ministry.[23] At the end of 1956, Coe announced plans for a new television series. He asked his supporters, "Help put Jack Coe on 100 TV-stations." "Starting Feb. 3, 1957," the evangelist wrote, "vast audiences from coast to coast will be seeing Jack Coe's television films . . . taken right *beside* him as he preached and prayed for the sick!" Coe appealed to his faithful supporters: ·

Our agent has worked hard and faithfully to line up the best possible stations available at economical rates . . . but, even so, the costs are tremendous!

[6 1

However, God has shown us that it is worth everything it will cost in time, money and effort.[24]

It was not to be.

In 1956 two events centering on Coe were among the most critical in the first decade of the revival.

In February while preaching in Miami, Florida, Coe was charged with practicing medicine without a license. He was jailed and released on $5,000 bond. The trial received national publicity. Suddenly, the revival seemed jeopardized. Coe telegraphed and telephoned evangelists all over the world to come quick to Miami to testify in his defense.[25] Dozens came to take the witness stand, most notably Gordon Lindsay, Raymond T. Richey, Gayle Jackson, and Richard Vinyard. The two-day trial was tense but when it was over the judge had ruled that he could not "condemn the defendant or anyone who in good faith advocates and practices Divine Healing." [26] He dismissed the case.

Coe charged that the trial was the result of a conspiracy of atheists, newsmen, and the Churches of Christ, whose ministers were among his main assailants in Miami. Some of his enemies seemed concerned that divine healing was a threat to public health. The enmity of some seemed to result from a clash of social classes. To others, the issue was a strong religious disagreement. Each of these forms of opposition was typical of that faced by Coe and other evangelists.

Then in December came perhaps the greatest shock in the history of the healing revival. While preaching in Hot Springs, Arkansas, Coe became critically ill. He had been working as always on a brutal schedule and had been careless of his health. He was badly overweight. At first he was thought to be suffering from exhaustion but soon his disease was diagnosed as polio. Of all the early evangelists, Coe was the most outspoken against medical treatment but he gave his wife permission to admit him to the hospital, as she later revealed, to satisfy her own conscience. Coe himself, having conducted his life as a race against time, seemed to feel that he was reaching the finish line.[27] A supporter wrote of him in hospital:

He is unconscious part of the time, but occasionally rallies and makes known some desires. He cannot speak. . . . He is in very serious condition . . . but we know that God can and WILL deliver him.[28]

When Coe died in early 1957, the revivalists could not ignore the puzzling question: "Why was Jack Coe taken in the midst of his ministry?" Gordon Lindsay believed that things might have been different had someone been able to pray for Coe, but the stricken evangelist had been quarantined.[29] Evangelist O. L. Jaggers scolded Mrs. Coe for not calling him to effect her husband's healing and told the widow he would come and raise him from the dead if she would only request his assistance.[30] But, wrote Lindsay, the death obviously had been God's will or providence would have allowed someone to pray for him. It was difficult to understand, but Coe's ministry had simply been fulfilled.[31]

Juanita Coe announced that she and the department heads of the ministry would continue the work that her husband had started. She was an able person; she had played a public role in the ministry from the beginning. Attractive and articulate, she served as assistant pastor of the Dallas Revival Center. She continued for a time to conduct healing campaigns. Many felt that she could have sustained a major revival ministry, but she chose to allow that phase of the ministry to taper off.[32] More and more Juanita Coe directed her energies to the support of foreign missions and the development of her children's home, which now sheltered sixty boys and girls. In 1958, she was joined by John Douglas, Sr., in an effort to coordinate a major missionary fund.

The Jack Coe ministry remained a large work—in 1958 the *Herald of Healing* circulated to 300,000 readers—but the death of the evangelist had pushed it from the mainstream of the revival.[33]

T. L. OSBORN

The man who came closest to carving out a unique ministry during the early years of the revival was a young Oklahoma evangelist, Tommy L. Osborn. In the process, Osborn pioneered many new techniques for independent foreign evangelism and won the respect of most of his contemporary evangelists. When the revival declined in the late 1950s, many others, in efforts to survive, followed the trails Osborn blazed.

One of thirteen children, Osborn was raised in the poverty of a depression farm in Oklahoma where he learned a deep trust in God. In 1937, when he was fourteen, he believed that God spoke to him and told him that he would preach. Although he finished only the eighth grade, he became a minister in the small Pentecostal Church of God. In 1946, he spent a discouraging year in India as a missionary. He returned sick and disappointed and settled into a small local church in McMinnville, Oregon. At best Osborn's early years as a minister were a limited success.[1]

[63

In Oregon, a disillusioned Tommy L. Osborn awaited the fateful arrival of the William Branham party in the summer of 1947. On the first night of the Branham campaign in Portland, Osborn's wife was in the audience. Daisy Osborn, a bright and forceful person in her own right, persuaded her husband to attend the next evening. Osborn later wrote:

> As I watched Brother Branham minister to the sick, I was especially captivated by the deliverance of a little deaf-mute girl over whom he prayed thus: "Thou deaf and dumb spirit, I adjure thee in Jesus' name, leave the child," and when he snapped his fingers, the girl heard and spoke perfectly. When I witnessed this, there seemed to be a thousand voices speaking to me at once, all in one accord saying over and over, "You can do that." [2]

Out of this experience "was born a unique missionary ministry that has reached tens of thousands for God." [3]

Osborn launched his independent ministry the next spring, and the help of Gordon Lindsay was crucial in his early success. Lindsay early recognized that Osborn had "a bold faith and an exceptional ability," but he also knew that the young minister needed financial backing and publicity. Lindsay helped provide both. He began to publicize Osborn's meetings and also teamed with him during a campaign in Pennsylvania. He wrote:

> This meeting made history in that area. . . . Enough funds were raised in the campaign to purchase the tent that had been used for the meeting. From that time on this evangelist had large audiences wherever he went in America. Overseas, however, proved to be the theater of his greatest accomplishments.[4]

In many ways Osborn was less controversial and more respected by other evangelists than any other man. For many years Gordon Lindsay remained his major promoter, but every powerful evangelist in the field gave Osborn free publicity. Oral Roberts affectionately recommended him as "a Tulsa boy." [5] William Branham was proud that he had influenced Osborn to start his independent ministry:

> I think he is a wonderful man. He is a dear friend of mine and I love him with a deep love. I think this program of his . . . is a wonderful thing and I am very thankful for it.[6]

Even in the late 1950s, when world pentecostal leaders began to be wary of the independent ministries, *Pentecost* magazine still published reports from T. L. Osborn.[7]

There was a moral seriousness about the Osborn ministry and about the Osborns themselves which impressed their peers; the same quality led them increasingly into foreign work. This move had beneficial side

64]

effects. As Osborn increasingly turned his attention to overseas campaigns, he also withdrew from the growing competition among the healing revivalists in the United States. Not until the revival began to collapse in America did the major evangelists once again begin to look upon Osborn as a competitor.

Osborn studiously avoided the clashes between the evangelists and the pentecostal churches in the 1950s. When intense pressure was applied in the mid-1950s to isolate such radicals as Jack Coe and A. A. Allen, however, Osborn took a firm stand for the freedom of the deliverance ministries. "Those who must wait for organizational sanction upon every new sign of God's presence," he wrote, "will find themselves hesitating in the pews of skepticism while courageous men and women of faith advance and do exploits in His name." [8] Osborn worked for peace, and his foreign work closely identified him with the organized mission efforts of pentecostal denominations.

From the beginning of his ministry Osborn reported tremendous successes in foreign campaigns. In his first five years he conducted crusades in eleven countries and preached to millions.[9] Very early in his career he held an "island-shaking" revival in Cuba in which "over 50,000 persons professed to accept Christ." [10] In Chile, as many as 100,000 persons packed the stadium to attend a single Osborn service.[11] As a result, Osborn wrote that he was moved by the "alarming challenge of the heathen masses everywhere dying without Christ" and felt "compelled by the Spirit" to "bear a miraculous gospel" to all the world.[12]

Osborn's concern for the heathen crystallized in 1953 when he received "the vision for native evangelism." He became convinced that native workers should be trained to follow up the mass crusades held by the healing evangelists and formed the Association for Native Evangelism. The original organization included on its advisory board officials of the Assemblies of God, Church of God, and Foursquare churches, though clearly Osborn was not dominated by any organization. In fact, the growing treasury at his disposal made him a man to be courted by the mission boards of the denominations.[13]

Osborn's success was lasting, and the growth of his ministry was steady. In 1956, he began to publish his own magazine, *Faith Digest*, and withdrew from the Voice of Healing family. The relationship between Osborn and Lindsay remained cordial but it had become apparent that while *The Voice of Healing* was an enormously effective organ for Osborn's fund raising, Osborn did relatively little to aid the financial growth of the magazine. By 1956, the Osborn ministry included seventeen workers, a modest building in Tulsa, and an impressive program of foreign mission work. Two years later, the ministry reported astonishing growth. *Faith Digest*, which had begun with a circulation of 12,000, was being printed at a rate of 250,000 copies per month. Osborn had produced and was circulating a movie dramatizing his work and had begun a radio ministry costing $10,000 per month.[14] As the revival lost momentum in the late 1950s, Osborn clearly considered diversifying his efforts even further, but instead he returned decisively to his old emphasis on missions. In May 1958, he abruptly announced the end of his radio series:

> I feel that God has given us the greatest calling on earth—that of Evangelism among the unreached. When the truths of faith and healing were revealed to me, God impressed me to take the message to the Heathen as Paul did. . . . That is why God has so abundantly blessed our lives.[15]

Osborn's decision to abandon his expensive radio ministry was a good example of his decisiveness. Supported by his wife, Osborn contributed much to the early years of the revival. Confronted with crowds of countless thousands at his foreign revivals, Osborn developed the technique described as "praying for the sick en masse, thus eliminating the long healing lines and human limitations." [16] The healings and miracles that took place in his campaigns were often sensational, although the major publicists of the revival felt he was a scrupulously honest reporter.[17] During "almost every service" in a campaign in Java in 1956 "someone saw the Lord." Osborn "testified that he felt Christ's presence in an unusual way, although he himself did not see the Lord as He appeared." [18] Osborn later wrote that "The Lord Jesus Christ has appeared at least once" in nearly "every campaign we have conducted overseas." [19] Combining a profound appreciation of the miraculous, a good preaching ability, and a bold common sense, Osborn faced the future in 1958 with a distinctive ministry and a loyal base of supporters.

A. A. ALLEN

The later history of the movement showed Asa A. Allen to have been one of the most important revivalists to emerge in the early days. Gifted, dramatic, and controversial, Allen's was the Horatio Alger story of spiritual and financial success in a movement filled with self-made men. A relative latecomer, "Triple A" clawed his way to the leadership of one wing of the revival by the end of the 1950s.

Born in Sulphur Rock, Arkansas, in 1911, he was reared in an environment of poverty, dissipation and back-breaking work. His father was a drunkard. His mother lived with a series of men; a light-skinned black man named John was her consort during Allen's youth. "By the time I was twenty-one," recalled Allen, "I was a nervous wreck. I couldn't get a cigarette to my lip with one hand. . . . I was a confirmed drunkard." [1] Two years later he served a jail sentence for stealing corn in the midst of the depression and thought of himself as "an exjailbird drifting aimlessly through life." [2] At this low point in his life Allen was converted in a "tongues speaking" Methodist church in 1934. While working in Colorado, Allen met his wife, Lexie, who whetted his religious interest and was a powerful influence in shaping him for the ministry he later built.

About 1936, Allen became a licensed Assemblies of God minister and began preaching at a small church in Colorado. Like most pentecostal preachers during the depression, Allen lived in base poverty despite a growing reputation as a preacher of considerable ability. For four-and-a-half years during World War II, Allen worked as a full-time revivalist, a position of considerable prestige in the Assemblies of God, but financially life remained hard for a man with a family of four young children. Allen later recalled that the compensation for his first revival had been thirty-five cents. He was billed as the musical evangelist: "I was song leader and musician combined. The music was a Montgomery Ward $12 guitar slung around my shoulder. I could play in one key, the key of C." [3] Allen's discouragement gave way to despair: "My ministry hadn't caught fire, and long years of small meetings in small town after small town appeared to be my fate." [4] In 1947, when an offer came to be the pastor of a stable Assemblies of God church in Corpus Christi, Texas, Allen abandoned his nomadic life and got a brief taste of the frustrations of security.

Shortly after settling in Texas, Allen heard rumors of the beginning of the revival. A friend gave him a copy of *The Voice of Healing*. Allen remembered that he "laughed in ridicule" at the magazine and labeled the revivalists "fanatics." [5] But most likely Allen's vivid imagination was stirred. In 1949, he drove to Dallas to attend an Oral Roberts campaign. He was captivated by Roberts' power over the audience and left convinced that the revival was from God. "As we sat watching the prayer line," wrote his wife, "he heard again the voice of God." [6] Surely, these were the times for which A. A. Allen was made.

Meanwhile, Allen was restive as a local pastor. When his church board refused to sponsor a radio program, he could no longer contain his energy and resigned. By the end of 1949 he was once again holding revivals in churches and hoping to expand into a major healing ministry.

In May 1950, from Oakland, California, he sent his first report to *The Voice of Healing*. With caution, yet with a touch of the later Allen style, he reported, "Many say this is the greatest Revival in the history of Oakland":

> Although I do not claim to possess the gift of healing, hundreds are being miraculously healed in this meeting of every known disease. I do not claim to possess a single gift of the Spirit nor to have the power to impart any gift to others, yet in this meeting, as well as in other recent meetings, all the gifts of the Spirit are being received and exercised night after night.[7]

Once he had committed himself to the healing ministry, Allen moved swiftly and deftly. He observed, "The evangelists who were drawing the largest audiences were doing so under tents," and determined that he must launch a tent ministry. Such a financial commitment was a major risk:

> It was incredible in that period if love offerings were sizeable enough to carry an evangelist to his next meeting, allow him to pay for food, shelter, the monthly car installment, much less to provide the money for a need as large as a tent.

In the summer of 1951, Allen made the leap; he paid $1,500 down and committed himself to pay a balance of $7,000 at a rate of $100 for each night the tent was used.[8]

Allen's ministry grew steadily. He established his headquarters in Dallas, and in 1953 successfully launched the *Allen Revival Hour* on radio. He conducted campaigns in Cuba and Mexico regularly, and by 1955 was broadcasting on seventeen Latin American radio stations as well as eighteen American ones. Allen's reports were always optimistic; he wrote to *The Voice of Healing* that his 1954 "campaigns broke all records."[9] In spring 1956, Allen proudly announced that he was constructing a new headquarters building at a cost of $18,000.[10]

Allen's growing reputation was based on his native shrewdness, unparalleled showmanship, and startling miraculous claims. After Jack Coe died, he had no rival as the boldest of the bold. In his late thirties when the revival began, Allen was always a powerful preacher, with a compelling presence. "When he walked into the tent," said his successor Don Stewart, "every eye was on him. They knew he was there."[11]

From the beginning Allen was a prophet of the poor people—he knew their moods and needs in a way that few public figures do. "The people he responded to," recalled his daughter Mary Allen Smith, "were the persons that were really destitute or handicapped."[12] The common people sensed Allen's identification with them and, whatever his faults, they never deserted him. "He may have had a weakness," said an admiring contemporary evangelist, "but he made no difference, none, among people. I liked that. . . . When you see ten thousand people, and you see Jews, Italians, Negroes, whites, rich, overalls, suits, silk, Cadillacs, Fords, wired together, okay, I like that. I like that type of ministry." [13]

Miracle became the key word in the Allen revivals; no one outstripped his supernatural claims. When Allen's troubles with the Assemblies of God officials became heated in the mid-1950s, his miraculous claims became increasingly sensational. His detractors accused him of creating a carnival atmosphere in his meetings; he generally countered such criticisms with dramatic announcements of new miracles. Allen seemed challenged to heal the hard diseases and frequently reported resurrections of the dead. In 1956, "miracle oil" began to flow from the heads and hands of those attending the Allen revivals. Allen found ample justification for this controversial phenomenon in Biblical passages such as Hebrews 1:9: "Thou hast loved righteousness, and hated iniquity. Therefore God, even thy God, hath anointed thee with the oil of gladness above thy fellows." [14] A little later the mark of a cross appeared on Allen's brow and others' in his revival, a sign, according to Allen, predicted in Ezekiel 9:4. The leaders of the major pentecostal churches found such sensationalism embarrassing, but by then they had lost control of the radical revivalists.[15]

Allen's success was not based only on his sensational miracle claims. He preached an old-time pentecostal message with consummate skill. His harsh condemnations of immorality rang true to those reared in the stern environment of depression pentecostalism:

> I remember back in the old flapper days it was short skirts, and every one of the women had an excuse for wearing their skirts six inches above their knees, and some Pentecostal women were just as bad as anybody else. But every one of them had an excuse. They couldn't find any long enough because that was the style, and that's the only kind of dresses they could buy. . . . I'd say, "Let me look at the hem. You've got four inches there. You could just let it out, you old hypocrites!" [16]

Allen also spoke the language of a prophet with rousing skill; ominous warnings of the "destruction of America" and "invasions from hell" were well designed to stir the minds of the people.[17]

A. A. Allen had an uncanny ability to turn adversity and opposition to his own advantage. He considered himself the most persecuted preacher in the world, but he seemed to thrive under pressure. His ministry was changed, however, by his repeated troubles. His erratic behavior brought crisis after crisis which alienated his old friends. Each new crisis seemed to threaten his career, and combined they contributed to apparent changes in his personality.

The charge that he drank abusively followed Allen like a dark cloud through much of his public ministry. He had been an excessive drinker as a youth, and many believed that he never overcame this weakness. Whether one believed the charges or not, said one evangelist, depended on whether one listened to his enemies or his friends,[18] but as pressures mounted in Allen's later career the evidence seemed strong enough to convince all but his staunchest supporters.

A major crisis occurred in Allen's ministry in fall 1955 when he was arrested for drunken driving while conducting a revival in Knoxville, Tennessee. The Knoxville press sharply attacked Allen and the beleaguered minister forfeited his bail rather than stand trial on the charge. A local sponsoring pastor called a news conference to announce that Allen was going to confess his guilt.[19] According to one influential minister, Allen "confessed the thing to the preachers up there." [20] But the facts remain somewhat obscure. According to one close associate, Allen told his friends that he had been kidnapped and knocked unconscious. When he awoke, he said, he was in a "smoke-filled room and somebody was pouring liquor down his throat." His subsequent denials were necessary because "the enemy" would obviously not believe the truth.[21]

Whatever Allen's first reaction may have been, he soon turned to the attack. He called the incident an "unprecedented persecution" aimed at ruining his ministry. *Miracle Magazine* published his defense:

> Allen declares that all this is but a trick of the devil to try to kill his ministry and his influence among his friends at a time when God has granted him greater miracles in his ministry than ever before. . . . If ministers pay the price of real MIRACLES today, they will meet with greater persecution than ever before. The only way to escape such persecution is to fold up and quit! But we are going on! Will you go on with us? [22]

Allen's predicament caused a crisis in the healing revival. Scandal ever hovered over the revival, and such publicity distressed all of the evangelists. Allen, supported by his wife, assured the Voice of Healing leaders that the story was not true, but the evidence lay heavily against him in the minds of many of his colleagues. Gordon Lindsay felt that the Voice of Healing had to take "a strong stand on ethics." [23] Allen resigned from the group rather than face expulsion and began his lonely career as a maverick. He immediately began publishing his own magazine, and, although he affected a cordial relationship with his former colleagues in the Voice of Healing, feelings remained strained.[24]

In some ways independence suited Allen. His daughter recalled:

> My dad really left . . . and went on his own because in the Voice of Healing there was such an effort to make decisions and control other people. You know, where they went and what they did. . . . The Voice of Healing at that time was an Assembly of God organization of evangelists, and they were trying real hard to work within the framework of the Assemblies of God. . . . You had to obey the rules.[25]

Allen was forced out—but he was probably ready to go.

The Knoxville episode also led to Allen's separation from the Assemblies of God. Shortly after the incident he received a letter from Ralph M. Riggs, superintendent of the general council of the church, suggesting that he "withdraw from the public ministry until the matter at Knoxville be settled." Mrs. Allen recalled that her husband was told, "go somewhere you aren't known and let it blow over," but that was patently impossible.[26] Allen believed his church had ungratefully deserted him when he was "in need of a friend." The embittered revivalist replied to Riggs:

> Although I have ministered with you for eighteen years with no question being raised at any time concerning my integrity, and although the city of Knoxville and its newspapers have a well established reputation for persecution against every evangelist who has attempted to work there for at least ten years, I did not expect that your organization would accept my statement of innocence.

Allen surrendered his credentials and announced that he considered doing so no great loss. He really had no alternative but to continue: "A withdrawal from public ministry at this time would ruin my ministry, for it would have the appearance of an admission of guilt." [27]

The battle between Allen and the authorities in the Assemblies of God got hotter in the following months. At first Allen hoped, "Even in the future we may be able to work in harmony with our Assemblies of God brethren as we have worked in harmony with brethren of other denominations in the past." [28] But the mood soon darkened. The church's officials apparently felt that Allen should be quarantined. Allen reported in his magazine that Assemblies of God ministers were being urged to "ignore him completely and let the Lord take care of the results." Church officials denied that Allen had been persecuted but insisted, "The arrest of an Assemblies of God minister is highly incongruous . . . and throws his ministry in a shadow." [29] A Church of

God minister who chose to turn in his "minister's license" in protest described what he called the slandering of Allen and other evangelists: "They say these ministers are liars, crooks, and thieves. . . . But I am sure that not all of these ministers are in that class, if any of them are!" [30] Mrs. Allen recalled that Allen was hounded and harassed: "they did everything they could to destroy him." [31]

Allen's clash with pentecostal leaders was not his only difficulty. Probably no other charismatic minister received so much adverse attention from the press. At times, it seemed to Allen that all of his enemies combined. In 1956, in Phoenix, Arizona, he claimed that reporters had shown him the "names, addresses and official positions in their denominations, of the ministers who had sought the cooperation of the Phoenix newspapers to 'put a stop' to the A. A. Allen Revival." [32]

After Knoxville, Allen remained an extremely controversial figure. That story was hard to put behind him and unsympathetic reporters hounded him in nearly every subsequent crusade. In 1956, the *Sacramento Bee* led an attack which resulted in a lawsuit against Allen for operating a business without a permit.[33] In 1957, the *Akron Journal* refused to publish his advertising and instead published a front page exposé.[34]

Again, Allen deftly turned adverse publicity to his advantage. He made his persecution a badge of martyrdom. His supporters were reminded, "Remember the early days of the Church of God, its ministers were falsely accused." [35] Allen reprinted many of the attacks of his detractors to prove to his supporters that the Devil was actively trying to stop his ministry, explaining on one occasion, "These articles were a collection of many of the criticisms that ungodly atheistic, communist tinted newspapers have printed, trying to kill the revival that is sweeping the country." Furthermore, Allen recognized the publicity value of even bad news. When attacked by the Akron papers, he announced that he had received "$25,000.00 worth of front page advertising, absolutely free." [36] He turned his California lawsuit into an occasion to raise money to save "every independent Church in America." [37]

Allen was helped by the inability of many critics of the revival to distinguish between the quite different techniques and personalities of the evangelists. He frequently shed attacks by pointing out that responsible and respectable figures such as Oral Roberts and Jack Coe were also being attacked—that the whole revival was under assault. The more moderate and respectable evangelists, who were struggling to escape the Elmer Gantry image, were welcomed by Allen as fellow martyrs.

By the mid-1950s Allen had declared war on his detractors—
including the churches. While many of the more moderate ministers
tried to continue to work with the pentecostal denominations—or at
least to remain friendly—Allen repeatedly attacked organized religion
and urged pentecostal ministers to establish independent churches which
would be free to support the revival.[38] He charged that the Sunday
school had replaced the altar in the pentecostal churches and that few
church members were filled with the Holy Ghost:

> Revivals are almost a thing of the past. Many pastors, and even evangelists,
> declare they will never try another one. They say it doesn't work. They are
> holding "Sunday School Conventions," "Teacher Training Courses," and
> social gatherings. With few exceptions the churches today are leaning more
> and more toward dependence upon organizational strength, and natural
> ability, and denominational "methods." They no longer expect to get their
> increase through the old fashioned revival altar bench, or through the miracle
> working power of God, but rather through the Sunday School.[39]

Besieged and angry, A. A. Allen fought for his life with the desperation
of a wounded man.

In some ways Allen's isolation was an asset to his ministry. He was
forced to consciously cultivate a circle of loyal followers outside the
framework of organized religion. He still tried to win the support of
pentecostal preachers—during a 1956 meeting in Phoenix he promi-
nently announced the support of "many full gospel denominations and
independent groups" [40]—but, in truth, his sponsors included only one
minister from a major pentecostal denomination. With characteristic
vigor, Allen moved to cultivate his own circle of ministers.

In fall 1956, Allen announced the formation of the Miracle Revival
Fellowship, an incorporated organization designed to license ministers
and to support missions. "After such hard hitting, convincing arguments
against denominational church membership," wrote Allen, "it hardly
seems fitting that I should close this book without offering my readers
the privilege of membership in a Christian Fellowship." [41] Theologically,
the fellowship welcomed all who accepted "the concept that Christ is the
only essential doctrine." [42] Allen urged laymen as well as ministers to join
his fellowship, through his "Every Member an Exhorter plan." Although
Allen announced that "MRF is not interested in dividing churches," [43]
he also disclosed that "the purpose of this corporation shall be to
encourage the establishing and the maintenance of independent local,
sovereign, indigenous, autonomous churches." [44] Anticipating charges
that the fellowship was his personal tool, Allen wrote,

> Although, at the insistence of ministers from all over America, I did join with
> others in the framing of Miracle Revival Fellowship, and by the choice of the

[73

incorporators, as they felt led by the Holy Ghost, I did accept the Presidency, MRF is in NO SENSE "my organization." [45]

Whatever the intention, the organization, which listed more than 500 ministers in its "first ordination," [46] was composed of a coterie of Allen supporters.

Under a withering attack at the time when other ministries were struggling and the revival was seemingly dying, Allen fought his way forward. *Miracle Magazine* was an immediate success; in 1956, at the end of a year's publication, it had a paid subscription of about 200,000, and, according to Mrs. Allen, was "the fastest growing subscription magazine in the world today." [47] In 1957, Allen began conducting the International Miracle Revival Training Camp, an embryonic ministerial training center. In 1958, he was given land in Arizona where he began building a permanent headquarters and training center. At the height of the 1958 crisis in the revival, Allen announced a five-pronged program for his ministry: tent revivals, the Allen Revival Hour radio broadcast, an overseas mission program, the Miracle Valley Training Center, and a "great number of dynamic books and faith inspiring tracts" published by the ministry.[48]

Allen's organization, however, merely tied down the success achieved by his "direct, personal ministry reaching thousands nearly every day and night of the year, in tents or auditoriums all over America." [49] The Allen revivals were deftly staged, and the Allen team, headed by Kent Rogers and Robert Schambach, was enormously gifted. In 1958, Allen, "unwanted, unrecognized by church organization," purchased Jack Coe's old tent and proudly announced that he was moving into the "largest tent in the world." [50] Where others looked for new methods to revive the revival, Allen reasserted his confidence in old-time revivalism. He was innovative, but old-time religion was his business, which he pursued with a tireless dedication that finally took an increasingly apparent toll on his health.

Finally, Allen survived because he was a superb money raiser. He was never subtle, but his ministry was to the poor and dollars came hard. Allen was one of the first in the revival to gain support by appealing to the financial dreams of his followers. Implicit in the revival was a conviction that God could grant not only physical but financial healing to His children. Allen early indicated that there was a scriptural secret to financial success. By the late 1950s, he had begun to stress the financial blessing theme which became a major part of the revival in the 1960s. He was fond of relating a story about a $410 printing bill he could not pay.

74]

He had nothing but a few one-dollar bills in his pocket when suddenly, in the midst of a prayer, the bills were changed to twenties:

> Of course, some of you do not believe this. Listen, you old skeptic, you don't have to believe it, because it doesn't have to happen to you. But it had to happen to me. I'll tell you why. I decreed a thing. . . . God said "Thou shall decree a thing, and it shall be established unto thee. . . ." I believe I can command God to perform a miracle for you financially. When you do, God can turn dollar bills into twenties.[51]

Clearly, such financial faith paid off for A. A. Allen.

The Flowering of the Revival

After the initial successes of William Branham and Oral Roberts in 1947 and 1948, scores of other evangelists launched full-time revivalistic ministries. Some lacked the talent or business acumen or physical stamina to last long; others became small successes, hedging their dreams with a hard-headed realism; a few were given incredible adulation and support. Many of the revivalists had meteoric careers, but only a few exerted a lasting influence.

William Freeman

For a time William Freeman surged near to the front of the revival. Born in a log cabin and reared in a poor but intensely religious environment in Stone County, Missouri, Freeman received visitations from God while still a lad.[1] Like many of the other revivalists, Freeman vaulted to success from an obscure and deprived background and years of grinding evangelistic disappointment. He later recalled, "I've walked and preached the Gospel in the rain and cold. I didn't have much, sometimes went to bed hungry; but I praise the Lord for it."[2] For twelve years he lived in poverty as a pentecostal pastor and evangelist. By 1946 personal tragedy seemed to surround him. He recounted how his wife had a nervous breakdown and "then a few months later my heart gave way on me and I thought I was finished, I handed my resignation in to my church in Porterville." "Later," he recalled, "a cancer came upon my leg, and it looked as if the enemy was going to get me again. . . . But I prayed unto the Lord again and He healed me." All the while, he "sought the Lord much," often praying until late into the night. His seeking was finally answered: "One night at about 11 o'clock, the Lord gave me a vision. In the vision I saw the Lord standing on a great cloud.

As I watched Him the scene seemed to change, and I was standing before a vast congregation." [3] Armed with this vision of his mission, in early 1947 Freeman once again took to the field as an independent revivalist.

At first, Freeman attracted little attention. His manager, Don Gossett, later wrote,

> It wasn't with a royal grandeur that his ministry was at first received. . . . Churches, missions, and small auditoriums were the scenes of the first of Freeman Campaigns. . . . There were some real financial struggles in those days.

But Freeman's ministry was accompanied by "amazing miracles, signs and wonders" and "word began to spread throughout the world of this 'unusual preacher with the gifts of healing.' " [4] Freeman's fame reached the ears of Gordon Lindsay, and when William Branham left the field in 1947, Lindsay visited the California evangelist:

> At that time my attention was called to a young man by the name of William Freeman. He had been holding meetings in small churches and his audiences were not unusually large. . . . Upon meeting Brother Freeman he at once asked me to work with him in a series of campaigns if I felt it was the will of God. [5]

Beginning in 1948 Lindsay featured Freeman in *The Voice of Healing* as he conducted a series of large campaigns on the West Coast and the Midwest.

Freeman's ministry developed as rapidly as that of any other revivalist. He attracted huge crowds and successfully carried the revival into the cities of the Midwest. He made Chicago, often called the evangelist's graveyard, into a favorite revival center. In campaigns in St. Louis and Chicago in 1953 Freeman listed 62,500 converts.[6] In 1949, he began publishing his own magazine, *The Healing Messenger*, and quickly assembled a permanent staff of workers. Freeman's description of the duties of his advance manager, who had formerly worked for Jack Coe, revealed his attention to organizational detail:

> Rev. Rogers' position with the Freeman Evangelistic Association will involve various duties, including advance advertising of the Freeman campaigns, meeting and organizing the various workers that will take part in each campaign (personal workers, ushers, ministers, etc.), and assisting in the service in various ways.[7]

In 1950, Freeman, as befitted a leading deliverance evangelist, took a rather large evangelistic party on a campaign to Scandinavia. By 1952 he claimed the largest tent in the world—a hotly contested title.[8] He also announced in 1952 that he could be heard "all over America every night" on the radio, although at the time he was broadcasting on only three powerful stations.[9]

Freeman early made friends with several influential businessmen who later became the nucleus of the Full Gospel Business Men's Fellowship and he was influential in encouraging the formation of the group. Demos Shakarian sponsored several early Freeman meetings; his wife was Freeman's pianist.[10] However, Freeman seemed unable to maintain his favored status with this group.

Freeman's effective revivals won the respect of his peers. Don Gossett believed that the "great divine visitation that God gave Bro. Freeman" endued him with "great power to marvelously heal the sick and afflicted."[11] During the early 1950s his magazine, like those of the other evangelists, was filled with testimonials of healings and documentary evidence supporting the claims.

His manager declared that the key to Freeman's early success was his fervent preaching:

> The third reason that the angels in heaven are made to rejoice so heartily during these great meetings is because Bro. Freeman preaches and expounds forth the straight Word of God. God has given him an ability to quote the Word of the Lord that is seldom exhibited anywhere else.[12]

Freeman's preaching was fervent (he believed Christ's second coming was near), but his services were orderly and businesslike.[13] His manager later recalled:

> Unlike many other mass scale evangelists, the ministry of William Freeman was simply on the basis of New Testament power—no carnal programs, entertainers, side line attractions, etc.[14]

In the early days of the revival, Freeman's earnest Biblical approach had much appeal, but when the fervor waned in the late 1950s, the Freeman ministry declined.

In 1956, Freeman was still on sixteen radio stations and was planning a trip abroad for the next year, but the financial burdens of his ministry were obviously great. In an appeal to his readers he announced that he would discontinue publication of *The Healing Messenger* because of flagging financial support and rising costs. Shortly thereafter, he retired from regular evangelistic work and settled in Chicago. According to one contemporary, Freeman remained a popular preacher, but he limited his ministry largely to the Chicago area.[15]

O. L. Jaggers

Another talented and successful leader of the revival who chose ultimately to establish a firm church base instead of remaining an itinerant evangelist was O. L. Jaggers. Jaggers, whose father was an Assemblies of God minister, began revivalistic work in 1941. He attended one of the early Branham campaigns in Arkansas, saw the potential of union meetings, and began holding auditorium revivals immediately. He soon was one of the leading figures in the Voice of Healing group.

Jaggers held successful meetings throughout the country, but in 1952 he settled down and became pastor of the World Church in Los Angeles. Jaggers called the "phenomenal rise and growth" of his church "the most remarkable success story of the 20th century." In 1956, he announced that the church had a membership over 10,000 and that "additional applications have also been submitted for membership which have not been passed upon." At that time the church had a seating capacity of 3,000 and Jaggers' plans were grandiose:

> Plans are now being pushed forward for the New World Church, the magnificence of which has never been equaled in the history of the world. This new structure will have a seating capacity of ten thousand. . . . However, God has subsequently spoken to Brother Jaggers and told him that the membership of the World Church in Los Angeles alone will be more than one hundred thousand! [16]

Jaggers was probably the most erratic and extreme of all the early revivalists. His contemporaries considered him a tremendous preacher, many believed him the greatest of the revival. But they also saw in him many of the chronic weaknesses which plagued the movement at its end. He was, according to one contemporary, "a man exceedingly full of pride." [17] Gordon Lindsay, and others associated with the Voice of Healing, became more and more skeptical of the exaggerated reports sent in by Jaggers and feared that frequently "his imagination went wild." Lindsay later recalled: "On the radio he would say, letters are coming in by the hundreds of thousands, by the millions and things like that." Lindsay recalled that Jaggers claimed, after appearing as a speaker at a Voice of Healing convention, that "supernaturally he had been on television all over the United States." Lindsay retorted that "no such thing happened." An open feud disrupted the supporters of the healing revival in California until a compromise was effected between the two men by Demos Shakarian. [18] Jaggers was also accused of loving expensive living. In 1958, the Los Angeles press charged that he was living in a parsonage valued at $390,000 and that he drove an $11,000 automobile.[19]

By the mid-1950s Jaggers found himself estranged from organized pentecostalism and even from many of his fellow evangelists. Nothing came of his 1956 plan to organize the leading healing evangelists; he urged that they "get together" in his World Fellowship.[20] Extremely acid in his criticisms of those who opposed his schemes, he set a style of anti-institutional invective otherwise approached only by A. A. Allen:

> Just as every move of God's spirit in the past which is recorded in the page of every history has had its opposition and persecution so The World Church has been attacked by the forces of evil which have included communism, the red conspiracy, ecclesiastical leaders, including full Gospel denominations whose ministry have met in closed sessions, scheming with their warped brains how they may destroy this tremendous church! All the opposition of Satan, however, to this time has been crushed under the feet of ten thousand members of The World Church.[21]

Jaggers not only attacked the pentecostal churches but also some of the leading figures in the revival.[22]

By the time the revival began to decline in the late 1950s, O. L. Jaggers had abandoned healing revivalism. He had isolated himself from the mainstream of the movement, and his doctrinal views became more and more extreme. He readily accepted such controversial teachings as the flowing of miracle oil and had begun to teach that Christians could have eternal life on earth: "The first time in 1900 years," he wrote, "an exact formula has been given as to how to attain physical immortality in this World!!!! The fountain of perpetual youth, longevity, and eternal life in a physical body, has now been discovered in this world." [23] William Branham publicly urged Jaggers, "Come back and stay with the Gospel," but the strong-willed revivalist continued to go his own way.[24] Since 1955, recalled one deliverance evangelist, "most of us have just sort of left him alone." [25] By the mid-1970s the World Church had become only a shadow of its former glory, but O. L. Jaggers was still its regular minister.

Tommy Hicks

Tommy Hicks became famous as an evangelist abroad. While he did not establish the type of organization which proved so important in T. L. Osborn's later career, Hicks conducted a series of fantastically successful foreign crusades in the mid-1950s. Perhaps the most famous single meeting in the history of the revival was Tommy Hicks' crusade in

Argentina in 1954. Arranged in a private conference with Juan Peron, Hicks conducted services in a large stadium. Reportedly as many as 400,000 persons attended a single service.[26] Hicks got along well with South American politicians and believed Peron to be "one of the finest, and kindest of men that I have ever met in all my life." [27] He claimed among his converts the vice president of Argentina, who along with his wife "came to Bro. Hicks' hotel room and there they were both saved." He reported that he healed the son of the vice president of Bolivia and met with "the richest woman in Argentina." [28] The drama of the Hicks revivals overseas won him support from the Full Gospel Business Men's Fellowship.[29]

Scores of other gifted evangelists became internationally famous by the mid-1950s. Velmer Gardner, a man with "a tremendous personality and a tremendous preaching ministry," launched a successful career after attending an Oral Roberts revival in 1949.[30] Already acquainted with Gordon Lindsay, he quickly became one of the central figures in the Voice of Healing group. W. V. Grant, an Arkansas farm boy, developed a strong following in the South, became a regular writer for *The Voice of Healing*, and became, after Gordon Lindsay, the most prolific and important writer in the revival.[31] For a time the reputation of Gayle Jackson was unsurpassed. Building on a series of large meetings in the South, Jackson effected a dramatic healing of fellow evangelist O. L. Jaggers and became the envy of his peers when he was featured in an article in *Look* magazine.[32] The most famous woman evangelist of the early healing revival was Louise Nankivell who preached in sackcloth because of a vow made in 1941 when she reported that God had healed her of pernicious anemia.[33]

The large ministries were only a part of the story of the revival. Scores of evangelists sustained smaller ministries. Some seemed satisfied year after year to bring miracle revivalism to the out-of-the-way places bypassed by the more famous. Some aspired to greatness: the older revivalists were constantly challenged by young preachers with talent, energy, and determination. The outburst of the revival rescued many itinerant pentecostal evangelists from dismal careers. In the beginning, availability was as important as talent. After 1950 the competition became much more heated.

Franklin Hall

One of the more interesting and influential of the smaller ministries was that of Franklin Hall. Hall grew up in rural poverty and was deeply religious. He recalled: "I used to pray quite a bit as a boy and I asked the Lord to give me a new ministry—different from anyone else—a ministry like Elijah." He left the Methodist church ("They didn't take to divine healing") and during the depression and World War II he traveled as an independent evangelist.[34]

When the revival erupted after World War II, Hall was there. He contributed to the revival a distinctive doctrine which, while it did not enrich him, had a major impact. In 1946, he published a brief book entitled *Atomic Power with God through Prayer and Fasting*. The book, which provided detailed information on the methods and benefits of fasting, was an immediate success and brought Hall a measure of fame.[35] According to Hall, all of the major evangelists began following his fasting regime and miracles erupted everywhere. Many observers of the early revival years agreed, as one said, "Every one of these men down through the years followed Franklin Hall's method of fasting." [36]

Franklin Hall himself never attracted a large following. He considered himself a teacher rather than a healing evangelist. He worked in combination with a series of preachers, including "Little David" Walker, the most famous early child evangelist: "I had a little David boy preaching with me, and he helped to get the crowd and then I'd give them this truth." [37] Thelma Chaney, a childhood acquaintance and a woman evangelist who established a moderate reputation, traveled with him for a time. According to her, the results of Hall's teaching were amazing: "Multitudes fasted. Many in our meetings fasted ten, twenty, thirty and forty days. Miracles, signs and wonders followed." [38]

Hall's work remained small, and as time passed it drifted further and further from the mainstream of the revival. His views on fasting seemed extreme to the more moderate leaders of the revival, and the organized pentecostal churches opposed him:

When we began to get this truth spread everywhere, we became persecuted. People began to withdraw and they didn't want to have anything to do with us. They considered it a false doctrine. . . . A lot of people fasted 10 to 21 days. And they had tremendous success with the Lord. But when we got under persecution so much, Gordon Lindsay, he was under attack too because of my books, my writing and my ministry. So he said not because we don't believe the message of fasting at all and not because you are not a good soldier of the cross and have a good reputation, but one of the denominations of pentecost . . . just won't go along with me and they turn down my subscriptions and so I'd rather just not advertise your book and rather not even announce your meetings.[39]

Isolated by a somewhat deviant doctrine and less talented as a preacher than many of his competitors, Franklin Hall hung on through the fifties with the same tenacity that had helped him survive during the depression. In small churches and auditoriums across the nation he continued to teach with fervor his message of prayer and fasting and healing. When hard times came to the revival in the late 1950s, it was nothing new to Franklin Hall. He had an instinct for survival. Scores like him roamed the countryside.

David Nunn

David Nunn was a typical example of the fresh new talent raised by the revival. Born and raised in a pentecostal environment, Nunn believed he had been miraculously healed when he stuck a nail in his foot as a boy. Later he said that he "backslid and stayed away from the Lord for a long time," and that by the age of 22 he was an alcoholic. After World War II, he said, he was "delivered from the bondage of drink and all the evil habits of my life" and felt called to preach in the Assemblies of God.[40] As a local pastor in Texas in 1948 and 1949, Nunn sponsored the meetings of a number of the deliverance evangelists and was deeply influenced by them. He developed a reputation as a good preacher in the local churches of his area and had some dramatic healing successes. He effected a dramatic healing of a paralyzed child in one of his meetings. It seemed to him "a definite act of God . . . to say, 'Son, I've called you.' "[41] Nunn often told his audiences of his vivid impression of a call to the revival ministry in January 1950: "God spoke to me again and said: 'Get up from here and go into every city, heal the sick therein and preach the kingdom of Heaven is at hand.' "[42]

Nunn's decision to start an independent ministry was forced on him by the official position of the Assemblies of God. "I stepped out," he later reminisced, "for about the same reason that Martin Luther left the Catholic church. . . . Not because of my desire, but because their policies demanded that I do this." In 1950, he was accused of insubordination by his state superintendent because he supported the independent revivalists, and he felt compelled to resign his pulpit. This confrontation, he believed, turned "out to be an act of God" because "from there on God projected me into a higher state of this ministry."[43] Always a moderate, he never openly expressed resentment against the churches. He associated himself with the Voice of Healing group and became a trusted coworker of Gordon Lindsay.

Nunn established his own evangelistic association in 1952 and shared in the great climax of the revival in the early 1950s. He later recalled that he had seen "as many as twenty-five totally blind receive their sight in one single service" and "in one single campaign I counted thirty-three people who were healed of paralysis or of a crippled condition." [44] For a time Nunn was the radio speaker for a Voice of Healing broadcast, but with the decline of interest in the revival in the late fifties the program had to be abandoned. In 1958, he was still convinced that the revival was in its youth.

The healing-deliverance revival probably crested around 1952. In 1953, Gordon Lindsay published a book entitled, *Men Who Heard from Heaven*. It included sketches of twenty-two ministers: Morris Cerullo, Clifton Erickson, Velmer Gardner, W. V. Grant, Philip N. Green, L. D. Hall, H. E. Hardt, Alton L. Hayes, Gayle Jackson, Richard Jeffrey, Stanley Karol, Walter Litzman, Michael Mastro, W. B. McKay, Louise Nankivell, David Nunn, Wilbur Ogilvie, T. L. Osborn, Everett B. Parrott, Raymond T. Ritchey, A. C. Valdez, Jr., and Richard Vinyard. The list was only a beginning. During the peak years from 1950 to 1956 over a hundred evangelists were associated with the Voice of Healing. Scores of others operated independently—some large enough not to need the support of Lindsay and others too weak or too young or too eccentric to receive his sanction. After 1956 the battle to survive became desperate. Those who were still active in 1960 had to be talented and adaptable.

5

Promises and Problems

The Ministry of Healing

THE GREAT OUTBURST OF HEALING momentarily became the center of the pentecostal world. Gordon Lindsay believed that the healing meetings had been raised up in the providence of God to encourage world-wide revival. The Full Gospel movement, he wrote, owed "to a great extent, its existence to this ministry." [1]

A belief in divine healing has always been a cardinal truth in the pentecostal message, but it had been less marked in early revivalism than the baptism of the Holy Spirit and glossolalia. [2] As the pentecostal denominations grew more sophisticated, they minimized the miraculous, but even in recent years, the campaigning revivalists had difficulty playing down their role as healers. One seasoned campaigner said, "It looks like . . . the people expect prayer for the sick. . . . It culminates in what people are not receiving in the organized churches they seek for elsewhere." [3]

The pentecostal theology of divine healing was based on a broad sampling of biblical teaching. [4] Jack Coe listed a series of texts he considered important:

Hebrews 13:8—"Jesus Christ the same yesterday, and today, and forever."
Isaiah 53:5—"But he was wounded for our transgressions, he was bruised for

our iniquities: the chastisement of our peace was upon him; and with his stripes we are healed." Exodus 15:26—"I am the Lord that healeth thee." Psalms 34:19—"Many are the afflictions of the righteousness [*sic*]: but the Lord delivereth them out of them all." John 14:12—"Verily, verily, I say unto you, He that believeth in me, the works that I do shall he do also: and greater works than these shall he do: because I go unto my Father." John 15:7—"If ye abide in me, and my word abide in you, ye shall ask what ye will, and it shall be done unto you." James 5:15—"And the prayer of faith shall save the sick, and the Lord shall raise him up." James 4:10—"Humble yourself in the sight of God and He shall lift you up!" [5]

Generally, pentecostals believed, "Deliverance from physical sickness is provided for in the atonement and is the privilege of all believers." [6] Jesus' death "purchased healing for both soul and body." [7] It was a "very serious offense," wrote Gordon Lindsay, to "deny that divine healing is in the Atonement." [8] The promise of divine healing did not protect against eventual death, but it did mean that "you don't have to be sick to die." [9] In most cases, the revivalists believed, God would allow His people a lifespan of seventy to eighty years. [10] In any case, wrote evangelist W. V. Grant, Christians could be assured that they would not be "taken away in the midst of their days." [11]

A. A. Allen carefully outlined God's promise of good health in his book *How to Renew Your Youth Without Medicines, Drugs or Surgery*, written in 1953: "It is my firm belief, and this belief is based upon the scriptures, that God created man healthy and strong, and that God meant for him to continue in that state. And it is my firm belief that God wants everyone of us to prosper and be in health UNTIL WE FULFILL THE NUMBER OF OUR DAYS. And it is also my belief that when the number of our days has been fulfilled, it is God's perfect will that we should die a Bible death." This did not mean, explained Allen, "that a person 75 years old can actually *be* 20." On the other hand, God had promised to "renew our YOUTH." This meant, concluded Allen, that God would "take away the sickness, the disease, the infirmity, even the deformity, that cause one to feel, act, think, and live like an old person." [12]

The crucial condition for the receiving of divine healing was an appropriating faith. However powerful the gifts of an evangelist, the basis for healing was always individual faith. "The Divine gifts of healing," reminded William Branham, "don't give any man power to heal anyone he chooses." [13] In his testimony at the famous Coe trial, Gordon Lindsay emphasized that a sick person must meet "the conditions upon which Divine healing is based." "No minister of Divine healing makes a guarantee that people who are not serving God, will be healed, either they or their children." [14] Evangelist Kenneth Hagin, castigating the faithless in a sermon, declared, "You can lay your hands on folks like that until you've wore every hair off the top of their head and all they're going to get out of it will be a bald head." [15] Only a strong faith could lead the ailing to receive the healing that God made available for them. David Nunn urged his audiences to abandon every reservation to faith: "God wants to heal you. . . . Some of these people keep praying, 'if it be Thy will, oh God, heal me.' . . . If they're going to pray that way—that old faith-paralyzing prayer 'if it be Thy will'—then they ought to submit to it . . . by not taking any medicine. . . . That old nonsense went out with hoop skirts. . . . There's not a nickel's worth of faith in that prayer." [16]

If faith was the kindling that brought spiritual healing, the gift of the evangelist was the spark to set it off. All of the revivalists emphasized that healing could come only from God (a doctrine which legally protected them from charges of practicing medicine), but they believed that God's anointed ministers were catalysts in the healing process. All Christians could receive the baptism of the Holy Spirit and speak with tongues, but "the gift of healing was exclusive." [17] By the mid-1950s the teaching on the nine gifts of the spirit had become much more sophisticated than in the early days of the revival. As the revival matured an evangelist was likely to claim only one or two gifts—perhaps the gift of healing and prophecy or of healing and miracles (required to raise the dead)—but in the early days an anointed evangelist was likely to assume a more general power to perform miracles.

Each minister had to "minister according to the gift God has given to him." [18] The evidence of his anointing was different for each evangelist— a feeling in his hand, an audible voice speaking to him, a vision, the presence of an angelic helper, or some other miraculous circumstance. Generally, a minister used his gift by the "laying on of hands," based on the biblical passage in James 5:14–18. But a gift could also be used impersonally, by mail or through radio and television. The practice of sending out anointed or blessed cloths soon became one of the trademarks of the revival. Evangelist David Nunn taught that the three basic methods of divine healing were the laying on of hands (Mark 16:17), the prayer of agreement (Matt. 18:19), and the use of blessed cloths (Acts 19:11, 12).[19]

The revival techniques of the evangelists varied considerably. Many required that those seeking healing fill out prayer cards and then, in an orderly way, selected certain cases to be prayed for during a service. Some evangelists seemed to avoid the hard cases, such as the blind and the deformed, but others, most notably Jack Coe and A. A. Allen, seemed to thrive on them. Some prayed slowly and agonizingly over each case; others used the "fast line," a technique which many believed "in most cases produced only erratic results." [20] T. L. Osborn originated praying *en masse* for thousands at one time, believing that every one could be healed in the same moment.[21]

Evangelist W. V. Grant summarized some of the differences: "One evangelist prays a simple prayer. Another anoints with oil and lays his hands on people. One prays over the radio. One has people healed over television. One minister sees instant healings more than another. One minister sees more gradual healings. . . . Crutches and braces are discarded in one meeting, while another man has faith for a gradual deliverance." Such diversity in no way diminished the unity of the revival: "They praise the Lord for each other's ministry and do not criticize another. If they have more faith they have it to themselves and to God and do not brag too much about it." [22]

For the first ten years of the revival the lifeblood of the deliverance ministries was the healing testimonials. Hundreds of thousands of testimonials were published—frequently in indelicate detail. Evangelist LeRoy Jenkins recorded a typical description of a cancer healing:

> The next night the Lord spoke to me and told me she had a cancer. He told me to have her bring a jar to church and she would spit up the cancer. For three nights she brought that jar in a little old brown paper sack. On the third night God spoke to me and said, "This is her night to be healed." After prayer, she was healed. She spit up a bloody cancer which had long roots on it. She had a terrible time as it almost choked her to death while it was coming up. She has not had any trouble since.[23]

The range of illnesses healed was as broad as medical science, although the evangelists had their own homespun medical jargon which combined many ailments under such terms as a heart condition, nervous disorders, and cancerous tumors. Frequently sufferers reported multiple healings, as in this somewhat extreme example from a grateful believer:

> I shall try to enumerate some of the things the Spirit revealed and the healing power of Jesus delivered me from them. Blood clot, mastoid trouble, sciatic nerve trouble, many pains in body because of the injury thirteen years before, chronic throat trouble, chronic sores that bled inside my nose, stigmatism in my eyes and nervous jerking in right eyelid due to strain. I also was healed of kidney trouble, sinus, gastric condition in the bowels, athlete's foot, and a bad rectal trouble. I also suffered an injury to my ankle during the revival and the Lord healed that, also a very tired feeling in my shoulders. Many are telling

me how much better I look, and I thank God I can tell them how much better I feel. Surely the Lord has given me a general overhauling.[24]

Many of the evangelists, particularly the more radical ones, emphasized the bizarre, but a large number of the healings involved such commonplace illnesses as headaches, nervous conditions, and alcoholism. Perhaps the rarest and most spectacular claims were the occasional reports of the resurrection of a dead person. In a typical case in 1956, an evangelist reported, "Seventeen witnesses declare Mrs. Katherine Powers was restored to life, in answer to prayer, after being dead for twenty-five minutes." [25] Most of the revivalists believed that they had seen a few resurrections, but only the most extreme systematically challenged such an apparently unyielding enemy.[26]

The exorcism of demons required a specialized type of healing ministry. Pentecostals believed in a great variety of demons—"demons of sickness, of lies, of fornication, Hitler demons and divorce demons" [27]— the healing revivalists were fascinated by the belief. In his early years Oral Roberts emphasized demon possession as a cause of illness and was noted for his power in casting out evil spirits. Many of the revivalists, including Gordon Lindsay, made special studies of demonology, but A. A. Allen was probably the leading specialist at driving out demons.[28]

Allen believed that demons had "filled the insane asylums, penitentiaries, prisons, and courts to over capacity." [29] In 1963, in a book which closely associated demon possession with mental illness, Allen published eighteen pictures of demons as seen and drawn by a demon possessed woman. "If you will go through your Bible," wrote Allen, "you will find that in every case where Jesus met a person who was suffering with mental sickness, insane, there was a demon connected with that sickness. . . . These Satanic beings have power to torment you mentally and physically until you are driven into the insane asylum, and the Lord permits it when disobedience is continued." Allen urged those possessed to send for a special blessed cloth to receive healing:

In writing the author for these blessed cloths, please follow these instructions carefully:

1. Please do not make your letter any longer than is necessary to explain your need.

2. If you are demon possessed or oppressed, name the kind of demon from which you desire to be set free, (if known).

3. Do not enclose a handkerchief or apron. These generally are bulky and require extra postage. We have small squares of cloths that we furnish for this purpose.

4. For convenience, please enclose in your letter a self-addressed, stamped envelope.

5. After you have been delivered, send me your testimony accompanied by a good clear photograph, or "glossy" print, to the address in the front of this book. Give the following information:

    a. Explain your past demon possession or oppression. Tell how long you suffered.

    c.[*sic*, b.] If you received medical aid; what was the doctor's opinion of your case? Give all information possible to prove your deliverance, such as doctor's statements, etc. . . .

    THERE IS NO CHARGE FOR THESE BLESSED CLOTHS. . . . However, your offering will be gratefully accepted and will help us carry the financial burden of this great God-ordained ministry.[30]

The miracles of healing were reinforced by an assortment of other miraculous claims. In a miracle which loomed large in the minds of William Branham's followers, Branham resurrected a fish which had been killed by a companion.[31] Miraculous photographs were first used to support the Branham ministry. Such miraculous claims increasingly came to be associated with the more radical revivalists. A picture printed by A. A. Allen in 1956 showed streaks of white surrounding Allen and several other people. *Miracle Magazine* explained:

> This is an unretouched photograph, showing spiritual things which were not visible to the natural eye, but which God permitted to become visible to the eye of the camera. . . . Two drunken reporters were creating disturbance near the end of the ramp. J. H. Hatton, head usher, was attempting to clear up the situation. . . .
>
> Hovering above the platform, covering it completely, is the bright cloud of God's glory. Surrounding the drunken reporters are formations of serpent like creatures. (Remember, Satan came to Eve in the form of a serpent.) As the forward formation turns to strike at Hatton, they are suddenly dissolved in a burst of light, only the heads and tails showing.[32]

By the mid-1950s, the more extreme miraculous claims had clearly become a source of division in the movement.

Although few evangelists squarely faced the issue in the first decade of the revival, the problem of failure haunted the strongest supporters of divine healing. Generally, failure was charged to a weakness in faith. When W. V. Grant was asked whether an evangelist who wore glasses could pray for the sick, he answered, "I knew a man who pastored a church who had a hernia. Many people were healed as he prayed for them. This did not mean that the Lord did not want to heal that pastor. It only meant that the Word still stands: 'According to your faith, be it unto you.' All things are possible to him that believes." [33] A weak Christian, warned William Branham, could lose his healing because the victory was "based altogether upon faith." [34] Evangelist Kenneth Hagin told his audiences the story of a faithless woman who was raised off her wheelchair by the power of God but, nevertheless, refused to "accept her healing." [35]

A variety of other reasons could account for apparent failures. "If the healing of a sick person does not take place," wrote pentecostal historian Hollenweger, "this can be the result of one of ten, fifteen or twenty reasons why prayers are not heard (unbelief, sin, etc., on the part of the persons seeking healing)." [36] Some evangelists emphasized gradual healing and urged the faithful to be patient when an immediate miracle did not occur.[37] Some of the leaders of the revival believed that the more extreme techniques used by the revivalists did not bring lasting healing. One healed by the power of positive faith, assured David Nunn, would keep his healing. On the other hand, "A fellow that comes in, he may get a sensational thing that happens to him there in the line but tomorrow when all of the battles of faith come to him, he may just as easily lose that and I've seen them do that too." [38] Finally, almost all of the evangelists taught that divine healing could not "keep a Christian on this earth forever." [39]

In the final analysis, the persistent, goading presence of failure was simply one of those paradoxes inherent in every theological system. Pentecostal historian John T. Nichol wrote: "One of the dilemmas that periodically confronts the Pentecostals is that some people who desire healing are not healed. A typical response to this seemingly incongruous situation is that a doctrine of divine healing in the work of the atonement must leave a place for permitted sickness as an expression of divine wisdom or divine purpose, inscrutable though it may be." [40] Not until recent years have some of the more thoughtful charismatic evangelists honestly and openly confronted the problem of failure.[41]

The problem of offering documentary proof of the miraculous was both a challenge and a dangerous trap for the evangelists. Some of the ministers, especially the more responsible ones, urged those who had been healed to seek medical verification of the miracle. Testimonials frequently reported that astonished medical experts had confirmed a healing. Before and after x rays, a highly valued proof, were frequently published. The evangelists often solicited return visits from people permanently healed in earlier revivals.

If the quantity of evidence was overwhelming, the quality was often very poor. In order to protect themselves legally, most of the revivalists began disclaiming responsibility for the accuracy of the testimonials printed in their literature. W. V. Grant developed a statement which was typical of those published in the major magazines:

> All printed testimonies have been reproduced as reported, with editing being limited to construction of grammar. We assume no legal responsibility for the veracity or permanency of reported healings, miracles or other happenings. All supernatural events and blessings are contingent upon spiritual condition, relative to the individual, and any deviation from the intended Divine plan could result in mental, physical, and/or spiritual setback. John 5:14.[42]

The trial of Jack Coe made the evangelists particularly careful to deny responsibility for the results when a person "trusted God for his healing."

The proof offered by the evangelists was constantly assailed by their enemies. "Had you ever noticed," wrote one critic, "that the claim is always made concerning an inward goiter or some trouble that is not outwardly apparent, or some trouble that people usually recover from naturally. *No glass eyes or cork legs are ever replaced!*" [43] Increasingly, the revivalists refused to be drawn into disputes with such "doubt-builders." W. V. Grant wrote: "I'd like to say that we have plenty of proof for God's children who are honest, and want to know that God is actually working, and answering prayer. . . . We do not have to have doctors' certificates, notary public statements, pastors' signatures, and proven testimonies." Grant's point was that the whole issue was a matter of faith. Those who wanted to believe could see the proof; those who did not could never see it. "If these doubt-builders," Grant declared, "cannot accept the testimony of two million people of many different denominations, who have experienced divine healing, neither would they have believed the five hundred who saw Jesus after he rose from the dead." [44]

Whatever one believed about the efficacy of divine healing, the evangelists approached it with a psychology that was never very subtle. The power of suggestion was ever present in the meetings and in the literature of the revival. The sick were carefully prepared to receive their healing with long tales of other miracles and the testimony of those who had previously been healed. Harold Woodson, a talented young evangelist working with Don Stewart, skillfully readied an audience for a healing service: "How many of you believe that same miracle working power is in this tent tonight? Lift your hands to heaven. . . . I believe the miracle working power of God is here tonight. To set men and women free, to deliver, to heal, to open the eyes of the blind." When evangelist Stewart greeted his expectant audience, he added to the spirit of anticipation: "Now the Lord has already spoken to me tonight about what he is going to do. In a few minutes we are going to feel the glory of God begin to rise in this service, Jesus Christ is going to come with healing in his wings. . . . The power of God is going to touch you." [45]

Thus were those seeking healing given careful instructions on what to expect. In 1950, William Freeman published a list of four steps to healing. The sick were urged to "stand on the atonement," trusting that with Jesus' "stripes we are healed." Second, they were told to "know that it is God's perfect will to heal you." Third, they needed to "understand that sickness is the devil's oppression." Finally, the believer was told, "Set the time of your deliverance." [46] A typical set of instructions were those published by Oral Roberts' associate minister, R. F. DeWeese:

> If I were coming to the crusade for healing, I would begin now to prepare myself. If I did not know Jesus Christ as my Savior, I would ask Him to forgive my sins, and to come into my life. . . . I would concentrate on God's love for me and that He wants to heal me.
>
> I would pray and read several chapters in the Gospels and Acts each day. As I read the accounts of healing by our Lord, I would put myself in the place of those Jesus healed and try to believe as they did.
>
> I would study the Scripture concerning healing and also read Brother Roberts' book, *If You Need Healing, Do These Things*. . . .
>
> I would plan to attend every service of the crusade. . . .
>
> As I filled out my prayer card . . . I would be willing to be healed any time or place that pleased God, whether on the ramp, down in the prayer line, or just sitting in the audience.
>
> Faith alone is not enough. We must know how to release our faith in order to receive healing. We can do this through a point of contact. This is something you do, and when you do it, you release your faith toward God for healing. When Brother Roberts lays hands on you, this may be your point of contact. . . .
>
> To sum up, if I were you: I would come expecting a miracle, I would believe that it is God's will for me to be healed. I would build up my faith by attending both afternoon and evening services and listening to the Word of God preached. I would use a point of contact to release my faith. And, I would let my faith go to God and accept my healing from Him.[47]

The ecstatic mood of the audience, frequently thousands strong, added to the sense of expectancy. LeRoy Jenkins candidly reported that unless an audience felt the fervor of the Spirit little healing could be effected, but "after the Spirit of God comes into the services, you will see people jump out of wheelchairs." [48] The enthusiasm of the crowd, the excitement of the music, the testimony of those who had been delivered from sickness, and the presence of the anointed evangelist combined to provide a powerful psychological stimulus for a believer to release his faith. Given a final point of contact—such as the laying on of the evangelist's hands or touching one's radio—the sufferer was urged to accept his immediate healing. The possibilities for psychosomatic healing in this environment were obvious.

In the first decade of the revival no evangelist explored the role of psychology in divine healing. In the 1960s, a few tried to look honestly at the question, although all believed that psychological explanations of divine healing were inadequate to account for what they had witnessed.

In 1957, Donald Gee, heralding a new mood of introspection, openly speculated that the sensationalism of the revival was attracting the mentally unstable. He found especially distasteful the emphasis on demon possession. On the other hand, he recognized that the whole revival, indeed pentecostalism, was based on the unbridled leadings of the Spirit. He wrote:

> Leaders of Pentecostal meetings need great tact and patience when the mentally unstable invade their borders, for they find in many of our meetings just that opportunity for disordered self-expression that they crave. . . . On the other hand we must guard our priceless heritage of true liberty by the Spirit of the Lord at all costs. Flight into deliberate formalism is a poor remedy for its occasional abuse and marks of poor leadership. The demands upon leaders of Pentecostal meetings for wisdom, love and power are tremendous. But they are the inescapable price of being within a Revival.[49]

Gee's article signaled the growing desire to leave behind extreme claims and preoccupation with the bizarre and to find a reasonable basis for faith in divine healing. As the revival simmered down, its more sophisticated leaders caught their breath and began to assess what had taken place.

Evangelism and Ecumenicity

The revival of the postwar period was never simply a healing revival. Salvation of the lost was theoretically the purpose of the outpouring of miracles. "The revival ministry," wrote Gordon Lindsay, "involves a missionary vision." [1] Pioneer revivalist Raymond Richey reportedly observed that healing was "like ringing the dinner bell" to lure sinners to salvation.[2] Many of the revivalists emphasized the baptism of the Holy Spirit; conversions were counted and advertised with almost the same vigor as healings. The revival gave an impetus to pentecostal evangelism all over the world which was to outlast the furor over miracles. The revival contributed greatly to the growth of organized pentecostal churches abroad in the 1950s and 1960s, and the emphasis on evangelism gave many of the deliverance ministries a way to build a new base of support.

From the beginning the major ministers paid some attention to evangelism in their mass meetings. Roberts repeatedly predicted "a new foreign missionary drive through mighty signs and wonders." [3] Branham early announced that "the vision of world missions" was his reason for traveling overseas.[4] Such leaders saw the healing revivals as a tool to convert the world. "To reach these people," wrote T. L. Osborn, "the Church must bear a miraculous gospel." [5]

Osborn was the first to realize the potential of massive foreign campaigr.s. His promotion of foreign evangelism won wide support from other leaders of the revival, and Osborn quickly steered his ministry in that direction. Lindsay, Roberts, Branham, and other leading ministers rallied to his support. Others soon picked up the theme of world missions. By 1958 Lindsay was presenting the Voice of Healing as a mission organization. This burst of independent mission work—remarkably vital in contrast to the sluggish and impoverished mission programs of most denominations—resulted in stunning growth for world-wide pentecostalism. The success of miracle-based evangelism seemed to pentecostal leaders one more confirmation that God was behind the revival. "It cannot be attributed to anything else," wrote David J. duPlessis, "than the spontaneous move of the Holy Spirit upon all flesh." [6]

Foreign crusades continued with unabated success in the late 1950s, after the American revival had begun to wane. Increasingly, the major revivalists turned to overseas tours—many of them in the backward nations—for their revival triumphs. Especially in Africa and Latin America they could still write of speaking "to tens of thousands a night," bringing to "the heathen a living savior in the power of His spirit." [7] By the late fifties almost all of the independent ministries, plagued by declining home support, began to look seriously at the attractions of foreign mission work.

The great crusades, both at home and abroad, added to the ecumenism of the revival, although the independent mission programs were sometimes resented by organized pentecostal churches. Pentecostals were encouraged to think in undenominational terms. Gordon Lindsay wrote:

In another sense these great meetings have a missionary character. The large population in the country rarely touched by Full Gospel meetings is reached in the Branham campaigns. . . . Although they do not return to swell the numbers of the local churches, they are, nevertheless, a priceless addition to the kingdom of God. It goes without saying, of course, that many from other cities are also converted and become candidates to increase the congregations of enterprising pastors who have the initiative to follow up and encourage these converts.[8]

All of the early leaders of the movement stressed the ecumenical nature of their work. Gordon Lindsay repeatedly reminded the healing revivalists that they must have "a vision of the unity of God's people." [9] Most of the revivalists resisted forming a denomination and insisted that their work was meant to aid the established full gospel churches. Several years of refreshing peace resulted among the pentecostal churches, marked by a sharing of the "same spirit." [10] Publicized on a world scale by Donald Gee's *Pentecost* magazine, the healing revivalists became the cord that bound the diverse movement together.[11]

The union spirit provided a time of healing for the fragmented pentecostal movement. Former doctrinal enemies were caught up in the fervor of the revival. Jack Moore's daughter, Anna Jeanne, described the change in attitudes:

> There was a time, not too long past, when most of us thought of "fellowship" as the pleasant associations we enjoyed with those who believed exactly as we, belonged to our same organization, and said "Shibboleth" just as we have been taught to say it . . . and toward those on the outside of our religious circle we held a sort of acrimonious tolerance, wondering how God could fellowship them when we didn't, or maybe not even admitting that *He* did.
>
> But a new day has dawned! Spirit-filled believers the world over have come to learn that *real fellowship* is that lovely state of appreciation we can enter into for those who *do not* believe as we do . . . but by the Birth of the Spirit are our Blood kin! [12]

The ecumenical achievements of the healing revivalists were based on the new willingness of many pentecostals to "avoid doctrinal hair splitting." Gordon Lindsay repeatedly warned, "Contentions over minor matters of water Baptism, predestination, meats, holy days, novel prophetic views, subordinate doctrinal points, are usually not edifying." [13] Of course, determining what was minor was the problem. Lindsay attempted to outline a theological platform for interdenominational fellowship.[14] In 1950, he submitted a seven point doctrinal statement that he believed would suffice:

1. Missionary work (Mk. 16:15). 2. Salvation to believer, damnation to unbeliever (V. 16). 3. Obedience in water Baptism (Mk. 16:16). 4. Mani-

festation of the sign-gifts among believers (Mk. 16:17–20). 5. That this Great Commission was not to be amended during Church Age (Matt. 28:20). 6. Baptism of the Holy Ghost for all believers (Acts 1:4–8). 7. That Christ would return in like manner as He went away (Acts 1:8).[15]

By the mid-1950s the ecumenical spirit was weakening. It had been sustained primarily by the enthusiasm of the early union meetings. As the revival began to decline, old doctrinal loyalties reappeared. The pentecostal denominations once again began to look to their own interests and reemphasized their doctrinal differences. Some sects tried to use the independent evangelists for their own purposes. Branham reported in 1955, "For instance, a few days ago I accepted an invitation to preach in a large church. When I got there I found that the purpose of having me come was to use what influence I had to get members out of another church. The other church had also given me an invitation for the same purpose. I would not go to either one." [16] Increasingly, the evangelists who stood for unity were liable to be branded compromisers. Branham continued to plead, "We have got to take a little and give a little, and make the blanket stretch to the other side of the bed to our brethren"; but many felt that he himself was becoming more and more dogmatic.[17] Finally, as the tension increased between the evangelists and the pentecostal churches, some of the more radical revivalists turned militantly anti-institutional and threatened open war inside the revival. Responsible revival leaders tried to quell the feud, but by the late 1950s the unity of the pentecostal revival was a thing of the past.

As pentecostal unity crumbled, the independent evangelists became conscious that they were attracting a new clientele. In its early years the revival was supported only by full gospel churches, but some of its leaders had always had a larger vision of unity. Very early Oral Roberts emphasized that he "recognized good in all denominations." While he preached the full gospel experience, he declared that he worked with many denominations. "He is called to bring deliverance to *The People*," wrote his friend Lee Braxton, "and he has no quarrel with some who might not see eye to eye with him on some fine point of theology or doctrine." [18] More and more the revivalists tried to reach the receptive in the traditional denominations. The spirit which led them out of a denominational ministry into independent revivalism prepared many of them for a wider fellowship. "The way a man gets to God is immaterial to me," said one of the evangelists, "if he gets to God being baptized in a Catholic church, wherever a man gets to God and it changes his life, okay." [19]

Minor Themes

A number of minor themes were present in the healing revival. Gordon Lindsay's warning against novel prophetic views suggested the importance of this gift to some evangelists. In a movement which thrived on the leading of the Spirit, an intense eschatology, and a deep sense of the miraculous presence of God in the world, prophecy and its interpretation offered rare opportunities to stir the faithful.

The prophetic speculations of the deliverance ministries fell into two main categories. First, many of the evangelists made dramatic applications of Bible prophecies to contemporary society. Second, many of the evangelists claimed to have received prophetic revelations.

In the midst of the early Cold War, the evangelists frequently speculated about an impending world confrontation between Russia and the United States. The prophecies were usually general, but were sometimes detailed. A typical prophetic revelation was A. A. Allen's *My Vision of the Destruction of America*, published in 1954. The book told of a supernatural vision-revelation given to Allen when he visited the top of the Empire State building during a New York City crusade:

> Suddenly, the Lord showed me all the North American continent, spread before me as a map on a table. From far to the North, a great black cloud in the form of a skeleton reached its tentacle arms toward America to embrace her in the embrace of death. From the gaping mouth and nostrils drifted white vapors, enveloping the cities, and strangely affecting the Statue of Liberty! Guided missiles, like fish leaping out of the water of the oceans, leap toward America, carrying their cargos of death. As the various phases of the vision unfolded before me, God's voice spoke to me, explaining the vision in the words of the scripture.

His research revealed, wrote Allen, that the vision was not only scriptural but also scientifically accurate. "One military man," he wrote, "upon hearing this vision given in a sermon, declared, 'Either this man has truly received a vision from God, or else has somehow come upon some of the Army's top military secrets!' " Allen was somewhat vague about the exact meaning of all of the images in his vision. He speculated: "What were these white vapors? Could they signify bacteriological warfare, that could destroy multitudes of people in a few moments time? Or could they be the new G-gas, the horrible nerve gas recently made known to the American public?" [1]

Allen graphically described the effects of the gas on the Statue of Liberty:

> As I watched the coughing grew worse. It sounded like a person about to cough out his lungs. The Statue of Liberty was moaning and groaning. She

was in mortal agony. The pain must have been terrific, as again and again, she tried to clear her lungs of those horrible white vapors. I watched her there in the Gulf, as she staggered, clutching her lungs and her breast with her hands. Then she fell to her knees. In a moment she gave one final cough, made a last desperate effort to rise from her knees, and then fell face forward into the waters of the Gulf, and lay still—still as death. Tears ran down my face as I realized that she was dead! [2]

Though the meaning of all of this still was not spelled out, it seemed ominous. But what exactly did it mean? Allen answered:

Can a country which has denied God a place in its government, its schools, its business, its homes and its churches escape the judgement and the wrath of God? No. A million times no! America will not escape God's wrath. She has sinned, and she must reap exactly what she has sown.
The reaping?
The reaping is in the future. [3]

Speculation about the imminent end of the world was perhaps the most important prophetic theme during the revival. Nearly all of the evangelists believed that the revival was a sign that the end of time was near. Branham was sure that his commission was one of the signs of the nearness of Jesus' coming, [4] and the second coming loomed large in the early preaching of Roberts. As the fires of revival began to burn lower in the mid-1950s, the evangelists fanned the flames with fervent appeals to Jesus' "soon-coming." [5] A few ventured to make fairly specific predictions, but exactness was generally considered irresponsible and was obviously not a good long-range tactic.

A second, somewhat surprising, minor theme in the early salvation-healing revival was a general social nonconformity and a specific racial openness. It was fitting that in the first Branham meeting in St. Louis in 1946 a Negro minister was healed. [6] Oral Roberts insisted that blacks be allowed to attend his first southern campaign in 1948. [7] From the beginning, the revival, supported largely by poor whites, bypassed many of the customs of racial prejudice. [8]

Such atypical social behavior had always been part of the extreme forms of pentecostal revivalism. In the 1880s, Mrs. Woodworth-Etter conducted integrated revivals in the South—to the astonishment of local whites. [9] An Aimee Semple McPherson supporter once expressed surprise at the "riffraff quality of Aimee's clientele." Her biographer related a story that would have fit well into the pattern of the postwar revivalists:

It is to her credit that she never denied [her early supporters] or looked down on them in later years when the social and financial level of her adherents was somewhat higher. She accepted a written invitation to conduct a revival in the town of Corona, Long Island, and was not in the least abashed, though she was astonished, to find her hostess a colored woman without influence to obtain backing for the projected meeting. . . . The absence of race prejudice was sincere and without condescension.[10]

In the early years of the revival the minimizing of racial barriers was spontaneous and uncalculated. Almost from the beginning the revivalists preached to mixed audiences, although in the South the races were generally seated separately until the late 1950s. The number of blacks attracted varied directly with the radicalism of the revivalist; Jack Coe's and A. A. Allen's audiences were more heavily black than those of Oral Roberts.[11] When the crisis came in the revival in the mid-1950s, many of the ministers increasingly courted black support in an effort to survive.

In no way did the early race mixing signify that the revivalists were social activists. The participation of blacks in the revival had simply happened and was accepted by the revivalists and their pentecostal supporters. Generally, the biracial nature of the revival did not lead to questions concerning the customs of segregation that existed, and most of the evangelists, when they spoke directly on the racial issue, were essentially conservative.

The first minister to emphasize that his ministry was interracial was A. A. Allen. When Allen held an integrated revival in Little Rock, Arkansas, in 1958, he termed it a "miracle in Black and White" and committed himself to a program of interracial work which many others followed but none equaled.[12] In the 1960s, Allen was the first evangelist to make racial liberalism an effective theological plank in his ministry. His open appeal for black support led him to campaign innovations which greatly influenced the revivalism of the 1960s.

Problems: External and Internal

During its first decade, the healing revival was clearly outside the boundaries of respectable religion in America. It bore the raggedy image of shoddy pentecostal buildings and holy roller services. The long, ecstatic meetings seemed not only curious but unstable to middle-class America. The charismatic faith healer was much attacked in the 1950s—mostly by people who had little knowledge of the revival.

Prominent American religious leaders considered the healing revival clearly deplorable. In 1955, the *Christian Century* labeled Oral Roberts a "Ringling press agent" and warned, "This Oral Roberts sort of thing

. . . can do the cause of vital religion . . . harm." [1] In 1956, the National Council of Churches of Christ, in an obvious slap at Roberts, "challenged the ethics of selling air time to healers." [2] Roberts was the most visible of the healers in the early fifties, but others occasionally drew the fire of national religious leaders as "racketeers" and practitioners of "religious quackery." [3]

More disconcerting than the disapproval of the liberal religious establishment was the open hostility of many prominent evangelicals. Most Baptists belligerently opposed the healing revival; in 1950 Bosworth debated a conservative Baptist clergyman in Houston. The Southern Presbyterian church warned against "evangelists motivated by self-glorification and publicity." [4] Other conservatives, even those who believed in divine healing, generally condemned the independent ministers. Roman Catholics readily accepted the miracles at Lourdes, but rejected what one publication termed the "so-called miracles of the itinerant Pentecostal preachers." [5]

The religious group which most fiercely challenged the teaching of the revivalists was the Churches of Christ, a church especially strong in the South. Militant and aggressive in their own teachings, Churches of Christ spokesmen believed that miraculous gifts had ceased. The revivalists occasionally won a supporter from the Churches of Christ, but in general its ministers led the fight against the evangelists wherever they went. Churches of Christ frequently bought advertisements in local newspapers challenging the healers to publish evidence that miracles did occur in their meetings and offering cash rewards for proof.[6] They repeatedly sought public debates and published a flood of polemical literature challenging the claims of the healing revivalists. They openly labeled the revivalists "fake healers." [7] *ignore*

By and large, the revivalists tried to igore such attacks. As we have noted, W. V. Grant readily admitted that it was virtually impossible to get the kind of hard evidence his attackers wanted. "Medical doctors are businessmen," wrote Grant; "they are not in the habit of signing their name to statements and getting tangled up in religious quarrels. . . . They will not swear that they *know* God healed him. This the fighters of God's power know." [8] Jack Coe branded the Churches of Christ "Bolsheviks" and "religious bigots" and flatly refused to debate any challengers: "There are two kinds of people I never waste time on. One is the disbeliever in God and the other is the disbeliever in God's word. . . . I'm too busy working for God to waste my time trying to convince the blind leaders who see God moving and hear sincere people testify to His miraculous healing grace." If one wanted to know the truth, wrote

Coe, there were "scores of testimonies and healing in evidence today." [9] Another healer said philosophically: "There's three and a half billion people in the world and why should I worry about a billion that . . . hates our guts? . . . There's two and a half billion more." [10]

In addition to religious opposition, the revivalists met resistance from the medical profession. At the request of the Church of England, in 1956 the British Medical Association issued a report questioning the claims of special divine healing. Many physicians felt that the ministers gave false hope to people who should have been under medical care. *Life* magazine reported that the American Medical Association took the general position that all miracle cures were the result of either suggestion, spontaneous remission, or wrong diagnosis. [11]

The pentecostal movement was divided on the worth of medical treatment. The more extreme pentecostals believed it was sinful to consult a physician, while moderates believed in both divine and natural healing. The revivalists divided along the same lines. Some were adamantly opposed to the medical profession. Jack Coe taught that the day would come when those who consulted physicians would have to take the "mark of the beast" and that men were clearly looking to the wrong source for healing when they consulted doctors. [12] Coe may have been making extreme statements for their effect in the galleries, but his tough stand against doctors was typical of his approach, and this view was preached by many of the other evangelists.

On the other hand, the moderate evangelists counselled respect for doctors, were even solicitous on occasion. Oral Roberts always advised his followers to consult a physician to confirm their healings. He, and others, frequently boasted that there were physicians among their supporters. Such revivalists generally distinguished their work from that of a physician. One revivalist explained, "I'm merely telling you that doctors cannot heal. They can keep you alive and I thank God for them. I wouldn't want to live in a city without them. I believe in them. But I don't believe they can heal." [13] In short, a physician could treat symptoms and assist nature but could not do what God's power could do. Neither was an evangelist working in the realm of the physician—he was not practicing medicine. A physician's work might be useful, but God's healing gift was infinitely more important. [14] The moderate evangelists believed that doctors and preachers both were fighting the evil of sickness and should not be enemies.

In many ways, the most powerful enemy the revivalists confronted was the press. All through the 1950s, the revival was a favorite target for exposé journalism. Only occasionally would a local paper be sympathetic. Most newspapers criticized the evangelists, and some refused even to print advertisements. The national press coverage of the revival was almost universally unfavorable.

The most famous clash between the press and a major evangelist came during the Oral Roberts campaign in Melbourne, Australia, in 1956. Battered by hostile publicity, which Roberts felt was promoted partly by what he called communists, the evangelist closed his crusade and announced that he was returning to America to "save lives." [15] Every major revivalist faced similar pressures; they all developed a deep-seated distrust of the press, which they expressed in different ways.

Oral Roberts remained aloof; he tried to maintain a dignified silence. When deeply stung in 1956, Roberts defended himself with a serious open letter to newspaper editors.[16] He later revealed that the hostility of the press during the first decade of his ministry had had a traumatic effect on his life and caused him repeatedly to reassess his convictions. He remained proud that he never struck back in anger.[17]

On the other hand, many of the more radical revivalists welcomed the attention of the press. Lesser known preachers were proud to be grouped with Oral Roberts as worthy of persecution; they frequently explained their own troubles by pointing to slurs and distorted facts published about Roberts.[18] Many of the evangelists quickly learned that even bad news had its publicity value.

The evangelists were also harassed by frequent minor brushes with the law in small towns. Not only their healing claims were objected to: their ecstatic, noisy services left them open to charges of disturbing the peace. Unfriendly local officials often imposed unreasonable requirements when the evangelists applied for permits to erect their tents.[19]

More ominous threats hung over their heads. The Internal Revenue Service suspiciously eyed the successful revivalists and subjected them to repeated audits. As William Branham learned, good records were a necessity. Charges of mail fraud were a constant danger.[20] Jack Coe's trial for practicing medicine without a license made every evangelist feel vulnerable. In 1960, Roberts was threatened with a similar suit in Miami.[21] In Sacramento, California, in 1956 A. A. Allen was charged with operating a business without a license and convicted in a local court. Allen appealed to the Superior Court of California, which ruled, "Because all people may not subscribe to the same forms of religious activity does not cause them to be any less religious in their nature." [22] Allen was acquitted, but such a court fight was expensive. He claimed that his cost was over $8,000.[23] Allen's operation was a large and fairly prosperous one, but the smaller evangelists lived in mortal fear that such litigation might ruin them. Revivalist O. L. Jaggers warned in 1956: "There will come a time soon . . . when the combined efforts of the newspapers, magazines, federations and councils of churches have done their deadliest and reached their zenith in creating smear campaigns and other methods of liquidation, which they now have in mind." [24]

Internal dissension ultimately proved even more destructive to the revival than outside opposition. The single most divisive issue was money. Financial success was likely to bring suspicion upon a revivalist. Frequently his success was sustained by techniques which alienated the churches, but willy-nilly, the day-to-day survival of an independent ministry became more and more a test of fund-raising skill. Mass evangelism was an expensive business and many of the most gifted ministers failed as financiers.

In the early stages of the revival, the ability to inspire large collections in the meetings was crucial. The nightly offerings were a highlight of the services. Oral Roberts may have been in a position, as he reported, to allow only "three minutes to state the need, offer prayer, and send the ushers to receive the offerings," but most of the evangelists were forced to press hard for money. Nor could most afford the ethical luxury of Roberts' practice of giving a strict accounting to a local committee for all of the funds received.[25]

The revivalists' hard-sell fund raising irritated local pastors, who frequently suffered diminishing church collections in the wake of a successful revival. In the early Voice of Healing conventions this issue was heatedly discussed. A suggestion by Jack Coe that the revivalists hold no Sunday meetings brought a temporary truce. Coe proposed, "The friends and converts could go to the local churches on Sundays and get acquainted with the pastors right along. Then the pastors could lift their Sunday morning and evening offering as usual, and there was no need to suffer." Coe said that when this plan was followed, his Monday night meetings were always the best and usually "made good what the evangelists miss on Sunday." [26] As the relations between the evangelists and the organized pentecostal churches became more and more strained in the mid-1950s, such compromises became less satisfactory.

Money raising tactics varied as broadly as the personalities of the evangelists. Some set a quota for a nightly meeting and pleaded with their audiences until that amount was raised. One evangelist pointed out that this was also a safeguard against greed: "Last week there was over 400 more [ready to contribute], the people had been standing in line, and I sent them back because it was more than we asked for. You may not believe that, but it's true anyway." [27] Others seemed less interested in the nightly collections than in the long-range support raised from pledges. A particularly good evening in the campaign of a successful evangelist could yield hundreds of pledges for donations of $100 to $1,000. Although in some sections of the country, particularly the South, no more than 10 percent of such amounts might actually be collected, it represented continuing support that was coveted by all of the ministers.

The aid of sustaining supporters, or "partners," became the cornerstone of the more successful ministries. Roberts was especially adept at attracting prominent backers, as well as winning the loyalty of thousands of the poor and humble. Less prominent ministers sought supporters wherever they could. They begged for the tithes and gift offerings of those dissatisfied with organized religion. Evangelist Thelma Chaney wrote, "If God's ministers that we minister to through the printed page would send us a small portion of their tithe we would not have to worry about paper, ink and postage." [28] A few looked far enough ahead to encourage estate planning, but there was something slightly incongruous in a discussion of death in the midst of the heady atmosphere of the healing revival.

Each evangelist tried to persuade a group of followers to become financially loyal to his particular work. The competition for such support was fierce, and the marginal evangelist usually accompanied the appeal for help with pointed promises:

> Many in foreign lands want these new books but we cannot send them, they must go free and when we have to borrow money to print them, we must get some offerings from them to be able to pay our debts that we incur for the printing of them. . . . God bless you and, now we command Holy Ghost fire to come upon each one that reads this book, in Jesus Name. Look up and shout Hallelujah! And you will feel the garment of power begin to wrap around you by the Holy Ghost.[29]

Most evangelists simply tried to magnify the achievements of their ministry. In 1958, A. A. Allen spelled out his case for support:

> A few years ago, I took a number of our party on an evangelistic tour in a Latin country. While we were there, we saw multitudes come to the Lord and repent of their sins, and get saved in the old fashioned way. According to the amount of money we spent and the number of conversions on that tour, the souls that were saved in that campaign cost only twenty-five cents each, or FOUR FOR A DOLLAR! . . .
>
> After returning home, I read in a periodical of another evangelist that his cost of winning souls averaged $2.00 each. Another group estimated that their cost was even higher. And some "missionary " activities just don't expect to win souls any more! . . .

As a wise "Investor" for God, use a part of your missionary dollar in this way, but be sure at least a part of your missionary dollar is reaching out into genuine, active, productive soul winning, building up your account in heaven NOW! [30]

From the beginning the evangelists taught that prosperity was a blessing that belonged to God's people. Individual prosperity, however, could be expected only if one gave generously to God's work. As early as 1954 Oral Roberts was predicting a sevenfold return to those who supported his ministry: "And God impressed me to pray that our contributors will have their money multiplied to them a perfect number of times, putting back into their hands every dollar their needs require." [31] Roberts called tithing a "sure way for God to deliver you from poverty." [32] By the 1960s, the promise of prosperity had come to rival healing as a major theme of the revival.

At no point were the evangelists more sensitive to criticism than on the question of their financial methods. Roberts, Branham, and many of the other revivalists decried the "improper emphasis on money" which admittedly marred many of the healing campaigns. [33] The responsible leaders of the revival repudiated high pressure tactics and the practice of accepting personal gifts from those healed. [34] Nevertheless, the huge cash collections, the regular love offerings received by the evanglists, and the desire of many of the faithful to shower gifts on the revivalists provided ample opportunities for misappropriation of funds. Investigation by the Internal Revenue Service and the precarious financial condition of most of the ministries made the personal misuse of funds a dangerous practice, but financial chicanery, as well as irresponsibility, was clearly present from the beginning of the revival. [35] As early as 1949 Gordon Lindsay warned against a covetous spirit: "But this revival can be greatly retarded if there is a continual auctioneering for money in the campaigns. There are some who are short-sighted enough to have destroyed their usefulness to the kingdom of God by an offensive handling of finances." [36]

More often than not, high pressure fund raising methods were a product of desperation, not greed. The financial pressures on the evangelists who aspired to national reputations were enormous. By the late 1950s the monthly cost of a modest ministry—including a monthly periodical, a network of about thirty radio stations, and a regular campaign schedule—was around $3,000. [37] An early worker in the Allen revivals outlined the financial risks in the larger ministries: "A lot of people think [the revivalists] are making a lot of money but they don't realize—I've seen them spend ten or fifteen thousand dollars before they ever preach the first sermon. . . . I can remember the time when Allen every spring would borrow ten thousand dollars from a man to start out in the spring with." [38]

In 1948, just as the revival was beginning, Gordon Lindsay had given his good advice to the new evangelists: "It is better for one to go slow. Get your ministry on a solid foundation. . . . By all means avoid Hollywood press agent stuff." [39] But only a select few managed to build a solid foundation before the revival began to lose momentum. When even William Branham suddenly found it difficult to meet expenses in 1955, the future looked dim indeed for lesser figures. In 1957, evangelist Alfred Allen of Memphis, Tennessee, who had been, he said, a "full time evangelist for the past three and one-half years," announced that he was "leaving the full time evangelistic ministry for awhile." The following notice, which illustrated the problems of the less prominent revivalists, appeared in the *Herald of Faith*:

> Bro. and Sister Allen are open for a pastorate anywhere in the United States. They are independent and preach the good old fashioned Bible; both have gifted Deliverance ministries. They are open for pastors or assistant pastor to a good church—(Sister Allen is qualified to run a church office efficiently) or they are willing to build or will accept an established congregation. . . . They will prayerfully consider every invitation. Open immediately. [40]

The mortality rate among the independent ministries was high enough to intimidate all but the boldest.

The early leaders of the revival agreed that outstanding ministries were not built on gifts alone but on the financial and organizational skills of the evangelists. Oral Roberts, T. L. Osborn, Gordon Lindsay, and A. A. Allen had instinctive business sense; in the cases of the latter three especially, their wives were important business partners. On the other hand, the history of the revival is littered with bankrupt organizations— the failures of men with great gifts but little talent for business. "One man had a great ministry," recalled Gordon Lindsay, "but he didn't last very long because he didn't have any business sense to go with it. He had never had a bank account before." [41]

The typical organization of the revival by the late 1950s was a nonprofit evangelistic association. The association was generally controlled by the evangelist, his wife, and several key supporters. All tax exempt contributions, except the love offerings which went directly to the evangelist, were accounted for by the evangelistic association. The association, in turn, funded the various works of the ministry. The evangelist might or might not receive a salary from the association. When he did, the salary was nominal because his needs were usually well supplied by love offerings. Only in the 1960s, when many of the ministers stopped active campaigning, did some of the evangelists become dependent on their associations for their income. In addition, some evangelists pastored home churches which either they or their associations owned. The local churches were sometimes lucrative sources of income. It was not unusual for them to be bought and sold.

The financial needs of the independent ministers ultimately led to direct confrontations with the pentecostal denominations. C. B. Hollis, a pioneer worker in the revival, recalled: "There has always been a gap between a pastor and an evangelist. . . . Of course, you can sum the whole thing up in one word—m-o-n-e-y—money. Because the pastor thought the evangelist was going to get too much money." [42] This clash was the most crucial weakness in the revival.

Among the many other causes of the rupture between the evangelists and the churches were denominational pride, doctrinal clashes, and financial jealousy.[43] In general, the churches welcomed the revival for about five years and tried to use it to build their own work. As late as 1952, the *Pentecostal Evangel*, the official organ of the Assemblies of God, included occasional reports on the campaigns of the more responsible revivalists. Nevertheless, from the beginning, church leaders tried to keep the healing meetings in proper perspective. In an article entitled "Some 'Weightier Matters,' " the *Pentecostal Evangel* advised, "Sanctification is relatively more important than divine healing," and, "The fruits of the Spirit are relatively more important than the gifts of the Spirit." The author concluded:

> The purpose of writing along these lines is to call attention to some "weightier matters" in view of the enthusiasm over present-day mass meetings and healing campaigns. That God is moving by His Spirit with fresh manifestations of the supernatural, particularly in the healing of the sick, is blessedly evident. . . . But this fresh emphasis on divine healing does call for consideration of some other things, particularly for those who have lost all sense of balance and relative values, thinking that signs and wonders are the very acme of Christian achievement. Such a view is far from the truth.[44]

Assemblies of God officials felt that the independent revivalists had blown out of proportion the Bible doctrine on healing; but responsible denominational leaders were in a difficult position. If they spoke out against an evangelist, they were branded as opposed to divine healing. Again and again, they proclaimed that their opposition to the independent revivalists was not doctrinal but, in the words of one, a matter of "motives, practice, commercialism, lack of credibility, and lack of ethics." [45]

The revivalists believed otherwise, however, and they had the ear of the people. One disgusted Assemblies of God minister, who pleaded with his denominational leaders to denounce the revivalists, admitted that many of the people "like this monkey-business." He recalled that when the matter was first discussed before the General Presbytery of his church, a policy of slow disassociation was approved:

> We should gradually pull away from the new radical left and lean slightly to the old conservative right. This was a tacit acknowledgement that the proverbial monkey's tail should be chopped off . . . carefully, of course, and by slow easy stages. Well, after these years, the monkey still has his very prominent appendage intact, and worse yet, the thing has grown to monstrous proportions. This has strengthened my convictions at the time that the "pull" and "lean" policy was a huge mistake.[46]

The Assemblies of God moved against the revivalists with increasing force in the early 1950s. The *Pentecostal Evangel* emphasized the importance of the local pastor and the availability of healing in the local churches. At the same time, the miraculous began to be played down. The paper also called for a renewed emphasis on financial responsibility. An article in April 1952, advised:

> We commend these pastors and evangelists who deliberately limit themselves to a modest salary in order to avoid the appearance of covetousness. It is reported that one well-known evangelist, who is winning thousands of souls to Christ, will not permit any love offerings to be taken for himself in his campaigns. He ceases to take offerings as soon as the campaign expenses, including a stipulated allowance for each member of the evangelistic party, have been met. A frank, sensible financial policy such as this must meet with the favor both of God and of men.[47]

In a move that was said to have incensed the supporters of the revival, the *Pentecostal Evangel* refused to print the evangelists' reports after about 1953.[48]

As early as 1951, the General Presbytery of the Assemblies of God asserted its authority to supervise all private corporations operated by the church's ministers.[49] When the pentecostal churches' leaders attacked the independent ministries, they did so, in their eyes, in an effort to discharge conscientiously their responsibility. In 1956, the General Presbytery of the Assemblies of God passed a resolution which summarized their objections to the independent ministries: 1. Many emphasized such unusual manifestations as the "exuding of oil or the appearance of blood." 2. There was no scriptural foundation for the public diagnosis of disease. 3. Some used questionable methods in raising funds, such as "offering prayers or anointed cloths in return for contributions, fantastic promises of financial reward, or threats of judgment or disaster upon those who do not respond to financial appeals." 4. Many of the evangelists were guilty of "sowing discord among the brethren." [50] These were guidelines that most of the evangelists were unwilling to accept.

No one worked harder to forestall an open breach between the revivalists and the pentecostal churches than Gordon Lindsay. In fact, some of the evangelists felt that Lindsay bowed servilely to every demand made by Assemblies of God officials. But while Lindsay repeatedly urged the evangelists to work closely with local pastors, and openly attacked free-lancers within the movement, he also condemned those who opposed the healing meetings which, he said, "have been so thoroughly endorsed by the Scriptures, as well as by the tremendous results obtained." [51]

Many of the independent ministers agreed with Lindsay. Roberts maintained cordial relations with all of the pentecostal groups and continued to court local pastors through the 1950s. Others honestly tried to reconcile the interests of the revivalists and the churches. Joseph Mattsson-Boze, editor of the *Herald of Faith*, pointed to a weakness and opportunity:

> Let us pray that we shall be able to find the solution to the follow-up work, that the Church shall be strong and that the Church shall harvest the great results from these marvelous campaigns. In the meantime let us not criticize and murmur and try to find faults with these men who are pressed by Satan every day because they fight the battles of God.[52]

Perhaps the most influential peacemaker in the mid-1950s was Donald Gee, editor of *Pentecost*. Gee observed that the healing campaigns had their hot enthusiasts and their cold critics but urged that neither group hastily condemn the other.[53] Gee viewed the confrontation as a clash between legitimate extremism and essential balance: "We need the extremist to start things moving, but we need the balanced teacher to keep them moving in the right direction. We need extremism for a miracle of healing, but we need balanced sanity for health. We need extreme fervor to launch a movement, but we need repudiation of extremes to save it from self-destruction. Only a wisdom from above can reveal the perfect synthesis." [54]

In perhaps his most practical effort to head off open strife between the independent ministers and the churches, in 1954 Gee urged the churches to recognize the revivalists' independence:

> On behalf of these strong personalities who seem as if they MUST strike out on their own rather than work in cooperation with their brethren, it ought to be recognized that often they conscientiously believe that it is the only way by which they can fulfill all the purposes of God for their own appointed ministry. They are sincere when they chafe at methods of consultation with brethren and submitting to the wish of a majority. Sometimes their responsibilities become so big that no organization would be willing to adopt them. . . . All in all it seems as though some gifted personalities in the Church just HAVE to be individualists to fulfill their ministry.

On the other hand, Gee had stern advice for the evangelists: "They sin against the brethren when they ride rough-shod over the ethics of ministerial courtesy, and ultimately there will always come a day of reckoning when they will need friends and find they are left alone. But also there should be no bitter speaking on the part of the individualist or the organization one against the other." [55]

One independent evangelist spoke for many when he said, "I think that part of it was jealousy. . . . He's having bigger crowds than we are. Or I'm the head of this organization . . . and who does he think he is. . . . They felt that [the revivalists] were getting money from the organizational people that they represented and they had no control of it and that this ought not to be." [56] Another revival leader charged that the churches were unreceptive to any idea that "didn't originate with headquarters." More and more the churches began to reemphasize their established doctrines and demand conformity from the evangelists.[57] The resurgence of denominational pride and doctrinal dogmatism killed the ecumenical spirit bred by the revival. "People see the evidences of a move," wrote evangelist Thelma Chaney, "but they are so wrapped around by certain doctrines that they cannot get loose to follow on to know the Lord." [58] To denominational leaders the struggle was to save the sheep from false teachers; to the revivalists it was a return to the petty jealousy and doctrinal myopia which crippled the early pentecostal movement.

In later years some of the revivalists came to accept philosophically the opposition of the organized denominations. "Any great revival," commented H. Richard Hall, "has never come from the church as such, but it comes from individuals." [59] Evangelist Don Stewart surmised, "Real revival has always sprang outside of the denominations. . . . The system kills revival." [60] Donald Gee hoped that the revivalists and the churches could be "extreme wings in the army of Emanuel" and that their work would be complementary, not contradictory.[61] That was not to be.

Open warfare began in spring 1953 when the Assemblies of God challenged Jack Coe. Coe published a letter from church official J. Roswell Flower informing him that the Texas district of the Assemblies of God had resolved that they could no longer place their approval upon his ministry. The resolution read:

> The Committee reported that in view of intolerable conditions resulting from methods and practices of yourself and associates in Dallas and elsewhere they can no longer place approval upon your ministry. It was the feeling of the committee that your methods and activities bring reproach upon the General Council Ministry, indicate a spirit of insubordination, constitute a breach of fellowship, show lack of proper appreciation for Council fellowship. They also feel that you are antagonizing Dallas Civil Authorities and misleading the public. They are not asking that you be dropped from the fellowship but that we withhold the renewal of fellowship certificate.

The leaders of the Assemblies of God expressed regret at taking the action, but they had repeatedly discussed the evangelist's tactics with him, and they felt they must finally act decisively.[62]

Coe replied that the action did not come as a surprise: "one of the officials made the remark to me that he would not rest until he saw every man that was preaching divine healing in a deliverance ministry, separated from the General Council of the Assemblies of God." Coe claimed that Flower had opposed his highly successful campaign in Springfield the year before; he went along because, according to Coe, "it would make it hard for him with the churches if I did not go ahead and come." [63]

Coe saw two reasons for the attack on him. First, he insisted, many of the church's leaders had lost their faith in the miraculous. Coe reported that Flower told him that he "did not approve of messages in tongues and interpretations in the Congregation within large meetings." More to the point, Coe charged that one church official had publicly denied that divine healing was in the atonement.[64] Coe cited a tract that was, he said, circulated with the approval of the Texas District Council condemning an overemphasis on divine healing and miracles. The embattled evangelist wrote, "From this tract . . . you can see that there is a spirit of jealousy in this man's heart against people who are doing miracles in the name of Jesus." [65]

Such jealousy was the second factor motivating his attackers, Coe believed. As for charges of financial misdeeds, Coe responded, "Any time anybody would like to, they can go over my books. . . . My books are open to the public. . . . I have conscientiously used every penny that has been put into my hands, for the thing that the money was specified for." [66] He was infuriated by a fellow minister's accusation that some of the revivalists who had practically nothing before they started capitalizing on healing were living in $40,000 and $50,000 homes. In his magazine he printed pictures of four homes owned by Assemblies of God officials in Springfield, Missouri and the homes of Jack Coe, David Nunn, Alton Hayes, and William Freeman. The houses of the revivalists seemed considerably more modest than those of the church officials. [67]

Coe believed that the Assemblies of God were at a crossroads; he urged bold action at the next meeting of the General Council. The only solution to the church's problems was, he believed, "to remove the men from office who are fighting divine healing and the deliverance ministry." Coe directly attacked the hierarchy of the church, ending all hope of compromise:

> My first recommendation to the people who are reading this paper would be that we go to our knees and pray and ask God to guide us and direct us in what we do at the next General Council and to put a man in as superintendent, such as Earnest Williams, or Bro. Ralph Riggs, who believes in the old time power of God, and to remove from office, men like Gayle Lewis and J. O. Savell who have fought divine healing and the deliverance ministry. Another recommendation that I would like to make is that I would like to see Bro. J. Roswell Flowers retired from office and given a pension for the rest of his life. I feel like he has set in headquarters too long and has built up a political machine. If you had time to visit headquarters and go on the inside, you would find out a lot of things that are going on, for which Bro. Flowers is responsible for.

Coe believed that if his church did not change it would find itself outside the revival. "I believe that the people in the Assemblies of God," he wrote, "need to wake up to the fact that formalism and unbelief is sweeping in among a bunch of the men who are fighting with all they have to tear down and destroy what God is doing." [68]

By the time the air cleared in 1953, rigid lines had been drawn. The Assemblies of God had taken on its most powerful independent revivalist, censured him, and revoked his ministerial license. For lesser figures the pressure to conform was intense. More covertly, the same pressures were increasingly present in the other pentecostal denominations. "The organization," recalled one evangelist, "began to fight. . . .

I've attended meetings when the superintendent got up and they would name Jack Coe and Oral Roberts and ridicule them and run them down because they felt that they were taking advantage of the people." [69]

It became nearly impossible with few exceptions for an independent revivalist to get the support of local pentecostal pastors for a city-wide campaign. Even if they were sympathetic, local pastors risked disciplinary action by their denomination if they supported the more radical evangelists. "Countless numbers," recalled one evangelist, "would confidentially whisper to me, 'Brother Hall, I'm for you . . . but I can't bring it out publically in my church denomination.'" [70] When an evangelist did get broad support from local churches, he did so at the cost of relinquishing control of the campaign. One complained, "Well, they tie you in so many hog-tied knots that you couldn't even get up and do anything. And so it's not possible to work that way." [71] Jack Coe concurred: "Most pentecostal denominations have cried, 'Latter Rain, fanatic and heretic,' so often that their evangelists are afraid to follow the leading of the Holy Spirit if it doesn't conform strictly to the 'doctrine laid down by the brethren.'" [72] Sometimes an evangelist faced not only nonsupport but open competition. Often pentecostal churches would stage their own local church revivals when an evangelist came to town.

The more radical evangelists brought the conflict to a heated climax with bitter public attacks on the "PLENTY CROSSED churches." [73] In a 1956 article, "An Open Letter to the Deliverance Ministry," O. L. Jaggers urged a united front against the churches: "Many of the healing evangelists have been successful in bringing together pastors and churches in various parts of the world in combined so-called union meetings, which have given these evangelists large audiences to preach to"; nevertheless, he declared that such methods held little hope for the future. He warned, "The denominations of our day, whether fundamentalists, pentecostals, or otherwise, are not basically interested in the divine healing ministries of our time!" He advised abandoning the union approach and ceasing to be "puppets of this iron-clad machine." [74] Jaggers denounced what he called the "modern popes, presbyters, bishops, and man-chosen superintendents who stubbornly refused to accept the leadership of the Holy Ghost" in pentecostal religious services. He warned: "My dear friends, the sun of sectarian, Pentecostal bossism is sinking in the sky." [75]

Asa A. Allen led the onslaught against the pentecostal churches after the troubles which led to the cancellation of his ministerial license in 1953. He asserted, "About ten years ago, God just threw a revival into the lap of one of the largest Pentecostal denominations in the world [the Assemblies of God], and they cried, 'We will have nothing to do with it!' They began to fight those who preached signs, wonders and miracles, and to persecute and ridicule them, branding them as radicals and fanatics, in false doctrine." [76] In Allen's opinion, the older pentecostal denominations had lost their zeal and too often practiced "sin and religion at the same time." He wrote, "Instead of the old time revival service which brought men face to face with doom and caused them to turn from their sins, they offer forms, ceremonies, rituals, ordinances and commandments of men, programs, beautifully robed choirs, lovely anthems, physical effort, natural ability, and 'inoffensive' preaching." [77] Like Jaggers, Allen argued that the revivalists could not work as they should if they kept their ties with a denomination and were subject to its leaders: "Some evangelists advertise themselves as sign-gift ministers, conducting miracle revivals, healing-salvation revivals and yet, in their meetings, bring deliverance to only a small part of humanity which is a little more respected by their certain denomination. . . . God cannot be pleased with them when they limit their ministry." He continued, "THESE PREACHERS CANNOT MINISTER TO THE MULTITUDES . . . they will soon be dropped out of their denomination if they do!" [78]

In the summer of 1956, Donald Gee, still hoping for reconciliation, wrote an astute summary of the causes of the rupture:

> Such an upsurge of energy, frequently by independent evangelists, backed by all the technique of modern propaganda, attracting generous financial support, and providing a glamorous contrast with more pedestrian ministries is bound to produce tensions. Hasty claims have been made that these many campaigns represent nothing less than a new Revival which now supersedes its parent Pentecostal Revival of the last half-century. There has been a tendency to dub established Pentecostal organizations and more conservative brethren, as hidebound, timid and backslidden in zeal and vision. . . .
>
> On the other hand, there have been cases of local pastors or officials who have allowed themselves to become sour in spirit about the whole business. They have seen and felt the inevitable temporary deflection of funds—for these campaigns are a costly business. They have become, perhaps unconsciously, envious at the glamorous popularity of the healing-evangelists while they themselves have laboured faithfully for years with only moderate results. It has been easy for them to fasten on features open to criticism by those who want to criticize, such as exaggerated claims for numbers, the ephemeral nature of many of the boasted conversions or healings, or the final lack of lasting fruit in the building up of the local churches.[79]

Thus, repelled by the extreme techniques and claims of some revivalists, responsible church leaders recoiled from the entire revival.

Threatened by the loss of support, the revivalists made increasingly grandiose claims. Each new aspiring revivalist felt obliged to do more marvelous miracles than the established evangelists. Even Gordon Lindsay became disgusted with the "gimmicks" and "counterfeits" that he perceived in the revival.[80] Donald Gee observed in 1954 a swing from quality to quantity in the ministries.[81] He wanted to believe the best but finally admitted that some of the sensational miracle claims simply made "too large drafts upon mere credulity." [82] The display of miracles by the mid-1950s had become mind-boggling. One historian reported: "The healing evangelists live in a constant dialogue with angels and demons, the Holy Spirit and the spirits of diseases from the abyss; some experience electric currents through their hands when they pray with the sick, others have a halo around their heads when they are photographed, and others again have oil appearing on their hands when they pray." [83]

Again and again the moderate leaders of the revival warned the evangelists to weigh their claims carefully. Gordon Lindsay pleaded for clear thinking and the avoidance of fanaticism: "For example, we understand that [some] have laid hands on missionary recruits, promising them that they should receive the gift of languages by which they would be able to preach the gospel to the heathen. Although it is possible for God to do this or anything else, we find no Scriptural basis for making missionaries in this way." [84] Donald Gee repeatedly urged that exaggeration stop: "I want to think the best of my fellow-labourers unto the kingdom of God. . . . I do not want to ever think, although sometimes I seem reluctantly compelled so to do, that an element of seeking our own glory enters in. A bubble-reputation built on exaggerated reports is bound to burst in shame and futility sooner or later, and I am certain that the anointing of the Spirit leaves those who do not state the truth." [85] Gee tried to keep an open mind, but two years later he reissued his warning to the revivalists: "Over-desire is only another term for lust, and there can be an unhealthy lusting after signs and wonders that desires them for their own sake rather than the glory of God and the work of the Gospel." [86]

Many of the revivalists, on the other hand, called such skepticism, "Satan's strategy . . . to divide the people who proclaim deliverance." T. L. Osborn, who tried to remain within the moderate stream, warned against groups which accept "one supernatural sign of God's presence among His people, while they turn around and deny another as false because it happens in some man's ministry 'who followeth not with us.' " Osborn urged the churches not to draw lines of segregation among the deliverance ministries and flatly declared that he would "rather be considered fanatical than to be skeptical." [87]

While the bickering of the mid-1950s centered on the independence of the revivalists and their radical claims, older theological issues lurked just beneath the surface. The bitter battle between oneness and trinitarian pentecostals began to surface, particularly in the ministry of William Branham. The churches insisted more and more that their members attend only revivals conducted by their own ministers. Increasingly, those who had lived through the glory days solemnly were asking, "Is the revival dead?"

William Branham in Houston, January 1950. Perhaps the most famous picture of the revival. The light above Branham's head was explained as a supernatural halo.

Oral Roberts holds the discarded brace of Aline Green. Her 1947 healing of infantile paralysis in Muskogee, Oklahoma, helped launch his charismatic ministry.

A *Voice of Healing* magazine cover picturing the prominent evangelists
and editors associated with the organization in the early 1950s. First row:
A. A. Allen, William Branham, Jack Coe, Clifton Erickson, Velmer
Gardner. Second row: W. V. Grant, Dale Hansen, H. E. Hardt, Fern
Huffstutler, Gayle Jackson. Third row: Gordon Lindsay, Jack Moore,
Louise Nankievell, Wilber Ogilvie, T. L. Osborn. Fourth row: Raymond
T. Richey, A. C. Valdez, Jr., R. R. Vinyard, Mildred Wicks, Doyle
Zachery.

Oral Roberts visits the Branham team in Kansas City, March 1949. Left to right: Young Brown, Jack Moore, William Branham, Oral Roberts, Gordon Lindsay.

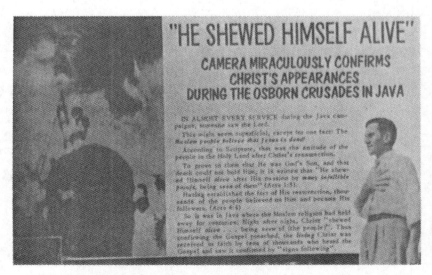

A T. L. Osborn campaign story, depicting a cloud formation that occurred in Djakarta, Java, in 1956.

Jack Coe being arraigned in Miami, Florida, February 1956.

A. A. Allen discards a crutch during a healing service,
January 1969.

Evangelist W. V. Grant, April 1954.

Evangelist Morris Cerullo of San Diego, 1973.

Evangelist William Freeman, center, arrives in Stockholm for a campaign in the early 1950s. Behind him is the long-time pentecostal leader, Joseph Mattsson-Boze.

Demos Shakarian accompanies Vice-President Richard Nixon, about to address the Full Gospel Business Men's Fellowship International in 1954.

Evangelist O. L. Jaggers, 1949.

Evangelist Tommy Hicks with President Juan Perón during a revival in Argentina, 1954.

Evangelist Franklin Hall, 1975.

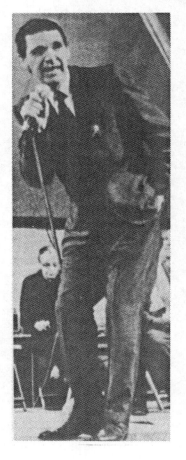

Evangelist H. Richard Hall, 1969.

Derek and Lydia Prince, 1975.

Evangelist David Nunn and family, 1960. Such poses are seen frequently, perhaps influenced by I Timothy 3:4.

Evangelist Robert W. Schambach, 1973.

Evangelist Jimmy Swaggart of Baton
Rouge, 1973.

Aerial view of Jack Coe's tent, 1951.

Evangelist David Terrell in a March 1974 service.

Publicity picture of the interior of Jack Coe's tent.

Inside the William Freeman tent, Los Angeles, 1950. Note the integrated congregation.

A demon drawn, according to A. A. Allen, by a demon-possessed woman. This one seems to teach history.

The Charismatic Revival

1958–1974

PROLOGUE

HOWEVER COMPELLING THE NEED OF the huge independent revival organizations to find new forms that would allow them to survive into the 1960s, their day was not over. The revival had set loose new forces that would revitalize the independent ministries.

One of those forces was a body of people disenchanted by what they deemed the limited vision and autocratic leadership in their pentecostal denominations. They offered permanent support to the independent ministers and became their financial patrons while they devised new programs. In addition, hundreds of thousands of members of traditional churches had been attracted to the revivalists by the end of the 1950s. The rapid growth of the Full Gospel Business Men's Fellowship International, founded in 1952 by Demos Shakarian, clearly indicated the potent appeal of the charismatic message outside organized pentecostalism. The 1960s saw a charismatic, or neopentecostal, revival as remarkable as its predecessor. The death of the old revival and the birth of the new are discussed in chapter 6.

Few revivalists continued their full-time campaigning into the 1960s. Some stopped holding revivals altogether; others pruned their schedules and diversified their activities. They anxiously waited on God to see what new moves they might be led to make.

The influx of more sophisticated people into the charismatic revival called for new skills. Increasingly, gifted preachers and healers were replaced by talented teachers. Organizational skill became infinitely more important than platform ability. Some important ministries of the past—most notably that of William Branham—were left in the backwash of the charismatic movement. Many older ministries survived only as small mission organizations supported by pentecostal friends who remembered the days of glory.

A few of the successful revivalists adapted their organizations to meet the challenges of neopentecostalism. Oral Roberts proved to be an even more daring and innovative administrator than evangelist. Gordon

Lindsay and T. L. Osborn built flourishing organizations which appealed to both old and new pentecostals.

In addition, scores of young ministers established new independent evangelistic associations in the 1960s. Some, such as David Wilkerson, had pentecostal backgrounds, but many were spirit-filled ordained ministers from the traditional churches. These new leaders brought to the charismatic revival teaching skills and theological training which had not been evident in the healing revival. New names crowded the speakers' lists at FGBMFI conventions—Derek Prince, Kenneth Hagin, John Osteen, Bob Mumford, and scores of others. The force of the new revival astonished American religious leaders. The fellowship became a major evangelistic organization in its own right, sponsoring a weekly television program, *Good News*, on more than a hundred stations. Major new publishing enterprises appeared, the most important of which was Logos International, and Christian radio and television stations flooded the country with the message of the miraculous power of the Holy Spirit.

These old and new independent ministers who led the charismatic revival were joined by several influential figures who had long been on the fringe of Holy Spirit revivalism. The ministry of Thomas and Evelyn Wyatt pioneered many of the techniques used by the charismatic ministers. Rex Humbard and Kathryn Kuhlman were highly successful independent ministers who never associated themselves with the healing revival but who were thrust into positions of honor and leadership by the neopentecostals. Although many of the pioneers of the healing revival were in the midst of the nebulous charismatic movement, the only names on the program of the World Convention of the FGBMFI in 1973 which would have been recognized by a 1950 believer were Oral Roberts and, perhaps, Rex Humbard. Chapter 7 describes a sampling of the variety of spiritual entrepreneurs who were the prophets of the charismatic revival.

While independent ministers pushed the charismatic revival into every major American church, other children of the healing revival continued to minister to the nation's religious outcasts. Chapter 8 discusses the evangelists who continued on the campaign trail. For the talented and the bold, there were still supporters, mostly among people on the fringes of pentecostalism or drifting outside the boundaries of organized religion—blacks, Indians, Puerto Ricans, and poor whites. This post-1958 generation of roving preachers (some old and some new) carried the mark of the old revival, but their reach was more limited and their message less spontaneous.

For a time, A. A. Allen was the only major American campaigner, although many other small revivalists never folded their tents. Their number grew. When Allen died in 1970, he left a legacy in such young preachers as Don Stewart, Robert Schambach, and LeRoy Jenkins. By the late 1960s, others were launching miracle revival ministries to increasing interest and support.

Some of the revival ministries that survived in the 1960s were quite different from A. A. Allen's. Morris Cerullo, a Jewish Christian who was an Assemblies of God minister, began preaching early in the healing revival and continued to hold impressive meetings abroad throughout the 1960s. In the 1970s, he returned to the United States and showed an unusual capacity to blend healing revivalism and charismatic teaching. More than any other man, he succeeded in attracting support from the religiously dispossessed, classical pentecostals, and neopentecostals.

Other impressive new revival ministries emerged in the 1970s. The independent ministry of Jimmy Swaggart, an Assemblies of God minister, opened a new era of cooperative revivalism among old-line pentecostals. Swaggart's success seemed to signal a new willingness among classical pentecostals to support responsible mass revivalism.

The healing revival was thus shattered into a kaleidoscopic pattern. The message of the charismatic revival came to include many doctrines besides divine healing. Some ministers emphasized healing, others demonology, or speaking in tongues, or prosperity, or prophecy. The movement comprised people with little knowledge of each other, people of vastly different cultural backgrounds, with different modes of worship, different moral standards, and different perceptions of the charismatic experience. The amorphous revival was united only by history and by the independent ministers who, free from denominational restraint, roamed the entire movement, speaking to any who would receive their message.

Chapter 9 analyzes the charismatic revival in the mid-1970s. It seemed beset by problems more perplexing than those that killed the healing revival. Some of the dilemmas were old ones—the problem of public misunderstanding and the corruption of spiritual leaders. But the internal diversity of the revival raised more fundamental questions about its survival as a coherent movement. As the revival came to include the sophisticated, it also became increasingly introspective. Candid self-analysis revealed deep contradictions and tensions.

6

From Healing Revival to

Charismatic Revival

Bitter Examination

BY THE EARLY 1960S, THE healing revival obviously had faltered. At the end of the previous decade, evangelist David Nunn could write, "The Holy Spirit has revealed to me by revelation that the greater part of the revival is yet to come." [1] Evangelist Velmer Gardner could assure his followers, "This present healing revival will not taper off—but up. . . . Never have I seen such a hunger for God. . . . We are having the largest crowds we've ever had." [2] Now the increasingly dominant mood was the disappointed concern expressed by Donald Gee:

> Mass healing campaigns have lost their novelty, especially in their homelands, and the evangelists are looking for new worlds to conquer. We wish them well. Much good can come from individualist missionary enterprises and individualist academic interests. Yet we look cautiously at all individualism, for we have lived long enough to see the wrecks of time. The crowds will always be ready to idolize, but the spiritual dangers are tremendous. [3]

As the revival became increasingly self-conscious and introspective, the participants tried to isolate the cause of its decline. Franklin Hall, deeply committed to the doctrine of fasting, believed that the revival faltered when the revivalists quit fasting and began "living on a coasting experience." [4] Others believed that the evangelists had left behind the power of God and had come to depend on gimmicks.[5] Gordon Lindsay observed that many ministers stopped "fasting and waiting before God." [6] The market was glutted with miracles, and showmen had replaced spiritual leaders. "Today we have too much division among ministers," said Indian evangelist W. A. Raiford at the 1962 Voice of Healing convention; "We have too many chiefs and not enough Indians." [7] Speaking to a Full Gospel Business Men's meeting in Chicago in 1961, William Branham denounced much of what was going on under the name of divine healing: "They come in and bleed the people and go out and what have they got?" he asked, and urged his listeners not to sponsor a meeting in their city.[8]

The new internal dissension and criticism shook the revival's most stable leaders. They were prepared for the attacks of outsiders; they quickly became inured to the criticism of the pentecostal churches; but the self-appraisal of the late fifties and early sixties could not be dismissed.

Gordon Lindsay, who continued to believe that the revival was a great move of God, increasingly denounced the "personal ambition and jockeying for position" among the evangelists. In 1962, he admitted that many evangelists had adopted questionable methods and he condemned those who continually played on highly sensational themes.[9] Evangelist David Nunn recalled that Lindsay told him privately, "The day of the evangelist is over." [10] Many of the ministries had declined, according to Lindsay, "largely because of a lack of humility and because of a tendency to self-exaltation." [11] He was sickened by the increasing emphasis on money.[12] The public, Lindsay believed, had every reason to believe that the revival was "phony"; the unethical conduct of some of the evangelists had become a serious obstacle to the charismatic message.[13] Lindsay later concluded that even at the height of the revival many of the evangelists "hadn't prayed through, they hadn't touched God for their ministry, they just put up their banner." [14] By the late 1950s he was deeply displeased and discouraged.[15]

Donald Gee came to believe that the movement had harbored frauds and promoted exploitation: "It has to be confessed that in a few regrettable cases commercialism vitiated the testimony. The tragic volume of human physical suffering tempts exploitation by those who claim power to heal." [16] These abuses, lamented the respected editor, had "produced a tremendous crop of tares." [17]

Gee even questioned the worth of the great revival. He believed that the revival had depended much too heavily on the excitement of the miraculous: "Once the novelty of the miraculous begins to wane, as wane it must, the soul is left with nothing to sustain it in the battle of life." [18] He admitted that the revival had been too credulous in its fascination with the supernatural: "The popular healing campaigns have produced over the years such grave scandals that it will need all the courage, and wisdom, and humility that God can give Pentecostal leadership to cleanse them away. What ought to have been our glory has become our shame." The time had come, he believed, to distinguish between the supernatural and the purely psychological: "When people are 'conditioned' for miracles, and want them at any price, they usually can be provided with them." He was convinced that miracles were still taking place, but amidst the presence of excess and fraud.[19]

Gee doubted the usefulness of the revival-spawned independent missionary associations, which could create chaos on the mission field: "Missionary societies that duplicate each other in their fields have approached a scandal at times. It means much unnecessary expense in organization and propaganda. . . . In small societies the leaders are often the founders. All kinds of personal loyalties are at stake." [20] Gee suspected that the sole reason for the existence of some such enterprises was the financial well-being of the founder of the association.

Montgomery's Attack

The troubled conscience of the healing revival was bared in 1962 by G. H. Montgomery, one of the most prominent leaders of the revival. A former editor of the magazine of the Pentecostal Holiness church, he became in the early 1950s one of the trusted advisors of Oral Roberts. For nearly a decade Montgomery edited Roberts' magazine, but in 1961 the two parted bitterly and Montgomery joined Juanita Coe's organization. In early 1962, Montgomery published a series of angry articles in the *International Healing Magazine* entitled "Enemies of the Cross." He apparently threatened to release to the press a file which would discredit Roberts. Mrs. Coe was inundated by appeals from her fellow charismatic leaders to stop the articles.[21]

Montgomery's precise analysis of the revival reflected his years of experience in the center of the action. "As irregular practices continue to rise in the current revival of deliverance," he wrote, "we feel that we cannot keep silent about these things and still be true to God in the great upsurge of spiritual power with which He has visited the world in these last days." Montgomery believed that his writing had done as much to promote the revival and make it acceptable as any other single force and that he had the right to expose the evil that had contaminated God's work.[22] He had been warned, he said, that he was "going against a ruthless group of men" who had millions of dollars to fight with, but with Mrs. Coe's support, he was determined to complete his series.[23]

Montgomery was critical of the pentecostal churches as well as of the independent revivalists. He believed that the jealousy and short-sightedness of the denominations had contributed to the worst excesses of the revival. The churches, instead of controlling the revival, had forced the evangelists to extremes—sometimes actually trying to find ways to excommunicate them.[24] Montgomery's balance made his critique all the more telling. His was the protest of a sympathetic insider and a true believer.

Montgomery cited the independence of the evangelistic associations as the prime source of the excesses of the revival. All formed in a common pattern, they were subject to many abuses: "Usually, the evangelist himself became the president of the association. His wife was a member of the board. Then some very close friend, who could be trusted to do what the evangelist wanted done, completed the board. Essentially, there was nothing wrong with this system. . . . However, *the door was open to many dangers,* and it is this fact which makes necessary the writing of these articles." The practical result, he said, was that each evangelist became a law unto himself. Perhaps Montgomery most openly revealed his personal feelings about his years of service in the Roberts' organization, although he did not name Roberts, when he wrote, "He hired men and women to help him, but he used these men and women as tools, not as the children of God with brains, gifts and callings as clear and distinct as his own." [25]

Montgomery's list of abuses confirmed the worst suspicions of the critics of the revival. He refused to print any names (and could well have drawn libel suits if he had), but he directly assaulted the character and motives of the evangelists. He was disgusted by their all-too-common penchant for comfort and ease. He declared, "Men who preach the meek and lowly Nazarene to a lost and dying world, and yet live in palatial homes built on money contributed by God's poor people, cannot call themselves followers of Jesus." [26] Not only did the evangelists live in comfort, Montgomery charged, some of the ministers were little more than derelicts. A disillusioned worker for one revivalist had told him, "We had heard reports about this evangelist drinking, but we discredited these reports for the Gospel's sake. He would disappear from time to time for two or three days, and no one knew where he was. Then one night in Sioux City, Iowa, he came to his own revival meeting so drunk he no longer cared who knew it. When he walked in like that, I walked out." Montgomery revealed that another well-known evangelist abused his wife, was being blackmailed by an inmate of the penitentiary, drank and used drugs and associated with "the lowest type of women imaginable." [27]

Montgomery also denounced the exaggerated claims of the evangelists. Each one seemed determined that no other should get ahead of him, and so padded his claims of miracles and conversions "according to the demand of the moment." The public would not "pay big money for straight, honest work," wrote Montgomery, so the evangelists resorted to "great swelling words." The rule became, "The bigger the report, the bigger the collections." Montgomery observed that in a two-year period the evangelists reported over 3,000,000 converts in Jamaica, while the population of the island was only 1,600,000. He commented, "We use this absurdity to illustrate the lying practices of men who pad their reports to get gain and glory." [28]

Montgomery raised the thorny problem of fraudulent miraculous claims. He was certain that he had seen miracles during the revival, but he was also sure he had seen "dishonest psychology." [29] He was appalled by the gimmicks which had been used to "make merchandise" of the people; he listed twenty-three different miraculous commodities hawked by the various evangelists—including a pinch of dirt from the Holy Land, a few drops of water from the river Jordan, and pieces from Jack Coe's tent. Of the latter he added, "I took this to Mrs. Coe and she told me that the man who was distributing pieces of Jack Coe's tent had actually purchased the tent from her after Jack's death and had never paid for it." [30] The healing claims of the revivalists, wrote Montgomery, were frequently simple falsehoods: "Some of these same evangelists reported that literally hundreds of deaf people were healed and received their hearing in the Jamaica meetings. Now, it so happens that we have a missionary daughter in Jamaica who works exclusively with deaf people. In five years of work with these people, neither she nor her colleagues have ever found so much as one person who was healed of total deafness." [31]

Montgomery reserved his most devastating attacks for the financial tactics of the evangelists. One revivalist received in one year more than four million dollars.[32] Sometimes, charged Montgomery, this incredible wealth was gained by outright fraud, but more often the evangelists merely resorted to gimmicks offered on the radio, television, and by letter. The personal attention offered during fervent radio and television appeals to those who wrote to the evangelists was an outright falsehood in Montgomery's eyes. Only in the most symbolic sense could the heads of highly mechanized ministries, handling thousands of letters daily, give personal attention to prayer requests. In some cases, callous disregard was a more fitting description. But, like most victims of con men, those who were thus "criminally exploited" were reluctant to protest lest they admit that they were "suckers." [33]

Most galling to Montgomery was the diversion of financial support from the purposes for which it was solicited. He wrote angrily, "When men raise money under the pretext of using it for God's service and then channel it to their own comfort and ease, they're no better than bank embezzlers or confidence men of any rank." The money raised by the evangelists was supposed to go for the work of God, but did it?

> In the last three years, one evangelist secured pledges in an amount upwards of one million dollars for a certain phase of his ministry. I have in my possession at this moment an inventory of the product for which that money was used and which was available no longer ago than December 1961. Of the nearly one million dollars raised in pledges and cash for this one project, the inventory (which was given to me by one of the men who worked for this evangelist) showed that far less than fifty thousand dollars had been used for the purpose for which it had been raised. Less than 5% of all money pledged for that ministry actually went into the work for which the people gave it.

"Where does all this vast wealth go?" he asked. Too often, to support "the comfort and ease of the evangelist." [34]

At the conclusion of his series, Montgomery declared, "No man in this world will ever know what it has cost us to tell the people the truth about the existence of sin and crime in present day evangelism." He hoped he had not done harm to honest evangelists and editors. He harbored no illusions that he had "stopped the evil or put crooked evangelists out of business." "Poor people," he wrote, "will continue to send money to luxury-lined evangelists." But he had a clear conscience.[35]

After the publication of his articles, Montgomery was considered a turncoat by many of the leaders of the revival. Some never forgave Juanita Coe for publishing the attack in her magazine. A rumor circulated that Montgomery was himself guilty of personal indiscretions and was inordinately ambitious and vain. But whatever his motives, his articles put in the open some crucial problems which the supporters of the revival needed to face.

Montgomery's articles did not kill the revival; the city-wide, salvation-deliverance, signs-gifts revival had already slowly died in the late 1950s.

Montgomery performed the autopsy. It was a dirty, ugly examination that explained much of the mortal illness that killed the revival. The bitter facts did not obscure for Montgomery, and others like him, the glorious memory of the past, but the revival had grown old and sick—the time had come to lay it to rest. The question of the 1960s was: "Where do we go from here?"

New Moves

As the enthusiasm for the revival waned in the late 1950s, the hundreds of revivalists who were veterans of thousands of campaigns throughout the country could hardly believe that the end had come. The smaller ministers, and the more radical ones, found themselves increasingly isolated. The more successful and financially independent ministries insulated themselves and more and more withdrew from active campaigning. When Gordon Lindsay decided to change the emphasis of his ministry in the late 1960s, the last bond that held the revival together was loosed. When the Voice of Healing ceased to serve as a clearing-house and publicity voice for the revival, nothing remained but a virile variety of free-lancers.

In 1958, in an effort to preserve the cohesiveness of the revival, a number of the leading campaigners who had been associated with the Voice of Healing organized the World Convention of Deliverance Evangelists and held a successful convention in Canton, Ohio. The convention was sponsored by four stalwarts of the revival, David Nunn, Morris Cerullo, R. W. Culpepper, and W. V. Grant.[1] For a time these annual conventions seemed to go well and were well-attended. The list of speakers at the first included the names of many ministers long associated with the revival—Velmer Gardner, Wilbur Ogilvie, "Little David" Walker, Richard Vinyard, Juanita Coe, and Gayle Jackson. Conspicuously missing were the giants of the early 1950s—Oral Roberts, William Branham, T. L. Osborn, A. A. Allen, O. L. Jaggers, William Freeman.[2]

The leaders of the World Convention hoped to avoid the loss of common identity and purpose among the revivalists. They recognized that isolation led to excess. The estrangement of the evangelists from the churches and the subsequent fragmentation of the revival itself had made each man a lone wolf. Alone, many had gone to extremes or become merely eccentric. Without a national platform, the older evangelists were hard-pressed to sustain a national image; younger ministers had an even greater need for public exposure. David Nunn

144]

summarized the purpose of the World Convention: "We felt that by doing it and by bringing enough of the international evangelists in that some of the younger preachers coming up could get inspired . . . and also get a chance to get projected before an audience they'd never get a chance at. It might give them the boost that they needed." [3]

The conventions were expensive to conduct, however, and slowly enthusiasm died away. The last meeting was held in 1965. Healing revivalists simply were no longer a group by the mid-1960s. New fires might be built, but the old one was gone. Healing revivalism had become a lonely business.

Scattered they might be, but a talented and growing number of prophets remained in the field. During the late 1950s and early 1960s they sensed that their ministries were evolving naturally. As support within organized pentecostalism waned, interest among members of the traditional churches grew. Velmer Gardner wrote in 1958, "I realize many churches and pastors are rejecting this revival. But, thank God, hundreds more are accepting it. Scores of fine denominational pastors and churches are accepting the revival now and many of them are more Pentecostal than some of the PLENTY CROSSED churches." [4] Jack Coe, before he died, believed that he was seeing the "second call" as people from the traditional churches poured into his healing services.[5] One old-time revivalist declared, "This pentecostal thing . . . jumped the wall." [6]

In the early 1960s, when thousands of people in the older churches accepted the pentecostal teaching on speaking with other tongues and healing and hundreds of thousands seemed ready to listen, the pentecostal churches were perplexed, but the independent ministers readily accepted it as a new move of God. Donald Gee wrote, "There is this increasing new gale of the outpoured Spirit that is penetrating the old denominations with such intensity that we can hardly keep abreast of the news of all that is happening. Staid old-time Pentecostals are puzzled at the sovereignty of the Spirit. Happy are those modern 'Peters' who, even after a struggle, are ready to side with God. *The winds are blowing, let them blow.*" [7] Some pentecostal leaders believed that modernism had invaded their movement, but Gordon Lindsay disagreed: "This charge is so ridiculous that it scarcely needs refutation. . . . The inroads are in the *opposite direction!* Pentecost is being taken into the so-called liberal churches." [8]

The successful revivalists of the 1950s became more and more aware of the new potential supporters. They increasingly found backers among the affluent middle-class and interest among the sophisticated young.

Donald Gee commented, "The Wind of the Spirit is now affecting students and penetrating into the precincts of our universities and seats of learning. . . . We have placed a premium upon ignorance too long." [9] Gee commended Oral Roberts' move into education: "Oral Roberts has been in the forefront where advocating miracles is concerned, but if a miracle-ministry goes on to this fuller gospel, it can be welcomed as being worthily Pentecostal in wholeness." [10] To be sure, Roberts sensed the changes in the air and moved dramatically, as he always had, to meet the new challenges. Many of the less successful—and somewhat less adaptable—also sensed the new opportunities. One old-line revivalist recalled: "I don't know what; there's something happened. . . . But people . . . they're more interested . . . in pentecostalism and the occult, mysticism, Buddhism, eastern religions. There's a tremendous interest in the unknown. And pentecostalism is a mystical thing." [11]

The FGBMFI

The organization which first began to give order to the new charismatic revival, and which, in company with Roberts, came to guide it in the 1960s, was the Full Gospel Business Men's Fellowship International. The fellowship grew naturally out of the postwar mass revivals, which had unified the leaders of pentecostalism all over the world. [12]

The founder and president was Demos Shakarian, a successful California dairyman who had been reared in a pentecostal home and began sponsoring revivals in 1940. He was a friend and disciple of Dr. Charles S. Price and was prepared by him to anticipate the outbreak of a postwar revival. He threw himself wholeheartedly into the campaigns of the postwar years and was an active supporter of the early revivals in the Los Angeles area. In 1951, he helped to organize the Oral Roberts campaign in Los Angeles, and out of this meeting grew the Full Gospel Business Men's Fellowship International. [13]

Roberts became the chief mentor of the new organization. He urged Shakarian to call a group of men together. Shakarian invited twenty-one business men who shared the full gospel experience and who chafed under the restrictions of old-line pentecostalism. They gathered at Clifton's Cafeteria in Los Angeles to hear Roberts speak. A loose organization was formed with Shakarian as president and Roberts' long-time associate, Lee Braxton, as vice-president. The founders announced that the organization "would be developed as the Lord leads." [14]

Roberts gave his full support. The potential uses of an organized group of business men, free from denominational restraint, were obvious. The Tulsa evangelist assured Shakarian that he would do all in his power to help; the presence of Braxton in the organization assured a close personal tie.[15] For many years, Roberts remained the most powerful supporter of the new group and probably benefitted most from its growth.

The nondenominational association of charismatic businessmen (clergymen were not accepted as members) rapidly spread across the country. Local chapters were often established during a campaign by one of the independent ministers. By 1953, the fellowship had established its own publication, *Voice*, edited by respected pentecostal editor, T. R. Nickel. In October 1953, its first annual convention was held in Los Angeles, attended by several thousand people. The roster of speakers was an honor roll of independent ministers: Oral Roberts, Jack Coe, Gordon Lindsay, Tommy Hicks, Raymond T. Richey, O. L. Jaggers, and many others.[16] A year later, at the second annual convention held in Washington, D. C., the speakers included Roberts, Coe, and William Branham, and the convention was visited by Vice-President Richard Nixon.[17]

The growth of the fellowship in the 1960s and 1970s was startling. By the mid-1960s it had established three hundred chapters with approximately 100,000 members. By the early 1970s, *Voice* had a circulation of over 250,000 and each issue carried news of new local chapters and increased membership. In 1972, Shakarian reported a membership of 300,000 and an annual operating budget of more than $1,000,000.[18] Shakarian had become the shepherd of a huge independent charismatic flock.

From the beginning, the pentecostal denominations looked askance at the new fellowship. Its very existence was due in part to the feeling of pentecostal laymen, particularly in the Assemblies of God, that they were excluded from decision making. The organization was thus both a subtle rebellion against denominational authority and a new competitor with the local churches for financial contributions.[19] Ralph Riggs, General Superintendent of the Assemblies of God, wished Shakarian well in a 1953 letter and said that he was following the fellowship's activities with interest,[20] but the interest could not remain entirely an admiring one.

The FGBMFI struck an immediate alliance with the independent revivalists. The fellowship offered a much-needed source of funds and business leadership, as well as a way to circumvent the jealous regulation of church officials. Nearly all the evangelists became unofficial promoters of new chapters during their campaigns.

Although the fellowship did not, as a policy, sponsor campaigns, many of the local chapters backed specific evangelists. William Branham was a favored speaker at conventions and the fellowship repeatedly honored him as one of the fathers of the healing revival. Other deliverance revivalists who received sustained support in the 1950s included Tommy Hicks, R. W. Culpepper, and O. L. Jaggers.

One recent pentecostal historian assumed that the FGBMFI replaced the Voice of Healing as the coordinating agency of the healing revival.[21] Many of the evangelists themselves initially believed that the fellowship was formed to sponsor meetings. But the fellowship was never wedded to revivalistic techniques, and many of the old-time revivalists were eventually disappointed with the directions in which the group developed.[22]

Increasingly, in the late 1950s and early 1960s the FGBMFI began to reach new types of audiences in settings far removed from the tents and sawdust of the early revival. According to a pentecostal historian: "At the banquets of the 'Full Gospel Business Men' [nonpentecostals] were brought together with Pentecostals in a context that fitted their place in society. In seeking thus to move sociologically beyond the stage of the sect, the Pentecostals made conversion very much easier." Local chapter meetings in leading hotels put on display charismatic fervor in a dignified setting before a much broader and more sophisticated audience than the revivalists ever reached. "The 'Full Gospel Business Men,'" wrote historian W. J. Hollenweger, "can claim credit for having gained a hearing for the healing evangelists in the non-Pentecostal churches." The fellowship, he continued, while freeing the evangelists financially from the narrow-mindedness and clericalism of the pentecostal denominations, made a decisive contribution towards the spreading of pentecostal ideas all over the world.[23] It was both a product of the healing revivals of the postwar years and a platform for many of the more innovative evangelists in the charismatic revival of the 1960s.

The fantastic growth of the fellowship marked the acceptance of charismatic religion by thousands of successful middle-class people. God seemed to be moving in new ways, and the old-time revivalists—each in his own way—were forced to come to terms with the new neopentecostal movement. Some clung to the old methods and old supporters; others accepted the new challenge. Some of the evangelists could adapt their healing message to the Hilton ballroom; others needed sawdust under their feet.

7

Innovators and
New Breeds

ORAL ROBERTS

N O MAN MEASURED THE PULSE of the emerging charismatic revival
more astutely than Oral Roberts. Roberts generally moved slowly
and cautiously, after much thought, but no innovation escaped his
scrutiny. Then, in moments of crisis, he would make shocking and
unexpected changes in his ministry. It was agonizing to abandon what
had worked in the past, but when hard pressed he acted again and again
decisively and with uncanny success. More than all other charismatic
evangelists combined, Oral Roberts put his mark on the neopentecostal
movement which grew out of the healing revival.

Faced with a shortage of funds in 1958 which threatened to halt
construction on his new headquarters building, Roberts resolutely
stepped up his own work schedule.[1] He pushed his evangelistic crusades
with renewed vigor. In 1959, he announced that he had reached the
half-way point in his campaign to convert ten million souls and appealed
for partners to win five million souls to Christ within three years. The
millions of converts came so quickly that Roberts' aim soon became
simply "souls unlimited." [2] Well into the 1960s, Roberts still called the
crusades "the heartbeat of his ministry." At the beginning of 1964, he

announced plans to increase the number of crusades in both America and overseas to "reach more people with God's healing and saving power." [3] Beginning in 1961, he greatly expanded his work abroad, and by the end of the decade had visited fifty-four countries.[4]

The achievements of the Roberts ministry in the early 1960s were large, and the organization continued to flourish. In 1962, *Abundant Life* had a circulation of 600,000 readers, many of whom were regular contributors to the evangelistic association. Roberts' television program was being aired on 132 stations; his radio network included 366 stations.[5]

Nevertheless, Roberts saw that the old methods were increasingly ineffective. He was ready to begin construction on his enormous new venture, Oral Roberts University in Tulsa. He also moved to take personal charge of every part of his organization. Early in 1962, he had installed himself as editor of *Abundant Life*. "God recently laid it upon my heart," he wrote, "to do even more writing in ABUNDANT LIFE magazine." He wanted to redesign the magazine to keep his readers informed on "how this ministry is *meeting the needs of the people.*" "People are being healed in every crusade," wrote Roberts, and he wanted the magazine to emphasize the old-time power of the ministry: "We intend to give you in detail every month, accounts of each of our soul-winning crusades." He also intended to remain permanently as editor-in-chief: "I do not want to lose this close touch with you, my faithful reader and partner." [6] In 1965, he revised his television series to include studio interviews, and in 1967 he introduced a new format on his radio programs.[7]

Roberts' revivals in the mid-1960s seemed much like the healing campaigns of fifteen years before, but this phase of the ministry was also being reevaluated. Reluctant to abandon personal evangelism altogether, he vowed to try harder, year after year. In 1967 in a special message to his partners, he declared that God had told him, "Millions are waiting for you. Go to them. Did not I give you your name and your initials to spell GO (Granville Oral)?" [8] For a time, he sponsored a World Action program in which he and groups of student evangelists from his new university held campaigns throughout the world.[9]

During this transitional period, Roberts abandoned his national television program. He later wrote: "In the spring of 1967, after 13 years of nationwide television the Lord let me see that that phase of our ministry was ended." [10] Roberts called it one of the hardest decisions he ever made, but he was determined not to be wedded to an outdated method.[11] "I thought the world was coming to an end when he told me he was going off television," said his loyal advisor Lee Braxton.[12]

Since the early 1960s Roberts had been exploring a number of new ideas for his ministry—most of them related to the growing charismatic movement in the traditional churches. He held ecumenical ministers' seminars and laymen's seminars at Oral Roberts University. The audiences and the services in his campaigns had obviously changed in quality since the tent revivals of the 1950s:[13]

> Since the first crusade in the year of 1967, I became conscious that God was dealing with us in a very special way. I noticed, in my preaching, there was a new quietness and reverence in the crowd. . . . When I prayed for the sick, there was more of a spontaneous faith for healing. . . . There is something going on in our crusades now that is deeper. . . .
>
> The deepening that we now see in our crusades may be a result of my strong emphasis in the last few years upon the work of the Holy Spirit. It's a fact that thousands of people are receiving the baptism with the Holy Spirit through our crusades. . . . I see a great change among the ministers especially. Every ministers' seminar that we have held on the ORU campus has turned into a major emphasis upon the power and work of the Holy Spirit. Many of these men of different denominations have received the baptism with the Holy Spirit or have come into a new understanding of the work of the Spirit.[14]

Roberts' teaching was increasingly addressed to the neopentecostal fascination with the gifts of the Holy Spirit.[15]

Roberts most shocked religious leaders throughout the world and a vast majority of his supporters when in March 1968, he joined the prestigious Boston Avenue Methodist Church in Tulsa.[16] Stunning as the act seemed at the time, it was consistent with Roberts' growing identification with the neopentecostal movement. He later explained, "My concern was to follow the leadership of the Holy Spirit and to be true to the calling of God upon my life. I felt led to share this ministry of healing and to escape the tendency to denominationalize my full-gospel experience of the baptism with the Holy Spirit." [17] Roberts declared that he still loved the pentecostal denominations, but said he had long felt that his calling was "to deal with the individual, not the denomination." There also must have been a practical side to the decision. Where most of Roberts' early supporters had been pentecostals, his work came to depend heavily on sympathizers in the traditional churches. By the late 1960s, he felt that his strongest backing came from the Methodist community.[18]

Roberts' pentecostal friends were dismayed by his move. A young Pentecostal Holiness historian recently mentioned the switch in these words: "Roberts' defection from the church in which his father and mother had been pioneer ministers, and from the pentecostal movement

in general which had brought him to prominence, puzzled many." [19]
R. O. Corvin, a life-long friend and a prominent official in Roberts'
organization, was deeply offended.[20] Roberts was surprised when he
received letters of vilification from men he had grown up with and knew
closely. His organization was shaken; the ministry's income decreased by
more than one-third.[21] He had sought the counsel of few about the
switch and had rejected the advice of some of his most trusted advisors.[22]

Roberts' action illustrated the cleavage developing in the healing
revival. He once again felt called to serve a wider and more promising
mission. In his latest autobiography, Roberts astutely analyzed the
separating of the traditional pentecostal and the neopentecostal movements. He simply did not believe that the new charismatic movement
could or should be channeled into the pentecostal denominations.[23] The
evangelist felt that he had served the small Pentecostal Holiness church
well, but he would not limit his own potential by remaining inside its
narrow walls. Those who could think only as loyal church men would
have to leave his organization.[24]

The development of Oral Roberts University strongly influenced his
decision to leave the Pentecostal Holiness church. He was determined
that his new educational venture not be taken "down the denominational trail." [25] It is difficult to say when Roberts first began to think of
building a school. Lee Braxton, chairman of the Board of Regents and
long-time member of the Roberts team, once recalled that several years
before ORU was formally announced Roberts had pointed out to him a
parcel of land that would make a nice site for ORU. "I agreed and the
matter passed at that," wrote Braxton; "however, this statement stuck
with me and I would notice all that was said and done, until the time
had come to purchase the present campus land in 1961. I have always
believed that nothing can hold back an idea whose time has come." [26]
On March 2, 1962, ground was broken for the first building.

Roberts' concept of the school changed several times. His initial
intention, influenced by R. O. Corvin, who had been director of the
educational system of the Pentecostal Holiness church, was to establish
an Oral Roberts University of Evangelism. "In the University of
Evangelism," wrote Roberts in 1962, "our theme will be soul winning
and reviving of the spirit of evangelism, signs and wonders in America
and throughout all other nations." It was to be a "free school operated
by faith" and would assemble students on a highly selective basis from
many different denominations. Those who attended the university would
be graduates of conventional schools and would be instructed "on how

[153

to bring deliverance by the miracle power of God to the people." [27] The school was conceived as a boot-camp for potential ministers.[28]

But, Roberts wrote, "We soon saw that the whole of the vision was greater than the sum of its parts." [29] Soon the plan was to build a full-fledged university with a charismatic dimension rather than a professional ministerial school. Eventually, the Graduate School of Theology was dropped. These changes, commented Roberts, were not of purpose or goals, but of methods, and were made only after much "research, study, prayer, and meditation." [30] By 1965 the heart of the Oral Roberts ministry had become a university to educate the whole man—body, mind, and spirit. The huge financial resources of the ministry were harnessed to develop a reputable liberal arts college. In the 1970s, the Oral Roberts Evangelistic Association was funneling about $3,000,000 a year into the university.[31]

Roberts acknowledged that the decision to begin an educational institution caused an almost violent reaction among members of his team, some of whom felt the university would sap energy better devoted to evangelism. He listed several reasons for their reaction: "One, their religious and educational background was based on the traditional belief that the power of the Holy Spirit and higher education don't mix. Two, they knew me first as an evangelist. Any deviation from a full-time traveling tent or auditorium ministry was viewed as a threat to their own calling and career security." [32] These tensions—between the classical pentecostals and the neopentecostals, and between revivalists and educators—ultimately led to the departure from the Roberts ministry of such important figures as G. H. Montgomery, R. O. Corvin, and R. W. DeWeese. But Roberts persisted:

> Swayed by neither praise nor scorn, we pressed forward to carry on God's expressed will for the University. There was a crisis of some sort almost daily. One day it would be a financial crisis; on another it would be an academic problem, particularly as it related to the divine purpose of the school; on another it would be fear that something would happen to me. Then what would happen to the future of both the Evangelistic Association and the University? [33]

As well as opposition, Roberts received an immediate response from his partners and a series of large gifts which gave him great encouragement.[34] He asserted that he never believed in doing things "second-rate," and he threw himself unreservedly into his new venture. Some of his advisors hesitated when the plans called for an initial outlay of over three million dollars to build a Learning Resources building, but Roberts told them, "God said do it." [35] He began a major expansion of the school's facilities in 1970 with supreme confidence in his own skills and experience as a fund raiser: "I am in tune with God, with this whole ministry of world evangelism of which ORU is a vital part, and I know that every time we have felt something deeply and started, suddenly we found God moving in with a miracle." [36]

By the 1970s, Oral Roberts University, once a butt of derision in the educational world, had become a solid academic institution with superb facilities, a remarkable tribute to the talents of its president. The school was formally dedicated on April 2, 1967, when Billy Graham addressed a huge crowd of Roberts' supporters. In 1970, ORU enrolled over 1,100 students, and in 1971 the university received accreditation from the North Central Association of Colleges and Secondary Schools. Roberts proudly announced that he had completed his base and was ready to launch his greatest venture of faith. [37] By 1972 the campus included fifteen major buildings that had cost more than fifty-five million dollars. [38] The driving personality of Roberts was evident everywhere— pressing for greater recognition for his nationally-ranked basketball team, for solid academic standing, and for preserving the charismatic aspect of the school.

In 1969, with Oral Roberts University well established, Roberts announced that he was returning to television in a series of prime time television specials. He called it "one of the most important decisions of our entire ministry." The first special, featuring the World Action singers from Oral Roberts University and guest star Mahalia Jackson, was broadcast on 160 stations, including ones in the nation's ten largest population areas. Roberts estimated that the show had a potential audience of 192 million and that the air time alone would cost about $135,000. [39] The series, slickly directly and staged, was designed to reach all levels and ages. Of himself, Roberts said, "The Lord has given me a new anointing of the Holy Spirit." [40] The personalities appearing on his early shows included religious notables like Billy Graham and Kathryn Kuhlman, political figures like Mark Hatfield, and a stream of entertainers ranging from Pat Boone and Roy Rogers to unlikely guests like Jimmy Durante and Jerry Lewis. Such name guest stars were the reason that networks were willing to sell Roberts the necessary time, contended his supporters. [41]

In general, the television ministry was an enormous success. A few months after its inception, Roberts announced that over 300,000 new names had been added to his mailing list: [42] "Our mail is at an all-time high. Our audience is the largest ever. People in all walks of life write me telling how they are being won to Christ—they are being healed, they are receiving the infilling of the Holy Spirit, they are getting needs met in their lives as a result of viewing our TV programs." He was convinced: "At this moment in history the most effective way to reach the masses—in person—is through television." [43] He felt that the specials had taken him back to where he had started, on a one-to-one basis with his supporters. Television gave him a more personal contact with individuals than was ever possible under the big tent.[44] He explained to television interviewer Dick Cavett that he had not abandoned faith healing but had simply expanded his capacity to reach people.[45] Never had the adaptability of Roberts been more obvious.

His return to television in a modish new format may well have played a part in Roberts' decision to change churches. Certainly many of his old pentecostal friends were scandalized by the new specials.[46]

Throughout this period the Roberts organization remained a multi-faceted, multimillion dollar ministry. In 1966, it still included eight World Outreaches, designed to "bring God's healing power to this generation." [47] When some important figures left the organization, other early helpers, such as Lee Braxton, remained important members of the team. The staffing of the university fed new talent into the ministry. A recent, perhaps unimportant, development has been an increasing public presence of Roberts' son, Richard, in the organization.

The maturing and the continuity of the Roberts ministry may be best seen in the evangelist's work as a healer. Long sensitive to charges of fraud and deception because of his healing claims, Roberts had developed a complete philosophy of divine healing by the 1960s. He increasingly associated health with a positive mental attitude and the belief that "God is a good God." [48] In an interview with Mike Douglas in 1970, Roberts agreed that much of the healing he effected had to do with psychosomatic illness, but he insisted that it was nonetheless valuable.[49] Roberts acknowledged that many things about healing remain unknown and freely admitted that he had failed many times. The older Roberts could deal philosophically with the inscrutable presence of success and failure.[50]

Perhaps Roberts most candidly analyzed his healing ministry during his visit to the World Conference on Evangelism in 1967. Participating in a panel on healing, Roberts agreed that healing could be "stressed too much." He confessed disarmingly, "I would like to say I think that in the early part of my ministry I made mistakes. I had to learn the hard way. . . . For example, now in our ads we simply announce an Abundant Life Crusade. In the early part of our work, however, we stressed far more than that. I suppose it was the eagerness that we felt in our hearts. I know it was in mine; I wanted to help the people get what I had received." [51] As early as 1955, G. H. Montgomery had tried to counter charges that Roberts was "top-heavy on the healing idea";[52] in his maturity Roberts could see the point of his early critics.

At the same time, Roberts clearly demonstrated that he had not abandoned faith healing.[53] *Abundant Life* remained crammed with testimonies of healing and the Abundant Life Prayer Group continued to keep a twenty-four-hour prayer vigil in the tower on the campus of Oral Roberts University. The ministry published an endless stream of teaching on the subject, and "miracle faith" remained the central theme of the ministry. In 1971, the magazine readers were told, "When you need someone to pray . . . to care for your hurts and needs . . . remember the Abundant Life Prayer Group . . . because God has raised up this ministry to care and to pray for you . . . and to help you get your needs met—through God, the source of all healing and deliverance." [54] Nor was the healing ministry of the new Oral Roberts a nonmiraculous version of positive thinking. Mrs. Clarence Sanders, one of Roberts' supporters, testified in his magazine that God had healed her of terminal cancer at the moment she drove through the avenue of flags at the entrance of ORU.[55] The typical testimonials of the 1970s were no less miraculous than those of the 1950s.

At any rate, Oral Roberts began to gain a new respectability in the late 1960s. Long ridiculed and maligned, Roberts found an increasing number of doors open to his teaching. If Roberts moderated in his views, his change was less perceptible than that of the world around him. Even before the 1960s Roberts had won the respect of his local community. When *Life* magazine published a critical story on him in 1962, Jenkins Lloyd Jones, editor of the conservative and powerful *Tulsa Tribune*, came to the defense of his fellow Tulsan. Jones pointed out that faith in divine healing was by no means confined to pentecostals and the unsophisticated, and added,

> The Tribune editor is agnostic about the efficacy of faith-healing as far as genuine, organic ailments are concerned. There certainly is no doubt that confidence that health is coming back will evaporate all manner of psychosomatic illnesses, which are what most illnesses are. . . . And whether by divine power or by adroit mass psychology most people leave Roberts' tent with a vastly improved attitude of mind.

Jones observed that a large number of people had received "comfort and joy and confidence because of Oral Roberts." He concluded, "He needs no apology. We are proud to have him in Tulsa."

Jones also defended Oral Roberts' controversial financial success. The evangelist seemed to him to be financially responsible and to deserve whatever personal rewards he received: "Roberts lives well because of the flood of 'love offerings' that pours into his Tulsa headquarters. But he doesn't live anywhere near as well as the Archbishop of Canterbury or the Pope and he has personal contact with a lot more people." [56]

Roberts still had many critics in the 1970s, but none of them gainsaid his success. His organization operated with enviable efficiency. He pampered his partners, calling them the heart-beat of the ministry, and gave personal attention to his important financial supporters.[57] Few organizations were better equipped to explain their mission to prospective supporters than the Oral Roberts Evangelistic Association. By 1974, the operating budget of the entire Roberts empire was reportedly about $15,000,000 a year.[58]

Roberts had pioneered the idea that giving would produce prosperity for the donor; by 1971 his book on seed-faith had been distributed to over a million followers.[59] The key to prosperity, according to Roberts, was for a Christian to release his faith by planting a seed. In return, God would meet his need. *Abundant Life* magazine abounded in testimonies of successful seed-faith. A typical group of headings of personal testimonials in a 1970 issue read: "A Raise, Plus a Bonus," "New Job as General Manager," "A Bonus Surprise from Day to Day," "Sales Have Tripled." [60]

The growing acceptance of Roberts' ministry was demonstrated when, in 1966, he was invited by Billy Graham and Carl Henry, editor of *Christianity Today*, to participate in the World Congress on Evangelism in Berlin. Roberts was reluctant to go, wondering how his ministry would be accepted at such a gathering: "Healing and evangelism have been considered by some to be on the periphery of the great stream of evangelical Christianity." Scarred by two decades of criticism from the established religious community, Roberts stepped very timidly into the world of religious respectability. He had met and prayed with Billy Graham as early as 1950 and had called him the premier evangelist of our time. So Roberts went to Berlin and told the delegates, "I have surely come up in the religious world." [61]

Roberts and R. O. Corvin, who accompanied him, returned with a new evangelical fervor and convinced that a new day had arrived for his ministry.[62] In his comments at the conference, Roberts humbly thanked "Billy and Dr. Henry, for helping to open my eyes to the mainstream of Christianity." He was overwhelmed by his reception and announced to his supporters that he had been "conquered by love." His commitment to unity broadened to include all of evangelical Christianity. He earnestly prayed that Christians would "never look at each other again as . . . in the past, but as one family through the Lord Jesus Christ." [63] The conference both marked the arrival of Oral Roberts and also hurried the neopentecostal transition of his ministry.

Oral Roberts entered the 1970s with a new vitality. "Our mail is at an all-time high," he reported; "our audience is the largest ever. People in all walks of life write me telling how they are being won to Christ—they are being healed, they are receiving the infilling of the Holy Spirit." [64] Two decades of Roberts slogans had become the shouts of the neopentecostal, charismatic revival. Millions of Americans had learned Oral Roberts' favorite sayings: "Expect a Miracle," "Our God Is a Good God," and "Something Good Is Going to Happen to You." Hundreds of thousands committed themselves to have "Seed-Faith" and make a "Blessing Pact."

Perhaps most basic to the success of Oral Roberts has been his own capacity for introspection and his basic honesty. He looked with rare candor at the excesses of the early days of healing revivalism, even his own. But he did not let his past paralyze him; he simply looked to the future determined to do his best. The rough treatment he received during his early years seemed to have deepened his understanding of his own convictions. He wrote in 1967: "The press caused me to re-examine my life, my calling and my goals. I came down to the bedrock of what I was, what I believed and what I was attempting to do. I realized that I was sincere." [65] Always respected by his peers for his talent and his success, he was also a symbol of integrity. In a movement where the revivalists themselves were more conscious than anyone else of the pitfalls and the fallen, a smaller revivalist paid Roberts the ultimate tribute: "He's a gentleman. You can speak Roberts' name and not blush." [66]

WILLIAM BRANHAM

By the late 1950s William Branham's admirers had come to wonder why "the shout in the camp has died down to a whisper, and why the great shining light has faded to a distant glimmer in the dark." Branham himself described the decline of his ministry: "The multitudes that once thronged the services by the thousands have dwindled to a mere trickle of hundreds. The thousands who received healing in a single night, no longer move through the long prayer lines, but only a few are received on the platform each night." [1] Investigated by the Internal Revenue Service, and with no effective organization, Branham endured several hard years. "Where once he had gotten a thousand letters a day," wrote follower Pearry Green, "his mail had dropped down to 75. He didn't sell anything. He didn't promote anything. . . . And because he didn't promote . . . people in the natural way—they sought those that seemed to be more popular." [2] From one point of view, William Branham had passed the peak of his career; the massive auditorium meetings of the early decade were over, never to return. [3]

Branham apparently thought the decline temporary. He believed that he was still to have a great tent ministry. [4] He repeatedly announced that God was about to lead him into a new and greater work. In 1959, Branham said that he would abandon his emphasis on his "ability to read the very thoughts of men's hearts" and return to a healing ministry. He wrote, "My friends, I have read your loyal hearts and know your intense desire that there might be a return to what has been called the 'old ministry' and also a going on to an even greater ministry as has been indicated by a vision of the Lord." [5] Having preached in nearly every state and travelled abroad five times, he was ready for a new work:

> Now I feel that my ministry is going to change at any time; the third and last phase will come into being. I am returning to praying for the sick. I have every assurance that vast crowds will attend, and an even greater assurance that the most Christ-magnifying miracles will take place on an even greater scale than ever. I now propose to be away for a rest for a few months, waiting on God and gaining new strength. [6]

Branham talked often in the late 1950s and early 1960s about the "third pull" which was about to begin in his ministry. [7]

As the 1960s began, Branham's crusades were successful enough that many of his supporters thought old times were back again. "As it has been for many years in the Branham Campaigns," wrote a loyal follower in 1963, "the theme was 'Jesus Christ, the same yesterday, today and forever,' coupled with the theme song that has been sung in nearly every language around the world in the Branham meetings, 'Only Believe, All Things Are Possible.' " His meetings were reported to be some of the most glorious ever experienced. [8] Influential editor Joseph Mattsson-Boze, a loyal Branham supporter to the end, faithfully reported Branham's successes and echoed the yearning of Branham's disciples— "Just once more, Lord." [9] Mattsson-Boze reported after a 1964 Branham meeting in New York City: "It has been my privilege to take part in many of Rev. Branham's campaigns, but I dare say, this was the greatest. A free flow of glory went through the whole campaign, a humble, liberating Spirit, that made you search your own heart and seek God afresh." [10]

Branham still tried to get the cooperation of the pentecostal churches, but with limited success.[11] For a time the evangelist's most reliable support came from the Full Gospel Business Men's Fellowship International. Demos Shakarian and vice president Carl Williams of Phoenix respected Branham greatly, although in the late 1960s he became too controversial for some fellowship leaders. In 1961, the editor of *Voice* wrote, "In Bible Days, there were men of God who were Prophets and Seers. But in all the Sacred Records, none of these had a greater ministry than that of William Branham. . . . Branham has been used by God, in the Name of Jesus, to raise the dead!" [12] Branham meetings occasionally were underwritten by local chapters of the fellowship, and he became a frequent speaker at the group's regional and national meetings. The little evangelist felt more and more dependent on the organization. When he died, Demos Shakarian wrote, "Rev. Branham often made the statement that the only Fellowship to which he belonged was FGBMFI. Often, when called upon to speak at various conventions and chapter meetings, he has traveled long distances to keep those engagements. His spirit of service was an inspiration." [13]

The Branham ministry was severely pinched financially in the late 1950s and early 1960s. Large meetings became risky; it was easy for receipts to fall behind costs. Branham raised some funds through the selling of tapes of his sermons, the gratuities of the Full Gospel Business Men's Fellowship, and meetings in independent churches that accepted his doctrine.[14] Toward the end of his ministry, his doctrinal preaching became more controversial and he was used less and less by the FGBMFI. Pearry Green wrote, "He told me of how doors were being closed to his message, how many churches and camp meetings and conventions and things, that used to would have opened their doors to him as long as he was preaching divine healing, would gladly receive him, but once he came forth with 'Thus saith the Lord' on doctrine, they closed the doors." [15]

It seemed ironic that financial troubles should have fallen on the evangelist who had shunned the expensive life style so common among the deliverance revivalists. Branham's style was observed by an Australian disciple in 1959:

American preachers are very dress conscious, and usually look as if they have just "stepped out of a band box." In the evening service I noticed that

[1 6 1

Brother Branham had different pants to his coat, something that is just not done in the U.S.A., where clothes seem to mean so much and few are courageous to break with this. . . . On my last visit I mentioned how "car conscious" American preachers are, almost judging a man's success by the car he drives. At this particular conference, where Brother Branham was the principal speaker, they all came up in their nice cars, the picture of elegance, but Brother Branham drove up in his truck. He doesn't seem to worry about these things in this country, that, more than any I know, bends over backwards "to keep up with the Joneses." [16]

Branham shunned personal gain, but proved unable to protect himself from bad managers.

Of course, it was partly Branham's humility and simplicity which attracted so many followers. Gordon Lindsay told how he impressed audiences with his "utter and complete consecration." [17] The famous evangelist appeared almost timid before his audiences and spoke quietly and haltingly. "Brother Branham fully recognizes his limitations," wrote Lindsay, "and frequently apologizes to his audiences for his lack of cultural qualifications." [18] A modern pentecostal historian, who knew Branham personally, offered an extremely critical judgment:

To be fair, one must take into account his extremely limited education and his inadequate English. He seems to have been aware of his limitations in this direction, and in his writings asks for indulgence because of his poor education. However generously he is judged, it must be admitted that his sermons were not merely simple, but often naive as well, and that by contrast to what he claimed, only a small percentage of those who sought healing were in fact healed.[19]

Branham's sermons were indeed simple; hundreds of extant recordings demonstrate that. And yet, the power of a Branham service—and of Branham's stage presence—remains a legend unparalleled in the history of the charismatic movement. One observer wrote: "I marvelled at the simplicity of these messages as brought by His humble servant. It will always be remembered how he spoke with the voice of authority and yet in a gentle way pleaded with sinners to accept Jesus Christ as Saviour and then turning to the Christians, he would exhort them to line up with the Word of God and be prepared, for the coming of the Lord draweth nigh." [20] Joseph D. Mattsson-Boze tried to describe Branham's meetings: "I can picture the tremendous gatherings and the tremendous results in the great meetings in which I often sat on the platform with Rev. Branham. Sometimes I was scared because of the deep sense of holiness that penetrated the meetings, but I never failed to see the gift of God in operation through His servant and to feel the warmth of love that flowed through his ministry." [21]

In his early revivals, the evangelist had avoided wrangles over doctrine,[22] but by the 1960s he had become an extremely controversial teacher. Lindsay and other ecumenical-minded men defended him, but many of those who remained loyal did so in spite of his teachings. It was also charged that by the 1960s Branham had become surrounded by sychophants who damaged his reputation,[23] and that in his last years he was used by intellectually dishonest coworkers, for whose doctrinal positions he was not responsible.[24] One close friend said that Branham had told him that the crowds mixed him up and took as sacred the "little sermons" he never meant to be preserved.

Be that as it may, Branham increasingly lent his influence to a small group of followers who compiled and canonized his teaching before and after his death. He may have been used, but his recorded sermons demonstrate that his followers did not pervert his later teaching. Branham reached at last that status of unique prophet which he believed was his destiny.

Branham had long preached a rigid pentecostal moral code which became increasingly unpopular. He had no patience with "bobbed hair," "slacks," and other such "fads" and was rigidly opposed to women preachers.[25] On the other hand, he received a prophetic message allowing divorce, which offended some strict pentecostals.[26] But the controversy centered on his distinctive theology which alienated all the organized pentecostal churches. First, he began to press his conviction that denominationalism was the mark of the beast. During his early years, Branham, according to some reports, had equivocated on this divisive question. He reportedly told some trinitarians that he agreed with them, but that he felt obligated to the "Jesus only" pentecostals because they had supported him early in the revival.[27] But, by the 1960s he was teaching openly the oneness position.[28] In addition, Branham pushed his views on predestination. Always a Calvinist, Branham believed that the end of time was near and that the purpose of the church in the last days was to bring together the chosen seed so that the end could come. He made a series of startling predictions, including a warning that California was about to "slide into the sea." His followers believed that the prophet had predicted that the destruction of the United States would begin in the year 1977.[29]

Most important and most controversial was Branham's revelation, received in 1963, that the "End Time Messenger who was the Angel to the Seventh Church Age in these final closing days of time" had come in the "spirit of Elijah." [30] Branham wrote, "I DENY UPON THE INFALLIBLE

EVIDENCE OF THE WORD THAT THERE IS MORE THAN ONE MAJOR PROPHET MESSENGER." His prophetic message demanded the withdrawal of the elect from denominationalism and loyalty to the messenger. The healing revival had been a final step of preparation for all who would abandon the "dead churches" and come to "the message." Branham, who sometimes seemed unclear about the identity of the messenger, preached that his name would have the perfect number of letters (seven) and would have an "ending like Abraham." Though Branham's theology seemed complicated and bizarre to many people who admired him personally, it was compatible with his belief that he had been called to occupy a unique position in God's scheme.[31]

On December 18, 1965, the final eerie chapter in the fantastic saga of William Branham began to unfold. As he was driving to Arizona, his car was hit head-on by a drunken driver. He was rushed to a hospital in Amarillo, Texas, where he lay in a coma. A tracheotomy was performed, but Branham died on Christmas Eve. His wife was severely injured.[32] The tragedy shocked the entire pentecostal world. A number of old friends—Oral Roberts, Demos Shakarian, T. L. Osborn—telephoned their concern.[33] Funeral services were held in Jeffersonville on December 29; among those attending were Gordon Lindsay, Joseph Mattsson-Boze, T. L. Osborn, A. C. Valdez, and hundreds of the lesser healing revivalists who had drawn their inspiration from the humble little Baptist preacher.[34] A magazine called it "coronation day" for a "great soldier who fell in battle." [35]

One bizarre incident remained before William Branham's ministry divided into several feuding groups. Many of Branham's followers fervently believed that the revivalist came in the spirit of Elijah; some of his closest friends believed him to be God, born of a virgin.[36] In the confusion immediately after his death, there were anticipations that Branham would rise from the dead. The press reported, and perhaps distorted, these expectations of resurrection. A rumor was widely circulated that Branham's remains were "embalmed and refrigerated" rather than buried, but actually the body was stored in the attic of a Jeffersonville funeral home. On Easter Sunday special services were held at the Branham Tabernacle in Jeffersonville, which attracted about 2,000 followers. Disciple Pearry Green later said that the delayed burial was in deference to Mrs. Branham, whose injuries had delayed her decision on a burial site. But clearly some had hoped for Branham's return on Easter Day and his ultimate burial was accepted reluctantly.[37] He was finally interred on April 11, 1966.

Branham's followers continued his work by printing his sermons and distributing tapes of his sermons (over two hundred of them, and 300,000 copies in circulation), and by supporting a regular William Branham Hour on the radio. Some of his disciples still believed he was "the Lord Jesus Christ," while others honored him as "the last-days prophet" with the message for modern times. His taped messages were considered "oral scripture." [38] Several independent churches, most notably the Branham Tabernacle in Jeffersonville, Indiana, and the Tucson Tabernacle in Arizona, remained active in furthering his message. Pearry Green, the aggressive young minister of Tucson Tabernacle, visited over ninety foreign countries promoting the work, and his church sponsored a broad overseas program. Green listed over 300 pastors in the United States who believe Branham to be the "prophet of Malachi 4." [39] The Branham legacy in the mid-1970s was mostly these men and their followers. Scorned and shunned by those who revered the early healing ministry of Branham, they were nevertheless the legitimate offspring of his last years of preaching.

William Branham was preeminently the visionary of the healing revival. He lived in a miraculous world. Simple almost to the point of transparency, Branham ministered to a generation of credulous people, a man of his times. To a pentecostal world that craved marvels in the years immediately after World War II, he offered his sincerity and his fantastic array of personal spiritual experiences. To the modish charismatic movement of the 1960s, Branham was an outdated figure. He himself recognized he had little place there. He could not adapt to the new needs, nor compete with powerful organizations for funds. His lack of sophistication made him susceptible to those who wanted to use his reputation for their own financial or doctrinal benefit. Perhaps his death saved him from obscurity or further scandal. And yet, on the cutting edge of healing revivalism in the 1970s was a generation that remembered longingly the legendary power of William Branham. Young evangelists still wondered if the Lord might call them in a similar way. "Walk closely to the Lord as Elisha did Elijah," wrote one revivalist, "so that Br. Branham's mantle may fall on you . . . in the great revival just ahead." [40]

Gordon Lindsay

By the end of the 1950s, Gordon Lindsay saw that his Voice of Healing organization had become counter-productive. Its widely circulated magazine brought fame to healing revivalists, but the organization received little in return. In fact, as the evangelists became financially independent, they dropped the Voice of Healing and set up their own organizations and publications. In mid-decade, a series of them joined the organization for only a year or two and then, on the basis of their easily acquired reputations, launched out on their own.

Lindsay's efforts to consolidate around the healing work of the organization largely failed. Nothing came of plans announced in 1958 to change from an informal association of evangelists into a tightly-knit body.[1] By 1960 the schedules of only seven evangelists were being published in *The Voice of Healing*—Morris Cerullo, W. V. Grant, Louise Nankivell, Joseph De Grado, John and Olive M. Kellner, and "Little David" Walker. Grant, Cerullo, David Nunn, Richard Vinyard, and Lindsay himself continued to headline Voice of Healing conventions, which met until the mid-1960s, but missing were the giants of the past—Branham, Roberts, Jaggers, Allen, and Osborn.

It was the decision to move into T. L. Osborn's type of ministry that kept the Voice of Healing moving forward. Lindsay had long been interested in missionary work, having conducted campaigns in Mexico early in his career, and his mind naturally turned in that direction.[2] In 1956 Lindsay began a Winning the Nations Crusade, asking his supporters to contribute toward deliverance teams that would be sent all over the world by the Voice of Healing organization.[3] Early in 1968, he announced an all-out move for world evangelization[4] and for over a year called his magazine *World-Wide Revival*. The title reverted to *The Voice of Healing* in 1969 but the organization had changed permanently from one of healing revivalists into an important missionary society.[5]

In a final adaptation, Lindsay abandoned his role as publicist for the revival and became its historian and theologian.[6] By the late 1960s, he had developed the concept of producing evangelistic literature about the charismatic movement and message. He wrote about 250 historical and doctrinal books, many of them substantial manuscripts rather than the flimsy pamphlets usually hawked by the healing revivalists. Always a respected teacher, Lindsay developed a wide audience for his writings. He still believed that the message of healing was important to the salvation of the world, but he recognized that his own ministry had evolved. In 1967, he once again changed, this time permanently, the name of his magazine and gave a detailed explanation for the new title:

> You will notice that the new name of our magazine is *Christ for the Nations*. For twenty years God has blessed the ministry of the Voice of

Healing. It is through the ministry of healing that the great work of this ministry has been made possible. Our emphasis on it shall continue in the future. . . .

Actually the ministry of healing has made possible this great world outreach. Divine healing has opened the door to reach the multitudes with the message of Christ. And thus divine healing is the means, and *Christ for the Nations* is the objective—and has been our objective from the beginning. . . .

Of course our emphasis on the ministry of healing shall not diminish. It is only through the supernatural and the signs following that we can in a significant way bring Christ to the Nations.[7]

All through the 1960s the moderate mind of Lindsay led him out of the world of tents and shouting and into a world of sophisticated charismatic followers and thoughtful evangelism.

Lindsay's successful transition was eased by his early recognition of the force of the emerging neopentecostal movement. Lindsay was always ecumenical, and as early as 1958 he was willing publicly to support mission work among all Christians regardless of their church affiliations. The Voice of Healing would, he wrote, "continue to encourage the apostolic revival that is beginning to appear among such groups as the Lutherans, Presbyterians, Methodists, and Baptists, especially in foreign lands—groups which are welcoming our evangelists in their overseas revivals." [8]

Lindsay, in common with Roberts and a few of the other deliverance revivalists, clearly saw the potential of the neopentecostal movement in the traditional churches. As early as 1962 he announced that he intended for his work to have wider scope than evangelism alone. One of his major activities would be to encourage those engaged in getting the revival into the historical denominations.[9] In 1962, Lindsay, in conjunction with W. A. Raiford, organized the Full Gospel Fellowship, a loose association which they hoped could bridle the stampeding charismatic movement.[10] The effort was unsuccessful because the neopentecostal phenomenon was much too nebulous to take very much organization, and what fellowship was needed was already provided by the Full Gospel Business Men's Fellowship International. But Lindsay remained in close touch with the new movement and had many followers among the charismatic leaders.[11]

Gordon Lindsay entered the 1970s with a healthy and prosperous ministry. Although Lindsay had not built a fellowship, by 1972 he had established over 350 prayer groups nationally and received generous support. He had followers among many denominations; he was in the mainstream of the neopentecostal movement.[12] The Lindsay ministry by then included five main works: the native church program which by 1973 had dispensed funds to over 3,000 overseas church building programs in 83 nations; the native literature work which had distributed over 15 million books in 46 languages; a unique Jewish mission in Israel which was led by Lindsay's talented daughter, Carole; a rapidly growing Bible Training School in Dallas which offered one- and two-year religious courses; and a prayer and tape ministry which sent out about 2,000 teaching tapes each month to charismatic groups all over the world.[13] The Lindsay ministry operated on a thirty-acre Christ for the Nations office complex in Dallas.

Lindsay not only was well-known in neopentecostal circles but also maintained cordial relationships with the classical pentecostal denominations. Few other men rode out the storms of the 1960s on good terms with all segments of the divided movement. It was with justifiable pride that Gordon Lindsay could say after a visit to the headquarters of the Assemblies of God in 1971, "they put out the red carpet." [14]

Suddenly, on April 1, 1973, Gordon Lindsay died. His wife, Freda, was always the more important business partner in the Lindsay ministry. She stepped into the breach, and the well-established organization kept operating smoothly. In fact, the death of Lindsay brought a sympathetic financial support. Mrs. Lindsay and Carole toured twenty-six cities to publicize the work and received unparalleled support. Quickly, the organization retired over $150,000 in debts and expanded most of its programs.[15] A prolific writer until the end, Lindsay left nearly forty completed manuscripts for future publication to assure a lasting flow of literature from the ministry. More than any other major ministry to come out of the revival, Christ for the Nations rested on a firm institutional base and seemed entirely capable of surviving its founder.

The death of Gordon Lindsay closed a major chapter in the charismatic revival. No single man knew the revival and its leaders so well. No man understood its origins, its changes, and its diversity as did Lindsay. A shrewd manager and financier, Lindsay had been as nearly the coordinator of the healing revival as any man could be. When the revival began to wane, Lindsay was faced with a crisis more severe than those of most of the evangelists themselves. Never a dynamic preacher, he found himself virtually abandoned by his most successful protégés. But Lindsay proved able to adapt. Always a balanced person, Lindsay built a balanced and enduring ministry.

T. L. OSBORN

Like Lindsay, T. L. Osborn had a strong foundation upon which to build when hard times came in the late 1950s and early 1960s. He whittled the expenses of his mission ministry and constantly assured his friends, "We are making every dollar received count toward our goal of evangelizing the world in our generation." [1] In 1961, Osborn summarized the nine-point program of his wide-ranging ministry:

1. Mass evangelism. Osborn still held overseas campaigns which often drew crowds of 10,000 to 100,000 persons. "A careful analysis of our past foreign campaigns," his office reported, "indicates that we have won a soul for each 10¢ to 25¢ invested."
2. Native missionaries. "Each month," continued the report, "nearly $50,000.00 is sent . . . to assist an army of many hundreds of Native Missionaries preaching the Gospel in unreached areas of 70 countries under the supervision of missionaries of nearly 60 Full Gospel mission agencies."
3. Foreign literature. Osborn estimated that 14¢ invested in literature could save a soul and his organization was providing millions of pieces throughout the world.
4. A program of "co-evangelism," in which films were supplied to groups wishing to support his program.
5. Books and tracts, widely distributed in the United States.
6. Tapes and records of his sermons, sold and distributed.
7. *Faith Digest*, his monthly paper, circulated free to over a half-million homes in 113 countries.
8. Osborn films, supplied to foreign missionaries.
9. Correspondence. "Each month," continued the report, "thousands of letters are received asking for help and guidance in spiritual matters. Every letter is carefully considered and individually answered." [2]

All of this was pretty much in the pattern established in the early Osborn ministry, although his personal mass campaigns came to be overshadowed by other types of mission schemes. Osborn had an eye for the right place, and Osborn campaigns showed up at crucial times in such places as Vietnam and other areas of current interest. The Osborn work continued to flourish during the lean early 1960s. In 1963, he opened a striking new headquarters building in Tulsa. Osborn declared that none of the money for the construction of the building had been diverted from evangelism and also proudly announced that not "one dollar" had been borrowed to construct the building.[3]

Osborn was not one to stand pat. In 1969, an article in *Faith Digest* reminded, "Where tradition and caution have characterized many orthodox ministries, Osborn has often set the trends, established the pace, and stayed in the forefront of evangelism by sheer faith and divine audacity." [4] The occasion for this boast was the announcement of the beginning of the Osborn Foundation, a reorganization which would assure the work of the ministry "in perpetuity." Osborn faced the future in the 1970s with less uncertainty than any other old deliverance evangelist.

It was the simple truth that Osborn had moved with "divine audacity" during his career, particularly in the 1960s and early 1970s. He constantly did something new. In the late 1960s he temporarily turned his main attention from missions abroad to a youth revival in the United States. He barnstormed the country delivering a three-lesson series designed to save modern youth. It began with a lesson entitled "conversion," billed as "a mighty sermon for teen-agers on declining moral standards"; continued with a sermon entitled "God Is NOT Dead," a "devastating answer to atheism and false theology"; and concluded with a film featuring his overseas work entitled "The Healer of Trinidad." [5] Addressing himself to the disturbed parents of the 1960s, Osborn said that he was preaching differently from ever before in America and that he was having amazing results: "I'm slanting every message in language that makes sense to young people. Many of the vandals and sex-perverts who run our streets today like wild animals, will be voted into state and national offices tomorrow. We'd better talk on their level, while we still have the chance." [6]

With the coming of the youth emphasis, Osborn adopted the language of the young and used the "one way" slogan that came to be the mark of a national youth revival. He urged his old-time followers, "Think young in your faith." [7] Even the appearance of the evangelist changed. Beginning in 1969 the former pentecostal missionary's hair line descended and his dress became more and more modish. Still a youthful man in his mid-forties, T. L. Osborn came on as hip to the youth scene; he had moved with the revival to appeal to a quite different audience.

T. L. Osborn entered the 1970s as one of the most powerful and successful fund-raisers among the independent ministers. He once again began to emphasize his mission programs. His appeal to send the gospel overseas had always been powerful, and though he had many competitors by 1970, he had been the pioneer in the field. "It makes sense," said

Faith Digest in 1970, "to turn to a man with a proven ministry of successful, believing prayer—a man of faith. T. L. Osborn has a record unsurpassed." [8] In 1972, Osborn announced that he was once again "returning to the harvest fields abroad." [9]

Osborn proved to be a good organizer and he, like Roberts, carefully cultivated his financial supporters in special meetings. In 1970, Osborn had jumped full scale into the prosperity message which was pervading the entire revival. Osborn had written that, "Like a little child," he had begun to comprehend God's other challenge in giving: Give and it shall be given unto you. Thus the PACT OF PLENTY concept was born.[10] *Faith Digest* was crowded with testimonials of financial blessings received through a Pact of Plenty made with the Osborn ministry.

Some supporters of the revival quietly criticized the stylish Osborn, whose impressive headquarters building in Tulsa not only housed a museum of valuable artifacts from all over the world but also an expensive collection of antique automobiles. But others were impressed by the results of his work. The Osborn ministry had been a powerful force in sponsoring pentecostal revivalism all over the world. Osborn's financial help to overseas missions, without denominational discrimination, had deflected from him the denominational attacks leveled against many of the deliverance ministers. Some of the pentecostal organizations did not like him or his work, but they respected his ability to aid their impoverished mission programs.

Osborn's record by the early 1970s was impressive. Still less than fifty, he had preached, noted Daisy Osborn in his magazine, in nearly fifty different countries; he had pioneered the support of native preachers and had supported such missionaires in nearly fifty thousand villages and areas. "More than one new church a day is established and becomes self-supporting through this one outreach alone," she wrote, "OVER 400 PER YEAR!" [11]

Whatever the lasting impact of such mission programs, and whatever can be made of such fund-raising propaganda, clearly the millions of dollars that flowed through the Osborn ministry had some impact. His effort to make the revival overseas into a truly native experience, instead of an American program, was an important contribution to the world pentecostal revival, and its success was one of his proudest achievements.[12] David Nunn, another of the deliverance evangelists who traveled widely overseas, wrote:

> He's got a great concept. To me, he provides . . . from the mission standpoint one of the greatest leaderships of any man to come up in the last

hundred years. In challenging the old line churches to change its old policies that never have worked properly. That brings down the people into servitude and makes them houseboys and to lift those men up to where they belong as children of God and proud of their national heritage with confidence in them that they've got ability and that they can carry out the work of evangelizing their own countries.[13]

T. L. Osborn had come a long way from the disillusioned young pentecostal pastor who had visited a Branham crusade in Portland, Oregon. His ministry could not be categorized as belonging in any one wing of the modern revival; he attracted supporters from all segments of the divided movement. Osborn did not make a clear transition to neopentecostalism. He remained, more than Roberts or Lindsay or the other important ministers, in touch with the young evangelists still conducting campaigns. When he went to Miracle Valley, Arizona, in 1971 to aid young Don Stewart after the death of A. A. Allen, he was probably the only successful pioneer revivalist who would risk associating his name with the ghost of A. A. Allen. More obviously than most of the large and successful deliverance evangelists, T. L. Osborn remembered where he came from. Enjoying the luxury of a financially secure ministry, T. L. Osborn was very much his own man.

W. V. GRANT

One of the more important ministries to survive the 1960s was that of W. V. Grant of Dallas, Texas. Born in 1913 in rural Arkansas (in the same community as Rex Humbard), Grant was a successful business man before becoming an Assemblies of God minister in the late 1940s. He launched an independent ministry in 1949 and became one of the early leaders of the revival. In 1956, Grant was forced to sell his tent and retire from campaigning because of failing health, but he remained a prominent figure in the movement. For six years he was vice-president of the Voice of Healing organization and a prolific writer for the magazine. He also pastored Jack Coe's church in Dallas and continued to conduct occasional campaigns.[1]

As Gordon Lindsay ceased to act as publicist of the revival in the early 1960s, W. V. Grant came more and more to fill that role. Grant, like Lindsay, was a tireless writer, although he by no means wrote with the same felicity. Both men were moderate in their approach to the organized pentecostal denominations; Grant remained a licensed Assemblies of God minister until 1963, when he allowed his ministerial papers to lapse. Both men recognized publicity as the key to the success of the revival. As Lindsay changed the emphasis of his ministry, many of the remaining healing evangelists turned to Grant to seek advertisement.

Lindsay and Grant were very different personalities. Lindsay was quite capable of becoming a leader in the more sophisticated charismatic movement; Grant's talents were best fitted for the work required in the days of the healing revival. Grant had been a pioneer in taking the early revival into small towns and proudly called himself "the ploughboy preacher from Arkansas." Gordon Lindsay agreed: "He appeals to Arkansawyers. . . . There is a class of people in America who kind of take to an Arkansas style. He practically monopolizes that field." [2] Grant was never ashamed to admit, "I don't attract the theologians." [3] But no one retained the loyalty of the common people of the healing revival, or of the old-time revivalists, as he did.

Grant's ministry in the 1960s and 1970s was diverse. He still conducted an average of two revivals each month and still believed that successful campaigning was as possible as ever. "I'd still be out there with that tent if I had the strength," he declared.[4] Grant also knew the advantages of pastoring a large church and in the early 1960s built a large revival center in Dallas. In recent years Grant has acquired ownership of seven additional churches. In addition, he sponsored some limited mission programs and did some radio preaching. In a 1966 summary of his work he wrote: "We have built hundreds of churches and supported native evangelists for years. For years I preached to millions of people each day on radio. I have traveled over 47 states and about 100 nations and seen tens of thousands of people filled with the Holy Ghost." [5] Grant considered beginning a television ministry in the late 1960s but abandoned the idea as economically unsound.[6]

W. V. Grant's forte, and the heart of his continuing ministry, was his writing. In 1966, he claimed to have written 156 books; by 1974 the figure had passed 300 and was growing by at least one new volume each month. Grant said candidly, "I went to an extreme on publications." [7] In order to publicize his books, in 1962 Grant began to publish a monthly magazine, *The Voice of Deliverance.* By 1973 his monthly magazine had reached a circulation of over 2,000,000 and had become the most widely circulated journal in the movement. Often little more than an advertising circular, *The Voice of Deliverance* was nonetheless a sign of the continuing power of the healing revival.

In some ways the booming Grant ministry seemed an anachronism in the 1970s. His brief books, the unprofessional makeup of *The Voice of Deliverance,* his hard-line pentecostal theology, even his Arkansas twang, all seemed curiously out of place beside the glamorous charismatic movement. But Grant's ministry was proof of the continuing strength of the original motifs of the revival and he himself was a classic example of the survival of a wily and cautious religious entrepreneur. Admitting only to an "Arkansas country merchant style" [8] of business acumen, Grant managed his ministry with a skill that many of the more sophisticated evangelists would have done well to imitate. In the early 1960s, Grant tried to buy advertising space in *Life* and *Look* magazines for his books but was refused. There was more than a hint of pride in his recent statement, "Both of them is out of business now and my magazine is going into 2,000,000 full gospel homes." [9] W. V. Grant had skillfully retained the loyalty of thousands in the rapidly changing world of healing revivalism.

Other Innovators

Many of the older ministers retired from tent and auditorium revivalism in the early 1960s. Some, like Velmer Gardner, were forced by ill health to abandon the strenuous life of a revivalist.[1] Others established powerful churches in areas where they were well known, as William Freeman and O. L. Jaggers had done earlier. These independent churches, generally owned outright by the minister, provided comfortable retirements. Some ministries became "missionary societies" or "benevolent societies," often modeled after the work of T. L. Osborn. Some did not totally abandon revivalism but changed the major direction of the ministry.

Juanita Coe

In some cases change was inescapable. Juanita Coe filled some of Jack Coe's revival commitments immediately after his death (some observers believed she could have been a powerful evangelist in her own right), but she chose not to be a full-time campaigner. Mrs. Coe, along with her second husband, Dan Hope, continued to pastor the Dallas Revival Center until the early 1970s. But increasingly she turned her energy toward administration. She established the Coe Foundation and in the early 1960s wrote that her reports were being sent to 100,000 "Coe-partners." She successfully paid off a $270,000 debt left at the death of her husband and solidified the ministry around the orphan home established by her husband.[2] A number of influential people in the charismatic revival, including G. H. Montgomery and John Douglas, Sr., worked with Mrs. Coe, but she and Dan Hope kept the management of the ministry in their own hands.

As the memory of Jack Coe faded, it became increasingly difficult to sustain the ministry. By 1973, the Coe ministry was struggling even to maintain the orphanage then housing about twenty children in Waxahatchie, Texas. Although some of the supporters of the 1950s had remained loyal, financial problems were ever present.[3]

John E. Douglas, Sr.

A large number of important mission and benevolent ministries grew out of the healing revival. By 1973 one of the most successful was World Missionary Evangelism, the ministry of John E. Douglas, Sr. Douglas, a successful businessman and a Methodist, was converted by A. A. Allen and for a number of years worked in the Allen organization. He later was associated with the Coe ministry. In 1959, he launched his own work—"not loving his former associates less, but seeking God, and believing Him more!" [4] Douglas began publishing a monthly magazine, *World Evangelism*, to solicit funds and launched a remarkably successful radio ministry. By the 1970s the Douglas message was heard regularly on more than three hundred radio stations; and the ministry reportedly was supporting fully more than sixty orphanages and schools, more than two thousand native evangelists and Bible teachers, besides a ministry to the lepers and to the starving.[5]

The success of the Douglas ministry demonstrated the maturing of the revival and the ascendance of a new type personality to leadership. Douglas was never a charismatic preacher, although he did for a time direct the morning services in A. A. Allen's revivals. But he exuded sincerity and honesty and built his ministry on a promise of sound management. His motto was: "First to be True Christians, pay our debts, to be truthful in all our dealings. To be good Stewards for the Lord Jesus Christ. Our lives are dedicated to reaching the Christless Millions." [6] Douglas promised: "All funds are handled with utmost care and business is conducted in a Christian manner so as to make each dollar accomplish the greatest possible good." [7] Colleagues and competitors agreed that Douglas was an effective worker. "No matter where I go overseas," said one evangelist, "I see Douglas' work. . . . You can't say that about all of them." [8] There was apparently a powerful appeal in Douglas' plaintive radio cry: "Will you help us?" and the tragic case histories related by his "darling daughter" Yvonne.

[175

M. A. Daoud

A successful overseas revivalist all through the 1950s, especially in Africa, was M. A. Daoud of Dallas, Texas.[9] As late as 1965, Daoud sent glowing reports to his readers of revival in Madagascar: "God gave us great outpourings and mighty miracles and the masses turned out by 30,000 to 60,000 every meeting to hear and witness the power of God." [10] His magazine, *Miracles and Mission Digest*, which he began in 1955, furnished his supporters with a constant stream of such news.

W. T. Jeffers and Bob Daniels

In 1960, two members of the Oral Roberts organization launched the New Frontiers of Faith ministry, intended especially to benefit neglected and afflicted children around the world.[11] W. T. Jeffers and Bob Daniels proposed a program to support children in established orphan homes all over the world. While the ministry broadened somewhat through the years, its main aim, and the financial appeal, remained the support of orphans.[12]

R. W. Culpepper

Many of the older deliverance evangelists slowly changed their ministries into general purpose religious organizations. R. W. Culpepper was a good example. Culpepper began preaching in 1945 and soon became a successful healing campaigner. In 1961, he announced that he had preached throughout the United States and in thirty-five foreign countries.[13] From 1959 through 1961 Culpepper served as Director of Conventions of the Voice of Healing. In common with most of the evangelists, Culpepper insisted that his revival ministry was not declining in the early 1960s: "It is impossible to answer all the invitations that we receive to conduct campaigns." [14] Nevertheless, in late 1961 he decided to relinquish his position with the Voice of Healing and to begin supporting foreign missions. In 1968, Culpepper summarized the step-by-step progress of his ministry: "It all started in 1957—our real burning desire to do more for missions. For ten years I had been an evangelist. Our meetings had gone from successful church revivals to city-wide and union crusades. Then in 1957 God spoke to me to go overseas on a missionary tour. I didn't know then that I would be called upon to support native evangelists and missionaries from the most needy mission fields of the world. But I saw the need. God spoke, I obeyed." [15] Many others heard the same call.

Throughout the 1960s Culpepper supported native preachers and benevolent enterprises overseas; in 1968, he reported: "Today we support more than 90 missionaries and native evangelists around the world." [16] Culpepper also continued to conduct campaigns during these years and also held revivals in local churches. For several years he planned to build a headquarters in Dallas, but in 1970 he instead moved to Milwaukee where he became co-pastor with A. C. Valdez of the Milwaukee Evangelistic Temple. In making this move, Culpepper took the common step of shoring up a ministry by gaining the support of a large local church. By 1970 he had explored most of the options open to the average deliverance minister.[17]

A. C. Valdez

A. C. Valdez was also a pioneer of the revival.[18] He cooperated with Gordon Lindsay in 1963 in forming the Full Gospel Fellowship of Churches and Ministers International and served as its president. In 1958, Valdez began his own paper, the *Evangelistic Times*, which in 1963 reported a circulation of nearly 10,000, and frequently conducted campaigns overseas. His basic means of support was his Milwaukee Evangelistic Temple. Valdez was widely respected in the movement and was typical of many of the evangelists who settled into major local ministries while continuing to conduct occasional campaigns.[19]

Lester Sumrall

Another local pastor who built a strong diversified ministry in the 1960s was Lester Sumrall of South Bend, Indiana. During the peak of the revival in the 1950s Sumrall built large independent congregations, first in South Bend and later in Manila in the Philippines. He conducted deliverance crusades, although his talent as an organizer was always more important to his ministry. Occasionally he worked with Clifton Erickson, one of the powerful evangelists of the early years of the revival, and in 1962 the two began editing their own magazine, *World Harvest*. They soon parted, however, and Sumrall diversified into a typical ministry of the 1960s. On the list of World Harvest works by 1970 were intercession in prayer, crusades and seminars, counseling by telephone, counseling by mail, *World Harvest* magazine, radio ministry, literature, gospel films, gospel records and tapes, Bible land tours, orphans, and evangelistic centers.[20] In 1971, Sumrall established a World Harvest Advanced School of Evangelism in Indiana to "instruct ministers to exorcise spirits by faith in God," a subject which had long interested him. "The Lord has revealed to me," he wrote, "that there will be many millions of people in our modern world who will need deliverance from evil spirits in the days ahead of us." [21] Sumrall, like many of the pioneer evangelists, was impressed by the power of the new charismatic movement in the major denominations, but his own ministry, he insisted, would "never compromise the Full Gospel which is the hope of this generation." [22]

Joseph D. Mattsson-Boze

Scores of other personalities associated with the revival institutionalized their ministries. Joseph D. Mattsson-Boze, widely respected minister from Chicago and long-time editor of the influential journal, the *Herald of Faith*, spent most of his time overseas in mission work. Mattsson-Boze worked through an organized Herald of Faith ministry to raise funds for his overseas programs, primarily building training centers for native evangelists. Boze's career spanned the entire history of the revival. An early friend and supporter of William Branham, he was also influential in international pentecostalism and was one of the more important older evangelists to accept and participate in the neopentecostal movement.[23]

David Nunn

The important ministry of David Nunn also changed markedly in the 1960s. Nunn had been a member of the inner circle of the Voice of Healing family in the late 1950s. He remained with the organization until 1961 and was the speaker on the Voice of Healing radio broadcast until Lindsay decided not to underwrite the program any longer. In 1962, as it became more and more obvious that Gordon Lindsay was going to be forced to revamp his organization, Nunn decided to set out on his own. He established his own association, Bible Revival Incorporated, and began to publish *The Healing Messenger*. Nunn's magazine began with a circulation of 5,000 and rapidly expanded to over 60,000. By 1970 the circulation had passed 140,000. He also began to build a small and select radio network. After five years, he was regularly heard over nine stations, and after ten years, he was heard on nineteen.[24]

The heart of the Nunn organization, and its basic financial appeal, was the support of overseas missions. He continued to conduct healing revivals overseas throughout the 1960s and to a lesser extent in the 1970s.[25] He believed that the simple faith of the people in underdeveloped countries made them good prospects for a healing revival: "Great ministers with ministries from God are still reaching the heathen world where the heavenly message is still being confirmed with power." He wrote, "They cannot be reached by the old line conventional method, but only through the power of God will they be reached." [26] Nunn also sustained his ministry by raising money to support native ministers and Bible schools in backward areas. His ministry was relatively small, but he could say, "Every year we've given more to missions," and his 1972 budget provided over $200,000 a year for mission work.[27]

Nunn continued his healing ministry on a small scale in the United States, although he felt that the days of huge cooperative revivals were gone. His organization operated with a minimum staff; his support came from small but loyal contributors. At first he had employed a business manager to make advance preparations for his meetings but finally decided that it was a waste of effort. "You've got to be a Billy Graham or a Kathryn Kuhlman to get that kind of support," he said in 1972:

> A lot of the places where I have radio stations, I'll rent the auditorium and I'll go in and put my ads in the paper, and will announce it on the radio and we'll start the meeting. They're not as big as they used to be . . . but they grow and it's better to have a few that are with you than to have 15 churches behind you that are hacking you to pieces. I had 44 churches behind me in one meeting and all they did was gripe. It was the hardest meeting I ever had in my life. That's what changed me.[28]

In two decades David Nunn had changed his ministry markedly and yet had remained much the same in approach. He refused to establish an independent church. He remained throughout his career a member of an Assemblies of God congregation in Dallas. He saw the full implications of the charismatic movement, and was impressed by the numbers of people among his supporters from the traditional denominations, but he was not closely identified with the development of that movement. After some early associations with the Full Gospel Business Men's Fellowship International, he continued to reach out for the less sophisticated types of audiences that had been his supporters in the early days of the revival. The transformation of the Nunn ministry had to do largely with its institutionalization and broadened purposes rather than the changes in style typical of the leading innovators in the charismatic movement.

Kenneth Gaub

The career of evangelist Kenneth Gaub illustrates another interesting type of transition made by the revivalists in the 1960s. Gaub began preaching in 1955 and launched his career as a tent revivalist just as the revival began its sharp decline. In his early years he preached a hard-line pentecostal gospel and emphasized divine healing.[29] Gaub struggled through the early 1960s as a marginal success. He built the mailing list for his magazine, *Faith in Action*, to 120,000 by 1964 but was never able to expand his work as he planned.[30] In 1961, his radio network included only three stations; he repeatedly tried unsuccessfully to begin a television ministry.[31] In the late 1960s Gaub began to preach a distinctive patriotic message. He staged "patriotic rallies" that became extremely popular, especially among the Assemblies of God where he found more sponsoring pastors than ever before.[32]

Each of the independent ministers tried to save his evangelistic association in his own way. Some specialized in one type of message or work, while others engaged in broad programs which included missionary programs, benevolent work, the building of local churches, continued campaigning, and use of the mass media. Some of the evangelists appealed openly to the new charismatic movement for support; others built their base of support on the pentecostal people who had known and supported them for years. Few of the older evangelists made a complete transition to neopentecostalism—many did not have the capacity to do so. In many ways the evangelists of the 1960s became administrators rather than charismatic leaders, and the success or failure of their ministries depended on their abilities to raise funds and build efficient organizations. In fact, administrative leaders who had never had dramatic preaching ministries, people such as John E. Douglas, Sr., built important organizations in the aftermath of the healing revival.

New Breeds

A sense of enthusiasm and common purpose provided the unity of the early charismatic revival, as in the early days of the healing revival.[1] Derek Prince, one of the most perceptive leaders of the new movement, labeled the period from 1956 to 1966, the "testimony revival." [2] Thousands were spellbound by repeated tales of miraculous conversions, healings, and other spiritual wonders as told by growing groups of charismatic preachers and laymen. By the late 1950s the most popular speakers in the new movement were recently spirit-filled ministers and laymen from the traditional denominations. In a large part, such testimony is still the central theme of the meetings of the Full Gospel Business Men's Fellowship International.

The broadening of the revival created an urgent need for teachers. An intellectual elite emerged which was no longer satisfied with repetitious appeals to the miraculous and the bizarre. Many felt impelled to analyze the charismatic experience in the light of traditional Christian theology. Only a few of the older deliverance evangelists, most notably Roberts and Lindsay, were able to function as teachers; most of the others had little ability to dissect the experience they preached. The opportunity was open for new leaders to come forward.

The charismatic revival had few centers of power; one current leader estimated that the removal of its fifty leading preachers would not impede the revival.[3] The revival was particularly strong in the Roman Catholic church, but few American denominations escaped its influence. Studying the amorphous movement, according to Derek Prince, was like approaching the "verge of the ocean."[4]

Until the late 1960s the only institutional cohesion in the charismatic revival was supplied by the FGBMFI and its small magazine, Voice. Edited from 1953 to 1962 by Thomas R. Nickel, Voice chronicled the charismatic revival's spread among the traditional churches. In 1963, the fellowship began publishing a quarterly youth magazine named Vision. As the revival grew, it was spearheaded by new journals and publishing houses. The new organizations were generally founded by gifted preachers, but some had no such charismatic head. Several of the new journalistic leaders received their training while working on the staff of Voice or Vision.

In 1962, when Thomas R. Nickel begrudgingly retired as editor of Voice, he established a new organization, Great Commission International, and began to publish an attractive quarterly, Testimony, which was immediately associated with the neopentecostal revival. In 1960, John Meyers of Northbridge, California, began a quarterly, Voice in the Wilderness, with a clear neopentecostal appeal. Meyers' first mailing was only 774 copies, but after three years circulation had reached 15,000.[5] Several journals were begun to publicize the outbreak of the charismatic revival in specific denominations. Trinity in 1961 heralded the charismatic movement in the Episcopal church. Initially edited by Jean Stone, it included among its directors well-known charismatic leaders such as David duPlessis and Harold Bredesen. "He Is Able" was begun in 1961 as "a journal dedicated to aid the revival of the Ministry of Healing in the Methodist Church." Edited by Jimmie and Virginia Johnston in

Chattanooga, Tennessee, the journal in 1972 listed 181 Methodist churches "holding healing services or other services incorporating laying-on-of-hands." [6] *New Covenant*, a charismatic journal published by Roman Catholics, was begun in 1969.

A neopentecostal publication aimed at the young was *Campus Fellowship*, published in Waco, Texas, by Robert Ewing. Begun in 1967, the beautifully designed magazine was, it said, "published as the Lord instructs and provides," and was circulated without cost. In 1972, the editor wrote, "Campus Fellowship is emerging to help serve the needs of the rapidly increasing spirit-filled faculty and student nuclei in the universities, colleges, and seminaries." [7]

One of the most important new journals to emerge was *New Wine*, which began publication in Fort Lauderdale, Florida, in 1969, first under the auspices of the Holy Spirit Teaching Mission, and later under the direction of Christian Growth Ministries. These organizations, and the journal, represented a collection of several of the most important new teaching ministries in the charismatic movement. The editors of *New Wine* wrote, "Many of us could see the need for a vital experience in the Holy Spirit *plus* the necessary teaching which should follow. As most of our readers know, the Charismatic outpouring increases daily and so the teaching need expands." At first the group only intended to sponsor teaching seminars, but soon its vision enlarged: "The magnitude of the demands for teaching, however, has made it necessary to use electronic means of teaching, . . . this magazine and bi-annual Christian Growth Conferences. God has sovereignly brought the men, ministries and equipment together here in Ft. Lauderdale to establish a 'spiritual kitchen' in which He can provide for the needs of His people." [8]

A number of evangelists worked temporarily with Christian Growth Ministries, but its leadership came from Derek Prince, never a revivalist but a well-known figure in the healing movement; Don Basham, an ordained Disciples of Christ clergyman with a free-lance ministry of writing and speaking; Bob Mumford, who had formerly served as Dean and Professor of Bible and Missions at Elim Bible Institute; and Charles Simpson, a charismatic Baptist minister from Mobile, Alabama. [9] Other important new figures in the charismatic revival had passing relationships with the paper, including Eldon Purvis and Neil Frank. In addition, the journal publicized the work of older ministries such as those of Gordon Lindsay, Joseph D. Mattsson-Boze, Kenneth Hagin, Gerald Derstine, and Morris Cerullo.

The most important of the new charismatic magazines, *Logos Journal*, appeared in 1971. It grew out of Joseph D. Mattsson-Boze's

Herald of Faith, giving it a solid historical link to the early revival. During the 1950s the *Herald of Faith* was William Branham's chief publicity organ. In July 1970, the *Herald of Faith* was merged with *Harvest Time,* a journal edited by Gerald Derstine, a rising light in the neopentecostal world. The magazine was then issued under the title, *Herald of Faith–Harvest Time,* until August 1971, when *Logos Journal* began publication under the editorship of Daniel Malachuk, a widely-known publisher who had formerly worked with the Full Gospel Business Men's Fellowship International.

When he left the magazine, Mattsson-Boze predicted an immediate jump in circulation from 20,000 to 75,000 and added, "It is the conviction of Mrs. Mattsson-Boze and me that this change is born of God. It has been prophesied that HERALD OF FAITH–HARVEST TIME shall become the leading FULL GOSPEL magazine in the U.S. and we believe that by this new step of faith that it shall become a reality." [10] Under the able management of Malachuk, the magazine had a brilliant beginning. By the end of 1971 Malachuk reported that it was reaching "over 150,000 readers who are leaders in the Charismatic Renewal." [11] The journal set out to be the voice of the new revival: "Without apology, we state that LOGOS Journal is a charismatic magazine. We intend to serve Christians of all denominations. We believe that there is a Pentecostal explosion occurring in many Protestant Evangelical and Catholic communities. Our reports will be forthright and tending to the 'healing of the Body of Christ.' " [12]

The Logos organization expanded rapidly after its inception in 1971. Logos International became a prolific publisher of neopentecostal books. In 1973, Logos sponsored a World Conference on the Holy Spirit in Jerusalem. The ministries advertised and promoted by Logos were diverse, although the readership of the magazine were mostly sophisticated neopentecostals. According to Derek Prince, Logos provided an "umbrella under which any kind of charismatic literature or ministry can be projected." [13] In the 1970s Logos was as nearly a nucleus as existed in the nebulous charismatic movement. Its service to the charismatic revival resembled the central role of *The Voice of Healing* in the healing revival.

The charismatic revival continued to spawn new publications rapidly. In 1971, Eldon Purvis, formerly associated with *New Wine,* established *Heartbeat* as the organ of Charismatic Educational Centers. "Last August," he wrote, "the Lord indicated to me that He wanted a publication that would present the prophetic word without the doctrinal and traditional bondage of man." [14]

[1 8 3

In its decentralization, some of the most important centers of influence in the charismatic revival were in local Christian centers. These centers, essentially loosely-organized independent churches, sometimes included thousands of members and had large "outreach" programs. The Christian center in Anaheim, California, brought national attention to its leader, Ralph Wilkerson.

The proliferation of charismatic ministries in the late 1960s was much like the flurry that accompanied the initial outbreak of the healing revival in the late 1940s. Some of the ministers were linked to the past and had, in one way or another, been associated with the revival at its peak. Many were new breeds who had never seen the sawdust of the tent cathedrals of the early 1950s, and many knew little about the sources of the revival. They believed in healing and taught perceptively on the gifts of the Spirit, but their clientele was different from the old one, their message was more reasoned than charismatic, and their platform was more likely to be a banquet room in a Hilton hotel than a fairground.

Derek Prince

Derek Prince was a central figure among the emerging neopentecostal ministries. He had a long and respected record of service in the pentecostal movement. Born and raised in England, he had a conversion experience in 1941 and believed that he had been miraculously healed in 1943. Before his conversion, Prince received a fine education at Eton College and King's College, Cambridge, something that set him apart in pentecostal circles: "I studied philosophy for seven years, obtained B. A. and M. A. degrees, and was elected to a Fellowship (that is, virtually a Professorship) in philosophy at King's College, Cambridge, which I held for nine years." From 1956 to 1961, he worked under the auspices of the Pentecostal Assemblies of Canada, first as a missionary in Israel and then as dean of a teachers training college in Kenya, East Africa.[15]

Prince's friends early believed that he had "a divine anointing as a teacher"; by the 1960s the charismatic revival was ripe for his talents. He became a frequent speaker at meetings of the FGBMFI, but he felt that the meetings of the fellowship were too often devoted to shallow testimonies rather than to serious study. He more and more prepared his ministry to provide concentrated teaching for those who had had a powerful emotional experience but who had little spiritual knowledge.[16]

Prince's roots went deep into pentecostal tradition, and he had a keen understanding of the history of the revival. And yet, his education and studious manner always set him somewhat apart. His distinct

Cambridge accent made many pentecostals ill-at-ease. In addition, he was strongly antiinstitutional, insisting that his purpose was to build the body of Christ rather than a denomination. As his independent work grew in the 1960s, the established pentecostals were the ones who viewed him with the greatest reservations.[17] On the other hand, Prince's teaching talents were perfectly suited to the needs of the sophisticated converts in traditional churches who swelled the charismatic movement in the 1960s.

Prince's teaching, like that of most of the new charismatic ministers, emphasized the Biblical writings on the Holy Spirit. In the 1970s healing had become an increasingly important theme in Prince's lectures, but he had long been known as a specialist on exorcism. He traveled nationwide with "that message" and was a widely-recognized authority on the subject before the recent sensational popular interest. Contrary to conventional pentecostal doctrine, Prince taught that demons often inhabited apparently normal people; the need for exorcism, he believed, was broad and persistent.[18]

As noted earlier, Prince did not believe that powerful, independent organizations were the wave of the future.[19] He worked through Christian Growth Ministries, along with his friends Bob Mumford and Don Basham, to maintain an active itinerary of meetings both in the United States and abroad. At a recent Greater Los Angeles Bible Teaching Conference in Long Beach Municipal Auditorium, conducted by Prince, Mumford, and Basham, the attendance on the closing evening was estimated at almost 4,000.[20] Prince and his associates did not sustain major radio ministries, but they had a large tape and literature distribution. Much in demand as a speaker, Prince accepted only a fraction of the invitations he received to lecture on the miraculous.

Kenneth E. Hagin

The neopentecostal movement proved to be precisely the right climate for the ripening of several other older teaching ministries. Kenneth E. Hagin, whose offices were in Tulsa, Oklahoma, was raised in Baptist surroundings and preached in Southern Baptist churches for several years before becoming an Assemblies of God minister in 1938. He began a successful career as an evangelist in 1947. He strongly stressed divine healing; his belief that he had been cured of heart trouble at the age of sixteen led him into the full gospel ministry. Hagin preached and held meetings during the turbulent 1950s but he did not attempt to establish an independent ministry or conduct major campaigns. An able preacher with a homey and humorous Texas style, Hagin had nevertheless always been more a student and teacher than platform performer. He early sensed that the gift of teaching was a more enduring basis for his ministry. He recalled telling a group of colleagues in the 1950s: "When all these other things are gone, I'll be out there. Because the word never fails. I built on the word and they built on some kind of gift." While conceding that gifts had their place, he could see the day of the teacher and prophet coming. In 1962, Hagin formed his own association and gave up his ministerial papers in the Assemblies of God.[21]

More and more Hagin began to exercise his calling as a prophet. In a popular book published by Fleming H. Revell Company in 1972, Hagin told of repeated heavenly visions which had influenced his life and directed his ministry: "Then for the first time I actually looked into the eyes of Jesus. Many times when relating this experience I am asked, 'What did His eyes look like?' All I can say is that they looked like wells of living love. It seemed as if one could see a half mile deep into them, and the tender look of love is indescribable." [22] Frequently Hagin's prophetic gift operated during his services: "Many times I look out across a congregation when I minister and see what certain individuals were doing a couple of days before." [23]

Hagin's ministry blossomed after 1967. He kept his work small but efficient; his ministry in 1973 employed nineteen full-time workers. Hagin conducted teaching meetings in hotels and auditoriums throughout the country and maintained a flourishing business, circulating his literature and tapes. He also spoke on an expanding radio network and published a monthly newsletter, *The Word of Faith*.

David Wilkerson

A great variety of new ministries appeared in the early and mid-1960s. In 1963, David Wilkerson, a third generation Assemblies of God minister, published an extremely successful book, *The Cross and the Switchblade*.[24] Wilkerson's book, and a subsequent movie starring charismatic convert Pat Boone, led to the establishment of Teen Challenge, "an incorporated, spiritual program that offers help to delinquents, narcotic addicts and other troubled youths." [25] In 1962, Wilkerson began a regular newsletter, *The Cross and the Switchblade*, to report on his work. Appealing to supporters of the neopentecostal revival, Wilkerson's ministry grew rapidly and had a powerful influence on the decade's youth culture.

In some ways Wilkerson was not a typical neopentecostal leader, but his dramatic book about the adventures of an Assemblies of God evangelist working with New York's ghetto gangs made him a celebrity in the movement. By the 1970s no man's voice carried more authority in the charismatic revival than Wilkerson's. His influence launched a number of new ministries, including that of Nicky Cruz, a converted gang leader who was a central character in his book. By the 1970s Cruz had become a prominent charismatic speaker; he had all the flashy appeal of a modern revivalist, although his work was primarily with the young.[26]

John H. Osteen

John H. Osteen was an ordained Southern Baptist minister preaching at the Hibbard Memorial Baptist Church in Houston, Texas, when, as he said, he "received the Baptism of the Holy Ghost in fire in 1958." With a group of his followers, Osteen formed a new full gospel church, the Lakewood Baptist Church of Houston. Osteen's move was a great boost for the nascent charismatic outbreak in 1958 and received wide notice. In 1961, Osteen resigned his pastorate and, according to one account, began "to give his entire time to awakening the denominational world to the need of returning to the supernatural pattern set forth in the book of Acts." [27] His independent ministry was widely accepted by both the older deliverance ministers and by the growing neopentecostal movement. Called a "preaching machine" by one pentecostal leader, he was widely used by the FGBMFI and his tapes and literature were prominent among the teaching materials circulated in the charismatic movement. Osteen was a pioneer in a growing fraternity of spirit-filled ministers from the traditional churches.

Gerald Derstine

Gospel Crusades was an organization started by two charismatic Mennonites, Henry Brunk and Gerald Derstine. Derstine, who was spirit-baptized in 1954, quickly became a noteworthy figure in the new revival and attracted followers from among both the old-line pentecostals and the new charismatics. Derstine worked especially with young people; in 1970, after a service in his Revival Tabernacle in Sarasota, Florida, the wife of Joseph Mattsson-Boze marveled at Derstine's success in mixing the new and the old: "It was a great sight to see good 'Hippies' and 'good' church people both young and old hugging each other." [28] By the 1970s the organization owned property in Florida and Minnesota where retreats were held and was building a retirement center in Bradenton, Florida.[29]

Roxanne Brant

Another unique and interesting ministry was that of Roxanne Brant. Brant, an attractive young woman born in 1953, was reared in a comfortable family, her father was reputedly a well-to-do scientist. She advertised that she was "a product of the exclusive DANA HALL preparatory school" and that her "pianistic training" had led to "performances as soloist in *Carnegie Hall*, with *Arthur Fiedler* and the *Boston Symphony* and other orchestras." After receiving her B.A. degree, she studied "theology at HARVARD DIVINITY SCHOOL, BOSTON UNIVERSITY SCHOOL OF THEOLOGY and GORDON DIVINITY SCHOOL," receiving a Master of Divinity degree from the latter institution. Her denominational background was Presbyterian Congregational.[30] In 1970, Brant, who worked in coordination with other young charismatic ministers in teaching conferences, became president of the Outreach for Christ Foundation with headquarters in Orlando, Florida.

Brant's teaching was unemotional and logical, but she also emphasized the power of the spirit. *"This ministry is different,"* advertised the foundation in 1971, "in that it is not through the laying on of hands that miracles occur. Instead, the sovereign and unpredictable Spirit of God falls upon certain individuals and sections of the audience, healing people in their seats as their physical problems are called out through the gift of the 'word of knowledge.' "[31] Brant conducted seminars in churches and auditoriums throughout the country and also inaugurated a regular radio series. A newsman reported, "Some have said that Miss Brant may succeed to the position Miss Kuhlman has in this field."[32]

During the mid-1970s the proliferation of neopentecostal ministries continued. Many of the leaders of the charismatic revival were simply the leaders of successful local churches or centers, but the advantages, and the risks, of a totally independent ministry were as obvious as ever.

Fellow Travelers

Several important ministries in the 1970s were related to the healing revival and tended to merge with the charismatic movement. They did not systematically participate in the revival, but neither were they totally separate from it. The most significant were those of Thomas and Evelyn Wyatt on the West Coast, Kathryn Kuhlman in Pittsburgh, and Rex Humbard in Akron, Ohio.

Thomas Wyatt

The ministry of the Wyatts is most clearly linked with the salvation-healing revival. Thomas Wyatt pastored a number of small Methodist churches in the 1930s before "receiving the glorious baptism of the Holy Spirit" and launching a ministry of "pioneer evangelism" in the midst of the depression.[1] Wyatt roamed the Midwest, holding healing revivals, but revivalism was a hard business in the 1930s, and, in 1939, after a successful revival in Portland, Oregon, Wyatt established the Wings of Healing Temple and settled into a local ministry. At first his work seemed to falter, but in 1942 Wyatt began his successful Wings of Healing broadcast, "the pioneer of radio healing ministries." [2] In 1945, he began a monthly paper, the *March of Faith*. Wyatt's ministry in Portland continued to expand, and in 1946 he opened the Bethesda Bible Institute. His radio ministry grew slowly at first, but in a bold stroke in 1952 Wyatt asked his local supporters to raise $10,000 to sponsor his program on the ABC radio network.[3] A year later he added the Mutual network. In 1954, Wyatt proudly announced:

> Millions of listeners are finding new hope and living faith through the inspired ministry of Wings of Healing, heard every Sunday on more than five hundred stations. We have received hundreds of thousands of testimonies from folks whom God has healed through Wings of Healing. Thousands of heathens throughout the world have been saved and healed in the past year through the ministry of faith. Multitudes have been filled with the spirit and impowered with supernatural service.[4]

In 1959, the Wyatt ministry purchased the Embassy building in downtown Los Angeles and moved its offices there. Max Wyatt, Thomas' son, remained with the church in Portland.

In 1948 Wyatt predicted the coming of a great revival, which, according to his followers, "came in full force the following year." [5] Wyatt aided the beginning of the revival during the early Branham tour of the West Coast. He continued to encourage the revival and heartily endorsed it in the vibrant 1950s, but he was a marginal participant. Although Wyatt did conduct campaigns, by the time of the postwar healing revival his ministry was already highly institutionalized. During the decade, Wyatt explored many of the techniques later followed by faltering healing ministers: his success on the radio, his teaching on prosperity and healing, and his early efforts to support missions abroad. In the early 1950s, his ministry was strongly tinged with a right-wing political emphasis, but in later years he returned to his earlier charismatic theme and continued on his independent way.

In April 1964, Thomas Wyatt died and the ministry fell to Evelyn, his young wife. Mrs. Wyatt had been "the voice of testimony" on the radio program since 1945, and the transition to her leadership proved extremely smooth. Mrs. Wyatt, an articulate young woman, was a capable administrator. She continued the vast radio ministry, supervised a broad program of mission work overseas and conducted healing and deliverance rallies several times a year.[6] Summing up the work of the organization in 1969, the *March of Faith* reported:

> Wings of Healing is a nonprofit, religious and church organization, incorpo-rated for the purpose of proclaiming to all the world the Gospel of salvation, Holy Spirit baptism, and deliverance from sickness and oppression. The ministry of compassion includes radio, television, missionary evangelism, training of national ministers, literature, and children's homes, and is supported by an open fellowship of believers who unite their prayers, their finances, and often their lives, in a dedicated march of faith.[7]

Kathryn Kuhlman

A latecomer to the revival who captured an enormous audience by the 1960s was Kathryn Kuhlman. By the 1970s her career had blossomed into one of the most important in the charismatic revival. Her books, *I Believe in Miracles* and *God Can Do It Again*, became best-sellers; the old-time leaders of the revival, who had a profound respect for success, agreed that she had a fantastic ministry. Reportedly in her early sixties, Kuhlman seemed to have boundless stores of energy; according to her supporters, she was a "veritable one-woman shrine of Lourdes." [8]

Kathryn Kuhlman came to leadership in the charismatic movement indirectly. Reared in Concordia, Missouri, by a Methodist mother and a Baptist father, she decided at the age of sixteen that she was called to preach. "I went from community to community, sometimes having to hitchhike," she later said. "I would find any empty building, advertise the services, set up benches, and the people would come—strictly out of curiosity to see a red-headed, teen-age girl preacher." [9] She spent nearly two decades as an itinerant, free-lance evangelist before settling in the mid-1950s into a small church in Franklin, Pennsylvania. In the meantime, in 1946, she received the baptism of the Holy Spirit and began to teach extensively on that subject.

Kuhlman was not linked historically with the pentecostal revival, although she eonsidered herself pentecostal. She was ordained to the ministry by the Evangelical Church Alliance. Analyzing her teaching on the baptism of the Holy Spirit, one healing evangelist said, "She has the baptism but she don't really preach it like we do. . . . She softens it down a little." [10] She was repulsed by the usual tent healing services which were the mark of the early revival. "The long healing lines, filling out those cards," she later said, "it was an insult to your intelligence." [11] In fact, her healing techniques were much like those of William Branham.

In 1954, in Franklin, Pennsylvania, "members of Ms. Kuhlman's congregation suddenly began to claim spontaneous healings during her services." She increasingly preached on healing and her ministry began a fantastic spiral upward.[12] The following year she moved to Pittsburgh where she rented the auditorium of the Carnegie Library to conduct a miracle service; she was still there twenty years later. She was the target of some criticism during her early years in Pittsburgh, but she soon earned the respect of the community and the support of many local religious leaders. While Kuhlman's style was extremely theatrical, there was no fanaticism in her services: "Often there is such quietness that the faintest rustle of paper may be heard." She organized and became president of the Kathryn Kuhlman Foundation which is a major contributor to religious and benevolent charities in the United States and abroad. Housed in Pittsburgh's Carlton House Hotel, by the 1970s her ministry featured a large radio and television network and a growing number of regional personal appearances in key cities throughout the nation in which she conducted her miracle services.[13] By 1973, the annual budget of the ministry was reportedly approaching $2,000,000.[14]

Clearly only marginally related to the healing revival of the post-World War II period, Kathryn Kuhlman had become one of the most respected leaders of the charismatic revival by 1970. She had come to a healing ministry in her own way and had established a reputation of integrity and intellectual honesty greatly prized by neopentecostal leaders. No one typified the best hopes and aspirations of the movement better than Kathryn Kuhlman.

Rex Humbard

Another major independent ministry strongly related to the revival was that of Rex Humbard. Humbard, born in Little Rock, Arkansas, in 1919, grew up in a family of traveling pentecostal evangelists. Humbard joined the family team in a public relations capacity after graduating from high school. He was deeply influenced by the healing revival, although never clearly a part of it. In a moving personal experience, his son, Rex Jr., was healed in an early Oral Roberts campaign in Mobile, Alabama. Subsequently, Humbard bought an old Roberts tent to launch his own ministry.[15]

Humbard's remarkable success story began in 1952 when, after a successful tent revival by his family, he decided to stay in Akron, Ohio. He asked Kathryn Kuhlman, who had a large following in the area, to help him begin a church. In response, she reportedly attracted 18,000 people in one day. Humbard felt he was harassed by the newspapers of Akron, but he was well treated by the city officials and proceeded to build his Cathedral of Tomorrow, a modern building with a seating capacity of over 8,000. In the late 1960s and early 1970s his ministry mushroomed. By 1970 his Sunday morning services were carried on a network of 225 television stations, "reaching areas where some 150 millions of Americans live." [16] "Not satisfied with the great Cathedral of Tomorrow," wrote one reporter, "and the outreach by t.v. and radio, there are also camps for young people, retirement homes, and missionary endeavors." [17] Unexpectedly in 1973, Humbard suddenly appeared to be in deep financial troubles, but to many observers of the deliverance movement he still seemed to have the most dynamic ministry at the moment.[18]

Although he was an early friend of such figures as Oral Roberts and Kathryn Kuhlman, and was raised a pentecostal, Humbard never identified his work with the deliverance revival. From the beginning, he considered the Cathedral of Tomorrow strictly undenominational: "People from almost every denomination you can name feel free to join in worship with us." [19] The Director of Public Relations of the church wrote, "The Cathedral of Tomorrow is not Pentecostal; neither is the pastor or any of the staff. Neither are we affiliated with any Pentecostal organization, and the magazine is not slanted at the Pentecostal message at any time. We are an interdenominational evangelistic church." [20]

Humbard profited from the charismatic revival, however, and he was never ashamed of his charismatic friends and teachings. A statement of his beliefs in 1966 included "regeneration by the Holy Spirit" and "Divine healing through the redemptive work of Christ on the cross." [21] Not only did Humbard profit from his friendship with such figures as Roberts and Kuhlman, but he also encouraged the work of smaller revivalists.

Of all the important ministries of the late 1960s, the appeal of Rex

Humbard is most difficult to explain. Country and almost bland in personality, Humbard seemed able to identify with the common man. Furthermore, despite his financial difficulties, Humbard oozed integrity and honesty. As the hullabaloo of the early revival began to fade, these qualities became more important than talent. Humbard was not clearly a part of the charismatic revival, but he was a friendly fellow traveler.[22]

8

Old-Time Revivalism

A. A. ALLEN AND DON STEWART

A. A. ALLEN SAW CLEARLY the signs of change in the late 1950s, but his commitment to healing revivalism never wavered. Perhaps he had no choice. Estranged from the churches because of charges of personal misconduct and already embarked on a sensational miracle ministry, 'Allen could hardly have chosen to evolve into a charismatic teacher. Neither was it his style to institutionalize his ministry and build a secure financial base instead of tirelessly beating the campaign trail. "It was lean through the early sixties," recalled his young associate Don Stewart, "but Allen never slowed his pace." [1]

In the late 1960s, Allen analyzed the "era of the vanishing evangelist": Ten years before, he wrote, "there were more than two hundred evangelists in America with revival-centered healing ministries . . . and uncounted thousands *were* healed." But, he continued, "the devil's destroyed one evangelist after another." He charged that some of them, to survive, took "refuge in dying churches, where they are afraid to preach the Gospel." Others were "cowed by criticism and a fear of letting emotions flow during services," because emotionalism had become bad form in the more sophisticated circles of the charismatic revival. "There are a few still influential evangelists and ministers who enjoy large followings," he observed, "but they hold 'crusades,' 'campaigns,' 'seminars' and at their meetings they frequently do not even issue altar calls but weakly tell their hearers that an 'information booth' is available for anyone interested in God." Declared the tough old campaigner, "That isn't revival!" [2] It seemed to him that all his "competitors" were gone, and he alone was left to preach "Restoration Revival." [3]

Allen built his ministry on the conviction that the "old-time religion is still the newest thing around." [4] He and his closest advisors believed that the revival had deserted the principles central to its early success. Kent Rogers, Allen's handsome and distinguished associate evangelist, said: "The difference is we have stayed the same way. This ministry has not only pioneered the miracle aspects and the healing, we've kept the old-time pentecostal message alive." As the Allen people saw it, the pentecostal churches had changed; most of the early healing ministries had changed; the Allen ministry was the one large ministry to maintain its early emphasis. [5] Allen believed that the revival had left behind the people who needed it most. "My people," he wrote, would never be comfortable in "snob congregations" and neither would such churches welcome them. He concluded: "Thus we will continue to fill the gap between revealed truth and the butchered truth of denominational religion. Our revivals will continue to glorify God with singing, dancing, shouting, speaking in tongues, falling prostrate before the Lord." [6]

A. A. Allen's congregations rarely let him down. In 1969, he boasted, "The crowds who come to my meetings grow larger every year, my ministry grows stronger and more influential." [7] In 1958, a supporter, Urbane Leindecker, a rancher in southern Arizona, donated 1,250 acres of land near Bisbee to the Allen ministry. Allen bought an additional 1,250 acres and began building a community which he named Miracle Valley. During the 1960s Allen constructed a church that would seat about 4,000, a headquarters building, and several buildings to house a Bible Training Center. The structures might seem somewhat shoddily constructed and impermanent to some; to Allen they represented a major accomplishment:

> Miracle Valley is alive, pulsing with God's work, a totally spiritual community, unique in the world—private homes for scores of families who want to live in a godly atmosphere year-round, a training school for missionaries who will carry the message all over the world, employment base for 211 dedicated souls (it takes a lot of manpower to keep spreading the Gospel), the healing

pool of Bethesda, headquarters for our camp meetings and radio and television outreach which now circle the globe.[8]

Miracle Valley and the large organization supported by Allen gave stability to the ministry despite the frequent instability of the evangelist.

The heart of A. A. Allen's ministry remained tent revivalism. In 1960, when most had retired from the field, Allen unveiled a huge new white vinyl big top which he heralded as the only tent of its kind in the world and the world's largest.[9] Ten years later, in June 1970, *Miracle Magazine* again announced the unfurling of a new world's largest tent. Allen was a hardened campaigner whose constant innovations greatly influenced many new ministries that arose in the 1960s and 1970s.

By the end of the 1960s, the Allen ministry had matured and grown dramatically. Allen was delighted to be featured in *Look* magazine in 1969.[10] "God has brought us a mighty long way," he wrote in a rare mellow note for *Miracle Magazine* in 1969; "I like to recall the humble and meager beginning most of us had when we first started running for Jesus in this Christian race." He then recounted the impressive statistics amassed by his ministry during the past year: letters received from 90 countries; a *Miracle Magazine* circulation of 340,000; an average daily mailing from Miracle Valley of 216,000 pieces; 60,000 Miracle Revival records sold; a network of 58 radio stations supported at a cost of $355,068.43 a year; a 43-station network of television stations airing half-hour weekly broadcasts at a cost of $163,562.60. In addition, the ministry had sustained Miracle Valley Bible College, operated a fellowship which granted ministerial papers to 9,000 persons, and supported several missions and missionaries overseas. Allen had ministered in two major camp meetings, ten tent campaigns, and fourteen auditorium campaigns in twenty-four cities in the United States and conducted two revivals in the Philippines.[11] The A. A. Allen revival clearly was not dead.

Allen clawed and fought for every inch of his success. There was a ring of truth when he wrote, "I do not have a persecution complex, but what else can you call it but persecution when so many attempts have been made to silence me and destroy my ministry?" [12] Again and again in the 1960s Allen reminded his supporters of the threats faced by his ministry and others like it. "An ever increasing wave of religious persecution is sweeping across America," he wrote in 1962, "directed . . . at churches and ministers who declare the whole counsel of God, especially along the lines of His miraculous power through Deliverance and Divine Healing." Allen associated his troubles with "a far reaching, insidious conspiracy to undermine and destroy faith of God in America." [13] Allen, who understood the uses of mob hysteria, warned frequently of a Communist conspiracy, but he was never deeply influenced by right wing political thought. He was afraid that "new mental health laws" could be used to declare all "full gospel Christians insane" and apparently believed that some of his associates wanted him committed. [14]

Allen's major enemies remained those ancient foes of all healing revivalism. He continued his running battle with the press and in 1962 charged that the typical news coverage given his revivals included:

1. Criticism of the offerings.

2. Criticism of the manner of worship.

3. Ridicule of the evangelist—his clothing, his speech, his personal appearance, often including moral defamation.

4. Similar ridicule of other members of his staff.

5. Ridicule of the congregation—usually portraying them as a very ignorant, low-type, almost sub-human rabble.

6. Insinuations that the Revival is a "religious carnival," conducted for gain.

7. Complaints of "unfriendly attitude" toward the press! [15]

More serious was the intense scrutiny the ministry received from federal and local governments. In 1963, Allen was sued for over $300,000 in back taxes by the Internal Revenue Service, but he won a major battle in the courts to protect his association's tax exempt status. The courts ruled that the ministry's collections had not been used for the benefit of any private shareholder or individual and that the love offerings received by Allen and his wife were not "unreasonable when one considers the services performed by them for the organization." [16] But the pressure remained intense. In 1962, Allen summed up the bureaucratic "approaches" used against revival ministries:

1. They have attempted to put a stop to *tax exemption for many independent churches* and evangelistic associations.

2. They have urged local governments *to refuse permits to erect tents,* and to deny the use of public auditoriums. . . .

3. They have attempted to have the deliverance *revivals classified as "business"* or "commercial" enterprises, *rather than as church services,* and thereby to require business registration, payment of sales taxes, or "license to solicit."

4. They have brought pressure to bear upon *radio and TV stations,* threatening action through the FCC. Some of them have organized themselves *to demand that no time be sold to religious broadcasters,* but that time

rather be given as a "public service" to churches and religious programs selected and approved by them.

5. They have complained to the Post Office Department, *attempting to stop the use of the mails* by various healing ministries. This would be, without doubt, the most devastating blow of all.

Allen urged his followers to write immediately to their senators and representatives to protect their right to "hear their Church by radio and TV, without the censorship of any self-appointed religious council, representing itself to speak for religion in America." In addition, Allen urged any supporter whose contribution was questioned by tax examiners to write him immediately.[17]

A. A. Allen survived because of his innovations and daring. He picked up the tempo in his revival meetings; he added gospel rock music; he emphasized old-time pentecostal worship; he assembled a team of skilled entertainers to support him; and he reeled off an endless array of spectacular miracles. "He had insight," recalled his associate evangelist Don Stewart; "he was ten years ahead of his time. . . . He brought a little bit of the black beat in, and now it is the thing with the Jesus kids." Said Stewart, "The other boys, they didn't know anything but have a prayer line. And when things began to change they were left out in left field." [18]

Healing remained the mainstay of the Allen ministry, and *Miracle Magazine* was filled with sensational healing testimonials. A California "lady minister" who "swallowed an open safety pin a week before" an Allen revival testified that she "felt it rise into her mouth as Brother Allen preached the sermon." [19] W. W. Wilkins, "pastor of the Revival Center in Selma, California," told a remarkable story of healing: "When I made the statement that I wanted a ministry like Brother Allen's, Satan told me he was going to kill me with cancer. Tonight he tried, but God is greater! I felt the presence and power of God go through my body tonight." The next evening, "he returned to the tent with six cancers in a jar, which he had passed since his healing the night before." [20] Mrs. Alvester Williams of Las Vegas reported that she took 200 pounds off instantly using "God's reducing plan." The editor of the magazine added to her testimony the note, "This lady's body could be seen shrinking visibly, as she sat in the service. Many people commented on this." [21]

Bizarre healing testimonials were almost an Allen trademark. In 1961, *Miracle Magazine* reported in detail the healing of a forty-three year old "hermaphrodite," Hugh Chrisman. Chrisman testified that he had been to "at least ten psychiatrists and medical doctors and hospitalized in two hospitals in an effort to find help for my many problems," but not until he attended an Allen revival was he cured. He reported: "As I lay there on the ground [having been overcome by the Spirit], God changed me completely to a male. I left the other self there. The female spirit left! Even my large breasts had vanished." Chrisman happily related that others had "noticed the change in my appearance, the tone of my voice, even in the manner in which I can work. My boss says I go about my work now like a real man." Finally, Chrisman said, "There is another outward sign that indicates the vast change that has taken place inside my body. Down through the years, with the dual sex both controlling my body functions, it was only necessary for me to shave once every three days. Since God removed every trace of the feminine and has healed and strengthened the masculine organs, it has been necessary to shave every day." [22]

Allen reported that "there were two outstanding cases of women receiving their dead back to life" during the 1966 camp meeting at Miracle Valley. *Miracle Magazine* reported in some detail the circumstances surrounding the case of "little Carol Jones":

> Marjorie Dearman, the nurse, came at Sister Jones' call for help. They could find no pulse, no respiration. The color had left her lifeless little body. . . . It was 1:30 a.m., and the all night prayer meeting was going on in the great Miracle Valley Tabernacle. Sister Dearman rushed over and requested prayer and help. Several ministers left a praying multitude to go back with her to 'raise the dead'! As soon as they prayed, little Carol's eyes came back to normal. . . . God raised her and healed her! [23]

In the mid-1960s Allen launched a brief "raise the dead" program, but there were difficulties. Several of his disciples refused to bury dead loved ones and a number reportedly attempted to send bodies to Arizona. He shortly urged overzealous followers to "obey the law" and bury their dead in "a reasonable period of time." [24] He believed that resurrections were possible, but obviously God was not going to raise all Christians who died.

Allen also explored demon possession in considerable and sensational detail.[25] In a book published in 1963 he included eighteen pictures of demons "as seen and drawn by a demon-possessed woman." He linked demon possession with insanity: "These Satanic beings have power to torment you mentally and physically until you are driven into the insane asylum, and the Lord permits it when disobedience is continued." He urged those possessed to order a blessed cloth to effect a cure.[26]

"Miracle oil" continued to flow in the Allen revivals. *Miracle*

[199

Magazine reported in 1967: "To those who witness the outpouring of the oil, there can be no doubt of the validity of the phenomenon. It appears before your very eyes. Its shining surface reflects the light until it glistens. . . . It appears on hands, on feet, on the face, from the crown of the head! . . . We make no effort to explain why. This just happens to be one way God is edifying His Church today!" [27] When such miracles occurred, Allen generally found a way to share the blessing with his far-flung supporters. Reporting on the 1967 campmeeting at Miracle Valley, he wrote:

> As the people passed over the ramp to see the oil, Brother Allen anointed their heads with his own hands, and prayed for them all! Would you like one of these prayer cloths anointed with the Miracle Oil? Brother Allen thought of you! He realized many were unable to attend Camp Meeting who would want a specially anointed prayer cloth. If so, fill in the blank below and mail today.[28]

Allen had a flair for drama and the instincts of a carnival hawker, but his ingenuity seemed to captivate his followers. When dedicating a new tent in Philadelphia in 1967, reported *Miracle Magazine*, "In a moment of inspiration, Brother Allen scooped up some of the shaving from the ground and rejoiced in the Lord for God's blessing him once again with another lovely tent cathedral. . . . He offered to send a tent shaving to anyone who would use it in faith as a point of contact for their miracle! Miracle shaving! . . . You may request one when you write." [29]

Allen was an unsurpassed fund-raiser. In the early 1960s he increasingly emphasized the promise of prosperity for the children of God, an idea which had long been present in the revival. During a 1962 campaign in Philadelphia, Allen announced that God had given him "a new anointing and a new power to lay hands on the believers who gave $100.00 toward the support of our missionary outreach and bestow upon each of them POWER TO GET WEALTH." Allen was miffed when others quickly echoed his prosperity message:

> Humbly I tell you this, as reports are reaching my headquarters that ministers all over the country are preaching about the blessing of prosperity.
>
> The three things I want you to see are the same things I have always preached. Namely, first that God told me he had given me power to bestow power to get wealth. He did not say it was given to Tom, Dick and Harry, or to just anyone who says "Lord, Lord." God confirmed this as it caught on like wildfire and within weeks it had been confirmed thousands of times across the nation.
>
> Persons who know me well . . . will not think that I believe I am the only

man whom God uses to cast out devils, or through whom He can bestow "Spiritual Gifts," or that I am the only one He can use to bestow power to get wealth. No doubt, he has bestowed this power on others, and if not he may in days to come.

In March 1963, while conducting a campaign in Houston, Texas, another revelation came to Allen—"like a flash from heaven, a bolt out of the blue." "It was just as if a light had been turned on in the mind," he told his readers when the revelation was printed: "I am a wealthy God! Yea, I am not poor. . . . But I say unto thee, claim my wealth in thy hand, yea, in thy purse and in thy substance. For behold, I plan to do a new thing in the earth! . . . Yea, yea, yea, obey ye the servant of the Lord, for I have placed him in this place. Indeed I did call him forth from his mother's womb. And I have kept my hand upon my servant." [30] In the late 1960s testimonies of financial blessings came to outweigh reports of healing in *Miracle Magazine*. Among the urban poor, quick riches proved at least equally as powerful an allure as good health.

More and more Allen turned to the ghettoes for support. He preached increasingly to blacks and other minorities, although he never lost the backing of large numbers of poor whites in North and South. Allen had always boldly challenged traditional racial taboos, as had most of the more radical evangelists in the 1950s. As early as 1958 he held an integrated revival in Little Rock, Arkansas. He considered a meeting in Atlanta, Georgia, in 1960, in some ways the most important he had ever held: "It was a pathfinding revival, because it broke the religious color line in the Deep South, bringing together huge numbers of blacks and whites in unsegregated worship for the first time." While such experiments had occurred earlier, the meeting did represent the conscious commitment of a major ministry to biracial revivals. The integration of the Atlanta meeting was not a calculated arrangement, said Allen, but rather a spontaneous outbreak.[31] He quickly accepted a fully integrated ministry. By 1963, he spoke boldly against segregation—something which few of the more moderate ministries dared to do—and directed more and more of his efforts to winning black supporters.[32]

Allen's appeal to blacks was many-faceted. In 1961 he added to his team Gene Martin, an attractive, vivacious, and talented black singer. Allen himself established a remarkable rapport with his black audiences; they accepted his declaration: "I don't love the colored people a bit more than I do the white people, but I don't love the whites a bit more than I do the colored." He dealt frankly with touchy racial issues:

I saw a little lady up in New York City some time ago. . . . She was a colored lady, no covering it up. I mean she was black. You colored folks had better watch out or you'll get tired of being black. You'll want to be white. God made you black, and you better get the victory over it. Make heaven your home and just be willing to stay black. . . .

I was walking down the street—past this little colored woman, I could see she was just like a lot of our white folks. Some of them get that old tan stuff and smear it on them and make them brown. Some women have straight hair, but they don't want it straight. They spend all their time curling it. Holy Ghost night, on Saturday night, by the time some people go by I've worn the skin off my hands on those old bobby pins done up in pin curls. . . . And by the time the Holy Ghost line is over, my hand is as greasy as it can be from the palmade. Why? All of these colored folks putting that palmade on their hair trying to stretch it out and take the kink out. . . . You know I'm telling you the truth. You don't want to stay like God made you. If you've got red hair, you want it black. If it's black, you rinse it in henna so it will have a red color. . . .

You'll never have victory in your soul as long as you want to be somebody else instead of what God wants you to be.[33]

Allen's success was all the more notable because his erratic personal conduct continued to be a constant liability. The charge that he was a heavy drinker persisted; some of his most loyal supporters, while not accepting the news accounts of Allen's misconduct, became reconciled to the idea that Allen might have "a problem."[34] He began to miss revivals, turning the preaching responsibilities over to young Don Stewart. Sometimes he made extended trips alone to rest.

Most stunning was Allen's decision in 1967 to divorce his wife of many years, Lexie. Divorce was highly undesirable in radical religious circles, though sometimes permitted, and the move shook the Allen organization to the core. For years Mrs. Allen had been at the center of the ministry; some supporters suspected that "there were people who worked to gain his [Allen's] confidence for reasons of personal gain that felt she was a hindrance to what they saw in the future for themselves."[35] One insider felt the divorce was caused by incompetent drones who were draining the ministry. Another believed Allen was actually being blackmailed by unscrupulous subordinates. Few of his followers doubted that the scandal hurt the organization.[36]

As in life, Allen was controversial in death. He died alone in San Francisco in June 1970 in a Jack Tar Motel while his team was conducting a revival in Wheeling, West Virginia. News accounts reported sclerosis of the liver as the cause of death. "Rumors too wild to dignify by repeating, vilification too vicious to recount," wrote Don Stewart's biographer, "spread about his passing."[37] More to the point than one more scandal was the question whether such a personal ministry could survive the passing of its charismatic leader.

The task of carrying on the Allen ministry fell on thirty-year-old Don Stewart, who since 1958 had been Allen's associate evangelist. Stewart immediately announced, "We are going on for God . . . A. A. Allen was a great apostle in this last day; there will never be another A. A. Allen—never another as great. But, according to his own prediction, greater things were ahead!" [38] Stewart was backed by Allen's long-time associate minister, H. Kent Rogers, who assured the ministry's supporters that the Miracle Revival team would continue the work of deliverance evangelism.[39] In the immediate aftermath of Allen's death and the accompanying scandal, the ministry lost some support, but, according to Stewart, not a "large following." [40] The staff was cut in half, both for economy and efficiency, but the ministry remained strong financially. At the 1973 camp meeting in Miracle Valley, Stewart announced that the ministry's indebtedness had been halved.[41]

In some ways, Allen had prepared well for his succession. He left behind a group of stable institutions at Miracle Valley and a team of well-known crusade workers. At least a portion of the ministry's supporters were loyal not to Allen but to the program of work at Miracle Valley. Don Stewart forthrightly claimed Allen's mantle:

> God spoke to the heart of Reverend Allen and he had enough wisdom to begin to groom me, because he knew the plan of God. Even several years before he went on to be with the Lord, he knew his ministry was beginning to come to an end. That's the reason he began to train me and put me forth in the manner in which he did. . . . God planned it. You know why? Because God had to find somebody that would take this ministry on in the pattern that God had ordained. . . . That had enough guts to look the devil in the eye and say "Satan, you have to move back because God's ministry is moving forward." [42]

But Stewart's succession was not uncontested. A bitter two-year internal struggle ravaged the organization before the Don Stewart Evangelistic Association took over the remnant of the Allen organization. Firm control was gained only after a well-publicized battle in the Arizona courts, in which Stewart and his associates were charged with embezzling. Through loss of considerable financial support and rumors that the ministry was about to collapse, Stewart held on gamely. He told a 1972 camp meeting in Cincinnati:

> The past few weeks Satan has literally stuck his head up. Now Satan is trying to take and steal the mantle from me. He's trying to hijack the mantle, but

[203

Satan absolutely cannot. If God had wanted another man to stand in my shoes, God would have put that man there. If I was the wrong man in these shoes right now, God would kill me and remove me and put the right man in them. . . . But it just so happens that I'm the right man and some of them didn't know who they were tangling with.[43]

The fight over the Allen ministry was in part a simple power struggle between Stewart and his supporters and Gerald W. King, the executive director of the organization and Allen's brother-in-law. More important, it was a contest over whether the organization would remain a revivalistic ministry or become a missionary and educational organization. It was a struggle between institutional managers and the charismatic revival team. The crisis began when Stewart proposed that the organization spend $100,000 to promote a gigantic revival in Madison Square Garden in New York City. Stewart later said:

I laid my heart out to the board of directors and to our organization and to our people, and I told them what God had told me about going to Madison Square Garden. Reverend Rogers and Gene Martin and those that have worked close with me, said "Brother Stewart, if God has told you to go to Madison Square Garden, we're with you all the way. . . ." Thank God for men who speak the same spirit and the same anointing and the same unity as we speak. But then there were a few others, accustomed to sitting behind desks, looking over cold figures. "A hundred thousand dollars, we don't have a hundred thousand dollars," and I had to look at them and say, "listen, this ministry has always moved in faith. We never had any money to do anything. . . . I've never done anything with money. I have always had to do it with faith." [44]

Stewart held his New York crusade and won what he called, "the fight of my life." [45] After a shakeup of the board of directors, he emerged as the leader of a revival ministry. The Don Stewart Evangelistic Association was the first deliverance ministry to retain its original format after the passing of the charismatic leader.

The success of the Don Stewart ministry became increasingly dependent on the gifts of the young evangelist himself. A graduate of Allen's Miracle Valley school, Stewart had survived for several years as an independent campaigner when Allen asked him to become one of his associates. While Stewart lacked the totally uninhibited flair of his mentor, he was a powerful preacher and knew well how to appeal to the simple audiences that attended his crusades. In a typical appeal for support, Stewart said, "You don't care if I don't stand behind the pulpit very rigid and very sophisticated? You don't care if I mix up my grammar a little bit? . . . Just as long as I give you the bread of life . . . and his power and his anointing touches your life. You're not going to church to try to get impressed." [46]

Young Stewart recognized that the ministry he had inherited was the ultimate in pentecostalism, with all "the old-time shouting and praising God and dancing in the spirit and the manifestations of the Holy Ghost and the gifts of the spirit." [47] He openly dubbed his followers "outcasts" and said, "There are very few places they can go and worship the way we do. . . . We consider it a privilege and a blessing to be an outcast. . . . It puts you on the in-crowd with God." [48] He was well aware that others had "changed their methods, changed their attitudes, have even changed their publications," but he believed that as "long as God has the people that are hungry for the truth, we'll always have revivals." [49] Stewart told an audience in 1972:

> Now if you're not sick tonight and you got plenty of money and everything's all right, your mother-in-law's treating you okay . . . what I'm going to do tonight is not going to relate to you much. You don't need a physician. . . . If you're going to a nice lovely church and are full of self-righteousness, you don't need my message. But if you need help tonight and you need somebody to point you to the Christ of Calvary, I have a message for you tonight. . . . Jesus is here to touch you. . . . It's kind of like going to some of these churches. You might as well make up your mind that some of them wouldn't let you in the front door anyway, honey. But you can get to Jesus.[50]

Healing and the miraculous were less characteristic of Don Stewart's ministry than of his mentor's. Nonetheless healing remained a central theme in his revivals and testimonies of healing became more and more common in later issues of his magazine. In a revival in Brooklyn, Stewart reportedly healed a young man who had just been shot, the bullet being lodged "just a few centimeters from his heart." Instead of taking the young man home from the hospital to die, his mother brought him to "God's man, Don Stewart." When Stewart prayed, "the power of God hit Melton on the stretcher. He threw off the sheet and jumped to his feet! . . . The transformed young man embraced his mother and they walked arm and arm from the stage into the midst of the resounding shouts of praise to Christ the Healer!" [51]

Prosperity was also a strong theme in the Stewart ministry. Stewart's financial techniques were almost as hard-sell as A. A. Allen's had been. A Stewart revival could bring in hundreds of $100 pledges and scores for $1,000; Stewart provided his supporters the convenience of charging contributions on BankAmericard and Mastercharge. The ministry remained a multimillion dollar a year operation.

The Stewart ministry was diverse. All of the operations started by Allen were retained. The tent campaigns remained "the end of the spear," but the organization had many facets.[52] *Miracle Magazine* had a circulation of nearly 400,000. Miracle Valley Bible College, established by Allen in 1958, was a successful part of the ministry under the direction of Dean Roy M. Gray. Stewart also maintained Allen's sizeable mission work in the Philippines and a moderate radio network. By 1973 he had launched a small television work.

Don Stewart never considered himself simply a caretaker for A. A. Allen's projects; he recognized as well as other observers of the revival that no one could impersonate Allen. Fiercely loyal to Allen personally, Stewart was intent on establishing a ministry fitted to his own personality. He adopted the name "Compassion Explosion" for his crusades and soon began to establish a reputation as a more moderate and responsible figure than his mentor had been.

In February 1974, after over three years of searching for his own charismatic identity, Don Stewart announced a series of bold new changes in the ministry. The steps were clearly calculated to move Stewart a step closer to the moderate center of charismatic revivalism. Probably the most important change was the division of the old Allen revival team. The ministry began to support two teams, one headed by Stewart and the other made up of old-time Allen associates, H. Kent Rogers and black singer Gene Martin. More symbolic was the removal of the headquarters of the Don Stewart Evangelistic Association from Miracle Valley to Phoenix.[53] Don Stewart was no longer A. A. Allen's successor. He was, for better or for worse, his own man.

MORRIS CERULLO

If A. A. Allen was the most successful old-time revivalist of the 1960s, Morris Cerullo was probably the leading campaigner of the 1970s. Cerullo was the last of the first-generation healing ministers with a major campaigning ministry. Raised in an orthodox Jewish orphanage in New Jersey, Cerullo was converted and began preaching before he was fifteen years old. He became an Assemblies of God minister in the early 1950s and began a healing ministry in 1956. A powerful and dramatic speaker, Cerullo early became famous as a "converted Jew."[1] He remained with the Voice of Healing organization until the early 1960s, and then began building his own organization in San Diego. In 1963, he began to publish an attractive monthly magazine, *Deeper Life*, which by 1973 had a circulation of around 150,000. In 1966, his ministry included a crusade team of six people and a headquarters staff of seven, including Mrs. Cerullo. By 1973, his organization, called World Evangelism, employed about forty-five people.[2]

In the late 1960s, he developed a "seven-point master plan for souls" which included crusades in the United States and abroad and a broad program for the support of native missions. In addition, he launched an active "Israel outreach" which by 1970 had distributed 1,000,000 pieces of literature to Jews in Israel.[3] The primary thrust of the Cerullo ministry was personal evangelism, however, and in 1975 Cerullo, who had conspicuously avoided both radio and television, launched a major television series called *Helpline.* Slickly produced and widely distributed, it was the most ambitious television venture since Oral Roberts' new series.

Cerullo was second only to A. A. Allen in keeping alive healing revivalism in the 1960s. He held sensational meetings abroad, particularly in South America, where he was arrested several times because of his aggressive techniques.[4] Cerullo's methods and his successes recalled the classic days of the revival. In 1970, Velmer Gardner, long retired from the active ministry himself, wrote, "There is no doubt that God is using Brother Cerullo to reach more people on foreign fields than any ministry or organization today. I am praying that God will keep him humble and use him even in a greater way!"[5] Evangelist David Nunn said, "Morris Cerullo is still having tremendous meetings on the overseas trail. He has twenty, forty, fifty, sometimes a hundred thousand people in his meetings there."[6] World Evangelism estimated in 1973 that over 1,000,000 people had been converted in the Cerullo crusades.[7]

After 1971, Cerullo increasingly concentrated on training native evangelists to be "miracle workers." Through a National Evangelist Crusades program, he hoped to build an army of native preachers to replace American missionaries. Cerullo regularly conducted large schools of evangelism in South America and sponsored over 3,000 crusades conducted by native preachers.[8]

Cerullo also had great success in American revivals in the late 1960s and 1970s, increasingly turning his attention toward home. In a five-day crusade in Los Angeles in 1971, Cerullo preached to over 18,000 people and reported 2,000 healings.[9] He adopted many of the techniques used successfully by Oral Roberts in the 1950s. He courted local politicians and celebrities and tried hard to win the support of local pastors. He established open financial policies in his campaigns in an attempt to satisfy local pastors and insisted that his crusades were designed to "build, edify, and bless the local church." Although Cerullo did not escape criticism from the organized pentecostal denominations, he frequently won the cooperation of the Assemblies of God and other churches.[10]

While Morris Cerullo built a solid and growing crusade ministry during the 1960s, he was also in close touch with the emerging neopentecostal phenomenon. No one else worked so well with all of the elements in the charismatic movement. In 1966, he began conducting Deeper Life Conferences throughout the country, directed to the young and new charismatic converts. While speakers at the early conferences included men like William Branham and Joseph Mattsson-Boze, by the 1970s most prominent were neopentecostal celebrities like Pat Boone.[11] Cerullo's connections with the Full Gospel Business Men's Fellowship International seemed to be good; for a time Richard Shakarian, the son of Demos Shakarian, was his General Manager of World Evangelism.[12] Cerullo believed that his ministry had always been balanced; he recognized the diverse possibilities of the charismatic message.[13] According to his son, the evangelist consciously tried to stay in the middle-of-the-road.[14] On the other hand, some of his contemporaries believed that he had "semi-made it" into the charismatic camp. "He is 75 percent there," said one evangelist.[15]

Still in his early forties in 1975, Morris Cerullo was the most seasoned charismatic evangelist with a major campaign ministry. Finally entering the expensive but powerful medium of television, he was beginning a new five-year plan to carry revival to seventy-five American cities. A tireless worker, he often spent ten hours a day in active ministering, sustained, he believed, by a greater anointing than ever before.[16] Gifted, experienced, and energetic, Cerullo was also, in the words of one observer of the revival, "incredibly tough." [17]

Survivors

Revivalists such as David Nunn, R. W. Culpepper, A. C. Valdez, and Lester Sumrall remained active in the 1960s and 1970s, but each of them changed his methods considerably. A few old-timers could not or would not change and simply reconciled themselves to smaller crowds and thinner budgets. They continued to preach the same message of healing and deliverance in tents and auditoriums across the nation. Many of them had never experienced the dramatic success of the prominent evangelists; for them the lean years of the 1960s were business as usual.

H. Richard Hall

H. Richard Hall of Cleveland, Tennessee, was a good example of a successful small revivalist. He was born in rural poverty in the mountains of North Carolina and began preaching when he was only fourteen. He was deeply influenced by his mother, who was "one of the first in Pentecost in the western part of North Carolina." Hall remembered preaching in the "mountain parts" from his youth: "I would then stand upon chairs and preach, and also from street corners." [1] At twenty-four, he was ordained a minister in the Church of God of Prophecy and spent several years in Colorado as a state overseer in that church.

In 1952, Hall gave up his position in the church and became a full-time evangelist. A deep religious mystic, he believed that God had spoken to him three or four times. He made periodic journeys to what he called a secret place in the desert where he received "a visitation of His presence." On a number of occasions during these retreats, Hall said he was healed of a prolonged illness.[2]

Other forces also drove Richard Hall to establish an independent ministry. He was greatly impressed by the successes of the eary revival and remained an ardent admirer of William Branham. In addition, Hall seemed to crave to be somehow unique, as did other charismatic evangelists. He often recited for his mostly unsophisticated audiences the list of his academic accomplishments: "I have had three years of Bible School in Cleveland, Tennessee, also Webster University of Atlanta, Ga. I have a degree with them. For a short session, I attended a Knights of Columbus school in New York, which is Catholic. . . . I hold a degree in speech and expression—dramatics. I also hold a doctor's degree from Carter's Bible College in North Carolina. I studied pre-law for a short season—just before I came down with sickness." [3]

In 1952, according to Hall, God spoke in an "audible voice" to him and said: "*Homer Richard Hall* . . . I HAVE LAID MY HAND UPON YOU TO PREACH DIVINE DELIVERANCE TO ALL PEOPLE OF ALL CHURCHES." "The Lord showed Bro. Hall many things in that hour," reported his magazine, and he "immediately resigned his position and began to carry the message of deliverance." Hall believed that his ministry was to serve all people: "Jesus made Bro. Hall to know that his ministry was not to be crowded inside denominational walls . . . or it would be taken from him, but was to be taken to ALL God's people and to the sick and sinful of all races." [4]

Through the 1950s Hall crisscrossed the South holding tent revivals in the small towns missed by the larger evangelists. He seldom strayed from that region: a typical notice to his supporters read, "I would appreciate very much people in the states of North Carolina, Mississippi, Virginia, West Virginia, Eastern Kentucky to write me for the location of the tent revival meeting that is to be held in your state." [5] By 1960 Hall had developed a small organization with a radio work and a regularly published magazine. In a 1961 appeal for funds, he wrote, "By radio, through the ministry, by printed page and personal contact we work untiringly with this great burden upon us. The ANOINTED OF GOD ARE MEN OF DESTINY. It is those that have the message of DELIVERANCE." [6] By then Hall was heard on thirty radio stations—most of them in small towns in the South. In addition, he reported, "We mail over 15,000 letters, booklets and pieces of literature from Cleveland monthly." [7] He estimated the cost of this modest ministry at approximately $3,000 a month and he constantly solicited aid from his supporters. Hall worked, said his magazine, "in cooperation with Holiness, Pentecostal, and Full-Gospel Churches and all others of good will for the furtherance of the Gospel of Christ," but he never won substantial support from any major pentecostal denomination.[8]

Richard Hall was one of a few small ministers who learned to work within his limits. He cautiously explored new possibilities but never overextended himself. In 1968, he tried to extend his broadcasting lineup to one hundred radio stations, and issued a fervent appeal for support: "I don't know about you but I am going to GIVE EVERYTHING I HAVE to the Lord Jesus Christ and his work. I mean this: I am giving God all my time, all my strength, all my abilities, and EVERY POSSESSION I HAVE (worldly goods, money, property). That's it!" [9] But, in fact, his radio work declined in the 1960s as Hall increasingly diverted his attention to other things. By 1972 his magazine, *The Shield of Faith*, had a circulation of nearly 100,000 and his ministerial department had licensed over 2,000 ministers.[10]

On a smaller scale and in more remote places, Richard Hall used all the tactics tested by the big deliverance ministries. The heart of his ministry remained, however, a continual schedule of taxing tent and auditorium revival in localities such as Carbon Hill, Alabama; Bessemer, Alabama; and Concord, North Carolina, in addition to an occasional visit to a larger city such as Dallas. Although Hall insisted that he did not emphasize healing, he remained essentially a healing revivalist. He exercised the gift of knowledge successfully practiced by William Branham in the early 1950s by which he "was able by the revelation of the Spirit to tell the people what their sickness and diseases and trials were to help them believe God for their healing." [11]

Richard Hall appealed to the fringes of the pentecostal world. He identified with the social outcast. His ministry, he said, was "not helping that man that's up, it's helping the man that's down." He courted the marginal Christians abandoned by organized religion: "Most of the men preaching today in the organized church world know nothing about drugs, nothing about whiskey, alcoholism, they know nothing about that side. All they can do is rant and rave. But a man that's been that road can have compassion." Said Hall, "Our desire is to reach those that churches don't want." These sentiments led the southern-born Hall to "change his mind" on the race question and to welcome blacks into his revivals.[12]

Richard Hall was willing to change markedly to relate to the youth culture of the 1970s. A gaunt and somber character fit for a Grant Wood portrait, preaching with a deep Tennessee drawl, it seemed remarkable that he could find common ground with the young. But the evangelist saw in the youth rebellion of the 1960s a hunger he believed he could satisfy. "These boys are waiting for this special supernatural or charismatic move, mysticism," he said, "and we have it." With little apparent friction, Hall began preaching to audiences laced with old-time pentecostals and hippie-type youth: "We had thirty-seven of those long hairs and drug addicts at our altars just a few weeks ago. . . . We could understand how some of our contemporaries felt. . . . But if the speaker of the hour accepts it, usually the congregation will." [13]

Hall collected around him a number of attractive and capable young college students to campaign with him. Young Kent Sullivan became an important member of his staff and others worked regularly for the small ministry. At a recent meeting, Hall announced that "over 50 young ministers" would participate.[14] Hall believed that the "sign-gift thing is going to burst on to the colleges" and that his mission was to inspire young ministers. "They won't be accepted with their long hair and hippie clothes by the churches," said Hall, "but, after all, the churches don't need them." [15]

Through it all, H. Richard Hall changed very little. His hair grew down to his shoulders, but he looked more like a Tennessee senator than a convert to the youth culture. The country evangelist had won the confidence of his young followers on his own terms. There was a vast cultural difference between Hall and his old-time pentecostal supporters and the young converts of the 1970s. The merging of the two streams in Hall's ministry was a striking accomplishment.

Franklin Hall

The teaching of Franklin Hall on fasting had a wide influence among other ministries, but his own small scale work was a fascinating story of its own. He took part in the revival from its beginning, but was always so independent that he isolated himself from the larger endeavors. Even his position on fasting was moderated by the other ministries that accepted and practiced it; Hall's emphasis was considered somewhat extreme. On his part, Hall believed the more successful evangelists were not extreme enough: "The 1946–1947 deliverance preachers have [not] advanced with anything deeper than what the Lord gave them in that year." [16] The schism between Hall's doctrine and the mainstream of the revival widened through the years.

Hall continued his small teaching ministry in the 1960s with headquarters at his "bodyfelt salvation" church in Phoenix, Arizona. He regularly taught his views on divine healing at meetings throughout the country and trained and licensed preachers at his headquarters in Phoenix. Hall's wife, Helen, who was also a minister, often preached for her husband. By the 1970s their small ministry supported missions in Ghana and England. In 1971 Hall reportedly distributed a million of his tracts. His magazine, *Miracle Word*, reached a circulation of around 24,000. Through his years of campaigning Hall remained optimistic, believing that his work was about to blossom. "This is going to cover the whole world," he said in 1972; "it is a stone ministry that is going to grow and become a mountain. . . . Ministers are coming out everywhere. . . . The youth want something for thrills, for kicks, for the body. That's why they go to drugs. . . . We have the answer." [17]

Franklin Hall's "bodyfelt salvation" was the center of his appeal; he declared it to be "700% greater than ordinary healing power." In the early 1950s Hall noticed that people who were healed would feel a warmth coming on them. He later determined that it was "the Holy Ghost fire" and that it was designed to save men's bodies. "If we could get it all over them," he believed, it would free people from "sickness, tiredness, odor" and all human frailties.[18] According to Hall, it required "about thirty days to get this established and concentrated all over a person's body so that they can live completely above all tiredness and all sickness." Others taught deliverance from sickness and Holy Spirit baptism but, said Hall, "Nobody seems to want to understand what the fire is all about. . . . When you have the baptism we're talking about you don't get sick any more. . . . You can live above sickness just like you can live above sin. . . . You still get sick when you speak in tongues. . . .

Sister Hall has had no sickness in eighteen years. . . . She has had no tiredness in fifteen years." When one was clothed with the Holy Ghost fire, according to Hall, he no longer had any type of body odor. Disciple Thelma Moore of San Francisco testified that she wore the same hose for six months without washing them: "They never did get stiff. . . . They never had any unpleasant odor about them." [19] Hall's teaching raised the hope of "eternal life in a physical body now and a return to life of dead saints." [20]

Franklin Hall's meetings had a unique and mystical air. He insisted that his audience sit with "head up and eyes open" because after forty years' research he had determined that they would have "400 percent greater faith in coming to the Lord with head up and eyes open." Hall frequently mentioned the "glory cloud" that he saw hovering over his assemblies, and his disciples anticipated that, at any moment, Jesus would visualize himself before them. When his disciples raised their right hands and said "Hello, Jesus," the Holy Ghost fire descended on them. When they raised their left hand and said "Hello, Jesus," they smelled the fragrance of Jesus. "Now take a deep sniff," Hall told an audience in Phoenix, "Doesn't that smell good? Have any of you folks got a dog? If you've got a dog, you'll have to watch out, because you'll smell different. . . . Oh, you can take this fragrance with you and it will go all over the lot. It gets in your house, makes you bug proof. It makes you a Holy Ghost exterminator." [21]

Franklin Hall had always been a teacher rather than a charismatic preacher. His following was limited by the complexity and the extremity of his teaching. Although he made no major inroads among the young, he believed that his teachings were perfectly suited for them: "This is a thrilling thing for their body. It will make a superman out of them. They get a bigger kick out of this than they do out of heroin." Hall's appeal in the 1970s, however, seemed to be mostly to those estranged from organized religion—"people who are disappointed with their church group." [22] "When your old church elders won't speak to you, won't associate with you, won't have nothing to do with you, [Jesus] comes and says come on get in my way," preached evangelist Helen Hall.[23] Even among the disinherited Hall's following was small. His teachings demanded patient study and self-discipline. Hall reached out for black supporters but with only moderate success:

The colored people are a little more emotional and this ministry is different from A. A. Allen's in several ways. . . . He has more of emotional . . . demonstration and this ministry tries to get people to receive it by a teaching

[213]

ministry. In a teaching ministry the people have to learn to sit down and be quiet. Now some of the colored people are so emotional they don't seem to have patience enough to be willing to sit down. But we have lots of colored people. . . . And they seem to be seeing that there is something better than just dancing and shouting. . . . Which we are for but not to take the place of the teaching ministry.[24]

Franklin Hall's later career, as was his earlier, was dominated by his radical doctrine. Few of the other deliverance evangelists would associate with him. Gordon Lindsay believed that Hall ruined his influence because he became obsessed with particular doctrines and refused to use common sense to balance his views.[25] Another evangelist said, "That heat business is for the birds. . . . Anybody that feels heat all the time is just sick." [26] Nevertheless, as spokesman for the most psychically deprived group in American religion, Franklin Hall was a veteran of many battles with an uncanny capacity to survive.

The Young Lions

Deliverance revivalism is a young man's game. Time was hard on the older evangelists; few men sustained active healing ministries for two decades. As the older ministries faded in the 1960s, a group of talented young preachers brought new vitality to tent and auditorium revivalism. For them, old-time revivalism remained a promising field.

Jimmy Swaggart

The most spectacular new revival ministry of the 1970s was that of Jimmy Swaggart of Baton Rouge, Louisiana. Swaggart, an Assemblies of God minister, was a powerful preacher and a gifted entertainer. He was the cousin of singer Jerry Lee Lewis and one of the nation's top gospel recording stars. In 1972, his album, "There Is a River," became the most requested gospel album in America, and his recordings were among the leaders in their field.[1] A tireless worker, Swaggart was only thirty-four and ruggedly handsome when he began his independent ministry in 1969. In less than five years he had created one of the ten largest ministries in the country.

Preaching was the center of the Swaggart ministry. A typical campaign lasted only three days and often drew audiences of 4,000 to 5,000. In his meetings Swaggart emphasized the old-fashioned evangelistic appeal, but his services were never boisterous or unruly. "We don't try to work the people up," he said, but "we do have a lively service."

Swaggart stressed the importance of teaching: "The old-fashioned whoop and holler has its place . . . but people want something deeper." Probably the most powerful attraction was Swaggart's "ministry of music," which brought an enthusiastic response from his supporters. Although he taught much on healing and the gifts of the Spirit, he did not have a prayer line. Instead, he prayed a simple prayer at the end of his service for the sick.[2]

An Assemblies of God minister since 1960, Swaggart was a celebrated evangelist in that denomination before starting out on his own. He remained intensely loyal to his church, and he became the first independent revivalist since the early 1950s to receive the enthusiastic backing of the Assemblies of God. His meetings were generally sponsored by Assemblies pastors, but he always invited all pentecostal groups to participate. He felt he had broken out of denominational barriers without compromising his message.[3] Swaggart's ministry had great appeal to the neopentecostal movement. He had many friends in the Full Gospel Business Men's Fellowship International and as early as 1972 noted that over half his audiences were "denominational people hungry for the Holy Spirit." [4]

Swaggart's greatest success came in the mass media. He began his radio broadcast, *The Campmeeting Hour*, in 1969. After five months the expense and labor had become so great that he felt he could not continue,[5] but suddenly his support began to increase. By the beginning of 1974 the evangelist was heard on over 350 radio stations; his network of stations was one of the largest in the world. He called this growth the " 'radio miracle' of the twentieth century." [6] In 1972, Swaggart announced that he was beginning a television series. He moved quickly into this expensive media and by 1974 was seen on nearly 40 stations. His radio and television programs cost over $10,000 a day; almost overnight the Swaggart ministry had become a $3,000,000 a year business.[7] It seemed to be only beginning.

Swaggart's organization remained small and unsophisticated. He handled a tremendous volume of work (up to 5,000 letters a day) with a small staff in Baton Rouge and worked with only one campaign assistant, his long-time friend Harry Bouton. Swaggart stressed that his was a "faith ministry," and that all the money he received from gifts and the sale of his records was used to support his work. Swaggart was paid a salary by the association; he refused to accept love offerings as an additional source of income. He donated the royalties on his records to the support of the ministry.[8]

The Swaggart ministry was determinedly "honest" and "clean." His record seemed above reproach and his appeals for financial support were among the least frenetic in the history of the healing revival. Swaggart was openly critical of those who "perverted the prosperity message" to bilk the unfortunate. No minister since Oral Roberts in the 1950s was so successful in working out amicable financial arrangements with local pastors.[9]

Swaggart also preached a moderate message. Although he believed strongly in healing and urged his audiences to "come boldly to God" for their deliverance, he also admitted that some remained sick and he could not understand why. His sermons were laced with positive thinking ("The only thing you cannot do is what you say you cannot do"), but they also were filled with old-fashioned tales of God's miraculous healings. His lessons were loaded with pentecostal doctrine, but they were always presented in a positive "spirit of love." [10] Swaggart's Holy Spirit Impact Rallies, which he conducted on Sunday afternoons during his campaigns, were remarkably orderly, but he believed he had seen "as many people filled with the Holy Spirit as anyone in the world." [11]

Jimmy Swaggart brought mass revivalism back to life in the major pentecostal denominations. His appeal spread in all directions, and his future seemed bright. Swaggart seemed destined to rescue charismatic campaigning from its reputation of radicalism and irresponsibility.

Robert W. Schambach

One of the most important protégés of A. A. Allen was Robert W. Schambach. Born in 1926, Schambach became an Assemblies of God minister in 1951 before joining the A. A. Allen team as an associate minister in 1953. Schambach developed an intense personal loyalty to Allen; he left the Assemblies of God when Allen was disciplined by the church after his arrest in Knoxville. Schambach remained with the Allen team until 1959 when he decided to launch his own ministry. He left with the blessings of his mentor and remained close to the Allen family.[12] He patterned his own ministry after Allen's. "Everything I learned," he later recalled, "I learned at his side." [13] Schambach Miracle Revivals grew steadily in the 1960s, attracting a clientele much like the Allen originals.

Schambach built a firm foundation of support during the 1960s by founding four Miracle Temples. The first of his churches was begun in Newark after a successful revival in 1960. Subsequently, he began churches in Brooklyn, Chicago, and Philadelphia. Each church was pastored by a full-time assistant, but Schambach conducted periodic revivals to stimulate them. His four churches provided a base of financial support which was the backbone of the ministry.[14]

Schambach was primarily an old-fashioned revival minister. The evangelist had the same restless commitment to tent campaigning that characterized the early revivalists. In a typical three-month period, the Schambach team visited New York City, Newark, Miami, Mobile, Atlanta, Dallas, Chicago, Phoenix, and Gallup, New Mexico.[15] In 1974, he claimed that his $50,000 tent was the largest in use. "There is something about a tent," said Schambach, "that you can't get in an auditorium." [16]

The Schambach ministry grew rapidly in the 1970s. In 1970, he began a monthly magazine, *Power*, edited by Lexie Allen, the widow of A. A. Allen, and by 1974 the circulation of the magazine was approaching 100,000. His office was operated efficiently by a small staff in Elwood City, Pennsylvania. By 1974 Schambach's radio network included nearly fifty stations at a cost "approaching $50,000 a month." [17]

R. W. Schambach preached the old-time message of deliverance. He believed that "every child of God should be free from sickness" and his healing services were much like those of the early revival. His message was well-rounded, however; he preached "total deliverance for the total man." Perhaps the chief attraction of his services was the spontaneous audience participation and response. The "joy of worship" flowed freely under the big tent. Schambach was convinced, as was A. A. Allen, that the stigma against noise had killed the spiritual joy of most Christians.[18]

R. W. Schambach was a powerful charismatic preacher, and more— he was intelligent, open, and versatile. He established a good rapport with many ministers in the established pentecostal denominations and attracted some followers from the neopentecostal movement. But his basic talent, consciously cultivated, was to bring "positive teaching" to the "lower class." Critical of the prophets of doom common in the revival, Schambach insisted that his mission was to move the people "out of despair." [19] In the eyes of many, the mantle of A. A. Allen had fallen on R. W. Schambach.

LeRoy Jenkins

LeRoy Jenkins was one of the most controversial, and one of the most gifted, of the second generation healing revivalists. Even Jenkins' detractors within the revival generally believed that his ministry was accompanied by "fantastic miracles." [20] He was a successful young

Presbyterian businessman in Atlanta, Georgia, when he was healed in a 1960 revival. Inspired by Allen, he immediately began an independent ministry.[21] Jenkins' call came when a voice told him, "There is somebody up here that loves you." [22]

Jenkins' early success was unbroken. He stressed cooperation with the pentecostal churches. His promotional literature declared that he was "thoroughly Pentecostal in belief and doctrine, and he encourages all who are saved and blessed in his meetings to attend the *Pentecostal Church* of their choice as represented by the cooperating pastors on his platform." [23] Jenkins was a prized convert to the full gospel movement, and he succeeded in gaining the support of some of the major pentecostal denominations—a difficult task in the early 1960s. He courted the Full Gospel Business Men's Fellowship International and generally won the respect of his fellow evangelists. He explored a number of ways to expand his work, including a nursing home and a retirement center. For a time he pastored churches in Miami and Tampa but in the mid-1960s concluded that doing so was contrary to the calling of an evangelist.[24] He wanted to begin a television series but was never able to finance one in the 1960s. Throughout the decade he remained largely an itinerant tent revivalist. He owned a tent which seated over 10,000, and his crusades reportedly were still having tremendous results at the end of the 1960s.[25]

While most supporters of the revival believed he had a powerful gift, Jenkins' career was extremely stormy. His claims often seemed extravagant. He had frequent scrapes with local authorities; in 1964 he was detained in the Bahamas as an "undesirable person." [26] On more than one occasion Jenkins claimed divine purpose behind the death of a detractor.[27]

LeRoy Jenkins' greatest problem was his own ebullient personality. He had persistent difficulties with his close associates. On one occasion he wrote ruefully, "It was late at night, the service was over and most people were in bed. I was feeling God-forsaken. It seemed as if all of my employees were giving me trouble. Two of the men who really worked close with me in my ministry were leaving. Others didn't seem to care if the work went on or not. I had been having trouble with my wife. I was tired, mad and disgusted." [28] The evangelist won a reputation for wild living. Divorced from his wife and arrested on several occasions in cases involving the use of alcohol and drugs, the Jenkins ministry seemed bent on self-destruction.

However, in the 1970s a newly designed LeRoy Jenkins ministry showed surprising vigor. Jenkins began holding regular services in the

Ohio theater in Columbus, and dubbed his congregation "The Church of What's Happening Now." He unabashedly announced that the church was controlled by a "four man board: the Father, the Son, the Holy Spirit and me." [29] He used his church as a base of support for his new work which rapidly gained momentum. He launched a growing radio program, and by mid-1974 was preaching regularly on four television stations. His quarterly magazine, *Revival of America*, was mailed regularly to about 100,000 supporters.[30] Jenkins was determined not to reach too far in his ministry of the 1970s. "I don't have any empire here," he said, "but I don't have any big obligations." [31]

LeRoy Jenkins did not live down his reputation, but he learned to capitalize on being "the nation's most controversial evangelist." [32] He urged his followers not to listen to the "garbage collectors" who criticized him; at the same time, he said privately that such attention probably helped his work.[33] Jenkins' supporters were obviously captivated by his boyish charm and his slightly rouguish manner. He publicly denounced the "holier-than-thou attitude" of many Christians and admitted his own human weaknesses. Promising his congregation to furnish his own home-made wine for a communion service, Jenkins told his followers, "I don't know what it will do for you, but it got me arrested." [34]

Young, handsome, and talented, LeRoy Jenkins seemed to have found his place in the 1970s. He had contemplated other careers "outside religion," including an offer from Mae West to make motion pictures, but decided to "stick with the thing that helps the most people." [35] Jenkins' concept of religion "in the now" was totally foreign to the pentecostal meetings of the early revival. On the other hand, when Jenkins each week laid hands on the sick in the Ohio theater, his techniques and results were as nearly like the early revival as anything available in the mid-1970s.

David Terrell

The most austere and prophetic ministry of the 1970s may have been conducted by David Terrell of Greenville, South Carolina. Terrell was on the cutting edge of modern healing revivalism. Severe and threatening in message and manner, his appeal was limited to the most devout. But his ministry grew and was a monument to the vitality of radical revivalism in the 1970s.

According to one of his associates, Terrell frequently "agonized" in prayer—sometimes for as much as four hours a day.[36] Gordon Lindsay, and most of the other moderate charismatic leaders, believed that Terrell had a powerful anointing, but most believed that his bitter prophetic preaching was too extreme. Although Terrell conducted healing revivals in the pattern followed for decades, he emphasized his anointing as a prophet. He frequently issued prophecies about current events—including a prediction of the election of Richard Nixon in 1968—and sometimes prophesied in poetry.[37] In 1966, Terrell graphically described his call to a prophetic ministry:

> The ministry of a prophet is not an easy one. No man chooses to be a prophet, but the Lord chooses His man. . . . When the Lord first called me as Jeremiah I made excuses for I could not read or write. It seemed impossible for me to obey the calling, but God furnishes all that we need if we furnish a clean, consecrated yielded vessel. My baby sister spent many hours teaching me to read the Bible, and I believed every word of it. . . . By the time I was 22 years of age, my burden had become so heavy and my concern so great until I vowed my life to the Lord in a long fast, determined to get an answer or die trying. Even in this I received much criticism and practically no encouragement. During this fast I saw many visions and on the 30th day God spoke to me just as plain as anyone could speak. I actually heard His voice with my own ears and there's not a devil in hell or on earth that can make me doubt my calling or what I've been commissioned to do.[38]

Terrell's services were emotion-packed. His language was rustic; his message was dynamic, down-to-earth, clear, and hard.[39] Terrell openly condemned the more sophisticated charismatic ministries and proclaimed his new movement as the fulfillment of prophesy. "It is going to get so rough," he wrote, "until they will be forced to either join the Ecumenical movement or join up with Christ whole-heartedly as I have." [40] Terrell was frequently accused, in his words, of "fighting, tearing up churches, confusing people, and just about everything else in the book." He replied that he was not an ordinary preacher, but a "prophet with a message burning his soul for this generation." [41]

Most of Terrell's supporters were radically independent pentecostals. His ministry was especially strong in the deep South. Terrell was well-trained to be a prophet to the poor:

> Since I was poor [as a young man] and did not have sufficient clothes I was not allowed to preach in many Churches. When I went to Revivals the Lord would use me and many times the preachers would accuse me of trying to take over their services. For years I ministered without a pulpit. I cried, prayed, fasted, preached on street corners and anywhere I was asked to preach. It looked as if the Lord had forgotten His promises to me, but I realize now He was only preparing me before sending me forth.[42]

Obviously, the stark and rigid message of David Terrell met a real need. By 1966 his ministry had grown to include nine radio stations, a monthly magazine, and regular tent revivals; soon afterward it began to mushroom. In 1967 he announced that he was working under the world's largest gospel tent, and the other phases of his ministry also grew. By 1972 the circulation of his magazine had reached 85,000 and his revivals had begun to move outside the South. His radio network had expanded to sixty stations and cost approximately $35,000 a month. Tapes of his sermons were in such demand that $2,000 worth of new tape had to be bought each month.[43]

Many of the older ministers judged that Terrell's influence would not last. Because of his educational deficiencies, he makes statements that are "wild and crazy," said one charismatic leader.[44] Others believed that his extreme views on fasting led to false doctrines.[45] Clearly, Terrell's extremism was more than a recapturing of the early enthusiasm of the revival. It was a tough radicalism that won only the severely discontented.

Neal Frisby

The most bizarre prophet of the 1970s was Neal Frisby of Phoenix, Arizona. Born in rural poverty in Arkansas, Frisby lived a harsh life, finally becoming a barber at the age of eighteen. His wife was fifteen at their marriage. According to Frisby, after the birth of two children, she became subject to "moody spells." She was afflicted with a "suicide spirit," he believed, which caused her to shoot herself.[46]

Afterward, Frisby pursued hard drinking during several tormented years. He was finally committed to a mental institution where, he reported, he was told that he was in danger of "brain combustion." Upon his release, he resolved to never return to that "crazy-house with these nuts." [47]

Frisby began to "seek God" while institutionalized, not telling his doctors that he felt called to preach, but holding to his firm decision. He later wrote, "After the death of my wife the Lord called me alone for nearly six weeks without food and spoke several times to me concerning my future ministry. His words to me were 'There shall not anything stand before thee all the days of thy ministry. As I was with Moses I will be with thee! '. . . I saw the Lord so long my hair began to fall out and my bones were almost without flesh!" [48] During his forty-day fast, when Frisby was "shut up with the Lord," he believed he was called to be "a prophet in the last days to bring the fullness of Bible Deliverance." [49]

Frisby first came to notice in the deliverance revival in the early 1960s. Like David Terrell's, his early ministry was a struggle; he later freely told of the humbling experience of his days as a campaigner. He bought a large tent, but a series of storms destroyed it and left his ministry tottering on the brink of financial collapse: "My staff after seeing so many Miracles and the hand of God move in such a way in other things just didn't know what to think about the trials and the discouragement that came. The joy and laughter soon left us all as we saw we were confronted with an unscrupulous devil. . . . Some of the staff people thought maybe I had disobeyed the Lord." After consulting with a number of older evangelists, Frisby abandoned his ministry and began a long trek home to California. While passing through Arizona, he felt that "the spirit of the Lord moved" on him while he was resting under a "Juniper-type tree." He was told that God would give him a special group of partners to support his ministry. For five years in the late 1960s Frisby did not preach, but through the circulation of mystical prophetic "scrolls," an "Elijah Company" of supporters gathered around him.[50] By 1971 these loyal supporters had built a Temple of Destiny in Phoenix. Frisby ministered irregularly in his new temple and claimed "ninety-nine percent, we guess, have been healed as they come before God." [51]

Frisby's techniques, both while a tent campaigner and since, have been typical of the most radical fringe of the revival. His miracles came in grandiose dimensions: "Who is this man? That speaks the word only and demons scream, come out and cases of nerves or insanity are healed instantly? Who is this man that speaks and God creates parts to the human body? Who is this man with an anointing powerful enough to raise the dead and heal incurable diseases instantly? . . . Who is this man that makes headlines even on front pages of leading newspapers? Why do evil spirits of fear and worry and nervousness leave through his prayer cloths?" [52] At times, Frisby seemed fascinated with mental illnesses and his powers over the insane. His scrolls, which frequently were incoherent, offered hope to the mentally ill:

Due to motion picture dramas and world conditions, narcotics and rejecting Gods Power brings on a surge of demons from satan, because he knows his time is short. People will see horrifying creatures and spirits. Children plagued with new mental diseases, terrifying madness sets in on the world. The only chance a person will have is to (stay with Gods anointed servants!). Reading these scrolls will relieve and protect against mental nervous disorders. My Prayer cloth will set up a standard also. The churches that reject the anointing of Miracles will receive what has been mentioned. Remember (stay on God side!) no matter what the church says.[53]

Frisby's prophecies included frequent warnings against the neopentecostal movement. The conversion of many Catholics and "Nominals" was viewed by Frisby as "a clever snare" devised by Satan to cripple the revival.[54] In a typical message in Scroll #7, Frisby wrote:

Two of Gods Greatest Men know I am right, but because of money and sponsorship they are afraid to say anything. . . . Now this is to warn Gods chosen. Some of the Salvation Groups and some of the Pentecostal groups will be tricked shortly, into a massive confederation out of which eventually some will make up the anti-christ bride (fallen church) Is brought to him by the spirit of man, and dead organizations. Listen closely if you are a member of one of these groups don't get frightened. (But when you see them going in, come out from among them!) . . . The Leaders will be told they can 'pray for the sick,' and (preach like the Bible says!) This is used for bait to draw them into a trap. . . . But after they get in (the trap) like a snare shall it come on all of them. Then the Bible will be changed finally another one given, for Catholic, Jew and Protestant which is the word of the beast. . . . A law will be passed no more preaching or praying for the sick and a mark issued! . . . Remember only the wise will see it, my message is not to the foolish but to the (wise!) The wise will hear until they are endued with power from reading Gods Scrolls. The Lord told me this message would bring some financial loss and persecution to me, but oh Sir, that great angel is standing by my side. . . . That's all He will let me tell you now.[55]

Frisby's prophetic ministry expanded broadly. A devout follower of William Branham, whom he called the Star Prophet, Frisby occasionally suggested that something very remarkable could happen regarding Branham's return.[56] His prophecies touched on a variety of moral and public issues. In 1970, he wrote:

A prophetic insight, I write not to be indecent but by command. The new music is not new but came from Asia and the islands. Spirit that produces the music there produces the music here. The music there is connected to idol worship. The heathen countries wear little or no clothes. The music here is one cause in the young, especially to keep shortening their dresses. . . . What is in the future is, if the music continues, morals will become like heathens and dresses shorter and finally, possibly none. . . . I saw a world plan underway to blend dope, music, sex into religion. . . . I foresaw America start through its most immoral seizure ever. Weird events will take place between 1975–77.). I don't know the date but be watching for the different, unusual and electrifying to happen to the future office of the presidency![57]

Frisby's prophetic ministry, and his retirement to Phoenix, illustrated the lonely end of charismatic revivalism. Fantastic as they may seem to his critics, Neal Frisby's prophetic scrolls were the most important message on earth to thousands of supporters.

The Diversity of Gifts

Hundreds of other independent ministers regularly toured the country displaying a wide variety of charismatic gifts. Many others— "Pastor" David Epley of Ft. Lauderdale, Ernest Angley of Akron, John Douglas, Jr., of Baltimore, Vic Coburn of Portland, Oregon—had growing and well-known ministries. For $2,000 in cash any aspirant could buy a small tent and hit the revival trail. Under the inspiration of an Allen revival, or a Schambach sermon, or a Terrell prophecy, scores of fiery young ministers resigned their pastorates (often risking excommunication) to test their anointing in fairgrounds and union halls across the nation. Their dreams were generally large. "God spoke" to young Don Powell in 1952 saying, "He had chosen me to take his message to the whole world by radio and television." [58] But the climb to the top was not easy. Dorothy Davis, an evangelist whose young ministry was inspired by Robert Schambach, was "caught up in the Spirit" for two-and-a-half hours during a recent visit to Birmingham, Alabama. The first words she "heard the Lord say" were prophetic indeed: "ONLY THE STRONG SHALL STAND." [59]

9

New Promises and Problems

THE CHARISMATIC REVIVAL—including all of its diverse manifestations —was a powerful force in American religion in the mid-1970s, overshadowing the small pentecostal denominations that spawned it. The movement was too nebulous to define, much less measure, but millions of Americans had been touched by it. The independent ministries were supported by gifts ranging between $30,000,000 and $50,000,000 a year. Many of the ministers were secretive about their incomes, but yearly budgets ranged from the marginal subsistence of the small tent revivalists to the reported $15,000,000 yearly budget of Oral Roberts' wide-ranging empire.

The charismatic preachers of the 1970s drew their support from a cross section of American society. The disciples of men like David Terrell were mostly independent pentecostals, the classic religiously disinherited. On the other end of the spectrum were the affluent and sophisticated supporters of the ministries of Oral Roberts, Kathryn Kuhlman, and the Full Gospel Business Men's Fellowship International. In between were the ministries aimed at other segments of American religious society, but no successful evangelist seemed able to escape capture by some group of supporters. Each evangelist who reached out to a new audience paid the price of leaving another behind.

[225

There was no doubt by the mid-1970s that old-time healing revivalism had recovered partially from the decline of the 1960s. Tents crisscrossed the nation, promising miracles, prophecies, healing, and deliverance, attracting crowds of thousands. "We're not only going to continue," said Don Stewart in 1972, "but we're going to broaden out, and grow, and do more of what we're doing. As long as people have needs . . . there's always going to be a place for this. . . . This is meeting a certain segment of society's needs." [1]

For all their similarities, there were distinct differences between the tent revivals of the 1970s and the campaigns of the late 1940s and early 1950s. With few exceptions—most notably Morris Cerullo and Jimmy Swaggart—the campaigners of the 1970s bore the mark of A. A. Allen. Their methods and their followers increasingly came to fit popular stereotypes. Ecumenical fervor was replaced by harsh antiinstitutionalism. The revivalists were more garish and boisterous, their miracles more extreme, and their financial techniques more frenetic. To many moderate charismatics, the typical campaigner of the 1970s retained the form of the early revival but not the spirit. But to hundreds of thousands of people, the miraculous presence of the Holy Spirit still hovered under the big tent.

The full dimensions of the charismatic revival were only beginning to focus in the mid-1970s. Preachers like Oral Roberts and Kathryn Kuhlman had taken the revival to millions of middle-class denominationalists. In technique and style, Oral Roberts had changed dramatically in twenty-five years, but Roberts himself did not feel that he had abandoned faith healing. [2] The neopentecostal independent ministers approached the question of healing with sophisticated theologies and honest insights, but they were no less interested in the miraculous than the revivalists of the early 1950s. While the neopentecostals had a broad interest in all of the workings of the Holy Spirit, divine healing remained primary in their thought. Demons, fasting, and divine healing were as central in the ministries of Derek Prince and Don Basham as they had been in the careers of William Branham and A. A. Allen. The neopentecostal preachers were more erudite, their message was more complicated and less given to novel and simplistic Biblical exegesis, their testimonies were more discreet, and their surroundings were more luxurious, but the issues they faced were the old ones. Don Basham's instructions for deliverance from demons had a thoroughly familiar ring: "1. Identify the specific spirit to be cast out. 2. Renounce the spirit by name. 3. Command the spirit to leave in the name of Jesus. 4. Expel the

Spirit." Basham found gagging or coughing to be useful because, "in most cases spirits seem to leave through the mouth." [3]

The success of the revival among the middle class not only put financial bonanzas within the reach of more moderate evangelists, it also pushed the charismatic message into the mainstream of American religion. Oral Roberts became a Methodist, and hundreds of clergymen in the traditional denominations—beginning in 1959 when the Episcopal priest Dennis Bennett of Van Nuys, California, announced to his congregation that he had undergone a charismatic experience—became filled with the Spirit. While some of these ministers established independent evangelistic associations, many remained within their denominations and tried to accommodate the charismatic experience to their own theological, liturgical, and ecclesiastical tradition. By 1966, a Presbyterian Charismatic Communion had been established and similar groups quickly appeared within Roman Catholicism and in most major Protestant churches. Even hardened opponents of the charismatic movement such as the Baptists and the Churches of Christ had active cells of spirit-filled members by the 1970s.[4]

Classical pentecostals by the 1970s had come to recognize that the winds of the Spirit were blowing freely outside the Pentecostal churches and to desire to "identify with what God is doing in the world today." While some still saw neopentecostals as extremists who overemphasized the importance of spiritual gifts and withheld approval from "that which is manifestly not scriptural in doctrine or conduct," the Assemblies of God announced in 1972 that it did not "categorically condemn everything that does not totally or immediately conform to our standards." [5] In addition, church leaders were willing to cooperate with the revival efforts of Jimmy Swaggart and a few of the other more responsible evangelists.

An observer in the 1950s—in the midst of the popular and religious disdain for faith healers—could hardly have guessed that the revival would have attained such respectability two decades later. By the 1970s the press was fascinated by the neopentecostal movement and even took occasional serious glances at the touring revivalists. Both the independent ministers and their critics had changed. Oral Roberts became a frequent guest on television talk shows. In his closing remarks before the World Congress on Evangelism in 1967, Roberts thanked Billy Graham for helping to open his eyes to the "mainstream of Christianity." [6] The divorce of the evangelists from classical pentecostalism had driven some to greater doctrinal extremes, but had a moderating effect on others. At the same time, by the 1960s American evangelical Christians were anxious to make peace with pentecostals. Roberts wrote, "There is a growing feeling in the evangelical church world that we should have greater healing emphasis in our evangelistic outreaches. There is a deeper feeling about the baptism of the Holy Spirit. In fact, there is a greater openness among all Christians that the charismatic power must be restored to God's people." [7]

The general American intellectual mood in the 1960s and 1970s was less dogmatic and less intellectually sure; curiosity and open-mindedness replaced scientific confidence and certainty. Francis MacNutt, a Roman Catholic priest with a vital healing ministry who was also a Harvard graduate and held a Ph.D. in theology, was typical of the intellectual believer: "My own experience leads me to the conclusion that healing is the most convincing demonstration to most people that God is *with us.*" While some considered such thinking prescientific, MacNutt pointed to some physicians in the 1970s who "practice a coordinated ministry of medicine and prayer" and observed that many physicians and intellectuals were no longer hostile to divine healing.[8] Especially within the Catholic community the concept of the wondrous seemed to many to be the resurgence of a very old truth.

Not only had the influence of the independent ministries reached many layers of American society, their impact was great outside of the United States. Millions of tracts and books were distributed throughout the world. The ministries supported thousands of native evangelists and built hundreds of schools, preacher training centers, and benevolent institutions. The overseas crusades of the major evangelists drew immense audiences. The permanent effect of such missionary work has not been measured, but the balance of world religion had been changed. Particularly in Latin America and in Africa, the pentecostal work was the most successful American mission movement after World War II—and it may well have been the most successful ever.

The evangelists were both shocked and fascinated by the youth revolt of the 1960s and directed much of their energy to preaching the power of the Holy Spirit to the young. The independent ministers reached out at every level. Men such as Oral Roberts and T. L. Osborn fashioned a modish image to attract young people—running the risk of alienating some older followers. Many of the tent revivalists anticipated that their revival would be joined by the budding Jesus movement. Old-time revival manager C. B. Hollis said, "Even though some of them [the young] do look terrible and I don't approve, but as they get full of the Holy Ghost, their lives begin to be cleaned up. They're going to be some of the greatest Christians the world has ever known." [9] The 1960s outbreak of fundamentalist religion among the young was influenced by the charismatic revival and raised the hopes of charismatic leaders, but the youth culture, like the other social subcultures in the revival, was rooted in its own unique circumstances and was composed of people quite different from the other types of pentecostals. Few independent revivalists made real inroads into the ranks of the Jesus people, with the major exception of David Wilkerson's youth-oriented Teen Challenge ministry.[10]

Perhaps the most important new idea of the charismatic revival was the emphasis on prosperity. The belief that God would grant prosperity to His people was an old tenet of the movement; even in the 1930s Thomas Wyatt had considered that doctrine the foundation of his ministry.[11] But in the 1960s the message almost supplanted the earlier emphasis on healing; every evangelist came to advertise his own "master key to financial success." [12] Third John 2 became the most quoted text in the revival: "Beloved, I wish above all things that thou mayest prosper and be in health, even as thy soul prospereth." While the promise of prosperity was handled with dignity by the moderate evangelists, the theme lent itself to high-pressure fund raising tactics. One young minister charged his audience:

Now there are fifteen people here tonight in this tent . . . because God has told me that he is going to give you an unlimited blessing. God told me that. God is going to speak to fifteen people to write a check, even if you have to postdate it for thirty days, God is going to talk to fifteen people to write a check or give $300 . . . tonight, right now. Now, if you don't believe he can do it for you, then you're not going to be one of them. . . . God is going to give you more money in 1972, from now to the end . . . of this year, than you ever made in any twelve month period of time. . . . You may use your Mastercharge, your BankAmericard.[13]

Whatever the intentions of the preachers, the prosperity message often came across like crass materialism.

The successes of the charismatic revival were impressive, but by the 1970s the independent ministers faced problems even more perplexing than those of two decades earlier. Campaigning revivalists still were harassed by local authorities, and faith healers were little more welcome in many communities in the 1970s than twenty years before. Postal authorities remained deadly enemies of religious hucksters; radio evangelist Charles Jessup was convicted of mail fraud and sentenced to prison.[14]

While the public image of charismatic ministers had improved greatly, popular exposé articles were still abundant in the nation's newspapers, magazines, and church periodicals. Most Americans still had honest reservations about the claims of even the most responsible revivalists. In 1975, Dr. William A. Nolen, a noted Minnesota surgeon and author, included the case histories of twenty-six persons who believed they had been healed through the ministering of Kathryn Kuhlman in his book: *Healing: a Doctor in Search of a Miracle*. Dr. Nolen concluded that "he couldn't find a single cured patient in the group." [15] The credibility of the revivalists also continued to be damaged by the inability of the public to distinguish between moderate and extremist ministers. Few popular writers understood the vast differences between the ministries of Jimmy Swaggart and David Terrell.

Nor had the charismatic revival been an unmixed success in the traditional churches. Many of the evangelical churches increased their opposition to the movement in the 1970s. The Churches of Christ produced thousands of tracts denying the Biblical validity of the charismatic experience. One editor labeled LeRoy Jenkins a "notorious fake healer and a con man"; another argued that the quality of miracles performed by modern revivalists in no way compared to those done by Jesus.[16] A team of enterprising ministers from Tulsa audited Oral Roberts' course on "The Holy Spirit in the Now" and offered to conduct exposés of it in Churches of Christ "to save souls from error." [17]

More dangerous to the independent ministries was the ability of the traditional churches to capture and domesticate most of their own charismatic members. Many of the major churches frowned on the charismatics in the 1960s, but by the mid-1970s the same bodies had taken a tolerant, if not supportive, position toward the experience. Neopentecostals were urged by their churches to disclaim the excesses associated with healing revivalism and to accommodate their charismatic experience to their own church tradition. Kilian McDonnell, one of the leading authorities on the Roman Catholic renewal, urged Catholic pentecostals to give due credit to the classical pentecostal origins of the revival but to beware other elements of that tradition:

> However, Catholic Pentecostals should make it clear that accepting and practicing the gift of healing does not mean that one must necessarily accept the style of healing ministry as practiced by the . . . healing evangelists. Here, as in many other areas, Catholic pentecostals have not always made the distinction between the manifestation of the Spirit through the gift of healing and the cultural baggage of classical Pentecostalism.[18]

The conception of the revival held by these church-oriented charismatics—who used the term neopentecostal to describe only the movement within the organized churches—clearly limited the usefulness of the independent ministries.

Most of the evangelists still felt estranged from the classical pentecostal denominations in the mid-1970s. Many remained convinced that real revival could not take place within the system. One leader of a large ministry charged that the leaders of the organized churches were "little people," incapable of accepting bold new programs. Small evangelists who tried to work within the churches lived in constant fear that they would be "busted." [19] On the other hand, one denominational leader labeled many of the healing claims of the revivalists "bunk" and wondered about the credibility of their claims of missionary successes.[20] In 1973, the Assemblies of God still had strict rules about the private ownership of religious institutions and tightly controlled the rights of the church's ministers to solicit funds.[21]

Perhaps most significant, the social changes that had taken place in the revival had estranged the evangelists from one another. During the early years of the healing revival personal acquaintance combined with a general uniformity in technique to unify the movement. By the 1970s many of the evangelists had never known the early leaders of the revival; a large number did not know one another. They were increasingly isolated. "I don't think Oral Roberts is really aware of what is going on in the inner guts of the charismatic movement," said one knowledgeable neopentecostal minister.[22] In time, lack of familiarity led to open criticism.

Most of the old-time revivalists were publicly reticent about the neopentecostal movement but privately critical. When they did criticize those who courted traditional Christians, their comments were veiled. When Oral Roberts joined the Methodist church, one deliverance minister pointedly told his supporters, "I will not join any church or organization not Full Gospel in doctrine and practice." [23] Many pentecostals were openly angered by Roberts' "compromise with the flesh." [24] Some of the campaigners ridiculed the charismatic seminars in modern hotel ballrooms and most admitted a growing estrangement between the revivalists and the Full Gospel Business Men's Fellowship International. Even those who remained sympathetic to the neopentecostals recognized deep cultural differences. "We're all for them," said one evangelist, "but I doubt that they would relate to our people. And probably we can't relate to them." [25] "We don't keep it in that minor key melody that they [neopentecostals] have," said another evangelist: "I want a little lively singing. I don't want 'Fill My Cup' all the time. . . . I want every once in a while 'I'm On My Way to Heaven Shouting Glory!' " [26] In their kindest evaluations, the modern campaigners wondered if the neopentecostal movement was not just a fad of religious dilettantes. The sterner prophets charged that those who had changed their style to minister to traditional middle-class Christians had "taken leprosy." [27] W. V. Grant concisely summed up the reservations of many old-timers: "You can't put live chickens under a dead hen." [28]

Moderate and neopentecostal ministers were just as skeptical of the work of the radical revivalists. Preachers like David Terrell and David Epley could find few supporters among the other independent ministers. Such preachers, said Gordon Lindsay, appealed to the grosser type of people and to the utterly naive.[29] Feeling themselves on the verge of respectability, neopentecostal leaders were appalled by the excesses of some campaigners. "I don't want to get mixed up with that crowd," said one moderate evangelist, "that crowd [that pleads] send me ten dollars and I'll heal you." [30] In his book that did much to publicize the pentecostal movement in the 1960s, John Sherrill saw charismatics faced with a choice between "the uncouth life of the Pentecostals and the aesthetic death of the older churches." He proposed as an alternative a synthesis on a higher plane than either.[31] Unfortunately, Sherrill's solution simply betrayed how deeply the movement was divided on social lines.

By the mid-1970s the charismatic revival had gone through a cultural evolution much like other historical religious movements. The independent ministries, once the spearhead of a simple revival with a powerful appeal to simple people, eventually adapted their styles to needs of vastly different social groups. What was once a well-defined and homogeneous revival became a heterogeneous movement, united only by a few doctrinal themes and a common heritage.

While the charismatic revival evolved in a variety of ways, most of the independent ministers remained classical cult-type religious leaders. Few of the charismatic revivalists showed any interest in gathering a denomination around them. The most powerful—Oral Roberts, Gordon Lindsay, Jack Coe, A. A. Allen—scrupulously eschewed such a path. The large independent ministries desired only to minister to a base of supporters throughout the Christian community. At the same time, like all cult movements, the healing revival was a seedbed for scores of new sects. The loyal followers of William Branham were in the early stages of sect formation, and many of the smaller revivalists established sect-type organizations. The more extreme revivalists, isolated from the organized churches, encouraged the founding of thousands of independent pentecostal tabernacles and gospel missions which surely will be the basis for future new sects. At the level of the neopentecostal revival, the emergence of large Christian centers in most major American cities may well prove the nascent beginnings of new churches.

The social pressures within the charismatic revival forced into view a growing number of old and new intellectual differences among pentecostals. Internal bickering existed at almost every level of the revival. Old doctrinal issues, such as the oneness belief and clashing codes of morality, again became major sources of friction. Sophisticated neopentecostals, particularly Roman Catholics, espoused a view linking charismatic gifts with the sacrament of baptism which was little understood by classical pentecostals.

The independent ministers of the 1970s also were threatened by the old nemesis of the revival—scandal. R. H. Montgomery's articles in the early 1960s had spotlighted the most fearful dilemma of miracle revivalism—how to account for its excesses and exaggerations. Every independent minister acknowledged that frauds existed in the revival; many related their own personal encounters with con men. Regularly among those healed by one evangelist in the 1960s was his tent manager. It was reported that the employee would jump from a stretcher (fully clothed) and dramatically run around the tent. Others allegedly discerned by communicating with a helper who had a short wave radio in his pocket.[32]

Marjoe Gortner

Public cynicism concerning the revival was further aroused in 1972 by Marjoe Gortner's exposé. Marjoe had been a relatively insignificant child evangelist in the 1950s, whose ministry had continued erratically as a young adult. He filmed his movie in a group of independent pentecostal churches on the radical fringe of the revival. According to one revivalist who frequently preached in the same churches, Marjoe's film could have brought out more scandal if he had broadened his perspective instead of concentrating "strictly on the sex and money" undertones of the revival. Not only had Marjoe missed much, he had created the appearance of scandal where none existed, charged his critic, by taking bits and parts of what was for most people a sincere experience and making it appear hypocritical.[33] Most of the leaders of the revival were angered by the Marjoe exposé; they believed that he had smeared the entire movement by the confession of his own sins. The carnival appeal of child evangelists which had developed during the height of the healing revival was widely disapproved of at the time, and few revivalists were shocked to learn that Marjoe had lacked conviction. But they did not believe that all revival ministries should be tarred with the same brush.

The leaders of the charismatic revival were dismayed by the instant celebrity gained by Marjoe. He became the television personality of the moment; his artistic and compelling critique of the revival reached a large audience. In their hearts, most of the evangelists knew that Marjoe's criticisms could easily be sustained. "He just got the wrong people," said one disgusted preacher.[34]

In fact, Marjoe said nothing that the revivalists had not said themselves. Every evangelist knew that some of their number had succumbed to the evil triumvirate—"women, money, and popularity." Admitted evangelist Kenneth Hagin, "It is no more than a con game with many." Another minister observed that he knew revivalists "by the dozen" who were adulterers: "You would be surprised if I started calling their names." Stories of the misappropriation of funds were common. Derek Prince judged that immorality was the greatest threat to the future of the revival.[35] Respected neopentecostal minister Don Basham acknowledged, "We have this problem of FALSE MINISTERS" who were guilty of dishonesty, immorality, and deception.[36] Despite all this, charismatic leaders repeatedly insisted that there was no evidence that independent evangelists as a whole were less ethical than other ministers.[37]

Reverend Ike

Perhaps more than Marjoe, the man who for a time seemed to threaten the integrity of the revival was the Reverend Frederick J. Eikerenkoetter II—usually known as Reverend Ike. The son of a South Carolina black Baptist preacher, Ike moved to Boston in 1964 and began a small storefront church. According to one evangelist, during the 1960s Ike visited the meetings of the most successful charismatic evangelists to study their techniques.[38] In 1966, he moved to New York City and purchased a large movie theater in Manhattan's Washington Heights which became the headquarters of his United Church and Science of Living Institute. Ike was a skilled healer, but in the late 1960s he began preaching prosperity almost exclusively. His ministry blossomed on radio and television in the 1970s. In 1973, he broadcast 350 times each week on radio and was carried weekly on 30 television stations in 18 states.[39]

Ike gaudily flaunted his success as a part of his message. "One trait especially distinguishes Ike," reported *Time* magazine in 1972, "his clear-eyed, unabashed love of money and other things material." [40] Ike's teaching, wrote one recent investigator, "makes Thomas Harris and Norman Vincent Peale sound like depressive paranoids with a bad case of the poor mouth." [41] Ike's prosperity message was summed up in his oft-repeated slogans: "You can't lose with the stuff I use"; "the lack of money is the root of all evil"; "money answers all things." Ike dispensed monthly "success ideas" to his regular supporters: "Send me the bottom part of this letter with your name still on it and I will send you this Fantastic Idea that will draw more money into your life. Don't be slow and don't be stingy." [42]

Such brash promises of financial reward, though only slightly more direct than those of other evangelists, made many charismatic leaders uncomfortable. Independent evangelists respected success, and Ike was a glowing example, but he increasingly became an embarrassment. Most of the evangelists were happy when Ike deserted fundamentalist Christian theology and began preaching the "Science of the Mind." Nearly all agreed that they belonged in a different category from Reverend Ike. [43]

The problems of the revival were, in general, the natural harvest of the personalities of the independent ministers. Their driving aspiration led them over and over again to innovation, to success, to excess, and to the brink of failure. If few were as brazen as Reverend Ike, most were equally ambitious. From the largest to the smallest, the reach of the evangelists often exceeded their grasp. The financial problems of Rex Humbard became national news, but they were typical of the struggles of hundreds of lesser evangelists. Every minister dreamed of launching a national television program. "The people that's on radio and television," said old-timer W. V. Grant, "is the ones that's getting the crowds." [44] The need for funds was endless; the competition was fierce. Hard-sell financial appeals were often the price of survival.

The small, marginal revivalists were sustained by a powerful combination of faith and hope. On one October Saturday evening in Birmingham, Alabama, evangelist Bob Phillips of Chattanooga, Tennessee, who advertised himself as the "leading deliverance evangelist of America," opened his service to an audience of less than twenty-five adults. [45] "No two revivals are alike," wrote a member of evangelist Dave Rich's team in 1972; "Some are like heaven on earth and the hot waves of glory roll, while others plunge to the stormy, icy depths of humility." He described with feeling a meeting in Madisonville, Kentucky:

Some nights here in Madisonville, the crowds are small and the offerings even smaller due to hazardous road conditions, flu and extremely cold weather.

[235

The spirit of God moves, however, and many people accept Jesus Christ, are filled with the Holy Ghost, healed, delivered, and are set free. And in God's mercy, somehow the financial burdens of the revival are met. After eight weeks, this meeting in Madisonville also closes. But the hundreds that intermittently attended and were blessed have scattered; the crowd is still small.[46]

Most clung to the belief that the Lord had a greater anointing for them in the future. There were indeed some con men and racketeers, but most of the evangelists shared the faith and hope of their followers.

It was their optimism and boldness that most singularly set apart the independent evangelists after World War II. From the mightiest to the lowliest they were, in the words of Gordon Lindsay, "rugged individualists." [47] Some, in the manner of Jack Coe, were recklessly bold; all were adventuresome. Most became independent understanding full well that they had become renegades.

Few religious movements in modern history boast more innovative or imaginative leaders. Most of the evangelists could give the same estimate that Franklin Hall gave of his own work: "This is the most unusual ministry, I believe, in the world today." [48] Charismatic preachers repeatedly staked their careers on a new vision or a new revelation. Few big business men would have been bold enough to make the dramatic policy changes inaugurated by Oral Roberts. In the large ministries a new leading of the Lord might be followed at the risk of millions of dollars; in the small ministries new moves were made at the risk of ultimate failure.

The heart of every independent ministry was the charisma of the evangelist. "In this type ministry," said a leader of the Allen organization, "the man out on the platform is the man. . . . That's where it all is." [49] The emotional pressures on the evangelists were enormous. The revivalists, said one perceptive observer, "are the loneliest men in the world." The victims of hero worshippers who demand super-father figures, the evangelists frequently found little outlet for their own human needs and weaknesses. One evangelist widely branded a hypocrite was, argued one close to him, a psychologically crippled man who found it impossible to live with his public image. His lapses into alcoholism and dissipation were as abhorrent to him as to others, but his turbulent personality drove him from the peaks of glory to the depths of sin. Incredibly burdened by work, adored by their disciples, tempted by floods of money, the successful revivalists became trapped men. "No one really knew him," said the wife of one evangelist.[50]

It is difficult to generalize about the sources of the unusual emotional strength of the evangelists. Many of them were products of tortured childhoods; a remarkable number were orphans. Jack Coe described being left by his mother: "I think I have known since that time just how Jesus felt when the world turned their backs on Him. I was just a little boy nine years old. . . . I thought my heart would break within me as I saw her going down the walk." [51] LeRoy Jenkins said of his childhood: "My mother was always busy working trying to support the children. Dad was always gone . . . out drinking and fighting. . . . In a sense I guess I never had a close mother or father. I never had a mother's or father's love which makes children feel wanted. . . . We were always ready to fight for our rights." [52] David Terrell wrote of his early life: "From my boyhood I have been different and could not understand myself, much less anyone else. At times I would desire to hide myself away from everyone and would sit for hours in deep concentration feeling the nearness of His presence. . . . I have lived a lonely, secluded life as far as the world is concerned, but I have seen many things in the Spirit that has enriched my life and ministry." [53] "He could never believe he was loved," said the wife of another evangelist, "and therefore never could accept love." [54] In the more militant ministers, their sense of rejection and persecution seemed clearly linked with the insecurity of their early lives. It also appeared to be the chief source of their personal magnetism.

Of course, not all the revivalists were children of tribulation. Oral Roberts' family, for instance, was poor but stable. Roberts was, however, the symbol of moderation in the revival. And even Oral Roberts often seemed introverted and insecure because of his pentecostal background, although he remained fiercely loyal to his convictions.[55] No twentieth century pentecostal totally escaped a feeling of rejection. "I know what it costs to be a pentecostal," said Derek Prince; "the pentecostal movement was the child of poverty and rejection." [56]

Every deliverance evangelist claimed a distinct call from God; most believed they had experienced a divine healing. To be "led by the Lord," or for Jesus to "speak to me in my heart," were conventional phrases in the movement that often meant little more than a strong personal conviction. But most evangelists believed that they had much more direct confrontations with God. "God spoke to me just as plain as anyone could speak," wrote evangelist David Terrell, "I actually heard His voice with my own ears and there's not a devil in hell or on earth that can make me doubt my calling." [57] Even with the passing of time and the advantage of hindsight, the most introspective evangelists remained convinced of their own personal experiences. With apparent candor H. Richard Hall described God's call to him: "I know He did. He really did. . . . Three or four times audibly. . . . Maybe it was a figment of my imagination. But if it was, all right, there had to be something. . . . And it was what I needed." [58]

Whatever one may think of the charismatic revival, almost to a man those who directed it were thoroughly convinced that they had seen the miracle power of God at work. Failure was ever present in the revival, and it troubled the more serious evangelists. "Oh, don't let any preacher or minister of healing tell you that he don't have any second thoughts," admitted evangelist H. Richard Hall.[59] "When you see failures, and you see them," said David Nunn, it could shake the faith of the boldest evangelist.[60] But the security of the true believer rested in the firm conviction that he had seen the deaf hear, the blind see, and the dead raised. And, in truth, under the big tents and in the crowded armories, individual lives were touched and changed in dramatic ways. No matter how calloused or depraved the minister, no one was more primed for the miracle, or more impressed by it, than the man who stretched out his hand to heal.

Some of the evangelists in the mid-1970s faced squarely the implications of psychosomatic healing. Every charismatic teacher believed that any illness could be healed by faith in God, but few would deny that the key to health could be in the power of the mind.[61] The teaching of many of the more sophisticated ministers was little more than a pentecostal version of positive thinking. Oral Roberts was quick to point out that psychosomatically ill people were ill nonetheless, and that their healing was an important blessing in their life.[62] Don Stewart argued that the revival was worthwhile regardless: "If no one was healed in my meeting . . . we're still doing a tremendous job. People are getting saved, people are getting blessed, people are getting other needs met." [63] Healing was important, but the revival had come to have a life of its own.

It seemed incredible in 1975 that the charismatic revival had risen to such heights. Chaotic and booming, it was the bright child of the ragged pentecostal movement of the early twentieth century. What of the future? Some were content to relive the glories of the past. To others, the time seemed ripe to conquer the world. The rapture drew near. In a recent stunning revelation, David Wilkerson, a towering figure in the neopentecostal world, predicted that a "persecution madness" was about to begin which would force the true gospel into retreat.[64]

Wilkerson's prophecy created a furor among many neopentecostal leaders who expressed grave reservations about such prophets of gloom and doom.[65] Wilkerson's vision, like those of prophets such as David

Terrell and Neal Frisby, revealed anew the extreme danger to the entire charismatic movement of subjectivism and individualism. A leading authority on Roman Catholic pentecostalism warned: "Both the more specific prophetic function and the more general desire to be 'led by the Spirit,' as all Pentecostals know, have been abused by willful or vain persons. The author has noted in some Catholic groups what amounts to gullibility with regard to prophetic utterance. Some accept a prophetic utterance, especially their own, with an absolute assurance that God has spoken." [66]

Divided, disorganized, haunted by its past, bewildered by its success, threatened by respectability, the charismatic revival plunged ahead. The late editor Alden West of *Logos Journal* asked, "Where is the Holy Spirit leading us?" [67] The voices of the prophets gave no sure answer. But modern charismatics remained undaunted in their faith that something greater was about to appear, something far surpassing the mighty works that earlier generations had witnessed. If one would only believe, all things were possible.

BIBLIOGRAPHICAL ESSAY

THE MOST IMPORTANT single source of information about healing revivalism is periodical literature. The evangelists early recognized the need for regular publications to keep their accomplishments before the public. A few magazines flourished which tried to report on the entire revival, but more often the successful evangelists published journals featuring their own ministries. The only significant collection of this material is the Pentecostal Collection at Oral Roberts University. Frequently, the evangelists themselves did not preserve files of their literature.

The most important single source of information about the early months of the revival is *The Voice of Healing*. Beginning in 1947, the monthly magazine was published in Shreveport, Louisiana, by Jack Moore and Gordon Lindsay to promote the ministry of William Branham. Lindsay edited the magazine with the help of Anna Jeanne Moore. In the 1950s the paper was published in Dallas and was the most powerful voice of the revival. In March 1958, Lindsay changed its name to *World-Wide Revival* but returned to the original name eighteen months later. By the 1960s it had become almost solely the organ of the Gordon Lindsay ministry. In May 1967, Lindsay changed the name to its present title, *Christ for the Nations*.

Oral Roberts established the first important magazine published by an independent ministry. His magazine went through a series of name changes: *Healing Waters* (November 1947–August 1953), *America's Healing Magazine* (September 1953–December 1955), *Healing* (January 1956–July 1956), and *Abundant Life* (July 1956–   ). Roberts' magazine had a number of able editors, but the evangelist himself exercised close control over its contents.

A number of other journals offer some insight into the early years of the revival. Until his death in 1947, *Golden Grain* (1926–1957) was the organ of pioneer evangelist Charles S. Price. For a decade afterward it was edited by Evelyn C. Carvell and featured the work of evangelist Lorne Fox. Price was probably the most astute observer of the beginnings of the revival.

Pentecost (1947–1966) was a quarterly edited by Donald Gee and published in London under the auspices of the World Conference of Pentecostal Churches. After the death of Gee, the magazine lapsed. In 1971, at the request of the conference, Percy Brewster began editing *World Pentecost* in Cardiff, Wales. Gee's comments on the revival in the 1950s furnish the most sophisticated assessment by a pentecostal.

Bibliographical Essay

The magazines of the organized pentecostal churches frequently carried reports of the meetings of the independent revivalists until about 1952. The two journals most directly concerned were the *Pentecostal Evangel* (1919–), the official organ of the Assemblies of God, and the *Pentecostal Holiness Advocate* (1917–), the magazine of the Pentecostal Holiness church. After the rift opened between the independent evangelists and the organized churches, the pentecostal periodicals ignored the revival. Church leaders obviously decided that their purposes were best served by avoiding awkward public confrontations.

During the 1950s the magazine most loyal to the work of William Branham was the *Herald of Faith* (1933–1970), published in Chicago by Joseph Mattsson-Boze. Over two hundred of Branham's sermons are available on tape and many have been transcribed. They are circulated by the Spoken Word Publications of Jeffersonville, Indiana. Issued in a magazine format under the title *The Spoken Word*, the booklets are published irregularly and without dates.

Most of the other early leaders of the revival published magazines. Jack Coe's magazine went through a series of names: *Herald of Healing* (1952–1954), *Jack Coe's International Healing Magazine* (1955–1962), and *The Christian Challenge* (1962–). *Miracle Magazine* was started by A. A. Allen in 1954. Initially edited by Allen's wife, Lexie, *Miracle Magazine* pioneered many techniques in reporting miracle revivalism. The magazine continued to be the voice of the Don Stewart Evangelistic Association after the death of Allen. T. L. Osborn's *Faith Digest* (1953–) was one of the most widely circulated papers. *The Healing Messenger* (1949–1956) was the voice of William Freeman Evangelistic Campaigns. O. L. Jaggers' paper was called *The World Fellowship News* (1956–?). Wings of Healing, Inc., the organization begun in the 1930s by Thomas Wyatt and continued by his widow, Evelyn, has published *The March of Faith* since 1942.

A large number of somewhat later and smaller journals are important sources of information. In 1962, W. V. Grant, who had long written regularly in *The Voice of Healing*, began publishing *The Voice of Deliverance* (1962–1965). Grant subsequently changed the name of his paper to *Evangelize* (1965–1966) and then to *TVD* (1967–). Grant's paper was important both because of Grant's broad acquaintance with the other revivalists and because he soon developed a huge mailing list of over 2,000,000 names. Evangelist David Nunn, whose headquarters were in Dallas, published *The Healing Messenger* (1963–) to feature his ministry. The voice of Missionary Evangelism, Inc., the ministry of John E. Douglas, Sr., was *World Evangelism* (1959–). R. W. Culpepper's World-Wide Revival Crusades, Inc., published *World-Wide Revival Reports* (1961–1970). The organ of the Lester Sumrall Evangelistic Assn., Inc., was *World Harvest* (1962–). *Evangelistic Times* (1961–) was the publication of A. C. Valdez. M. A. Daoud began early publicizing his meetings in *Miracles and Missions Digest* (1955–). H. Richard Hall began publishing a monthly magazine in 1956 which went through a series of names: *The Healing Broadcast* (1956–1960), *The Healing Digest* (1960–1962), *The Shield of Faith*

(1962–   ). Kenneth Gaub's magazine was *Faith in Action* (1959–   ). Franklin Hall published a large quarterly magazine, *Miracle Word* (1965–   ) in Phoenix, Arizona.

Most of the important campaigners still active in the 1970s had promotional magazines. The most impressive of the papers was *Deeper Life* (1964–   ), published by Morris Cerullo's World Evangelism. A professionally produced monthly, it was Cerullo's basic means of communication with his supporters. On the other extreme was *The Evangelist* (1970–   ), published by the Jimmy Swaggart Evangelistic Association. Swaggart, whose forte was radio and television, published a flimsy four-page report on his meetings each month. *The End Time Messenger* (1966–   ) was published by the New Testament Holiness Church, which was the organization of David Terrell. Neal Frisby's *20th Century Life* (1965–   ) was a bimonthly which was printed somewhat irregularly. LeRoy Jenkins' paper also was published irregularly. Originally issued under the name *Revivals* (1961), it later was called *Revival* (1961–1966?) and *Revival of America* (1968–   ). An attractive monthly titled *The Good Shepherd Magazine* (1970–   ) was published to promote the David Epley ministry. Reverend Ike's magazine, published semimonthly, was called *Action* (1966–   ). The publication of the Cathedral of Tomorrow, Rex Humbard's large church in Akron, was *The Answer* (1958–   ). It originally was published under the title *Echoes from Calvary* (1953–1958).

Scores of smaller ministries published regular magazines or newsletters. Some examples were: *Faith in Action* (1961–   ), edited by R. G. Hardy of Baltimore; *New Horizons* (1961–   ), the organ of the W. T. Jeffers ministry in Tulsa; *The Power of the Holy Ghost* (1955?–   ), published by Grace Cathedral in Akron, Ohio, pastored by Ernest Angley; *Deeper Faith* (1972?–   ), published by young evangelist Vic Coburn in Portland, Oregon; *New Day* (1970–   ), which succeeded *Missions Thru Faith* (1954–1970) as the organ of Don Powell of Indiana, Pennsylvania; *Living Hope* (1969–   ), the organ of Dave Rich Revival Crusades of Louisville, Kentucky; and *Faith and Vision Magazine* (1972–   ), published in Dallas in the interest of the ministry of Ray Bloomfield.

The neopentecostal movement of the 1960s produced a profusion of new journals. The most important was *Logos Journal* (1971–   ), founded and published by Daniel Malachuk and edited by Alden West. *Logos Journal* traced its history through the *Herald of Faith–Harvest Time* (1970–1971), which was a union of Joseph Mattsson-Boze's *Herald of Faith* and *Harvest Time*, a monthly edited by a charismatic Mennonite, Gerald Derstine. Through the *Herald of Faith*, *Logos Journal* was linked both to the Branham revival and to the pentecostal tradition of the prewar years.

Extremely important in the emergence of the neopentecostal movement was the small monthly, *The Full Gospel Business Men's Voice* (1953–   ). Until 1962, *Voice* was edited by Thomas R. Nickel and was the chief source of news of the revival after the decline of *The Voice of Healing*. In the mid-1960s *Voice* became a leading herald of neopentecostalism. In 1963, the FGBMFI began publishing a youth quarterly entitled *Vision* (1963–   ). Some of the most prominent names in neopentecostal publishing, including Nickel, Dan Malachuk, Jerry Jensen, and Raymond Becker, worked with the publications of the FGBMFI in the 1960s. As the official organ of the fellowship, *Voice* remained an important measure of that movement.

After his reportedly bitter departure from the editorship of *Voice* in 1962, Thomas R. Nickel began editing a small neopentecostal quarterly, *Testimony* (1962–   ). The paper was published by The Great Commission, International, an organization which promoted mission work and published religious literature. Quite a number of neopentecostal evangelists published papers promoting their ministries. David Wilkerson's organization, Teen Challenge, Inc., published a small bimonthly paper, *The Cross and the Switchblade* (1963–   ). Wilkerson's paper began as little more than a newsletter, but, as was the case with many of the publications, the magazine became more and more professional as the ministry grew. Evangelist John H. Osteen began publishing *Praise* in 1962. Kenneth E. Hagin published a small newsletter in Tulsa to promote his work, *The Word of Faith* (1967–   ). An attractive monthly, *Heartbeat* (1970–   ), was edited by Eldon Purvis in Ft. Lauderdale, Florida.

Perhaps the most important cooperative publishing effort among the neopentecostal independent ministers was *New Wine* (1969–   ), published by the Christian Growth Ministries, Inc., in Ft. Lauderdale, Florida. The magazine primarily was associated with the ministries of Derek Prince, Bob Mumford, and Don Basham, but many other neopentecostal ministers contributed to it.

A number of other individuals attempted to establish broad neopentecostal magazines. From 1960 to 1968 John Meyers of Northbridge, California, published a general neopentecostal quarterly under the title *Voice in the Wilderness*. *Acts* (1967–1969?) was a news magazine of the neopentecostal movement edited by Jerry Jensen, but it was short-lived. A beautiful magazine edited by Robert Ewing in Waco, Texas, *Campus Fellowship* (1967–   ), was aimed at promoting the charismatic movement on the college campus.

A number of journals were published to promote neopentecostalism within specific denominations. *Sharing* (1932–   ) was "an International Journal of Christian Healing" established by John Gaynor Banks. It was the organ of the Order of St. Luke within the Anglican church. More directly associated with the revival were "*He Is Able*," "a journal dedicated to aid the revival of the Ministry of Healing in the Methodist Church"; *Trinity* (1961–1963?), an Episcopal monthly which included neopentecostal leaders David duPlessis and Harold Bredesen on its staff; and *New Covenant* (1969–   ), the organ of the Roman Catholic charismatic renewal.

Two older journals which showed some sympathy for the revival were the *Herald of Hope* (1940–   ), published by the Christ Faith Mission in Los Angeles and the *Herald of His Coming* (1941–   ), which was an evangelical newspaper printed in Los Angeles.

In addition to these fairly conventional publications, the independent ministries after World War II published a staggering mass and variety of other material. Many of the ministries depended heavily on mail solicitations for their support. Some of the neopentecostal ministers published elaborate newsletters and sales catalogs: for instance, Bob Mumford's *Life Changers* and Derek Prince's *A Personal Message*. Some very unusual materials were published by the ministers. For four years Healing Waters, Inc., circulated a comic book series entitled *Oral Roberts' True Stories* (1956–1959). Since 1967 evangelist Neal Frisby has printed a series of prophetic "Scrolls" which assumed the dignity of scripture to his followers. Reverend Ike sent his followers monthly "success ideas" to enhance their "joy of living."

Since the early 1950s the independent ministers have preached thousands of sermons on radio and television. They have, as a result, left a large body of recorded and taped material. Many films and television tapes made in the 1950s are still extant and thousands of tapes of sermons are scattered throughout the country. Probably the best collection of this material is in the Pentecostal Collection at Oral Roberts University, but it is quite small. The followers of each evangelist are the best sources of information about such materials. The followers of William Branham were particularly zealous in recording his sermons in the last decade of his life and over 200 Branham sermons, most of them long, are available on tape. Of course, many of the evangelists were still active preachers in the mid-1970s, but it was impossible to recapture the mood of the early days of the revival. It is also very difficult to assess the quality of a charismatic ministry without witnessing the evangelist at work.

Personal contact with the participants in the revival—both the evangelists and the believers—was extremely helpful in writing this book. I attended over a hundred revival meetings and have discussed the revival with hundreds of people. I learned something about the meaning of the revival from most of them, although time had often dimmed memories of specific facts. Some of the leaders of the revival were reluctant to discuss their work with me, others were extremely open and helpful. In general, the independent ministers are wary of researchers, but are quite anxious to present their cases if they believe they will receive an unbiased hearing.

I taped formal interviews with twenty-six participants in the revivals. Copies of most of these tapes have been deposited in the Pentecostal Collection at Oral Roberts University. The interviews were conducted as follows: Lexie Allen, Dallas, Texas, December 6 and 7, 1973; Sven Blomberg, Miracle Valley, Arizona, February 9, 1973; Lee Braxton, Tulsa, Oklahoma, December 18, 1973; David Cerullo, San Diego, California, December 31, 1973; Thelma Chaney, Tulsa, Oklahoma, June 21, 1972; Pearry Green, Tucson, Arizona, December 27, 1973; W. V. Grant, Dallas, Texas, December 15, 1973; Kenneth Hagin, Birmingham, Alabama, May 24, 1973; Franklin Hall, Phoenix, Arizona, July 20, 1972; H. Richard Hall, Cleveland, Tennessee, May 31, 1972; C. B. Hollis, Dallas, Texas, July 28, 1972; Juanita Coe Hope, Waxahachie, Texas, December 6, 1973; LeRoy

Jenkins, Columbus, Ohio, April 7, 1974; Gayle F. Lewis, Springfield, Missouri, July 18, 1974; Freda Lindsay, Dallas, Texas, December 7, 1973; Gordon Lindsay, Dallas, Texas, July 27, 1972; Jack Moore, Shreveport, Louisiana, December 5, 1973; David Nunn, Little Rock, Arkansas, September 2, 1972; Anna Jeanne Price, Shreveport, Louisiana, December 5, 1973; Derek Prince, Ft. Lauderdale, Florida, January 31, 1974; Kent Rogers, Cincinnati, Ohio, July 7, 1972; R. W. Schambach, Miami, Florida, February 13, 1974; Mary Allen Smith, Miracle Valley, Arizona, July 24, 1972; Don Stewart, Cincinnati, Ohio, July 7, 1972; Jimmy Swaggart, Baton Rouge, Louisiana, November 29, 1973; Don Walker, Miracle Valley, Arizona, February 9, 1973.

A very large number of books, many of them little more than pamphlets, have been published by the participants in the revival. Much of their writing was doctrinal, but some of it was autobiographical and historical. The quality of this literature varied widely. In addition, a few of the major figures in the revival have been the subjects of popular and scholarly books.

The literature about the revivalists of the early twentieth century is very inadequate. Gordon Lindsay's *The Life of John Alexander Dowie* ([Dallas]: The Voice of Healing Publishing Co. [1951]) is the best available study of Dowie. The best book about Aimee Semple McPherson is Lately Thomas, *Storming Heaven* (New York: William Morrow and Company, 1970). Also useful are McPherson's autobiography, *The Story of My Life* (rev. ed.; Hollywood: An International Correspondents' Publication [1951]) and Nancy Barr Mavity, *Sister Aimee* (New York: Doubleday, Doran & Company, 1931). The only source of information about John G. Lake is Gordon Lindsay, ed., *The John G. Lake Sermons* (5th ed.; Dallas: The Voice of Healing Publishing Co. [1949]). Some biographical information can be gleaned from two books written by Mrs. M. B. Woodworth-Etter: *Questions and Answers on Divine Healing* (rev. and enl. ed.; Indianapolis: Mrs. M. B. Woodworth-Etter, n.d.) and *Marvels and Miracles* (Indianapolis: Mrs. M. B. Woodworth-Etter [1922]). Stanley Howard Frodsham wrote a popular biography of Smith Wigglesworth, *Smith Wigglesworth: Apostle of Faith* (reprint; London: Assemblies of God Publishing House, 1965). A small book about another English evangelist is Albert W. Edsor, *George Jeffreys, Man of God* (London: Ludgate Press Limited [1964]). An early biography of F. F. Bosworth is Eunice M. Perkins, *Joybringer Bosworth* (Dayton: John J. Scruby, 1921). A brief sketch of the work of Raymond T. Richey, originally published in 1925, is Eloise May Richey, *What God Hath Wrought in the Life of Raymond T. Richey* (rev. ed.; Houston: United Prayer and Workers League [1937]). The best source of information about the influential ministry of Charles S. Price is Charles S. Price, *The Story of My Life* (3rd ed.; Pasadena: Charles S. Price Publishing Co., 1944). A brief sketch of Lorne Fox, who was deeply influenced by Price, is found in Lorne F. Fox, *This Is My Story* (Naselle, Washington [Lorne Fox], n.d.). Because his ministry survived him, the life of Thomas Wyatt has been the subject of much writing. The best book about his work is Basil Miller, *Grappling with Destiny* (Los Angeles: Wings of Healing [1962]). Other good sources of information on this ministry include *A Memorial Tribute to Thomas Wyatt* (Los Angeles: Wings of Healing [1964]) and Thomas Wyatt, *Wings of Healing* (4th ed.; Portland, Oregon: Ryder Printing Co. [1944]).

A series of books about the life of Oral Roberts has been approved by his ministry. They tell much about the background of Roberts and also reflect the changing image of the ministry. The latest is Oral Roberts, *The Call* (New York: Doubleday & Company, 1972). Earlier useful books are Oral Roberts, *Oral Roberts' Life Story* (Tulsa: Oral Roberts [1952]); E. M. and Claudius Roberts, *Our Ministry and Our Son Oral* (Tulsa: Oral Roberts, 1960); and Oral Roberts, *My Story* (Tulsa and New York: Summit Book Company, 1961).

Much less has been written about William Branham. However, during the early years of the revival, the most popular single book was probably Gordon Lindsay's, *William Branham: A Man Sent from God* (4th ed.; Jeffersonville, Indiana: William Branham, 1950). Another important book about Branham's early work is Julius Stadsklev, *William Branham, A Prophet Visits South Africa* (Minneapolis: Julius Stadsklev [1952]). The best source of information on Branham's later years, although strongly colored by the views of its author, is Pearry Green, *The Acts of the Prophet* (Tucson: Tucson Tabernacle, n.d.).

Something has been written about most of the other major figures in the revival. Very useful is Gordon Lindsay's autobiography, *The Gordon Lindsay Story* (Dallas: The Voice of Healing Publishing Co., n.d.). A book which gives brief sketches of twenty-three evangelists is Gordon Lindsay, *Men Who Heard from Heaven* ([Dallas]: The Voice of Healing Publishing Co. [1953]). Two brief books about Jack Coe are Jack Coe, *The Story of Jack Coe* (Dallas: Herald of Healing [1955]) and Juanita Coe, *The Jack Coe I Know* ([Dallas]: Herald of Healing [1956]). The story of the Coe trial in Miami is told in [Jack Coe], *Tried . . . But Freed!* ([Dallas]: Herald of Healing [1956]). Two books which give some biographical information about T. L. Osborn are T. L. Osborn, *Revival Fires Sweep Cuba* (Tulsa: The Voice of Faith Ministry [1952]) and T. L. Osborn, *Young in Faith* (Tulsa: T. L. Osborn Evangelistic Association, 1964). A popularly written autobiography of A. A. Allen appeared shortly before his death: A. A. Allen with Walter Wagner, *Born to Lose, Bound to Win* (Garden City, N. Y.: Doubleday & Company, 1970). Earlier works about Allen which should be consulted are: Lexie E. Allen, *God's Man of Faith and Power* (Dallas: A. A. Allen, 1954) and A. A. Allen, *My Cross* ([n.p.: A. A. Allen, 1957]). The heir of the Allen ministry, Don Stewart, also published a popular autobiography: Don Stewart with Walter Wagner, *The Man from Miracle Valley* (Long Beach, Cal.: The Great Horizons Company [1971]).

Many of the other evangelists published materials about themselves. Some examples are: Velmer Gardner, *My Life Story* (Springfield, Mo.: Velmer Gardner Evangelistic Association [1954]); R. W. Culpepper, *100,000 Miles of Miracles* (Dallas: R. W. Culpepper, n.d.); T. M. Hicks, *Capturing the Nations in the Name of the Lord* ([Los Angeles: Manifest Deliverance and World Wide Evangelism, 1956]); and Tommy Hicks, *Millions Found Christ* (Los Angeles:

International Headquarters of Tommy Hicks Manifest Deliverance and World-wide Evangelism [1956]).

Many, though not all, of the evangelists now preaching have published autobiographical material. Two booklets by Morris Cerullo are helpful: *From Judaism to Christianity* (Dallas: The Voice of Healing [1957]) and *Portrait of a Prophet* (San Diego: World Evangelism [1965]). W. V. Grant has written an autobiographical book entitled *The Grace of God in My Life* (enl. ed. [Dallas]: W. V. Grant [1952]). LeRoy Jenkins also published an autobiographical sketch, *Somebody Up There Loves Me* (Tampa: LeRoy Jenkins Evangelistic Association, 1965). The best study of David Nunn is David Nunn, *The Life and Ministry of David Nunn* (Dallas: David Nunn, n.d.). W. V. Grant has written books about several of the smaller ministers. Grant's book, *Creative Miracles* ([Dallas: Faith Clinic, n.d.]), is the story of Neal Frisby; his *The Sign-Gift Ministry in the Twentieth Century* ([Dallas: Faith Clinic, n.d.]) is an interview with evangelist James Dunn. Some other examples of the type of biographical information available about the smaller evangelists are M. A. Daoud, *Bringing Back the King!* ([Dallas: Voice of Miracles and Missions, n.d.]); Don Powell, *My Struggle to Survive* (Daytona Beach, Fla.: World Evangelism Press, 1965); *Little David's Life Story* ([Norfolk]: no pub., n.d.); Mrs. R. R. Coyne, *When God Smiled on Ronald Coyne* (improved ed.; Pierce City, Mo.: Ronald R. Coyne, 1963).

Several of the more prominent neopentecostal ministries are the subjects of books. Kenneth E. Hagin has written an autobiography: *I Believe in Visions* (Old Tappan, N.J.: Fleming H. Revell Company [1972]). A study of the life of Rex Humbard is Rex Humbard and Joyce Parks, *Put God on Main Street* ([Akron: The Cathedral of Tomorrow, 1970]). Kathryn Kuhlman has written a number of books. Two of the most influential are *I Believe in Miracles* (11th printing; Englewood Cliffs, N.J.: Prentice-Hall, 1968) and *God Can Do It Again* (Englewood Cliffs, N.J.: Prentice-Hall [1969]). The best book about the work of Kuhlman is Allen Spraggett, *Kathryn Kuhlman: The Woman Who Believes in Miracles* (New York: The World Publishing Company, 1970). A short book about another major figure in the neopentecostal revival is Thomas R. Nickel, *The Shakarian Story* (2nd ed.; Los Angeles: Full Gospel Business Men's Fellowship International [1964]). Basic books on the ministry of David Wilkerson include: David Wilkerson and John and Elizabeth Sherrill, *The Cross and the Switchblade* ([New York]: Bernard Geis Associate Gospel Publishing House Edition [1963]); Ruth Wilkerson Harris, *It Was Good Enough for Father* (Old Tappan, N.J.: Fleming H. Revell Company [1969]); David Wilkerson, *The Story of Teen Challenge* ([Brooklyn: Teen Challenge], n.d.). The most important ministry to grow out of Wilkerson's work is described in Nicky Cruz and Jamie Buckingham, *Run Baby Run* (Plainfield, N.J.: Logos International [1968]).

Hundreds of books on healing have come out of the revival. Most of the material is repetitious but sometimes a minister developed a unique turn in his teaching. The most important doctrinal statement in the early days of the revival

[247

was probably Oral Roberts, *If You Need Healing Do These Things* (rev. ed.; 8th printing; Tulsa: Oral Roberts, 1956). A list of other books on this subject by the early evangelists includes: Oral Roberts, *Your Healing Problems and How to Solve Them* (Tulsa: Oral Roberts, 1966); Oral Roberts, *The Miracle Book* (Tulsa: Pinook Publications [1972]); Jack Coe, *Wilt Thou Be Made Whole?* (Dallas: Herald of Healing, n.d.); Jack Coe, *Curing the Incurable* (Dallas: Herald of Healing, n.d.); T. L. Osborn, *Healing en Masse* (Tulsa: T. L. Osborn [1958]); T. L. Osborn, *Healing the Sick* (14th ed.; Tulsa: T. L. Osborn Evangelistic Association [1959]); T. L. Osborn, *Frontier Evangelism* (3rd ed.; Tulsa: T. L. Osborn [1962]); W. V. Grant, *Raising the Dead* ([Dallas: W. V. Grant], n.d.); W. V. Grant, *Must I Pray for a Miracle?* ([Dallas: W. V. Grant], n.d.); David Nunn, *Declaration Faith* (Dallas: Bible Revival Evangelistic Assoc., n.d.); T. M. Hicks, *Manifest Deliverance for You Now!* (Lancaster, Cal. [T. M. Hicks, 1952]). O. L. Jaggers' doctrine on immortality is discussed in his book *Life and Immortality in the Book of St. John* ([Los Angeles: O. L. Jaggers, 1959]). Franklin Hall's unique teaching on the healing power of Holy Ghost fire may be studied in two books by Hall: *Formula for Raising the Dead* (San Diego: Franklin Hall [1960]) and *Our Divine Healing Obligation* (rev. ed. [Phoenix: Franklin Hall], n.d.). A plea for moderation is made in Donald Gee, *Trophimus I Left Sick* (London: Elim Publishing Co., 1952). Two recent books on healing by neopentecostal ministers are John H. Osteen, *How to Release the Power of God* (Humble, Texas: John H. Osteen [1968]) and Derek Prince, *Prayer and Fasting* (Old Tappan, N.J.: Fleming H. Revell Company, 1973). A detailed study of healing by a Roman Catholic charismatic is Francis MacNutt, O.P., *Healing* (Notre Dame, Indiana: Ave Maria Press [1974]).

Quite a number of the revivalists have published books on the prosperity theme. Two widely-circulated books on this subject are Oral Roberts and G. H. Montgomery, eds., *God's Formula for Success and Prosperity* (Tulsa: Oral Roberts [1955]) and Gordon Lindsay, *God's Master Key to Success and Prosperity* (Dallas: The Voice of Healing Publishing Company, 1959). A. A. Allen published a variety of books on the subject of prosperity and its relation to giving: A. A. Allen, *The Secret to Scriptural Financial Success* (Miracle Valley, Ariz.: A. A. Allen Publications [1953]); A. A. Allen, *Your Christian Dollar* (Dallas: A. A. Allen [1958]); A. A. Allen, *Time Does Not End at Sunset* (Miracle Valley, Ariz.: A. A. Allen, n.d.); A. A. Allen, *Power to Get Wealth* (Miracle Valley, Ariz.: A. A. Allen Revivals [1963]); and A. A. Allen, *God's Guarantee to Bless and Prosper You Financially* (Miracle Valley, Ariz.: A. A. Allen Revivals [1968]).

A subject which appears repeatedly in the literature of the revival is demonology. Two early books on the subject are Thomas Wyatt, *The Work of Demons* (Portland, Oregon: Wings of Healing [1948]) and W. V. Grant, *Power to Detect Demons* ([Dallas: Grant's Faith Clinic], n.d.). Three typical books on the subject by A. A. Allen are *Invasion from Hell* (Miracle Valley, A. A. Allen Publications [1953]), *The Curse of Madness* (Miracle Valley, Ariz.: A. A. Allen

Publications [1963]), and *The Burning Demon of Lust* (Miracle Valley, Ariz.: [A. A. Allen, 1963]). Two other books on this subject by early evangelists are Lester Sumrall, *Seven Ways to Recognize Demon Power Today* (2nd ed. [South Bend, Ind.: Lester Sumrall Evangelistic Association], n.d.) and Thelma Chaney, *The Downfall of Demons* (Tulsa: H. A. and Thelma Chaney [1953]).

The neopentecostal movement also has been marked by a fascination with demon possession. Gordon Lindsay explored the subject in two multivolume series: *The Chaos of Psychics* (4 vols.; Dallas: Christ for the Nations, 1970) and *Sorcery in America* (3 vols.; Dallas: Christ for the Nations, 1971). Three books on demons by prominent neopentecostal leaders are: Kenneth E. Hagin, *The Origin and Operation of Demons* (Tulsa: Kenneth E. Hagin, n.d.); Derek Prince, *Expelling Demons* ([Seattle: Derek Prince], n.d.); and Don Basham, *Deliver Us from Evil* (Washington Depot, Conn.: Chosen Books [1972]).

Hundreds of prophetic books have been written by charismatic ministers. Sometimes the evangelists wrote interpretations of Biblical prophecies and sometimes they revealed prophetic visions of their own. Interpretations of Biblical prophecies were particularly important in the thought of William Branham. Three of the most important of Branham's prophetic interpretations are: *An Exposition of the Seven Church Ages* ([Tucson: Rev. William Branham], n.d.); *The Revelation of the Seven Seals* (Tucson: Spoken Word Publications, 1967); and *The Laodicean Church Age* (no publication information). Two other examples of early books of prophecy are A. A. Allen, *My Vision of the Destruction of America* (Miracle Valley, Ariz.: A. A. Allen Publications [1954]) and David O. Nunn, *When America Fights Russia* ([Dallas]: Bible Revival Evangelistic Ass'n. [1964]). Gordon Lindsay was particularly interested in prophetic interpretation. For an example of his writing on this subject, see Gordon Lindsay, *The World Today in Prophecy* ([Dallas]: The Voice of Healing Publishing Co. [1953]). While the neopentecostal revival has not produced the same amount of prophetic literature, it is by no means totally lacking. David Wilkerson's controversial prophetic book *The Vision* (Old Tappan, N.J.: Fleming H. Revell Company [1973]) is a good example.

A number of good books have been published outlining pentecostal teaching about the baptism of the Holy Spirit and the gifts of the Spirit. An older book on this subject which is still useful is Donald Gee, *The Ministry-Gifts of Christ* (Springfield, Mo.: Gospel Publishing House [1930]). Two books on the subject by early leaders of the revival are Oral Roberts, *The Baptism with the Holy Spirit* (Tulsa: Oral Roberts [1964]) and Gordon Lindsay, *All About the Gifts of the Spirit* (Dallas: The World Correspondence Course, 1962). Three good books on the subject by neopentecostal ministers are Derek Prince, *Purposes of Pentecost* ([Seattle: Derek Prince], n.d.); John H. Osteen, *The Supernatural Gifts of the Spirit* (Houston: John H. Osteen Evangelistic Association [1961]); and Don A. Basham, *A Handbook on Holy Spirit Baptism* (Reading and Berkshire, G.B.: Gateway Outreach [1969]).

Hundreds of other doctrinal books have been published by the independent revivalists. A good summary of Oral Roberts' emphasis on positive thinking may be found in Oral Roberts, *God Is a Good God* (Indianapolis and New York: The Bobbs-Merrill Company [1960]). Gordon Lindsay's role as peacemaker is outlined in Gordon Lindsay, *Crusade for World Fellowship* (Dallas: The Voice of Healing Publishing Co., n.d.). A good sample of Jack Coe's rustic style and his bitterness toward organized religion may be found in Jack Coe, *Apostles and Prophets . . . in the Church Today?* (Dallas: Herald of Healing, 1954). A. A. Allen was one of the most prolific writers among the revivalists. For a sampling of his books, see *My Besetting Sin* (Dallas: A. A. Allen, n.d.); *The Fatal Word That Will Jam Hell to the Doors* (Dallas: A. A. Allen Publications, n.d.); *How to Take the Answer from God* ([Miracle Valley, Ariz.: A. A. Allen Publications], n.d.); and *Prisons with Stained Glass Windows* (Miracle Valley, Ariz.: A. A. Allen Revivals, 1963).

Franklin Hall wrote a number of doctrinal books on dieting and body-felt salvation. His book *Atomic Power with God* (4th ed. [Phoenix: Franklin Hall, 1965]) was originally published in 1946 and sold several hundred thousand copies. Other doctrinal books by Hall include *Glorified Fasting* (rev. ed.; San Diego: Franklin Hall, 1961); *The Fasting Prayer* (3rd ed.; Phoenix: Franklin Hall, 1967); *Sex Facts for Christians* (San Diego: Franklin Hall, 1956); and *The Body-Felt Salvation* (Phoenix: Hall Deliverance Foundation, 1968). Hall's wife, Helen, is the author of *The New Diet* ([Phoenix: Helen Hall, 1970]).

Many of the books published by the independent ministries combine doctrinal, historical and biographical materials. Those interested in the Morris Cerullo ministry should read Morris Cerullo, *Proof Producers* (San Diego: World Evangelism [1972]) and Morris Cerullo, *Wind Over the 20th Century* (San Diego: World Evangelism [1973]). An informative book by LeRoy Jenkins is *God Will Burn Your Barley Fields* (Tampa: LeRoy Jenkins Evangelistic Association [1965]). A rare pamphlet published by Neal Frisby is *The Spiritual Veil Opens* ([Phoenix]: 20th Century Life, 1972). A pamphlet on the problems of women preachers was written by Juanita Coe Hope, *Should Women Preach* (Dallas: Christian Challenge, n.d.). Some of the smaller evangelists published good doctrinal studies. Two useful books by Ray H. Bloomfield are *Secrets of Faith* (Dallas: R. H. Bloomfield, 1971) and *How to Defeat Your Fears* (Dallas: R. H. Bloomfield, 1972). Thelma Chaney, whose small ministry is located in Tulsa, wrote widely about the history and doctrine of the revival. Some of her books are: *Babylon Marches Again* (Tulsa: Thelma Chaney, n.d.); *The Power of God on Exhibition* (Tulsa: TOPService, 1954); *The Church One Body* (Tulsa: H. A. and Thelma Chaney [1960]); *The Power of the Unveiled Son* (Tulsa: All Hours Business Service [1968]); and *The New Wine of the Kingdom* (Tulsa: Lighthouse Gospel Center, 1968).

One of the more specialized doctrinal statements to come out of the neopentecostal revival is David Wilkerson, *David Wilkerson's Jesus Person Maturity Manual* (4th printing; Glendale, Cal.: G/L Publications [1971]). Directed at ghetto youth, over 100,000 of the manuals had been distributed by 1971.

Bibliographical Essay

Two recent popular books gave somewhat distorted views of the revival. Steven S. Gaines' *The Life of Marjoe Gortner* (New York: Harper & Row, 1972) resurrected the Elmer Gantry stereotype of evangelical revivalism. James Morris' book, *The Preachers* (New York: St. Martin's Press, 1973), also seemed to supporters of the revival a hostile book. Morris, who apparently had little concept of the unity and distinctiveness of charismatic revivalism, discussed only the most visible of the healing revivalists (Roberts, Allen, Kuhlman, Humbard, and Rev. Ike).

Few people within the revival were equipped to make sophisticated analyses of the movement. Stanley H. Frodsham, editor of the *Pentecostal Evangel*, wrote a good description of early pentecostalism, *"With Signs Following"* (Springfield, Mo.: Gospel Publishing House [1926]). Two books which are useful discussions of the revival by participating evangelists are David Nunn and W. V. Grant, *The Coming World-Wide Revival* (Dallas: W. V. Grant, n.d.) and Buford Dowell, *The Prophetic Revival* (San Diego: Revival Time Evangelistic Campaigns, n.d.).

A number of good scholarly books have been written about pentecostalism in the last fifteen years. A few scholars have recognized the importance of the independent revivalists. Donald Gee was conscious of the influence of the revivalists in his two books, *All With One Accord* (Springfield: Gospel Publishing House [1961]) and *Wind and Flame* (rev. and enl. ed.; Croydon, G.B.: Heath Press, 1967). Probably the best study of pentecostalism is W. J. Hollenweger, *The Pentecostals* (1st U.S. ed.; Minneapolis: Augsburg Publishing House, 1972). An important study of pentecostal theology is Frederick Dale Bruner, "The Doctrine and Experience of the Holy Spirit in the Pentecostal Movement and Correspondingly in the New Testament" (unpublished dissertation, University of Hamburg, 1963). Two other useful studies are Nils Bloch-Hoell, *The Pentecostals* (Norway: Universitetsforlaget, 1964) and John Thomas Nichol, *Pentecostalism* (New York: Harper & Row [1966]). An early interpretation of the movement from the neopentecostal perspective is John L. Sherrill, *They Speak with Other Tongues* (New York: McGraw-Hill Book Company [1964]). A recent book which relates neopentecostalism to the traditional movement is Steve Durasoff, *Bright Wind of the Spirit* (Englewood Cliffs, N.J.: Prentice-Hall [1972]). An assessment of the movement by a Roman Catholic is Prudencio Damboriena, *Tongues As of Fire* (Washington and Cleveland: Corpus Books [1969]). A study of the influence of the charismatic movement on Lutheranism is Laurence Christenson, *Speaking in Tongues* (Minneapolis: Bethany Fellowship, 1968). A book which associates some of the revivalists with the occult is Kurt Koch, *Occult Bondage and Deliverance* (Grand Rapids, Mich.: Kregel Publications [1970]). A study which encompasses the entire field of psychic healing is Sybil Leek, *The Story of Faith Healing* (New York: Macmillan Publishing Co. [1973]).

A considerable body of literature has grown up around the Roman Catholic charismatic renewal. Basic books on this movement include Kevin and Dorothy

Ranaghan, *Catholic Pentecostals* (Paramus, N.J.: Paulist Press [1969]); Edward O'Conner, *The Pentecostal Movement in the Catholic Church* (Notre Dame, Ind.: Ave Maria Press, 1971); Kevin and Dorothy Ranaghan, eds., *As the Spirit Leads Us* (New York: Paulist Press, 1971); and Kilian McDonnell, *Catholic Pentecostalism: Problems in Evaluation* (Pecos, N.M.: Dove Publications [1970]). A good view of the present status of the movement in the Roman Catholic church is contained in a statement drafted by Kilian McDonnell for a conference of churchmen held in Malines, Belgium, in May 1974: *Theological and Pastoral Orientations on the Catholic Charismatic Renewal* ([Notre Dame, Ind.: The World of Life, 1974]).

A study of the growth of the major pentecostal denominations is Vinson Synan, *The Holiness–Pentecostal Movement in the United States* (Grand Rapids, Mich.: William B. Eerdmans Publishing Company [1971]). Three books which emphasize the Assemblies of God are William W. Menzies, *Anointed to Serve* (Springfield, Mo.: Gospel Publishing House [1971]); Klaude Kendrick, *The Promise Fulfilled* (Springfield, Mo.: Gospel Publishing House [1961]); and Carl Brumback, *Suddenly . . . from Heaven* (Springfield, Mo.: Gospel Publishing House [1961]). A useful study of the largest oneness pentecostal church is Arthur L. Clanton, *United We Stand* (Hazelwood, Mo.: The Pentecostal Publishing House, 1970).

Popular writing about faith healers has been abundant through the years, but generally has been shallow and sensational. Three exposé-type articles in popular magazines are John Kobler, "The Truth About Faith Healers," *McCalls* (February 1957), 39–42; Richard Carter, "That Old-Time Religion Comes Back," *Coronet* (February 1958), 125–130; and "Beware the Commercialized Faith Healers," *Reader's Digest* (June 1971), 179–180. An example of a more sympathetic notice of the movement in the 1950s is Henry P. Van Dusen, "The Third Force in Christendom," *Life* (June 9, 1958), 113–122, 124.

Generally, only the more prominent evangelists received attention in the popular press. Oral Roberts was the most widely known charismatic preacher. Some typical articles about Roberts are: "Faith Healer at Work," *Look* (June 29, 1954), 88–94; "Thrill of My Life," *Newsweek* (October 24, 1955), 104; "Deadline from God," *Time* (July 11, 1955), 41; "Travail of the Healer," *Newsweek* (March 19, 1956), 82; "Frenzy of Faith in a Man's Touch," *Life* (August 3, 1962), 12–21; and Hayes B. Jacobs, "Oral Roberts: High Priest of Faith Healing," *Harper's Magazine* (February 1962), 37–43. Jack Coe's arrest and trial brought him some national publicity: "Coe's Cure," *Newsweek* (February 27, 1956), 56; "A Failure of Faith in a Faith Healer," *Life* (March 5, 1956), 63–64. In the late 1960s A. A. Allen was discovered by the popular press: "Getting Back Double from God," *Time* (March 7, 1969), 64; William Hedgepeth, "Brother A. A. Allen on the Gospel Trail," *Look* (October 7, 1969), 23–31. In the 1970s the most visible independent ministers, in addition to Roberts, were probably Rex Humbard, Kathryn Kuhlman, and Reverend Ike: "Electronic Evangelist," *Time* (May 17, 1971), 70–72; "Rex in the Red," *Time* (March 5, 1973), 66; Clayton Riley, "The

Golden Gospel of Reverend Ike," *New York Times Magazine,* March 9, 1975, 12; William C. Martin, "This Man Says He's the Divine Sweetheart of the Universe," *Esquire* (June 1974), 76; "That T-Bone Religion," *Time* (December 11, 1972), 97; "Miracle Woman," *Time* (September 14, 1970), 62.

Church magazines abound in articles about the independent ministers. A few examples of articles critical of the evangelists are: "Faith Healing Over T.V.," *America* 94 (March 17, 1956), 652; "Sideglances," *Liguorian* 44 (February 1956), 114–115; "But What About Hicks?" *Christian Century* 71 (July 7, 1954), 814–815; "Oklahoma Faith Healer Draws a Following," *Christian Century* 72 (June 29, 1955), 749–750; W. E. Mann, "What About Oral Roberts?" *Christian Century* 73 (September 5, 1956), 1018–1021; and Walter H. Boggs, Jr., "Bible and Modern Religions: Faith Healing Cults," *Interpretation* 11 (January 1957), 55–70. Denominational journals were filled with critical articles, especially until the mid-1960s. Two typical evangelical tracts contesting the claims of the revivalists are Fred C. Melton, *Try That Spirit* (Tonbridge, G.B.: Fred C. Melton, n.d.) and A. G. Hobbs, *Have Miracles Ceased?* (30th ed.; Ft. Worth: Hobbs Publications, n.d.).

In recent years the more liberal religious press has shown a growing respect for the charismatic movement. A few examples of this changed attitude are: Alan Walker, "Where Pentecostalism Is Mushrooming," *Christian Century* 85 (January 17, 1968), 81–82; W. J. Hollenweger, "The Pentecostal Movement and the World Council of Churches," *Ecumenical Review* 18 (July 1966), 310–320; "The Gift of Tongues," *Christianity Today* (April 11, 1969), 27–28; "Pentecostals Celebrate the World Flame," *Christianity Today* (December 4, 1970), 36; Jeffrey L. Klaiber, "Pentecostal Breakthrough," *America* 122 (January 31, 1970), 99–102; and Kilian McDonnell, "Holy Spirit and Pentecostalism," *Commonweal* 89 (November 8, 1968), 198–204. An article which examined this changing mood is Donald G. Bloesch, "The Charismatic Revival," *Religion in Life* 35 (Summer 1966), 364–380.

Scholarly investigations of the independent ministries are almost nonexistent. The racial attitudes of the revivalists were studied in David Edwin Harrell, Jr., *White Sects and Black Men in the Recent South* (Nashville: Vanderbilt University Press, 1971). A good sociological study of the Allen ministry is Howard Elinson, "The Implications of Pentecostal Religion for Intellectualism, Politics, and Race Relations," *American Journal of Sociology* 70 (January 1965), 403–415. The general literature on the sociology of religion provides many useful models for a student of the revival but little first-hand information about the healing ministries. A sociological view of charisma may be found in Edward Shils, "Charisma, Order and Status," *American Sociological Review* 30 (April 1965), 199–213. An anthropological study of the pentecostal experience is Luther P. Gerlach and Virginia H. Hine, *People, Power, Change: Movements of Social Transformation* (Indianapolis and New York: The Bobbs-Merrill Company [1970]). For a valuable summary of the current state of psychological investigation of pentecostalism, see Kilian McDonnell, "Tongues and the Churches: a

Psychological Survey and Evaluation" (unpublished manuscript, read by permission of the author).

Several books deal in a sophisticated way with the theological and psychological implications of divine healing. Some sympathetic studies include: Bernard Martin, *The Healing Ministry in the Church* (Richmond: John Knox Press [1960]); Morton T. Kelsey, *Healing and Christianity* (New York: Harper & Row [1973]); Emily Gardiner Neal, *The Healing Power of Christ* (New York: Hawthorn Books [1972]); Bernard Martin, *Healing for You* (Richmond: John Knox Press [1965]). An important critical study of healing by a physician is William A. Nolen, *Healing: a Doctor in Search of a Miracle* (New York: Random House, 1975). A study by a medical doctor sympathetic to healing is Edwin Hudson, trans., Paul Taurnier, *A Doctor's Casebook* (1st Am. ed.; New York: Harper & Row, 1960).

NOTES

ABBREVIATIONS OF PERIODICAL TITLES

AHM—*America's Healing Magazine*
AL—*Abundant Life*
C&S—*The Cross and the Switchblade*
CC—*The Christian Century*
CCH—*The Christian Challenge*
CF—*Campus Fellowship*
CFN—*Christ for the Nations*
DL—*Deeper Life*
ET—*Evangelistic Times*
FD—*Faith Digest*
FIA—*Faith in Action*
GG—*Golden Grain*
HOF—*Herald of Faith*
HOF–HT—*Herald of Faith–Harvest Time*
HOH—*Herald of Healing*
HT—*Harvest Time*
HW—*Healing Waters*
IHM—*International Healing Magazine*
LH—*Living Hope*
LJ—*Logos Journal*
MM—*Miracle Magazine*
MMD—*Miracles and Missions Digest*
MOF—*March of Faith*
MTF—*Missions Thru Faith*
MW—*Miracle Word*

NH—*New Horizons*
NW—*New Wine*
PE—*Pentecostal Evangel*
ROA—*Revival of America*
SOF—*Shield of Faith*
TA—*The Answer*
TCL—*20th Century Life*
TE—*The Evangelist*
TETM—*The End Time Messenger*
THB—*The Healing Broadcast*
THD—*The Healing Digest*
THM—*The Healing Messenger* (William Freeman)
THM (Nunn)—*The Healing Messenger* (David Nunn)
TSW—*The Spoken Word*
TVD—*The Voice of Deliverance*
TVH—*The Voice of Healing*
VW—*Voice in the Wilderness*
WE—*World Evangelism*
WFN—*World Fellowship News*
WH—*World Harvest*
WP—*World Pentecost*
WWR—*World-Wide Revival*
WWRR—*World-Wide Revival Reports*

Chapter 1 / Introduction

1. See Steven S. Gaines, *The Life of Marjoe Gortner* (New York: Harper and Row, 1972).

2. See Martin E. Marty, "Billy, Et AL," *Christian Century* 91 (September 4–11, 1974), 831; and Martin E. Marty, "Name Games," *Christian Century* 91 (October 16, 1974), 975.

Chapter 2 / Origins

1. Kilian McDonnell, *Theological and Pastoral Orientations on the Catholic Charismatic Renewal* ([Notre Dame, Ind.: Word of Life, 1974]), 61–62.

2. Donald Gee, *Wind and Flame* (rev. and enl. ed.; Croydon, Surrey: Heath Press Ltd., 1967), 3; see 1–6.

3. For a good summary of the growth of pentecostal churches in America see Vinson Synan, *The Holiness-Pentecostal Movement in the United States* (Grand Rapids, Michigan: William B. Eerdmans Publishing Company [1971]).

4. Gee, *Wind and Flame*, 8. W. J. Hollenweger's book, *The Pentecostals* (1st United States ed.; Minneapolis: Augsburg Publishing House, 1972), is probably the best doctrinal summary of pentecostalism. See also W. J. Hollenweger, "The Pentecostal Movement and the World Council of Churches," *Ecumenical Review* (July 1966), 310–320.

5. Three traditional, though slightly different, studies on this subject are Gordon Lindsay, *All About the Gifts of the Spirit* (Dallas: The World Correspondence Course, 1962); Donald Gee, *The Ministry-Gifts of Christ* (Springfield: Gospel Publishing House, [1930]); John H. Osteen, *The Supernatural Gifts of the Spirit* (Houston: John H. Osteen Evangelistic Association [1961]).

6. Steve Durasoff, *Bright Wind of the Spirit* (Englewood Cliffs, N.J.: Prentice-Hall [1972]), 5.

7. For information on the "oneness" pentecostals see Arthur L. Clanton, *United We Stand* (Hazelwood, Mo.: The Pentecostal Publishing House, 1970).

8. See Gordon Lindsay, *The Life of John Alexander Dowie* ([Dallas]: The Voice of Healing Publishing Co. [1951]).

9. Ibid., 271.

10. Stanley Howard Frodsham, *Smith Wigglesworth: Apostle of Faith* (Reprinted; London: Assemblies of God Publishing House, 1965), 93.

11. See Eunice M. Perkins, *Joybringer Bosworth* (Dayton: John J. Scruby, 1921).

12. Oscar Blomgren, Jr., "Fred F. Bosworth," *HOF* (April 1964), 23.

13. Gordon Lindsay, *William Branham: A Man Sent from God* (4th ed.; Jeffersonville, Indiana: William Branham, 1950), 130.

14. Oscar Blomgren, Jr., "Fred F. Bosworth," *HOF* (May 1964), 14–15.

15. "Soul Winning," *MM* 17 (May 1972), 2.

16. Gordon Lindsay, editorial note, *TVH* (March 1966), 4. See also, Gordon Lindsay, *The John G. Lake Sermons* (5th ed.; [Dallas]: The Voice of Healing Publishing Co. [1949]).

17. See "Sketches from Marvels and Miracles," *TVH* (October 1949), 4–5, 16; M. B. Woodworth-Etter, *Marvels and Miracles* (Indianapolis: Mrs. M. B. W. Etter [1922]); M. B. Woodworth-Etter, *Questions and Answers on Divine Healing* (rev. and enl. ed.; Indianapolis: Mrs. M. B. Woodworth-Etter, n.d.).

18. See Thomas R. Nickel, "Evan. Raymond T. Ritchey Now Is with His Lord," *Testimony* (2nd quarter, 1968), 9.

19. See Gordon Lindsay, *Men Who Heard from Heaven* ([Dallas]: The Voice of Healing Publishing Co. [1953]), 129–42.

20. See Eloise May Richey, "The Story of Raymond T. Richey," *TVH* (October 1951), 19, 21; Eloise May Richey, *What God Hath Wrought in the Life of Raymond T. Richey* (rev. ed.; Houston: United Prayer and Workers League [1937]).

21. Lately Thomas, *Storming Heaven* (New York: William Morrow and Company, 1970), 330.

22. See ibid. and Nancy Barr Mavity, *Sister Aimee* (New York: Doubleday, Doran & Company, 1931).

23. See Charles S. Price, *The Story of My Life* (3rd ed.; Pasadena: Charles S. Price Publishing Co., 1944).

24. "The Editor's Desk," GG (April 1928), 30.

25. "The Editor's Desk," GG (March 1937), 28–29.

26. "The Editor's Desk," GG (February 1947), 31.

27. See "The Editor's Desk," GG (May 1948), 28–29; "The Editor's Desk," GG (April 1947), 31; "The Story of the Conversion and Healing Ministry of Dr. Charles S. Price," *TVH* (June 1949), 10–11, 16; Lorne Fox, "From Bondage to Freedom," *TVH* (March 1949), 8–9.

28. Gordon Lindsay, *The Gordon Lindsay Story* (Dallas: The Voice of Healing Publishing Co., n.d.), 273.

29. David Nunn and W. V. Grant, *The Coming World-Wide Revival* ([Dallas: W. V. Grant, n.d.]), 23.

30. "The Editor's Desk," GG (August 1936), 24.

31. R. O. Corvin, "Pentecost in Three Dimensions," WP (first issue, 1971), 12.

32. David Nunn, "God's Order of the Day . . . Revive, Restore, Reap!" *THM* (Nunn) (August 1963), 2. See also, "The Editor's Desk," GG (February 1947), 31; Nunn and Grant, *Coming Revival*, 23; interview.

33. "The Story of the Great Restoration Revival," WWR (March 1958), 4.

34. "Renewed Emphasis upon Divine Healing," *Pentecost* No. 9 (September 1949), 14.

35. See John Thomas Nichol, *Pentecostalism* (New York: Harper and Row [1966]), 226–36 and Hollenweger, *The Pentecostals*, 34.

36. Nichol, *Pentecostalism*, 209.

37. R. O. Corvin, "Pentecost in Three Dimensions," WP (first issue, 1971), 12.

38. "World-Wide Pentecostal Revivals, 1906–1956," *TVH* (July 1956), 13.

39. "Report of International Pentecostal Convention, Des Moines, Iowa," HW (December 1948), 16.

40. See Hollenweger, *The Pentecostals*, 29–46.

41. "The Deliverance Campaigns," *Pentecost* No. 36 (June 1956), 17. See also, Gordon Lindsay, "A Look in the Past and the Future," *TVH* (February

1966), 2; Velmer Gardner, *My Life Story* (Springfield, Mo.: Velmer Gardner Evangelistic Association [1954]), 21–23.

42. Gordon Lindsay, "A Look in the Past and the Future," *TVH* (February 1966), 2.

43. Nichol, *Pentecostalism*, 221.

44. David J. duPlessis, "World-Wide Pentecostal Revivals, 1906–1956," *TVH* (July 1956), 13.

45. Letter from Frodsham to S. Juanita Walker, June 18, 1964, Pentecostal Collection, Oral Roberts University. See also, Stanley Howard Frodsham, "Remarkable Healing Campaigns," *Pentecost* No. 4 (June 1948), 5; Stanley Howard Frodsham, "Greater Things Shall Ye Do," *HW* (July 1949), 2, 15. A summary of the controversial ideas associated with the "latter rain" may be found in *Minutes* of the 1949 General Council . . . [Assemblies of God] ([Springfield, Mo.: Assemblies of God, 1949]), 26–27.

46. "The Deliverance Campaigns," *Pentecost* No. 36 (June 1956), 17.

Chapter 3 / Two Giants

WILLIAM MARRION BRANHAM

1. Gordon Lindsay, *William Branham: A Man Sent from God* (4th ed.; Jeffersonville, Indiana: William Branham, 1950), 9. See this book for the best account of Branham's early life.

2. Lindsay, *Branham*, 77.

3. "Brother Bill Comes Home," *TVH* (August 1950), 5.

4. Lindsay, *Branham*, 81–82. See also, Julius Stadsklev, *William Branham: A Prophet Visits South Africa* (Minneapolis: Julius Stadsklev [1952]), 1–5.

5. "William Branham's Life Story," *HOF* (February 1960), 10.

6. Lindsay, *Branham*, 43.

7. Ibid., 43, 71; Pearry Green, *The Acts of the Prophet* (Tucson: Tucson Tabernacle, mimeographed book, n.d.), chap. 6, p. 2.

8. Green, *Acts of Prophet*, chap. 7, pp. 2–3; "William Branham's Life Story," *HOF* (March 1960), 2.

9. R. E. Davis, Sr., "Wm. Branham's First Pastor," *TVH* (October 1950), 14.

10. Lindsay, *Branham*, 82.

11. Ibid., 81–82.

12. See Green, *Acts of Prophet*, chap. 8, p. 5.

13. Lindsay, *Branham*, 93; interview.

14. For information on Kidson, see Arthur L. Clanton, *United We Stand* (Hazelwood, Mo.: The Pentecostal Publishing House, 1970).

15. Anna Jeanne Moore, "William Branham Returns to Arkansas," *TVH* (February 1949), 1–2.

16. Lindsay, *Branham*, 101; interviews.

17. Anna Jeanne Price, "The Jack Moore Story, Installment II," *TVH* (November 1955), 9–10.

18. Gordon Lindsay, "The Story of the Great Restoration Revival," *WWR* (March 1958), 4–5; interview.

19. Ibid.

20. Lindsay, *Branham*, 100.

21. Interview.

22. Gordon Lindsay, "The Story of the Great Restoration Revival, Installment II," *WWR* (April 1958), 17.

23. Ibid.

24. See Stanley Howard Frodsham, "Remarkable Healing Campaign," *Pentecost* No. 4 (June 1948), 5.

25. Del Grant, "Branham Is 'Back,'" *TVH* (January 1949), 3.

26. Gordon Lindsay, "The Story of the Great Restoration Revival, Installment II," *WWR* (April 1958), 18; William Branham, "How the Voice of Healing Received Its Name," *TVH* (March 1950), 7.

27. Interview.

28. "Prayer for Rev. Wm. Branham," *HW* (July 1948), 8.

29. Del Grant, "Branham Is 'Back,'" *TVH* (January 1949), 3. See also, Green, *Acts of Prophet*, chap. 14, p. 6.

30. "Flash," *TVH* (October 1948), 1.

31. Gordon Lindsay, "The Story of the Great Restoration Revival, Installment IV," *WWR* (June 1958), 18.

32. "Conference with Brother Branham," *TVH* (January 1950), 2.

33. Ibid.

34. See David J. duPlessis, "News Briefs," *WWR* (April 1958), 10; Lindsay, *Branham*, 130–31; F. F. Bosworth, "How to Appropriate Healing," *TVH* (April 1949), 8–9, 16.

35. "God Vindicates Branham in Houston by Most Amazing Photograph Ever Taken," *TVH* (March 1950), 1, 4–5.

36. Gordon Lindsay, "The Story of the Great Restoration Revival, Installment IV," *WWR* (June 1958), 19.

37. See Anna Jeanne Moore, "William Branham Returns to Arkansas; Attracts Throngs to Hot Springs," *TVH* (February 1949), 1–2.

38. "Finland," *Pentecost*, No. 13 (September 1950), 8; see also, "Finland," *TVH* (June 1950), 1.

39. W. J. Hollenweger, *The Pentecostals* (1st United States ed.; Minneapolis: Augsburg Publishing House, 1972), 354.

40. See A. J. Schooman, "Great Revivals in Africa with Branham Party," *TVH* (January 1952), 8.

41. Interview.

42. "Crippled Congressman Walks from Branham Healing Service," *TVH* (April-May 1951), 2.

43. [Insert], *TVH* (February 1949), 3.

44. Interview; "Bro. Roberts with Rev. Branham and Party," *HW* (May 1948), 3.

45. "Branham Visits Roberts Campaign," *TVH* (April 1949), 2, 16.

46. Reg G. Hanson, "Wm. Branham Attends Roberts Campaign in Tampa, Florida," *HW* (March 1949), 6.

47. Interview; "In Memory of a Prophet," *SOF* (November and December 1969), 4.

48. Interview.

49. Interview.

50. "Looking at the Unseen," *TVH* (January 1950), 4.

51. "Gifts of Healing *Plus*," *TVH* (March 1950), 10.

52. F. F. Bosworth, "Looking at the Unseen," *TVH* (January 1950), 4.

53. "The Gifts of Healing *Plus*," *TVH* (March 1950), 10.

54. "An Interview with William Branham," *TVH* (October 1951), 8.

55. "The Gifts of Healing *Plus*," *TVH* (March 1950), 10–11.

56. Hollenweger, *The Pentecostals*, 354.

57. Donald Gee, *Wind and Flame* (rev. ed.; Croydon, England: Heath Press Ltd., 1967), 242.

58. Interview.

59. Interview.

60. Thomas H. Nelson, "Dowie's Followers Relive Glorious Days of Past as Branham and Bosworth Minister in Zion," *TVH* (May 1949), 10.

61. "Looking at the Unseen," *TVH* (January 1950), 5.

62. Lindsay, *Branham*, 14.

63. Len J. Jones, "I Visited a Branham Meeting," *TVH* (June 1954), 16.

64. "Renewed Emphasis Upon Divine Healing," *Pentecost* No. 9 (September 1949), 14.

65. Len J. Jones, "I Visited a Branham Meeting," *TVH* (June 1954), 16.

66. Lindsay, *Branham*, 13.

67. *Wind and Flame*, 242.

68. Interview.

69. Interview.

70. Thomas R. Nickel, "The Angel of the Lord Visits William Branham!" *Voice* (March 1956), 10.

71. Green, *Acts of Prophet*, chap. 15, pp. 6–7.

72. Interview.

73. Gordon Lindsay, "The Story of the Great Restoration Revival, Installment II," *WWR* (April 1958), 17.

74. Lindsay, *Branham*, 14.

75. Gordon Lindsay, "William Branham as I Knew Him," *TVH* (February 1966), 3.

76. "An Interview with William Branham," *TVH* (October 1951), 23.

77. See "Greetings from William Branham," *TVH* (September 1953), 5; "Interview with William Branham" *TVH* (May 1954), 22.

78. Green, *Acts of Prophet*, chap. 15, p. 7; see pp. 1–19.
79. Ibid., chap. 15, p. 2.
80. Ibid., chap. 8, pp. 6–7; chap. 9, p. 1; see pp. 1–9.
81. Gee, *Wind and Flame*, 242.
82. Thomas R. Nickel, "The Angel of the Lord Visits William Branham!" *Voice* (March 1956), 14.
83. Leo Mercier, "The Mount of God," *HOF* (March 1957), 3, 22–23.
84. "Rev. William Branham's Schedules," *HOF* (February and March 1958), 10.

GRANVILLE ORAL ROBERTS

1. Oral Roberts, *My Story* (Tulsa and New York: Summit Book Company, 1961), 221.
2. Interview.
3. "I'm Excited about the Whole Kingdom of God," *AL* (May 1967), 19.
4. See Roberts, *My Story*, 66–71; Oral Roberts, *Oral Roberts' Life Story* (Tulsa: Oral Roberts [1952]), 54–55.
5. See "Girl Healed of Infantile Paralysis," *HW* (November and December 1947), 3.
6. See Oral Roberts, "Oral Roberts Tells How the Founding of This Magazine Based on a Great Healing . . . ," *AL* (November 1969), 2–3.
7. "Partners for Deliverance," *HW* (November and December 1947), 5, 6.
8. "Great Healing Campaigns in America," *Pentecost* No. 12 (June 1950), 9; see also, "A Miracle in Masonry," *AHM* (November 1954), 5.
9. "Healing Waters Office Workers," *HW* (May 1948), 10.
10. "Miracle Seed-Faith, Part III," *AL* (December 1971), 9–11.
11. "Summary of the Oral Roberts Ministry in 1952," *HW* (February 1953), 13.
12. G. H. Montgomery, "Looking Forward with Oral Roberts in 1953," *HW* (February 1953), 10; G. H. Montgomery, "The March of Deliverance, *AHM* (February 1954), 4.
13. See "The Beautiful Healing Waters Office in Tulsa, Okla.," *HW* (November 1951), 1; "A Miracle in Masonry," *AHM* (November 1954), 5; "Abundant Life for Millions," *AL* (January 1958), 7.
14. "Visit to Great Roberts Tent Meet at Granite City, Ill.," *TVH* (September 1948), 7.
15. "I'm Excited about the Whole Kingdom of God," *AL* (May 1967), 20.
16. Oral Roberts, "My Plans for the Future," *HW* (November 1950), 4–5.
17. See O. E. Sproul, "The Largest Tent Ever Constructed for the Gospel Ministry," *HW* (January 1950), 15; G. H. Montgomery, "Looking Forward with Oral Roberts," *HW* (January 1952), 13.
18. "A Personal Report from Bro. Roberts," *HW* (October 1948), 2, 9.

19. G. H. Montgomery, "Looking Back Over 10 Years of Deliverance Ministry," *AL* (June 1957), 3–9.

20. "Summary of the Oral Roberts Ministry in 1952," *HW* (February 1953), 13.

21. See "Wanted: 20,000 Radio Partners," *HW* (June 1950), 10–11; "Summary of the Oral Roberts Ministry in 1952," *HW* (February 1953), 13; G. H. Montgomery, "The March of Deliverance," *AHM* (February 1954), 4.

22. See "To Whom It May Concern," *HW* (October 1951), 11; G. H. Montgomery, "Looking Forward with Oral Roberts," *HW* (January 1952), 13; "Venture of Faith," *HW* (August 1952), 8–9.

23. See G. H. Montgomery, "The March of Deliverance," *AHM* (February 1954), 4; Oral Roberts, "My Plans for Television," *AHM* (January 1954), 12–14, 16–17; "The Oral Roberts Television Network," *AHM* (July 1955), 3; G. H. Montgomery, "The March of Deliverance," *AHM* (January 1955), 4; "Oral Roberts' Television Guide," *AL* (March 1958), 29.

24. Interview.

25. See Lorne F. Fox, "The Christ We Forget," *HW* (February 1950), 4–5; "F. F. Bosworth Rejoices Over Roberts' Meeting in Miami, Florida," *HW* (February 1949), 4; Reg G. Hanson, "Wm. Branham Attends Roberts Campaign in Tampa, Florida," *HW* (March 1949), 6.

26. See "Announcements," *HW* (April 1950), 12; "Great Crowds Throng Union Full Gospel Meetings Across America," *HW* (January 1951), 12; "News of Last Day Revivals," *HW* (October 1950), 14; "Among Those Present," *HW* (July 1952), 7; interview.

27. Oral Roberts, "I've Made the Full Circle," *AL* (November 1970), 8.

28. "Preachers at the Crusade," *AL* (January 1962), 14.

29. See [picture caption], *HW* (July 1949), 4; "Sponsoring Pastors in Miami Campaign," *HW* (March 1950), 3; [picture caption], *HW* (June 1950), 15; "Among Those Present," *HW* (July 1952), 7.

30. "What's the Secret Behind Oral Roberts' Success," *HW* (November 1951), 7.

31. "For All People of All Churches," *AL* (March 1957), 24–25.

32. Oral Roberts, "To Touch Neither the Gold Nor the Glory," *HW* (October 1951), 4–5.

33. See Oral Roberts, "An Open Letter to Magazine and Newspaper Editors," *AL* (February 1957), 16–17, 28–29.

34. Ibid., 29.

35. Oral Roberts, "To Touch Neither the Gold Nor the Glory," *Healing* (March 1956), 5; see also, Roberts, *Life Story*, 80–87.

36. Ibid.

37. See Oral Roberts, "An Open Letter to Magazine and Newspaper Editors," *AL* (February 1957), 16–17, 28–29.

38. See Oral Roberts, *The Call* (New York: Doubleday and Company, 1972), 147–60.

39. Oral Roberts, "Do You Want God to Return Your Money Seven Times?" *AHM* (April 1954), 10.

40. Roberts, *My Story*, 161, 167.

41. See "Full Gospel Business Men of America Start New National Association," *HW* (January 1952), 12; "Full Gospel Business Men," *HW* (January 1953), 13. For a fuller discussion of the beginnings of the FGBMFI, see chap. 6.

42. See G. H. Montgomery, "Million Souls Crusade Draws Businessmen to Tulsa," *AHM* (October 1954), 14; Yvonne Nance, "Record Crowd Meets for Fourth Conference," *AL* (August 1957), 26–27. See also, Oral Roberts and G. H. Montgomery, eds., *God's Formula for Success and Prosperity* (Tulsa: Oral Roberts [1955]).

43. Oral Roberts, "What God Has Shown to Me," *AHM* (October 1954), 4–5.

44. "Branham Visits Roberts Campaign," *TVH* (April 1949), 16.

45. G. H. Montgomery, "God's Seven Messages to Oral Roberts," *AL* (April 1958), 25.

46. Oral Roberts, *If You Need Healing Do These Things* (rev. ed.; eighth printing; Tulsa: Oral Roberts, 1956), 15–41.

47. Reg G. Hanson, "Wm. Branham Attends Roberts Campaign in Tampa, Florida," *HW* (March 1949), 6.

48. "Demons," *AHM* (September 1954), 2.

49. "The Ministry of Casting Out Demons," *HW* (August 1948), 2, 8.

50. G. H. Montgomery, "God's Seven Messages to Oral Roberts," *AL* (April 1958), 14–15, 25–27.

51. Ibid.

52. G. H. Montgomery, "Looking Forward with Oral Roberts in 1953," *HW* (February 1953), 10.

53. Oral Roberts, "What God Has Shown to Me," *AHM* (October 1954), 4–5.

54. Oral Roberts, "The Burden of a Million Souls," *HW* (July 1953), 12–14.

55. Oral Roberts, "A Master Plan," *AL* (October 1956), 18–22.

56. G. H. Montgomery, "God's Seven Messages to Oral Roberts," *AL* (April 1958), 26–27.

57. Ibid.

58. Ibid.

59. "I'm Excited about the Whole Kingdom of God," *AL* (May 1967), 25.

60. Oral Roberts, "The Lord Told Me to Build," *AL* (April 1959), 4–6; interview.

61. See [masthead], *AL* (April 1957), 3; interview.

Chapter 4 / The Flowering of the Healing Revival

GORDON LINDSAY and The Voice of Healing

1. See Gordon Lindsay, *The Gordon Lindsay Story* (Dallas: The Voice of Healing Publishing Co., n.d.).

2. Gordon Lindsay, "The Story of the Great Restoration Revival, Part III," *WWR* (May 1958), 4.

3. Ibid., 3, 4.

4. "Special Message from the Editor, Gordon Lindsay," *TVH* (March 1949), 2.

5. See Anna Jeanne Moore, "Historic Conference of Evangelists Conducting Great Healing Campaigns Convened in Dallas December 22–23," *TVH* (February 1950), 1–3.

6. "The Purpose, Plan and Policy of the Voice of Healing Convention," *TVH* (December 1950), 2, 15; see "Second Voice of Healing Convention Draws 1,000 Ministers from 39 States," *TVH* (January 1951), 1.

7. David J. duPlessis, "A Convention with a Significant Voice," *TVH* (February 1952), 3. See also, David J. duPlessis, "Divine Healing Evangelists Confer in Kansas City," *Pentecost* No. 15 (1951), 10.

8. See Anna Jeanne Moore, "Voice of Healing Convention," *TVH* (February 1951), 2–3; "All Roads Lead to Dallas, Texas, Nov. 8–11," *TVH* (November 1955), 2–3; Anna Jeanne Moore, "Convention Diary," *TVH* (February 1952), 2–3; interview.

9. "Dallas—New Site of TVH Headquarters," *TVH* (June 1952), 2.

10. Gordon Lindsay, "An Open Letter to the Full Gospel People," *TVH* (August 1953), 2, 25.

11. See "Names Added—Removed—TVH Directory," *TVH* (January 1953), 3.

12. "Special Message from the Editor, Gordon Lindsay," *TVH* (March 1949), 2.

13. See "Bosworth-Osborn-Branham Meetings," *TVH* (August 1949), 1, 4; interview.

14. Interview.

15. Mrs. Gordon Lindsay, "The Oakland TVH Regional Convention Great Success," *TVH* (March 1956), 18–19.

16. Gordon Lindsay, "Report on World Revival Crusade," *TVH* (September 1954), 2.

17. "Concerning Other Ministries and Gifts Being Manifested," *TVH* (October 1948), 8.

18. "These Works That I Do Shall Ye Do Also, And Greater Works Than These Shall Ye Do," *TVH* (October 1949), 2–3.

19. Interview.

Notes

JACK COE

1. See Juanita Coe, *The Jack Coe I Know* ([Dallas]: Herald of Healing [1956]); Jack Coe, *The Story of Jack Coe* (Dallas: Herald of Healing [1955]), 60–66; interview.

2. See Coe, *Jack Coe I Know*, 54–55; Coe, *Story of Jack Coe*, 67.

3. Interview.

4. "Jack Coe," *TVH* (February 1957), 11.

5. Interviews.

6. "Jack Coe," *TVH* (February 1957), 9–12.

7. See Jack Coe, *Apostles and Prophets . . . in the Church Today* (Dallas: Herald of Healing, 1954); Coe, *Jack Coe I Know*, 100.

8. See Herbert Fuller, "Philadelphia Victory Story," *HOH* (June 1954), 9, 15; Jack Coe, "Mayor Hixon of Tampa Dies," *IHM* (June 1956), 13.

9. Interview.

10. Coe, *Jack Coe I Know*, 52.

11. Interview.

12. "Our Cover Picture," *TVH* (July 1951), 3.

13. Interview.

14. Jack Coe, "Which Evangelist Has the World's Largest Gospel Tent?" *IHM* (July 1956), 5, 16.

15. Coe, *The Jack Coe I Know*, 36, 100.

16. [Masthead], *HOH* (October, 1952), 1.

17. See Coe, *The Jack Coe I Know*, 55–58; [masthead], *HOH* (April–May 1953), 4.

18. J. L. Schaffer, "Springfield Stirred by Healings in City-Wide Revival," *PE* No. 1974 (March 9, 1952), 13.

19. "Jack Coe Holds Second Great Revival at Springfield, Mo.," *TVH* (September 1952), 8.

20. "Coe Revival Stirs Springfield, Mo.," *TVH* (March 1952), 13.

21. See "Letters," *HOH* (April–May 1953), 23–27; "Recommendations for the Next General Council," *HOH* (June 1953), 2, 11; "Who Is Capitalizing on the Christian's Money," *HOH* (November 1953), 8–9; "The Fundamental Assemblies to Begin One Hour Broadcast on ABC Network About Jan. 1," *HOH* (January 1954), 13; Coe, *Apostles and Prophets, passim.*

22. See Coe, *The Jack Coe I Know*, 58, 114; Norman Gordon, "New Era of God's Power," *HOH* (April 1954), 7; [Gordon Lindsay], "In Memory of Jack Coe," *TVH* (January 1957), 2.

23. Coe, *Story of Jack Coe*, 110–11.

24. "Many TV Films of Sermons and Healings Are Ready to Show," *IHM* (November 1956), 10.

25. Interview. For samples of national press coverage, see "Coe's Cure," *Newsweek* (February 27, 1956), 56; "Failure of a Faith Healer," *Life* (March 5, 1956), 86.

26. Coe, *Tried . . . But Freed!* ([Dallas]: Herald of Healing [1956]), 44, 126; Norman Gordon, "Medical Treatment . . . or Act of Faith," *IHM* (March 1956), 3–7, 16–17.

27. Interview.

28. J. E. Wilson, "Jack Coe . . . Front Line Casualty," *IHM* (December 1956), 14.

29. Interview.

30. Interview.

31. See Gordon Lindsay, "Why Was Jack Coe Taken in the Midst of His Ministry?" *TVH* (February 1957), 2, 20.

32. See Coe, *The Story of Jack Coe*, 115; "Mrs. Jack Coe Carries on the Gospel Work Started by Her Husband," *IHM* (May 1957), 8; "Jack Coe's Ministry Will Continue," *IHM* (January 1957), 12; Mrs. Jack Coe, "Women Preachers," *IHM* (September 1957), 5, 15.

33. See "Getting Acquainted with the Herald of Healing," *IHM* (October 1958), 14; "Coming to These Cities," *IHM* (April 1957), 9; "Spirit-Filled Services Bring Need for Fellowship," *IHM* (November 1958), 14.

T. L. OSBORN

1. See T. L. Osborn, *Young in Faith* (Tulsa: T. L. Osborn Evangelistic Association, 1964), 57–65; Drew Graham, "Ministry with a Million Faces," *FD* (March 1969), 2–5; William A. Caldwell, "God Has Spoken Again," *FD* (November 1959), 2–3, 12.

2. T. L. Osborn, "My Life Story and Call to the Healing Ministry, Part II," *TVH* (October 1949), 9. See also, Osborn, *Young in Faith*, 47–48, 66–67.

3. Gordon Lindsay, "The Story of the Great Restoration Revival, Installment II," *WWR* (April 1958), 17.

4. Gordon Lindsay, "The Story of the Great Restoration Revival, Installment IV," *WWR* (June 1958), 4.

5. "News of Last Day Revivals," *HW* (October 1950), 14.

6. "Interview with William Branham," *TVH* (April 1954), 14.

7. See "Immense Crowds Flock to T. L. Osborn's Meetings in Holland," *Pentecost* No. 46 (December 1958), 8.

8. "Concerning Our Association with The Voice of Healing," *FD* (June 1956), 17.

9. T. L. Osborn, "World Missions Crusade," *TVH* (July 1953), 10–11.

10. See T. L. Osborn, *Revival Fires Sweep Cuba* (Tulsa: The Voice of Faith Ministry [1952]).

11. Norman Gordon, "T. L. Osborn . . . Pioneer without Precedent," *FD* (September 1959), 3.

12. T. L. Osborn, " 'World Missions' Crusade," *TVH* (July 1953), 10–11; T. L. Osborn, "God's Message to the Church for This Hour," *TVH* (February 1953), 2–3, 21.

13. William A. Caldwell, "God Has Spoken Again," *FD* (November 1959), 3.

14. See "A Vision and 5 Years of Faith Ministry," *FD* (January 1956), 4–5; "Concerning Our Association with The Voice of Healing," *FD* (June 1956), 17; William A. Caldwell, "At Home and Abroad," *FD* (March 1958), 2–5.

15. "Home-Front Restricted and Front-Lines Unlimited," *FD* (May 1958), 3.

16. Norman Gordon, "T. L. Osborn . . . Pioneer without Precedent," *FD* (September 1959), 3.

17. Interview.

18. "He Showed Himself Alive," *FD* (June 1956), 12–13.

19. Osborn, *Young in Faith*, 48.

A. A. ALLEN

1. Lexie E. Allen, *God's Man of Faith Power* (Dallas: A. A. Allen, 1954), 57.

2. A. A. Allen with Walter Wagner, *Born to Lose, Bound to Win* (Garden City, N.Y.: Doubleday & Company, 1970), 64.

3. A. A. Allen, *My Cross* (no publication information), 23.

4. Allen and Wagner, *Born to Lose*, p. 94.

5. Allen, *God's Man of Faith*, 155.

6. Ibid., 161.

7. A. A. Allen, "Many Reports Appraise Ministry of A. A. Allen," *TVH* (May 1950), 4.

8. Allen and Wagner, *Born to Lose*, 129. See also, Allen, *God's Man of Faith*, 162.

9. "A. A. Allen Back under 'Big Top,'" *TVH* (May 1955), 20.

10. "Allen Revival Hour Requires Larger Quarters," *MM* (March 1956), 13.

11. Interview.

12. Interview.

13. Interview.

14. "The Miracle of the Outpouring of Oil," *MM* (January 1956), 2.

15. See O. L. Jaggers, "An Open Letter to Assembly of God Ministers and People," *MM* (October 1956), 10–11, 18, 20.

16. A. A. Allen, *My Besetting Sin* (Dallas: A. A. Allen, n.d.), 20.

17. See A. A. Allen, *My Vision of the Destruction of America* (Miracle Valley, Arizona: A. A. Allen Publications, 1954); A. A. Allen, *Invasion from Hell* (Miracle Valley, Arizona: A. A. Allen Publications, 1953).

18. Interview.

19. Interview.

20. Interview.

21. Interview.

22. "Under the 'Big Top,'" *MM* (November 1955), 8–9.

23. Interview.

24. See Mrs. A. A. Allen, "New Miracle Magazine Now Reporting Modern Miracles," *MM* (October 1955), 4–5.

25. Interview.

26. Interview.

27. "[Letter]," *MM* (December, 1955), 5.

28. Ibid.

29. "That the Truth May Be Known," *MM* (January 1957), 4–5; Robert W. Schambach, "Has A. A. Allen Been Persecuted," *MM* (May 1956), 5–6.

30. Virgil Stone, "Why I Left the Organized Church," *MM* (October 1956), 8.

31. Interview.

32. "Phoenix Reporters Reveal Source of Information," *MM* (May 1956), 5.

33. See Robert W. Schamback, "Has A. A. Allen Been Persecuted," *MM* (May 1956), 5–6.

34. See A. A. Allen, "If God Be for Us," *MM* (October 1957), 2–3.

35. See Allen, *Born to Lose*, 161–75; Virgil Stone, "Why I Left the Organized Church," *MM* (October 1956), 8.

36. A. A. Allen, "If God Be for Us," *MM* (October 1957), 2, 3.

37. A. A. Allen, "Will You Help Me Fight the Devil?" *MM* (July 1956), 2–3, 17–18; "Decision," *MM* (February 1957), 12–14.

38. See Virgil Stone, "Why I Left the Organized Church," *MM* (October 1956), 8.

39. A. A. Allen, *How to Take the Answer from God* (Miracle Valley, Arizona: A. A. Allen Publications, n.d.), 8. See also, A. A. Allen, *The Fatal Word That Will Jam Hell to the Doors* (Dallas: A. A. Allen Publications, n.d.), 26–28.

40. "Under the Gospel 'Big Top,'" *MM* (February 1956), 8–9.

41. *Prisons with Stained Glass Windows* (Miracle Valley, Arizona: A. A. Allen Revivals, 1963), 110.

42. "Miracle Valley Fellowship Points the Way!" *MM* (November 1956), 16.

43. "Miracle Revival Fellowship," *MM* (December 1956), 2.

44. *Prisons with Stained Glass Windows*, 110.

45. "Miracle Revival Fellowship," *MM* (December 1956), 3.

46. "Miracle Valley Fellowship Points the Way," *MM* (November 1956), 16.

47. Mrs. A. A. Allen, "The Most Thrilling Year of My Life," *MM* (August 1956), 3; A. A. Allen, "A Word for This Hour," *MM* (September 1956), 2–3.

48. A. A. Allen, *Time Does Not End at Sunset* (Miracle Valley, Arizona: A. A. Allen, n.d.), 6–8.

49. Ibid., 6.

50. "A. A. Allen Miracle Revival Moves into Largest Tent in the World," *MM* (August 1958), 16–17.

51. A. A. Allen, *The Secret to Scriptural Financial Success* (Miracle Valley, Arizona: A. A. Allen Publications, 1953).

Notes

The Flowering of the Revival

1. William Freeman, "My Life Story," *THM* (March 1949), 3.

2. William Freeman, "My Life Story," *THM* (May 1949), 4.

3. William Freeman, "When the Angel of the Lord Appeared to Me," *THM* (January 1956), 2–3.

4. [D. E. Gossett], "The Life and Ministry of William W. Freeman," *THM* (March 1954), 6.

5. Gordon Lindsay, "The Story of the Great Restoration Revival, Part III," *WWR* (May 1958), 4.

6. "65,500 Persons Accept Christ in Chicago and St. Louis Campaigns," *THM* (November 1953), 1.

7. "Rev. H. A. Rogers Joins Freeman Evangelistic Party as Advance Manager," *THM* (August 1952), 11.

8. See "Gigantic Gospel Tent for Nationwide Revivals," *THM* (September 1951), 3.

9. "William W. Freeman Can Be Heard All Over America Every Night," *THM* (May 1952), 14.

10. See Demos Shakarian, "My Impression of Rev. Freeman's Healing Campaign," *THM* (March 1949), 6–8; "Thousands Hit the Sawdust Trail for Salvation and Healing," *THM* (January 1951), 6–7.

11. "William W. Freeman, Evangelist," *THM* (February 1950), 8.

12. Ibid.

13. See William W. Freeman, "Christ Shall Come . . . I'm Looking for His Appearing," *THM* (May 1956), 4–5.

14. [D. E. Gossett], "The Life and Ministry of William W. Freeman," *THM* (March 1954), 7.

15. Interview.

16. The Phenomenal Rise and Growth of the World Church, *WFN* (June 1966), 2.

17. Interview.

18. Interview.

19. Los Angeles *Examiner*, July 2, 1958. See also, W. Branham, "The Godhead Explained," *TSW*, No. 24, 34–35.

20. O. L. Jaggers, "An Open Letter to the Deliverance Ministry," *WFN* (June 1956), 8–9, 12.

21. "The Phenomenal Rise and Growth of World Church," *WFN* (June 1956), 2–3.

22. Interview.

23. O. L. Jaggers, *Life and Immortality in the Book of St. John* ([Los Angeles: O. L. Jaggers, 1959]), 83.

24. Wm. Branham, "The Godhead Explained," *TSW*, No. 24, 35–37.

25. Interview.

26. See "400,000 in Single Service," *TVH* (August 1954), 19, 30. Tommy

Hicks, *Millions Found Christ* (Los Angeles: International Headquarters of Tommy Hicks, Manifest Deliverance and Worldwide Evangelistic, Inc. [1956]).

27. "400,000 in Single Service," *TVH* (August 1954), 19.

28. Thomas R. Nickel, "The Greatest Revival in All History," *Voice* (February–March 1955), 4–7. See also, "But What about Hicks?" *Christian Century* 71 (July 7, 1954), 814–15.

29. Tommy Hicks, "My Second World-Wide Mission Tour," *Voice* (October 1955), 3–18.

30. Interview; Velmer Gardner, "A Miracle-Working God," *AL* (June 1965), 6–9; Velmer Gardner, *My Life Story* (Springfield, Mo.: Velmer Gardner Evangelistic Association [1954]).

31. See "God's Will for You in 1966," *TVD* (January 1966), 4–5; Gordon Lindsay, *Men Who Heard from Heaven* ([Dallas]: The Voice of Healing Publishing Co. [1953]), 25–29.

32. See Lindsay, *Men Who Heard from Heaven*, 60–72; and Gordon Lindsay, "The Story of the Great Restoration Revival, Installment V," *WWR* (August 1959), 17.

33. See Louise Nankivell, "The Appearance of Christ to Me," *TVH* (October 1949), 12–13; Lindsay, *Men Who Heard from Heaven*, 106–07.

34. Interview.

35. See Franklin Hall, "The Power of Healing," *TVH* (October 1949), 11.

36. Interview.

37. Interview.

38. Thelma Chaney, *The Power of God or Exhibition* (Tulsa: TOP Service, 1954), 190.

39. Interview.

40. David Nunn, *The Life and Ministry of David Nunn* (Dallas: David Nunn, n.d.), 2.

41. Interview.

42. David Nunn, "How God Led Me into the Miracle Ministry," *TVH* (July 1960), 9.

43. Interview.

44. David Nunn, "How God Led Me into the Miracle Ministry," *TVH* (July 1960), 14.

Chapter 5 / Promises and Problems

The Ministry of Healing

1. "The Voice of Healing Convention—1951," *TVH* (December 1951), 8.

2. See John Thomas Nichol, *Pentecostalism* (New York: Harper & Row [1966]), 15–16; Nils Bloch-Hoell, *The Pentecostal Movement* (Norway: Universitetsforlaget, 1964), 147–51.

3. Interview.

4. See W. J. Hollenweger, *The Pentecostals* (Minneapolis: Augsburg Publishing House, 1972), 357.

5. *The Story of Jack Coe* (Dallas: Herald of Healing [1955]), 73.

6. Nichol, *Pentecostalism*, 16; see also, Bloch-Hoell, *The Pentecostal Movement*, 147–51.

7. Block-Hoell, *The Pentecostal Movement*, 149.

8. "The Voice of Healing Convention—1951," TVH (December 1951), 8–9.

9. Interview.

10. "Why Was Jack Coe Taken in the Midst of His Ministry?" *TVH* (February 1957), 2.

11. *Raising the Dead* ([Dallas: W. V. Grant, n.d.]), 32.

12. (Miracle Valley, Arizona: A. A. Allen Publications [1953]), 14–19.

13. "Divine Healing," HOF (November 1965), 9, 24.

14. "TVH Backs Jack Coe in Historic Trial at Miami," TVH (April 1956), 5.

15. Sermon, Birmingham, Alabama, May 22, 1973.

16. Sermon, Little Rock, Arkansas, September 1, 1972.

17. Block-Hoell, *The Pentecostal Movement*, 149.

18. W. V. Grant, *A Miracle Ministry* (Dallas: The Voice of Healing, n.d.), 7.

19. "God's Means of Healing," THM (Nunn) (November 1970), 4–7.

20. "Ten Rules We Must Obey If We Are to See a World-Shaking Revival," *TVH* (November 1949), 12–13.

21. See *Healing En Masse* (Tulsa: T. L. Osborn [1958]).

22. Grant, *A Miracle Ministry*, 6–7.

23. LeRoy Jenkins, *Somebody Up There Loves Me* (Tampa: LeRoy Jenkins Evangelistic Association, 1965), 27–28.

24. Thelma Chaney, *The Power of God on Exhibition* (Tulsa: TOPService, 1954).

25. "Woman Raised from the Dead," TVH (January 1956), 9.

26. See Grant, *Raising the Dead*, 32.

27. See Hollenweger, *The Pentecostals*, 377; Bloch-Hoell, *The Pentecostal Movement*, 147–51; Thomas Wyatt, *The Work of Demons* (Portland: Wings of Healing [1948]).

28. See Hollenweger, *The Pentecostals*, 377; interview.

29. A. A. Allen, *Invasion from Hell* (Miracle Valley, Arizona: A. A. Allen [1953]), 6.

30. A. A. Allen, *The Curse of Madness* (Miracle Valley, Arizona: A. A. Allen Publications [1963]), 55–73.

31. Pearry Green, *The Acts of the Prophet* (Tucson: Tucson Tabernacle mimeographed book, n.d.), chap. 9, pp. 3–4.

32. "Phoenix Reporters Reveal Source of Information," MM (May 1956), 5.

33. "Grant's Faith Clinic," TVH (June 1960), 10.

34. "An Interview with William Branham," TVH (October 1951), 8.

35. Sermon, Birmingham, Alabama, May 2, 1973.

36. Hollenweger, *The Pentecostals*, 357.

37. See Jack Coe, *Curing the Incurable* (Dallas: Herald of Healing, n.d.), 14–19.

38. Interview.

39. "Why Was Jack Coe Taken in the Midst of His Ministry," *TVH* (February 1957), 2.

40. Nichol, *Pentecostalism*, 16–17.

41. See Oral Roberts, *The Call* (New York: Doubleday and Company, 1972), 45–56.

42. [Masthead], *TVD* (November–December 1973), [1].

43. A. G. Hobbs, *Have Miracles Ceased?* (30th ed.; Fort Worth, Texas: Hobbs Publications, n.d.), 17–18.

44. W. V. Grant, *Must I Pray for a Miracle* ([Dallas: W. V. Grant, n.d.]), 12.

45. Stewart service, Cincinnati, Ohio, July 7, 1972.

46. William W. Freeman, "Four Steps to Healing," *THM* (November 1950), 5.

47. "If I Were Coming to the Crusade for Healing," *AL* (September 1966), 9. See also, Oral Roberts, *Your Healing Problems and How to Solve Them* (Tulsa: Oral Roberts, 1966), 89–93.

48. LeRoy Jenkins, *Somebody Up There*, 25.

49. "Mental Illness and Pentecostal Religion," *Pentecost* No. 39 (March 1957), 17.

Evangelism and Ecumenicity

1. "Ten Rules We Must Obey If We Are to See a World-Shaking Revival," *TVH* (November 1949), 12.

2. Hagin sermon, May 22, 1973.

3. Oral Roberts, "What God Has Shown to Me," *AHM* (October 1954), 4–5.

4. "Interview with William Branham," *TVH* (April 1954), 14.

5. "God's Message to the Church for This Hour," *TVH* (February 1953), 3.

6. "World-Wide Pentecostal Revivals, 1906–1956," *TVH* (July 1956), 13.

7. David Nunn, "God's Order of the Day, Revive, Restore, Reap!" *THM* (Nunn) (September 1963), 3. See also, "Winning the Nations Crusade," *TVH* (July 1956), 2–3; Vernon Pettenger, "50,000 Hear Velmer Gardner in South Africa," *Pentecost* No. 39 (March 1957), 11.

8. Gordon Lindsay, *William Branham: A Man Sent from God* (4th ed.; Jeffersonville, Indiana: William Branham, 1950), 15.

9. "Concerning Other Ministries and Gifts Being Manifested," *TVH* (October 1948), 8.

10. David duPlessis, "Christian Fellowship Convention," *HOF* (July 1957), 9–10.

11. See "Among the Healing Campaigns," *Pentecost* No. 30 (December 1954), 14.

12. Anna Jeanne Moore, "Convention Diary," *TVH* (February 1952), 2–3.

13. Gordon Lindsay, "Ten Rules We Must Obey If We Are to See a World-Shaking Revival," *TVH* (November 1949), 12.

14. See Gordon Lindsay, *Crusade for World Fellowship* (Dallas: The Voice of Healing Publishing Co., n.d.).

15. "The True Path to the Unity of Believers," *TVH* (January 1950), 6.

16. "William Branham's Message to the Church," *TVH* (March 1955), 6.

17. "William Branham's Message to the Church, Installment III," *TVH* (May 1955), 19.

18. "What's the Secret Behind Oral Roberts' Success," *HW* (November 1951), 7.

19. Interview.

Minor Themes

1. *My Vision of the Destruction of America* (Miracle Valley, Arizona: A. A. Allen Publications [1954]), 5, 28.

2. Ibid., 38.

3. Ibid., 74.

4. Lindsay, *Branham*, 79.

5. See William W. Freeman, "Christ Shall Come . . . I'm Looking for His Appearing," *THM* (May 1956), 4–5; G. H. M [ontgomery], "Looking Forward with Oral Roberts in 1953," *HW* (February 1953), 10.

6. Lindsay, *Branham*, 92.

7. Oral Roberts, *The Call* (New York: Doubleday and Company, 1972), 93–112.

8. See David Edwin Harrell, Jr., *White Sects and Black Men in the Recent South* (Nashville: Vanderbilt University Press, 1971).

9. Mrs. M. B. Woodworth-Etter, *Marvels and Miracles* (Indianapolis: Mrs. M. B. Woodworth-Etter [1922]), 57–59.

10. Nancy Barr Mavity, *Sister Aimee* (New York: Doubleday, Doran & Company, 1931), 38.

11. See "Jack Coe Returns to Pittsburgh," *HOH* (October 1953), 14–15; "Birmingham Pastors Acclaim Jack Coe Revival Campaign as Greatest Ever Held in Alabama!" *IHM* (June 1955), 14–15; Herbert Fuller, "The Greatest Religious Revival Ever Held in Philadelphia," *IHM* (June 1955), 10–11, 15.

12. "Miracle in Black and White," *MM* (August 1958), 10.

Problems: External and Internal

1. "Oklahoma Faith-Healer Draws a Following," *CC* 62 (June 29, 1955), 749–50. See also, W. E. Mann, "What About Oral Roberts," *CC* 63 (September 5, 1956), 1018–21.

2. "Travail of a Healer," *Newsweek* (March 19, 1956), 82. See also, *New York Times*, February 19, 1956, II, 11; March 4, 1956, II, 9. These assessments are typical of those published constantly in the newspapers throughout the country.

3. See, for example, "Disunity Decried in World Missions," *New York Times*, November 27, 1956, 8; "Religious Quackery," *Time* (February 9, 1962), 42; "Failure of Faith in a Faith Healer," *Life* (March 5, 1956), 64; J. Kobler, "Truth About Faith Healers," *McCalls* (February 1957), 39.

4. See "Faith Healing Is Declared True Healing," *New York Times*, May 24, 1960, 3; "Faith 'Cures' Stir Warning in South Birmingham," *New York Times*, April 28, 1957, 3; "Church Cautions on Faith Healing," *New York Times*, February 3, 1962, 4.

5. "Sideglances," *Liguorian* 44 (February 1956), 114–15.

6. Jack Coe, *Tried . . . But Freed* ([Dallas]: Herald of Healing [1956]), 35–40; Roberts, *The Call*, 52; Norman Gordon, "Modern Day 'Pharisees' Still Resist Those Who Pray for God to Heal the Sick," *IHM* (March 1956), 3; W. V. Grant, *Must I Pray for a Miracle?* ([Dallas: W. V. Grant, n.d.]), 12–15; "For Divine Healing," *Newsweek* (February 2, 1955), 86.

7. See Connie W. Adams, *Faith or Fake* (Marion, Ind.: *Truth Magazine*, n.d.), 17.

8. Grant, *Must I Pray for a Miracle*, 12–13.

9. "Church of Christ Bolsheviks," *HOH* (December 1953), 13–14. See also, Coe, *Tried . . . But Freed*, 34; Grant, *Must I Pray for a Miracle*.

10. Interview.

11. Bloch-Hoell, *The Pentecostal Movement*, 150. See also, "Church Cautions on Faith Healing," *New York Times*, February 3, 1962, 10; J. Kobler, "The Truth About Faith Healers," *McCalls* (February 1957), 39, 74–82; "Frenzy of Faith in a Man's Touch," *Life* (August 3, 1962), 19.

12. See Jack Coe, "Doctors, Demons and Pills," *HOH* (December 1953), 2–4, 6.

13. Interview.

14. See Gordon Lindsay, "On the Witness Stand in the Jack Coe Hearing at Miami, Florida," *TVH* (April 1956), 8, 23.

15. See Oral Roberts, *My Story* (Tulsa and New York: Summit Book Company, 1961), 172–90; Oral Roberts, "My Personal Story about the Melbourne Campaign," *Healing* (April 1956), 14; Roberts, *The Call*, 73–84; "Travail of a Healer," *Newsweek* (March 19, 1956), 81.

16. Oral Roberts, "An Open Letter to Magazine and Newspaper Editors," *AL* (February 1957), 16–17, 28–29.

17. See Roberts, *My Story*, 171.

18. See "Publicity-Minded Newspaper Prints Many Slurs and Distorted Facts about Oral Roberts," *IHM* (May 1956), 14; O. L. Jaggers, "An Open Letter to the Deliverance Ministry," *WFN* (June 1956), 8–9, 12.

19. See Gordon Lindsay, "TVH Backs Jack Coe in Historic Trial at Miami," *TVH* (April 1956), 7; Coe, *Story of Jack Coe*, 78–79; interviews.

20. See *New York Times*, April 10, 1958, 34.

21. Roberts, *The Call*, 57–60.

22. "Decision," *MM* (February 1957), 14.

23. A. A. Allen, "Will You Help Me Fight the Devil?" *MM* (July 1956), 18.

24. "An Open Letter to the Deliverance Ministry," *WFN* (June 1956), 9.

25. "To Touch Neither the Gold Nor the Glory," *Healing* (March 1956), 5.

26. Anna Jeanne Moore, "Voice of Healing Convention," *TVH* (February 1951), 2.

27. Interview.

28. *The Way to Prosperity* (Tulsa: Thelma Chaney, n.d.), 5.

29. Thelma Chaney, *The New Wine of the Kingdom* (Tulsa: Lighthouse Gospel Center, 1968), 91.

30. A. A. Allen, *Your Christian Dollar* (Dallas: A. A. Allen [1958]), 28–29.

31. Oral Roberts, "Do You Want God to Return Your Money Seven Times?" *AHM* (April 1954), 10.

32. Myron Sackett, "Deliverance from Poverty," *AL* (April 1958), 19.

33. See Oral Roberts, "To Touch Neither the Gold Nor the Glory," *HW* (March 1956), 3.

34. See Oral Roberts, "An Open Letter to Magazine and Newspaper Editors," *AL* (February 1957), 16–17, 28–29.

35. Interviews.

36. Gordon Lindsay, "Ten Rules We Must Follow If We Are to See a World-Shaking Revival," *TVH* (November 1949), 12.

37. See "We March Forward in Faith," *THD* (January 1961), 11.

38. Interview.

39. "Concerning Other Ministries and Gifts Being Manifested," *TVH* (October 1948), 8.

40. "Evangelist Alfred Allen, Memphis, Tenn.," *HOF* (March 1957), 8.

41. Interview.

42. Interview.

43. See Hollenweger, *The Pentecostals*, 357.

44. Walter H. Beuttler, "Some 'Weightier Matters,' " *PE* No. 1977 (March 30, 1952), 11.

45. Interview.

46. W. T. Gaston to Ralph M. Riggs, March 29, 1956, Assemblies of God Headquarters, Springfield, Missouri.

47. E. M. Wadsworth, "Miracle Without Money," *PE* No. 1980 (April 20, 1952), 4.

48. Carl Brumback, *Suddenly . . . From Heaven* (Springield, Mo.: Gospel Publishing House [1961]), 334.

49. See *Minutes* of the . . . General Council of the Assemblies of God (Springfield, Mo.: Assemblies of God, 1931), 40.

50. Typed copy of General Presbytery Minutes of 1956, 34.

51. See Gordon Lindsay, "Ten Rules We Must Follow If We Are to See a

World-Shaking Revival," *TVH* (November 1949), 12; "The Purpose, Plan and Policy of the Voice of Healing Convention," *TVH* (December 1950), 2, 15; "The Voice of Healing Convention—1951," *TVH* (December 1951), 8.

52. "Editorial," *HOF* (August 1957), 3.

53. "Wide Interest in Divine Healing," *TVH* (February 1953), 20.

54. "Extremes Are Sometimes Necessary," *TVH* (April 1953), 9. See also, "Healing Campaigns and Bible Schools," *Pentecost* No. 23 (March 1953), 17.

55. "Personality and Unity," *TVH* (December 1954), 12.

56. Interview.

57. Interview.

58. *The Church One Body* (Tulsa: H. A. and Thelma Chaney [1960]), 38.

59. Interview.

60. Interview.

61. Donald Gee, *All with One Accord* (Springfield, Mo.: Gospel Publishing House [1961]), 42.

62. [Letters], *HOH* (April–May 1953), 23.

63. Ibid., 25.

64. Ibid.

65. "The Awful Truth!" *HOH* (June 1953), 10–11.

66. [Letter], *HOH* (April–May, 1953), 26.

67. "Who Is Capitalizing on the Chrisitan's Money," *HOH* (November 1953), 8–9.

68. "Recommendation for the Next General Council," *HOH* (June 1953), 11.

69. Interview.

70. Interview.

71. Interview.

72. *Apostles and Prophets . . . in the Church Today?* (Dallas: Herald of Healing, 1954), 21. See also, Thelma Chaney, *The Power of the Unveiled Son* (Tulsa: All Hour Business Service [1968]), 28.

73. Velmer Gardner, "Will This Present Healing Revival Taper Off?" *WWR* (June 1958), 9.

74. O. L. Jaggers, "An Open Letter to the Deliverance Ministry," *WFN* (June 1956), 8–9, 12.

75. O. L. Jaggers, "An Open Letter to Assembly of God Ministers and People!" *MM* (October 1956), 10–11, 18, 20.

76. *Prisons with Stained Glass Windows* (Miracle Valley, Arizona: A. A. Allen Revivals, 1963), 95–96.

77. *The Fatal Word That Will Jam Hell to the Doors* (Dallas: A. A. Allen Publications, n.d.), 28. See also, A. A. Allen, *How to Take the Answer from God* ([Miracle Valley, Arizona: A. A. Allen Publications, n.d.]), 8.

78. *Prisons with Stained Glass Windows*, 15–16.

79. "The Deliverance Campaigns," *Pentecost* No. 36 (June 1956), 17.

80. Interview.

81. "Pentecost Re-Valued," *Pentecost* No. 28 (June 1954), 17.

82. *All with One Accord*, 42.
83. Hollenweger, *The Pentecostals*, 356–57.
84. "Ten Rules We Must Follow If We Are to See a World-Shaking Revival," *TVH* (November 1949), 12–13.
85. "Exaggeration," *TVH* (May 1954), 23.
86. "Attitudes Toward the Supernatural," *Pentecost* No. 38 (December 1956), 17.
87. "Concerning Our Association with The Voice of Healing," *FD* (June 1956), 17.

Chapter 6 / From Healing Revival to Charismatic Revival

Bitter Examination

1. "The Present Day Ministry of Deliverance," *TVH* (October 1956), 8.
2. "Will This Present Healing Revival Taper Off?" *WWR* (June 1958), 9.
3. [Donald Gee], "Pentecostal Winds of Change," *Pentecost* No. 67 (March–May 1964), 17.
4. Interview.
5. Interview.
6. Interview.
7. Mrs. Gordon Lindsay, "Highlights of the Fourteenth Annual Voice of Healing Convention," *TVH* (September 1962), 9.
8. "The Godhead Explained," *TSW*, no. 24, 35.
9. "Statement of the Scriptural Basis of Fellowship in the Body of Christ," *TVH* (July 1962), 4–5, 11, 13, 15.
10. Interview.
11. "Statement of the Scriptural Basis of Fellowship in the Body of Christ," *TVH* (July 1962), 4–5, 11, 13, 15.
12. Interview.
13. "Statement of the Scriptural Basis of Fellowship in the Body of Christ," *TVH* (July 1962), 4–5, 11, 13, 15.
14. Interview. See also, Gordon Lindsay, *The Gordon Lindsay Story* (Dallas: The Voice of Healing Publishing Co., n.d.), 272–73.
15. Interview.
16. *Wind and Flame* (rev. and enlarged ed. [Springfield]: Assemblies of God Publishing House, 1967).
17. "Wheat, Tares and 'Tongues,'" *Pentecost* No. 66 (December 1963–February 1964), 17.
18. "Miracles Are Not Enough," *Pentecost* No. 70 (December 1965–February 1966), 17.

19. "The Value of the Supernatural," *Pentecost* No. 62 (December 1962–February 1963), 17.

20. "Deserving Independent Existence," *Pentecost* No. 71 (March–May 1966), 17.

21. Interview.

22. "Their Glory Is Their Shame," *IHM* (March 1962), 3.

23. "Enemies of the Cross of Christ," *IHM* (February 1962), 3; "You're Going to Hurt Yourself," *IHM* (May 1962), 2.

24. "Their Glory Is Their Shame," *IHM* (March 1962), 3.

25. Ibid.

26. "Making Merchandise of You," *IHM* (May 1962), 15.

27. "Their Glory Is Their Shame," *IHM* (March 1962), 10–11.

28. "A Lying Spirit in the Mouth of the Prophets," *IHM* (April 1962), 6–7.

29. "Give Me This Power," *CCH* (June 1962), 10–13.

30. "Making Merchandise of You," *IHM* (May 1962), 14–15.

31. "A Lying Spirit in the Mouth of the Prophets," *IHM* (April 1962), 6.

32. "Their Glory Is Their Shame," *IHM* (March 1962), 10.

33. "Making Merchandise of You," *IHM* (May 1962), 11–15; see also, "A Lying Spirit in the Mouth of the Prophets," *IHM* (April 1962), 7.

34. Ibid.

35. "Where Do We Go from Here," *CCH* (July 1962), 11–15.

New Moves

1. See "Second World Convention of Deliverance Evangelists," *THM* (Nunn) (February 1964), 4–5; "Fourth World Convention of Deliverance Evangelists," *DL* (October 1965), 11.

2. Mrs. Gordon Lindsay, "World Convention Blesses Many," *TVH* (December 1959), 8–11, 13.

3. Interview.

4. "Will This Present Healing Revival Taper Off?" *WWR* (June 1958), 9.

5. Jack Coe, *Apostles and Prophets . . . in the Church Today?* (Dallas: Herald of Healing, 1954), 30.

6. Interview.

7. "Pentecostal Winds of Change," *Pentecost* No. 67 (March–May 1964), 17. See also [Donald Gee], "At the Crossroads," *Pentecost* No. 56 (June–August 1961), 17.

8. "The Truth about the Present Move of God in the Historical Churches," *TVH* (November 1961), 4.

9. "Pentecostal Winds of Change," *Pentecost* No. 67 (March–May 1964), 17.

10. "Miracles Are Not Enough," *Pentecost* No. 70 (December 1965–February 1966), 17.

11. Interview.

12. "The Story of Demos Shakarian and The Full Gospel Business Men's Fellowship," *TVH* (August 1953), 9.

13. See Thomas R. Nickel, *The Shakarian Story* (2nd ed.; Los Angeles: Full Gospel Business Men's Fellowship International [1964]); Demos D. Shakarian, "How Our Fellowship Came into Being," *Voice* (February 1953), 3–5.

14. "Full Gospel Business Men of America Start New National Association," *HW* (January 1952), 12.

15. Demos D. Shakarian, "How Our Fellowship Came into Being," *Voice* (February 1953), 4.

16. See Thomas R. Nickel, "God's Mighty Power Manifested at Our First Annual Convention," *Voice* (November 1953), 8–14.

17. "Full Gospel Business Men's Convention in Washington, D. C., Inspiring," *TVH* (August 1954), 18.

18. See "Growth of the Fellowship," *Voice* (June 1966), 8–11; John Thomas Nichol, *Pentecostalism* (New York: Harper & Row [1966]), 241–42; William C. Armstrong, "Demos Shakarian—A Man and His Message," *Logos* (September–October 1971), 13–14; "Pentecostal Unit Gains Followers," *Voice* (October 1972), 3.

19. See W. J. Hollenweger, *The Pentecostals* (1st U.S. ed.; Minneapolis: Augsburg Publishing House, 1972); and Donald Gee, "Should They Speak," *TVH* (October 1955), 18.

20. "From the Editor's Mail," *Voice* (February–March 1954), 12.

21. Hollenweger, *The Pentecostals*, 356.

22. Interview.

23. Hollenweger, *The Pentecostals*, 6–7.

Chapter 7 / Innovators and New Breeds

ORAL ROBERTS

1. See Oral Roberts, "The Lord Told Me to Build," *AL* (April 1959), 4–6.

2. "Will You Take My Hand in Partnership," *AL* (May 1959), 6–7.

3. Oral Roberts, "A Look at the New Year," *AL* (January 1964), 2.

4. Oral Roberts, "We Are Returning to Television," *AL* (February 1969), 2. For many years Roberts showed little interest in foreign evangelism. It is remarkable that he did not conduct a major campaign in Europe until 1961. See Oral Roberts, "My First European Crusade," *AL* (February 1969), 2–5.

5. See [Oral Roberts], "Seven Outstanding Achievements of the Ministry," *AL* (April 1962), 14–17; [Oral Roberts], "A Personal Statement," *AL* (November 1962), 7; "Keeping Posted," *AL* (February 1962), 13.

6. Oral Roberts, "The 'New Shape' of Abundant Life Magazine," *AL*

(February 1962), 2. As editor, G. H. Montgomery apparently felt the magazine should be more of a teaching medium, but Roberts wanted the magazine to report on his ministry.

7. See "New TV Program," *AL* (April 1965), 22–23; "New Radio Program," *AL* (January 1967), 5.

8. Oral Roberts, "A Special Message to My Partners," *AL* (May 1967), 28.

9. See Oral Roberts, "We Are Returning to Television," *AL* (February 1969), 2–7.

10. Ibid.

11. Oral Roberts, *The Call* (New York: Doubleday and Company, 1972), 186.

12. Interview.

13. See "Minister's Seminar," *AL* (April 1963), 2–11; "Laymen from Many States, 35 Denominations Find Spiritual Renewal," *AL* (June 1968), 19–21.

14. "I'm Excited About the Whole Kingdom of God," *AL* (May 1967), 25.

15. See Oral Roberts, *The Baptism with the Holy Spirit* (Tulsa: Oral Roberts [1964]).

16. See Roberts, *The Call*, 124–46.

17. Oral Roberts, "The President's Report," *AL* (February 1970), 7.

18. See Vinson Synan, *The Holiness-Pentecostal Movement in the United States* (Grand Rapids, Mich.: William B. Eerdman's Publishing Company [1971]), 210; Roberts, *The Call*, 128.

19. Synan, *The Holiness-Pentecostal Movement*, 210.

20. Interview.

21. Roberts, *The Call*, 136–37.

22. Interview.

23. Roberts, *The Call*, 130.

24. Interview.

25. See Roberts, *The Call*, 128, 197–216; interview.

26. "ORU Today," *AL* (February 1970), 21.

27. Oral Roberts, "A Spiritual Revolution Throughout the Earth," *AL* (May 1962), 6–10.

28. "Oral Roberts University Now Fully Accredited," *AL* (May 1971), 16.

29. Ibid.

30. Oral Roberts, "The President's Report," *AL* (February 1970), 7.

31. Interview.

32. Oral Roberts, "The President's Report," *AL* (February 1970), 7; interview.

33. Oral Roberts, "The President's Report," *AL* (February 1970), 6.

34. Ibid., 5–6.

35. "Oral Roberts University Now Fully Accredited," *AL* (May 1971), 16–19.

36. Robert Eskridge, "We Are Moving the Earth Again at ORU," *AL* (November 1970), 17.

37. "The Beginning of a Miracle," *AL* (February 1970), 2–4.

38. Oral Roberts, *The Miracle Book* (Tulsa: Pinook Publications [1972]), 63.

39. Oral Roberts and G. H. Montgomery, eds., *God's Formula for Success and Prosperity* (Tulsa: Oral Roberts [1955]), 150.

40. See Oral Roberts, "We Are Returning to Television," *AL* (February 1969), 2–7.

41. Interview.

42. Oral Roberts, "Oral Roberts Tells How the Founding of This Magazine Was Based on a Great Healing and the Amazing Results of Its 22 Years of 'A March of Faith' Across the World," *AL* (November 1969), 2–3.

43. Oral Roberts, "The President's Report," *AL* (February 1970), 8.

44. Oral Roberts, "I've Made the Full Circle," *AL* (November 1970), 8–9.

45. "Dick Cavett's Tough Questions," *AL* (June 1970), 10–12.

46. See Roberts, *The Call*, 190–96; interviews.

47. "The Oral Roberts Evangelistic Association, Inc.," *AL* (April 1966), 15.

48. See Oral Roberts, *God Is a Good God* (Indianapolis: The Bobbs-Merrill Company [1960]); "Next Question, Please?" *AL* (January 1968), 18–19.

49. "An Interview with Oral and Richard Roberts on the Mike Douglas Show," *AL* (December 1970), 10–12.

50. See Roberts, *The Call*, 45–56.

51. "Overflow Crowd of Delegates Bombards Panel with Questions on Healing," *AL* (February 1967), 21.

52. Oral Roberts and G. H. Montgomery, eds., *God's Formula for Success and Prosperity* (Tulsa: Oral Roberts [1955]), 150.

53. See "Dick Cavett's Tough Questions," *AL* (June 1970), 12; Roberts, *The Miracle Book*.

54. "Somebody's Got to Care," *AL* (December 1971), 5.

55. "God Healed Me of Terminal Cancer," *AL* (June 1972), 8–9.

56. R. F. deWeese, "A Statement," *AL* (October 1962), 22–23.

57. See Oral Roberts, "A Look at The New Year," *AL* (January 1964), 2–3; "One-Day Crusades with Our Partners," *AL* (July 1969), 15.

58. Interview.

59. "How I Discovered the Miracle of Seed-Faith and How It Works to Meet Needs in My Life Today," *AL* (October 1971), 2–17. See also, Roberts, *The Miracle Book*, 1.

60. "Do You Need a Beginning of Miracles in Your Life?," *AL* (February 1970), 23–27.

61. See Roberts, *The Call*, 113–24; "We Have Been Conquered by Love," *AL* (February 1967), 25.

62. Oral Roberts, "My Personal Impressions of the World Congress on Evangelism," *AL* (January 1970), 28–30.

63. Oral Roberts, "We Have Been Conquered by Love," *AL* (February 1967), 63.

64. Oral Roberts, "The President's Report," *AL* (February 1970), 8.

65. "I'm Excited About the 'Whole Kingdom of God,'" *AL* (May 1971), 22.

66. Interview.

WILLIAM BRANHAM

1. "Rev. William Branham and the Future," *HOF* (June 1959), 7.

2. Pearry Green, *The Acts of the Prophet* (mimeographed book; Tucson: Tucson Tabernacle [n.d.]), chapter 15, p. 8; interview.

3. See Joseph D. Mattsson-Boze, "William Branham," *HOF* (February 1966), 3.

4. See Green, *The Acts of the Prophet*, chap. 15.

5. "Rev. William Branham and the Future," *HOF* (June 1959), 7.

6. "Letter from William Branham," *WWR* (November 1958), 14.

7. See Green, *The Acts of the Prophet*, chap. 8, p. 6.

8. Roy Borders, "Report on Summer Campaign of William Branham," *HOF* (October 1962), 5.

9. See William Branham, "Just Once More, Lord!" *HOF* (January 1964), 5, 13, 17–18; "Schedule of Meetings for Rev. William Branham," *HOF* (July 1963), 4; William Branham, "The Greatest Battle Ever Fought," *HOF* (July 1962), 5–6, 12–13.

10. William Branham, "Just Once More, Lord!" *HOF* (January 1964), 5.

11. See Roy Borders, "Report on Summer Campaign of Rev. William Branham," *HOF* (October 1962), 5; "Branham Evangelistic-Healing Campaign Co-Sponsored by San Jose, Calif. Chapter," *Voice* (February 1960), 14–15.

12. "Concerning Photograph on Front Cover," *Voice* (February 1961), 3.

13. Demos Shakarian, "In Memorium," *Voice* (January–February 1966), 29.

14. See Green, *The Acts of the Prophet*, chap. 3, pp. 4–5; interview.

15. Ibid., chap. 15, p. 2.

16. Len J. Jones, "I Attended Another Branham Meeting," *HOF* (January 1959), 3.

17. Ibid.

18. Gordon Lindsay, *William Branham: A Man Sent from God* (4th ed.; Jeffersonville, Indiana: William Branham, 1950), 11.

19. W. J. Hollenweger, *The Pentecostals* (1st U.S. ed.; Minneapolis: Augsburg Publishing House, 1972), 355.

20. Roy Borders, "Report on Summer Campaign of Rev. William Branham," *HOF* (October 1962), 5.

21. "William Branham," *HOF* (February 1966), 3.

22. Gordon Lindsay, "William Branham As I Knew Him," *TVH* (February 1966), 11.

23. Interview.

24. Interview.

25. See William Branham, "Spiritual Amnesia," *HOF* (February 1965), 3–4, 16–17, 20–22; William Branham, "Divine Healing," *HOF* (November 1965), 9, 24.

26. See Green, *Acts of the Prophet*, chap. 5, p. 4; chap. 13, p. 6.
27. Interview.
28. See "The Godhead Explained," *TSW*, No. 24, n.d., 1–44.
29. See Green, *Acts of the Prophet*, chap. 12, p. 57; chap. 6, p. 6; interview.
30. William Marrion Branham, *An Exposition of the Seven Church Ages* ([Tucson: Rev. William Branham], n.d.), 329.
31. See Green, *Acts of the Prophet*, chap. 6, p. 3. For a discussion of the seals, see chap. 10, pp. 2–8.
32. Interviews.
33. Green, *Acts of the Prophet*, chap. 16, p. 10.
34. See Gordon Lindsay, "William Branham As I knew Him," *TVH* (February 1966), 3.
35. "Coronation Day," *TVD* (January 1966), 2.
36. See Green, *Acts of the Prophet*, chap. 19, pp. 5–8.
37. See ibid., chap. 17, pp. 1–15.
38. Interview.
39. Interview.
40. "Coronation Day," *TVD* (January 1966), 2.

GORDON LINDSAY

1. "Important Announcement," *TVH* (February 1958), 2.
2. Interview.
3. See "Winning the Nations Crusade," *TVH* (July 1956), 2–3; "Winning the Nations Crusade," *TVH* (August 1956), 9.
4. "Important Announcement," *TVH* (February 1958), 2.
5. See Gordon Lindsay, "New Developments and Plans for Winning the Nations Crusade," *TVH* (January 1962), 4–5, 15.
6. Interview.
7. "From the Editor's Desk," *CFN* (May 1967), 2.
8. "Important Announcement," *TVH* (February 1958), 2.
9. "A Most Important Announcement About the New Full Gospel Fellowship of Churches and Ministers International," *TVH* (September 1962), 2–3.
10. See ibid., and "Progress of 'The Full Gospel Fellowship,'" *TVH* (October 1962), 10.
11. See Gordon Lindsay and David duPlessis, "The Astounding Move of God in the Denominational Churches," *TVH* (January 1960), 4–5, 14–15; "The Objectives of the Voice of Healing," *TVH* (September 1964), 3, 15; "The Christ for the Nations' Library," *LJ* (January–February 1972), 11.
12. Gordon Lindsay, "Confidential Prayer Letter," March 1972, typed MS.
13. Interviews; see also, "From the Editor's Desk," *TVH* (March 1965), 2.
14. Interview.
15. Interview.

T. L. OSBORN

1. Henry L. Watson, "Am I Getting My Money's Worth," *FD* (August 1959), 10.

2. "T. L. Osborn's 9-Point Harvest Plan," *FD* (February 1961), 12–15.

3. William P. Sterne, "Dedicated to World Evangelism," *FD* (October 1963), 16–19.

4. "The Flaming Arch," *FD* (September 1969), 2–3.

5. "Attend a T. L. Osborn Crusade," *FD* (January 1968), 15.

6. "'67, Year of Opportunity," *FD* (January 1967), 3.

7. "God's *'Pact'* for You in '72!" *FD* (January 1972), 7.

8. "Man of Prayer and Faith," *FD* (April 1970), 4; see also, "Meet Us at the Big Tulsa Partners Homecoming," *FD* (July 1969), 16–17.

9. "T. L. Osborn Looks into the New Year . . . ," *FD* (January 1972), 6–7.

10. "Man of Prayer and Faith," *FD* (April 1970), 4; see also, "Meet Us at the Big Tulsa Partners Homecoming," *FD* (July 1969), 16–17.

11. Daisy M. Osborn, "Magnificent Revolution," *FD* (September 1971), 10–11.

12. Drew Graham, "Ministry with a Million Faces," *FD* (March 1969), 2–5.

13. Interview.

W. V. GRANT

1. See W. V. Grant, *The Grace of God in My Life* (enl. ed.; [Dallas]: W. V. Grant [1952]); interview.

2. Interview.

3. Interview.

4. Ibid.

5. "God's Will for You in 1966," *TVD* (January 1966), 4–5.

6. "Television," *TVD* (August 1968), 14–15; interview.

7. Interview.

8. Ibid.

9. Ibid.

Other Innovators

1. See Velmer Gardner, "A Miracle-Working God," *AL* (June, 1965), 6–9.

2. See [Juanita Coe], "See What God Has Done!" *CCH* (December 1962), 2.

3. See *The Christian Challenge* (February 1973), 2–10; interview.

4. Raymond G. Hoekstra, "Profile of a Man with a Purpose," *LJ* (January–February 1972), 47.

5. "From Our Hearts to You," *WE* (January 1971), 2; see also, John E. Douglas, Sr., "Missionary Radio Broadcast," *WE* (September 1972), 15.

6. "Our Motto," *WE* (December 1971), 2.

7. "Know Where Your Missionary Dollars Go!" *WE* (December 1971), 15.

8. Interview.

9. See M. A. Daoud, *Bringing Back the King!* ([Dallas: Voice Miracles and Missions, n.d.]).

10. "Please Decide for Us," *MMD* (January 1965), 11.

11. [Masthead], *NH* (April 1962), 2.

12. See "When You Give," *NH* (July–August 1969), 4–5.

13. R. W. Culpepper, "Why 'World-Wide Revival Reports,' " *WWRR* (November 1961), 2.

14. "R. W. Culpepper Makes Change in Schedule," *WWRR* (December 1961–January 1962), 2.

15. R. W. Culpepper, "Why 'World-Wide Revival Reports,' " *WWR* (December 1961–January 1962), 2.

16. "R. W. Culpepper Makes Change in Schedule," *WWRR* (December 1961–January 1962), 2.

17. See R. W. Culpepper, "Did You Know?" *WWRR* (April 1968), 4; R. W. Culpepper, *100,000 Miles of Miracles* (Dallas: R. W. Culpepper, n.d.); R. W. Culpepper, "Our Greatest Move in 10 Years," *WWRR* (January 1970), 2–3; [front page article], *WWRR* (February 1967), 1.

18. See Gordon Lindsay, *Men Who Heard from Heaven* ([Dallas]: The Voice of Healing Publishing Co. [1953]), 148–60.

19. See "Full Gospel Fellowship of Churches and Ministers International," *ET* (October 1963), 12; "Valdez Crusades in Foreign Countries," *ET* (October 1965), 6, 7; "First Annual Convention in Milwaukee Great Success," *ET* (September 1961), 6.

20. See Lester Sumrall, "How God Showed Me World Evangelization Must Be by Healing and Miracles," *TVH* (July 1955), 5, 17; "Editorial Comments," *WH* (April 1962), 2; Lester Sumrall, "Miracle of '1971,' " *WH* (December 1970–January 1971), 2–5.

21. "How I Learned to Cast Out Devils," *WH* (July–August 1971), 4; see also, Lester Sumrall, *Seven Ways to Recognize Demon Power Today* (2nd ed.; [South Bend: Lester Sumrall Evangelistic Assn.], n.d.).

22. "I Shall Not Compromise the Full Gospel," *WH* (June 1968), 2.

23. See Jos. D. Mattsson-Boze, "Victory Report," *HOF* (May 1966), 17–18; "Your Missionary Evangelist," *HOF* (June 1968), 13; "Two Glorious Training Centers—Honduras-Argentina," *HOF-HT* (April 1971), 18–20.

24. See "Anniversary Letter," *THM* (Nunn) (March 1965), 15; "Radio Schedule," *THM* (Nunn) (June 1967), 15; "Radio Schedule," *THM* (Nunn) (June 1972), 15; interview.

25. See [advertisement], *THM* (Nunn) (August 1967), 3; David Nunn, "From My Heart to the Hearts of My Friends," *THM* (Nunn) (February 1968), 6–11, 14; "Partnership Agreement," *THM* (Nunn) (July 1967), 13; "Thousands Converted in Africa Crusade!" *THM* (Nunn) (May 1968), 1; interview.

26. David Nunn, "The Move of God," *THM* (Nunn) (April 1972), 11.

27. See David O. Nunn, "We Have Come This Far by Faith," *THM* (Nunn) (January 1966), 2–4; interview.

28. Interview.

29. See Kenneth Gaub, "Do You Really Trust God for Healing???" *FIA* (July–December 1960), 5, 8.

30. Letter from Kenneth Gaub to S. Juanita Walker, February 29, 1964, Pentecostal Collection, Oral Roberts University.

31. See "Hear!!!" *FIA* (January–February 1961), 16; "Yes!!" *FIA* (October–December 1962), 10.

32. See "Attend Our Patriotic Rallies," *FIA* (May–June 1972), 2; "Sponsoring Pastors," *FIA* (May–June 1971), 7.

New Breeds

1. For a good summary of the neopentecostal movement, see Steve Durasoff, *Bright Wind of the Spirit* (Englewood Cliffs, N.J.: Prentice-Hall [1972]).

2. Interview.

3. Ibid.

4. Ibid.

5. "The Voice Magazine Vision," *VW* (April 1963), 1–3.

6. [Masthead], *"He Is Able,"* (May 1972), 23.

7. [Masthead], *CF* (March–April 1972), inside cover.

8. "Editorial," *NW* (March 1972), 3.

9. See Don Basham, "How It All Began," *NW* (June 1969), 7–8, 17; [masthead], *NW* (February 1970), 3.

10. Joseph Mattsson-Boze, "Important News Concerning The Herald of Faith," *HOF-HT* (July–August 1971), 5–6.

11. "Who Reads Logos Journal," *LJ* (November–December 1971), 57.

12. Dan Malachuk, "To Logos Journal Readers," *LJ* (September–October 1971), 34.

13. Interview.

14. "Editorial," *Heartbeat* (May 1971), 2.

15. See Derek Prince, "Philosophy, the Bible and the Supernatural," *HOF* (March 1966), 11–22; Derek Prince, *Teaching Tapes and Books* (Fort Lauderdale: Derek Prince Publications, n.d.), 1; Derek Prince, "The Baptism of the Holy Ghost," *HOF* (May 1960), 2, 12; Derek Prince, *Prayer and Fasting* (Old Tappan, N.J.: Fleming H. Revell Company, 1973).

16. Interview.

17. Ibid.

18. Ibid. See also, Derek Prince, *Expelling Demons* ([Seattle: Derek Prince, n.d.]); and Derek Prince, *Purpose of Pentecost* ([Seattle: Derek Prince, n.d.]).

19. Interview.

20. "A Personal Message," *A Personal Message* (Summer 1973), 2–3.

21. See Hagin sermon, May 22, 1973, Birmingham, Alabama; interview; Kenneth E. Hagin, *I Believe in Visions* (Old Tappan, N.J.: Fleming H. Revell Company, 1972).

22. See Hagin, *I Believe*, 48.

23. Kenneth Hagin, "God Called Me to the Ministry of a Prophet," *HOF* (June 1964), 9–10.

24. See David Wilkerson with John and Elisabeth Sherrill, *The Cross and the Switchblade* ([New York]: Bernard Geis Associate Gospel Publishing House Edition [1963]), and Ruth Wilkerson Harris, *It Was Good Enough for Father* (Old Tappan, N.J.: Fleming H. Revell Company [1969]).

25. [Masthead], *C&S* (April 1972), 2; see also, David Wilkerson, *The Story of Teen Challenge* ([Brooklyn: Teen Challenge, n.d.]).

26. "Jesus Gets Top Billing at Crusade," *Voice* (March 1974), 28–29; see also, Nicky Cruz with Jamie Buckingham, *Run Baby Run* (Plainfield, N.J.: Logos International [1968]).

27. "John Osteen Says," *Praise* (January–February 1963), 2.

28. Mrs. Daga Mattsson-Boze, "Revival Among the Hippies," *HOF-HT* (April 1970), 18.

29. "History Gospel Crusade," *HT* (special edition) [1972], 7–8.

30. "Introducing the Ministries of the Outreach for Christ Foundation," *LJ* (September–October 1971), 31.

31. Ibid.

32. *Birmingham Post-Herald*, February 19, 1972.

Fellow Travelers

1. The best study of Wyatt is Basil Miller, *Grappling with Destiny* (Los Angeles: Wings of Healing [1962]).

2. Thomas Wyatt, *Wings of Healing* (4th ed.; Portland: Ryder Printing Co., 1944), 16.

3. See "You Participated in a Miracle," *MOF* (May 1964), 6–7; *A Memorial Tribute to Thomas Wyatt* (Los Angeles: Wings of Healing [1964]).

4. "Wings of Healing," *MOF* (April 1954), 4.

5. "Twenty-Third Anniversary," *MOF* (May 1965), 2–4.

6. See "A Greater Year," *MOF* (January 1971), 4–5.

7. [Masthead], *MOF* (January 1969), 2.

8. "Miracle Woman," *Time* (September 14, 1970), 62.

9. Kathryn Kuhlman, "My First Healing," *Guideposts* (June 1971), 3. See also, Allen Spraggett, *Kathryn Kuhlman: The Woman Who Believes in Miracles* (New York: The World Publishing Company, 1970); James Morris, *The Preachers* (New York: St. Martin's Press, 1973), 235–56.

10. Interview.

11. "Miracle Woman," *Time* (September 14, 1970), 62.

12. See Kathryn Kuhlman, *I Believe in Miracles* (11th printing; Englewood Cliffs, N.J.: Prentice-Hall, 1968), 11.

13. Kathryn Kuhlman, "I Believe in Miracles," *Acts*, no. 3 [no date], 8, 23, 27; see, also, "Miracle Woman," *Time* (September 14, 1970), 62–63; "Kathryn Kuhlman's Television Radio Schedule," *HOF–HT* (May 1971), 14; Kathryn Kuhlman, "My First Healing," *LJ* (September–October 1971), 4–5.

14. See Morris, *The Preachers*, 252; "Miracle Woman," *Time* (September 14, 1970), 62–63.

15. See Rex Humbard, "Rex Humbard/Man with a Vision," *TA* (May 1964), 5, 14; Rex Humbard and Joyce Parks, *Put God on Main Street* ([Akron, Ohio: The Cathedral of Tomorrow, 1970]); Rex Humbard, "Rex Humbard/Man with a Vision," *TA* (March 1965), 6.

16. "Christ Is the Answer," *Acts* ([Spring, 1970]), 11–18.

17. Ibid., 12.

18. Interview.

19. Rex Humbard, "Rex Humbard/Man with a Vision," *TA* (March 1965), 18.

20. Letter from John K. Hope to S. Juanita Walker, May 16, 1968, Pentecostal Collection, Oral Roberts University.

21. Rex Humbard, "Rex Humbard/Man with a Vision," *TA* (January 1966), 4–6.

22. Several other old movements in American religion made some contact with the neopentecostal revival in the 1960s. The Order of St. Luke in San Diego, a divine healing movement within the Episcopal church which was established in the 1930s by John Gayner Banks, slowly became aware of its kinship with the charismatic revival during the 1960s. See "Ministry of Healing Literature," *Sharing*, (August 1968), 16. The Christ Faith Mission, with its organ, *The Herald of Hope*, was an independent ministry begun in 1940 by a woman disciple of Aimee Semple McPherson. The small ministry never actively participated in the revival but was clearly sympathetic with its aims. As the charismatic movement spread in the 1960s such small ministries found in it leaders they could support. See [masthead], *Herald of Hope* (Spring 1952), 1; "A History of Christ Faith Mission," *Herald of Hope* (September 1952), 3.

Chapter 8 / Old-Time Revivalism

A. A. ALLEN AND DON STEWART

1. Interview.

2. A. A. Allen with Walter Wagner, *Born to Lose, Bound to Win* (Garden City, N.Y.: Doubleday & Company, 1970), 161–63.

Notes

3. A. A. Allen, *God's Guarantee to Bless and Prosper You Financially* (Miracle Valley, Arizona: A. A. Allen Revivals [1968]), 130.

4. Allen, *Born to Lose*, 162.

5. Interview.

6. *Born to Lose*, 162–63.

7. Ibid., 162.

8. Ibid., 181. See also "Make Miracle Valley Your Home," *MM* (December 1963), 5.

9. "Miracle Revivalists Dedicate World's Largest Tent in Atlanta," *MM* (June 1960), 6.

10. See William Hedgepath, "He Feels, He Heals & He Turns You On with God," *MM* (October 1969), 13–20.

11. "From the Editor," *MM* (February 1969), 2.

12. *Born to Lose*, 167.

13. "It Can Happen Here," *MM* (June 1962), 4.

14. See "World's Psychiatrists Brand Jesus 'Insane!' " *MM* (November 1962), 4–6, 10; "Commitment of Political Opponent Gains World Attention," *MM* (October 1962), 6–7; interview.

15. "Typical News Coverage of the Healing Revival," *MM* (May 1962), 20–21; see also, "ABC Television Network Considers Allen in Columbus, Ohio, Important National News," *MM* (December 1969), 4–5.

16. "A. A. Allen Revivals, Inc., Wins Tax Case," *MM* (November 1963), 5, 7; see *Bisbee* (Arizona) *Daily Review*, October 19, 1963.

17. "Will You Be Crucified in 1962?" *MM* (May 1962), 12–14.

18. Interview.

19. "An Open Safety Pin Was Removed from My Stomach!" *MM* (January 1960), 4–5.

20. "I Took My Cancer to Church in a Jar," *MM* (January 1960), 7.

21. "I Lost Over 200 Pounds When I Used God's Reducing Plan," *MM* (January 1961), 3.

22. "I Was an Hermaphrodite," *MM* (March 1961), 6–7.

23. A. A. Allen, "Women Received Their Dead Raised to Life," *MM* (March 1966), 8–9.

24. "Statement Concerning Raising the Dead," *MM* (May 1966), 19.

25. See, for example, A. A. Allen, *The Burning Demon of Lust* (Miracle Valley, Arizona: [A. A. Allen, 1963]); A. A. Allen, *The Curse of Madness* (Miracle Valley, Arizona: A. A. Allen Publications [1963]).

26. Allen, *The Curse of Madness*, 81; see 55–73.

27. "Miracle Oil Continues Flowing," *MM* (June 1967), 6–7.

28. "Miracle Oil Flows at Camp Meeting," *MM* (August 1967), 8.

29. "New Miracle Revival Tent Dedicated in Philadelphia," *MM* (September 1967), 15.

30. A. A. Allen, *Power to Get Wealth* (Miracle Valley, Arizona: A. A. Allen Revivals [1963]), i–viii.

31. *Born to Lose*, 149–50.

32. See David Edwin Harrell, Jr., *White Sects and Black Men in the Recent South* (Nashville: Vanderbilt University Press, 1971); "How God Feels About Segregation," *MM* (May 1963), 8–9; "Integration for More Than a Decade," *MM* (September 1969), 12–13; A. A. Allen, "Did God Ever Call the White Man to Preach the Gospel to the Black Man?" *MM* (September 1969), 3, 6–7, 14–19.

33. A. A. Allen, *My Besetting Sin* (Dallas: A. A. Allen, n.d.), 37–42.

34. Interviews.

35. Interview.

36. Interviews.

37. Don Stewart with Walter Wagner, *The Man from Miracle Valley* (Long Beach, Cal.: The Great Horizons Company [1971]), 220.

38. Don Stewart, "We Are Going on for God," *MM* (August 1970), 2.

39. See H. K. Rogers, "Greater Revival Is Here," *MM* (September 1970), 8–9.

40. Interview.

41. Sermon, Miracle Valley, Arizona, January 31, 1973.

42. Stewart sermon, Cincinnati, Ohio, July 8, 1972.

43. Ibid.

44. Ibid.

45. Sermon, Miracle Valley, Arizona, January 31, 1973.

46. Stewart sermon, Cincinnati, Ohio, July 8, 1972.

47. Interview.

48. Ibid.

49. Stewart sermon, Cincinnati, Ohio, July 8, 1972.

50. Stewart sermon, Cincinnati, Ohio, July 7, 1972.

51. "Dying Gunshot Victim Saved, Healed, Holy Ghost Filled!" *MM* (November 1970), 9–12. See also, "Miracle Revival and Indian Camp Meeting," *MM* (August 1971), 13.

52. Interview.

53. See "Bold New Steps to Meet the Needs of Our Changing World," *MM* (February 1974), 2–3.

MORRIS CERULLO

1. For general information on Cerullo, see "A Little Jewish Boy Becomes a Christian," *TVH* (March 1957), 6–7, 22; Morris Cerullo, *From Judaism to Christianity* (Dallas: The Voice of Healing [1957]); Morris Cerullo, *Portrait of a Prophet* (San Diego, Cal.: World Evangelism [1965]); Morris Cerullo, *Proof Producers* (San Diego: World Evangelism [1972]).

2. See "Christmas Greetings from the Morris Cerullo World Evangelism Staff," *DL* (December 1966), 14–15; interview.

3. See "Special International Supplement of Deeper Life," *DL* (April 1969), 11–23; "World Evangelism Moves to New Headquarters," *DL* (January 1970), 3.

4. See "God's Servant Arrested Second Time," *DL* (January 1966), 10–11; Morris Cerullo, "The Corrientes Story," *DL* (February 1966), 8–11.

5. "You Can Live on the Mountain," *DL* (July–August 1970), 10–11.

6. Interview.

7. Interview.

8. Ibid.

9. David Balsiger, "Los Angeles," *DL* (October 1971), 10–11.

10. See [letter], *DL* (January–February 1972), cover; "Financial Policy Commended," *DL* (May 1971), 5; "Christian Leaders Report," *DL* (May 1968), 12, 13; "Your Opinion, Please," *DL* (April 1972), 8, 9.

11. See "Plan to Attend This Conference," *DL* (December 1965), 14, 15; "World Charismatic Conference Heard Pat Boone," *NW* (April 1971), 26; Morris Cerullo, "Faith with the Future," *DL* (April 1971), 2–5.

12. See "Morris Cerullo Team Profiles," *DL* (October 1971), 12.

13. See Morris Cerullo, *Wind Over the 20th Century* (San Diego: World Evangelism [1973]), 10–11.

14. Interview.

15. Interview.

16. Interview.

17. Interview.

Survivors

1. "Richard Hall—Prophet Unrealized," *SOF* (September–October 1965), 2.

2. See "Brother Hall Returns to the Desert," *SOF* (November–December 1967), 3; "Brother Hall Returns to Desert by Divine Appointment," *SOF* (May–June 1970), 1; interview.

3. "Richard Hall—Prophet Unrealized," *SOF* (September–October 1965), 2.

4. "Salvation—Divine Healing—Holy Ghost," *THD* (February–March 1961), 2.

5. "Tent Revival Season Is Here," *THB* (1956), 1.

6. "We March Forward in Faith," *THD* (January 1961), 11.

7. "Did You Know," *THD* (October 1961), 8–9.

8. "We March Forward in Faith," *THD* (January 1961), 8–9.

9. "From My Heart to Your Heart," *SOF* (January–February 1968), 3.

10. Margaret Minton, "Brief Resumé," unpublished MS. in possession of the author.

11. "Salvation—Divine Healing—Holy Ghost," *THD* (February and March 1961), 2.

12. Interview.

13. Interview.

14. "Great Tent Revival," *SOF* (July–August 1974), 8.

15. Interview.

16. Franklin Hall, *Formula for Raising the Dead* (San Diego: Franklin Hall [1960]), 51.

17. Interview. See also, "During July—Holy Ghost Seminar . . . ," *MW* (Winter 1970), 6.

18. Interview.

19. Franklin Hall service, Phoenix, Arizona, July 20, 1972.

20. Hall, *Formula for Raising the Dead*, 4. See also, Franklin Hall, *The Body-Felt Salvation* ([Phoenix]: Hall Deliverance Foundation [1968]), [1–3].

21. Franklin Hall service, Phoenix, Arizona, July 20, 1972.

22. Interview.

23. Franklin Hall service, Phoenix, Arizona, July 20, 1972.

24. Interview.

25. Interview.

26. Interview.

The Young Lions

1. See "No. '1' in America," *TE* (May 1972), 2.

2. Interview.

3. Ibid.

4. See "Editor's Notes," *TE* (December 1972), 2; interview.

5. "Editor's Notes," *TE* (November 1970), 2.

6. "Editor's Notes," *TE* (March 1974), 2.

7. See "Editor's Notes," *TE* (July 1972), 2; "Editor's Notes," *TE* (February 1974), 2; interview; Swaggart sermon, Virginia Beach, Virginia, January 18, 1974.

8. Interview.

9. Ibid.

10. Swaggart sermon, Virginia Beach, Virginia, January 18, 1974.

11. Interview.

12. See "Robert Schambach Graduates," *MM* (August 1959), 10.

13. Interview.

14. Ibid.

15. See "Schambach Miracle Revival," *Power* (January 1973), 16.

16. Interview.

17. See "Elwood City Ledger Reports Central Office Activity," *Power* (August 1972), 8; "The Hour of Deliverance," *Power* (February 1974), 9; interview.

18. Interview.

19. Ibid.

20. Interview.

21. See "Why Miracle Arm Revivals, Inc.?" *Revival* (October 1961), 2; LeRoy Jenkins, "How God Is Directing My Ministry," *Revival* (December 1966), 10–11; interview.

22. LeRoy Jenkins, *Somebody Up There Loves Me* (Tampa: LeRoy Jenkins Evangelistic Association, 1965), 5.

23. "Why Miracle Arm Revivals, Inc.?" *Revival* (October 1961), 2.

24. See LeRoy Jenkins, "The Harvest Is Truly Great," *Revival* (January 1964), 4–5, 8; "Brother Jenkins Spoke at the FGBMFI Luncheon in San Jose," *Revival* (July 1965), 8, 9; "Jenkins Revivals," *TVD* (June 1963), 5; "How God Is Directing My Ministry," *Revival* (December 1966), 10–11; LeRoy Jenkins, "Progress Report," *Revival* (April–May 1964), 10; [letter], *ROA* (November–December 1969), n.p.

25. See [letter], *ROA* (November–December 1969), n.p.; interview.

26. "Evangelist LeRoy Jenkins Detained in Nassau by Bahamian Governor," *Revival* (January 1964), 14, 15.

27. LeRoy Jenkins, *God Will Burn Your Barley Fields* (Tampa: LeRoy Jenkins Evangelistic Association [1965]), 7–9.

28. Jenkins, *Somebody Up There Loves Me*, 4. A former employee who worked with Jenkins for thirteen months described himself as a "long-termer."

29. Jenkins sermon, Columbus, Ohio, April 7, 1974.

30. See "And Then the End Shall Come," *ROA* (Winter 1973), 2–3; interview.

31. Interview.

32. "A Man and His God," *ROA* (Winter 1973), 16.

33. See "And Then Shall the End Come," *ROA* (Winter 1973), 2; interview.

34. Jenkins sermon, Columbus, Ohio, April 7, 1974.

35. Interview.

36. Interview.

37. See "Nixon's the One," *TETM* (November 1968), 1; "Birmingham Revival Report," *TETM* (August 1967), 8.

38. "The Ministry of a Prophet," *TETM* (July 1966), 2–5.

39. Interview.

40. "Methodists and Catholics Probe Unity," *TETM* (April 1968), 8–9.

41. "The Ministry of a Prophet," *TETM* (July 1966), 2–5.

42. Ibid., 3.

43. See "Radio Broadcast Schedule," *TETM* (April 1966), 6; "The World's Largest Gospel Tent," *TETM* (April 1967), 5; interviews.

44. Interview.

45. Interview.

46. W. V. Grant, *Creative Miracles* ([Dallas: Faith Clinic, n.d.]), 11.

47. Ibid., 11–13.

48. Neal Frisby, Scroll #35, printed scroll.

49. "Who Is This Man?" *TVD* (December 1962), 6.

50. "Scroll #15," *TCL* (November–December 1969), 7.

51. Neal Frisby, *The Spiritual Veil* ([Phoenix]: 20th Century Life, 1972), 3.

52. "Who Is This Man?" *TVD* (December 1962), 6.

53. Neal Frisby, Scroll #7, part 2, printed scroll.

54. Scroll #11, part 2, printed scroll. See also, "Our Partners Enjoyed These 2 'Review' Scrolls So Much That We Decided to Print Them Here for Everyone's Benefit," *TCL* (April–May 1969), 4–5.

55. Scroll #7, part 2, printed scroll.

56. See Scroll #32 and Scroll #14, printed scrolls.

57. "Important Questions and Viewpoints," *TCL* (January–February 1970), 6.

58. "Here's Our Plan!" *MTF* (May 1967), 2.

59. "Caught Up," *Praising the Lord* (September–October 1973), 3.

Chapter 9 / New Promises and Problems

1. Interview.

2. "Dick Cavett's Tough Questions," *AL* (June 1970), 12.

3. Don Basham, *Deliver Us from Evil* (Washington Depot, Conn.: Chosen Books [1972]), 206–207.

4. See John L. Sherrill, *They Speak with Other Tongues* (New York: McGraw-Hill Book Company [1964]) for an early assessment of neopentecostal success. A modern assessment of the movement may be found in Steve Durasoff, *Bright Wind of the Spirit* (Englewood Cliffs, N.J.: Prentice-Hall [1972]). See also, *New York Times*, September 8, 1974, 1, 42; "Events and People," *CC* (October 2, 1974), 9–13.

5. "Full Text of Charismatic Study Report by Executive Presbytery of Assemblies of God," mimeographed sheet, August 14, 1972, in possession of the author.

6. Oral Roberts, "We Have Been Conquered by Love," *AL* (February 1967), 23.

7. "I'm Excited about the Whole Kingdom of God," *AL* (May 1967), 25.

8. Francis MacNutt, *Healing* (Notre Dame, Indiana: Ave Maria Press [1974]), 24–25.

9. Interview.

10. For a survey of the "Jesus Revival," see Erling Jorstad, *That New-Time Religion* (Minneapolis: Augsburg Publishing House [1972]).

11. See Basil Miller, *Grappling with Destiny* (Los Angeles: Wings of Healing [1962]).

12. This was Gordon Lindsay's phrase. See Gordon Lindsay, "The Master Key to Financial Success," *TVH* (November 1965), 4.

13. Harold Woodson, Stewart service, Cincinnati, Ohio, July 7, 1972.

14. "Beware the Commercialized Faith Healers," *Reader's Digest* (June 1971), 179–80.

15. See *St. Cloud* (Minnesota) *Visitor*, September 12, 1974, 4; lecture, Collegeville, Minnesota, December 11, 1974.

16. See Connie W. Adams, "Reading the Papers," *Truth Magazine* (January 4, 1973), 10; Bob Reynolds, "An Examination of the Modern Faith Healer," *Gospel Advocate* 114 (October 26, 1972), 679–80; Ronny Milliner, "R. W. Schambach: Miracle Worker?" *Truth Magazine* (January 3, 1974), 11–12.

17. Mimeographed letter from L. W. Mayo and Gus Eoff [1973], in possession of the author.

18. *Catholic Pentecostalism: Problems in Evaluation* (Pecos, N.M.: Dove Publications [1970]), 22.

19. Interviews.

20. Interview.

21. See *Minutes* of the Thirty-Fifth General Council of the Assemblies of God ([Springfield: Assemblies of God, 1973]), 142–43.

22. Interview.

23. Lester Sumrall, "I Shall Not Compromise the Full Gospel," *WH* (June 1968), 2.

24. Interview.

25. Interview. See also A. A. Allen with Walter Wagner, *Born to Lose, Bound to Win* (Garden City, N.Y.: Doubleday & Company, 1970), 162–63.

26. Interview.

27. Interview.

28. Interview.

29. Interview..

30. Interview.

31. Sherrill, *They Speak with Other Tongues*, 162.

32. Interview.

33. Interview.

34. Interview.

35. See interviews.

36. "Let's Face It," *NW* (June 1973), 21–26.

37. Gordon Lindsay, *The Gordon Lindsay Story* (Dallas: The Voice of Healing Publishing Company, n.d.), 273.

38. Interview.

39. See "About the Prayer Cloth," *Action* (July 1974), 13; "Rev. Ike on TV and Radio," *Action* (October 1973), 12–13.

40. "That T-Bone Religion," *Time* (December 11, 1972), 97.

41. William C. Martin, "This Man Says He's the Divine Sweetheart of the Universe," *Esquire* (June 1973), 76. For general information on Reverend Ike, see this article and also Clayton Riley, "The Golden Gospel of Reverend Ike," *New York Times Magazine*, March 9, 1975, 12.

42. "A Special Message," *Action* (October 1973), 2–3.

43. Interview.

44. Interview.

45. See *Birmingham Post-Herald*, October 26, 1972, B2.

46. Joyce Jones, "The Sea of Blue Galilee," *LH* (January–March 1972), 3–4.

47. Interview.

48. Sermon, Phoenix, Arizona, July 20, 1972.

49. Interview.

50. Interviews.

51. Jack Coe, *The Story of Jack Coe* (Dallas: The Herald of Healing, 1955), 12.

52. LeRoy Jenkins, *Somebody Up There Loves Me* (Tampa: LeRoy Jenkins Evangelistic Association, 1965), 5–6.

53. "The Ministry of a Prophet," *TETM* (July 1966), 2–5.

54. Interview.

55. See Oral Roberts, "We Have Been Conquered by Love," *AL* (February 1967), 23.

56. Interview. A sophisticated survey of the psychology of pentecostalism is Kilian McDonnell, "Tongues and the Churches: a Psychological Survey and Evolution" (unpublished manuscript, read by permission of the author). Professor McDonnell argues persuasively that "emotional unstability does not characterize the Pentecostal-charismatic community," p. 96. It does appear to me, however, that psychological deprivation played a part in the personality development of most of the charismatic evangelists.

57. "The Ministry of a Prophet," *TETM* (July 1966), 3.

58. Interview.

59. Ibid.

60. Interview.

61. Interview.

62. "An Interview with Oral and Richard Roberts on The Mike Douglas Show," *AL* (December 1970), 10–12.

63. Interview.

64. See "Persecution Madness," *C&S* (October 1973), 4–6; David Wilkerson, *The Vision* (Old Tappan, N.J.: Fleming H. Revell Company [1973]).

65. Interview.

66. McDonnell, *Catholic Pentecostalism*, 32.

67. "Where Is the Holy Spirit Leading Us?," *LJ* (November–December 1973), 69–70.

INDEX

Abundant Life, 151, 157–58
Allen, Alfred, 106
Allen, Asa A., 66–75, 194–203: appeal to
poor, 8; battles with pentecostal
churches, 113–14; convicted of operating
business without license, 102; as exorcist,
88; fund-raising techniques of, 104–5,
200–1; and hard cases, 87; influence on
revivalists of 1970s, 226; interracialism at
meetings of, 99; legacy of, 136–37; mentioned, 6, 57, 61, 65, 79, 172, 175; ministry and personality of, 66–75, 194–203;
miraculous claims of, 89; *My Vision of
the Destruction of America*, 97–98; old-
time revivalism of, 194–203; quoted on
God and health, 85; Schambach a pro-
tégé of, 216; sensational testimonials to,
198–99; Stewart as successor to, 203–6
Allen, Lexie (Mrs. A.A.), 67, 70–72, 202, 217
American Medical Association, 101
Angelus Temple, 16
Angley, Ernest, 224
anointing of evangelists, 86, 199–201
Assemblies of God: and charismatic revival,
227; controls fund soliciting by ministers,
231; and FGBMFI, 147; mentioned, 11,
12, 14, 16, 20, 46, 54, 58, 59, 61, 71;
rupture with faith healers, 107–12; support of Swaggart, 214–15; Wilkerson's
experiences as minister of, 186–87
associations, evangelistic, 106–7, 141
*Atomic Power with God through Prayer
and Fasting*, 81
audience participation, 91–93

"baptism in the spirit," 11–12
Baptist opposition to revivalists, 100
Basham, Don: and Christian Growth Minis-
tries, 182, 185; instructions for deliver-
ance from demons, 226–27; quoted on
false ministers, 234
Baxter, W.J. Ern, 32, 34–35
Bennett, Dennis, 227

Best, W.E., 34
Bible Revival Incorporated, 178
Bible Training School, 168
biblical texts on healing, 84–85
blacks: integrated in revival movement, 59,
98–99, 201–2, 211; Reverend Ike and his
financial success, 234–35
blessed cloths, 86, 88, 199
body odor, control by Holy Ghost fire,
212–13
Boone, Pat, 155, 186, 208
Bosworth, Fred F., 14–15: accompanied
Branham, 34; debate with Baptist, 100;
mentioned, 55; ministry of, 14–15;
quoted on Branham, 36; and Roberts, 46
Bouton, Harry, 215
Branham, Billy Paul, 35
Branham, William Marrion, 27–41, 159–65:
admonition to Jaggers, 79; controversial
doctrine, 161, 163–64; death, expected
resurrection, 164; decline in ministry,
159–62; denunciation of some ministers,
139; in financial difficulties, 106; followers formed sect of, 232; and foreign
missions, 94; Frisby devout follower of,
223; FGBMFI support of, 148; Lindsay
as manager for, 54; and Mattsson-Boze,
178; mentioned, 6, 56, 57, 67, 76, 183,
226; ministry and personality of, 27–41,
159–65; in 1960s, 159–65; and Osborn, 64;
oneness vs. trinitarianism in ministry of,
116; photograph shows with halo, 34;
quoted on healing, 85, 90; quoted on
interchurch rivalry, 96; quoted on Roberts, 49; and Roberts, 42, 46; and second
coming, 98; stage presence, 162
Branham, Mrs. W.M., 164
Brant, Roxanne, 188
Braxton, Lee: and FGBMFI, 146–47;
quoted on Roberts, 47, 96, 151, 153; on
Roberts' team, 43–45, 49, 156
Bredesen, Harold, 181
Bridal Call, The, 16

VANGUARD COLLEGE LIBRARY
12140 - 103 STREET
EDMONTON, AB T5G 2J9